# FULL DISCLOSURE:

———— ∞ ————

*The New Lawyer's Must-Read Career Guide*

by

## Christen Civiletto Carey, Esq.

*Second Edition*

**2001**

**ALM Publishing**
**New York, New York**

The information contained in this book should not be con-
strued as legal advice. Readers are encouraged to consult
their own counsel regarding legal matters discussed in this
book.

**Library of Congress Cataloging in Publication Data**

Control No. 00-136160
ISBN 0-9705970-0-2

# DEDICATION

This book is for my husband, Mark, whose limitless love, patience, and support, are a constant blessing to me.

# ACKNOWLEDGMENT

I could not have written this book, or begun my training and development as a lawyer, without the assistance of my family and a great many other people. Words cannot express how grateful I am to my parents, Charles and Judy Civiletto, for their continual love, encouragement, and teaching (not to mention their brainstorming sessions and babysitting services). My appreciation is equally heartfelt to my siblings, Charles Mark Civiletto, Camille Civiletto, and, soon, Reyna Castillo. My in-laws provided additional help, especially Rebecca Carey Rook, a terrific editor in her own right. In their own unique way, my children, Julia, Mark, Jr. and baby-on-the-way, were and still are a constant source of inspiration for me.

A very special thank you to Yola Civiletto, my grandmother, Jeanette and Tony Scibilia, Cindy Krause, and other family members, for their support throughout law school, and, indeed, throughout my entire life. To those life-long friends who answered my many grammar questions or allowed me to talk, especially Barbara Luba, Jennifer Steinberg, Nicole Nowakowski, Susan Steffan, and Carol Haines.

I would like to thank the following friends—excellent lawyers all—who weighed in on various aspects of the book, even inspiring a few sections, and answering my endless questions: Kristen Yadlosky, Kristen D.A. Carpenter, Richard and Joan Green, Daniel Leary, Eric Johnson, L. Elizabeth Bowles, William Custer, and, of course, Mark Carey. Other lawyers, for whom I also have great respect, were kind enough to talk with me about specific aspects of practice, including Todd Bair, Leslie Jutzi, Angela Hsu, Andrew Galeizowski, Richard Galeema, Jackie Hutter, Richard Schroff, Sheri Keeling, Ralph Boniello, Sr., Diane Roberts, Beth Mayfield, and many others, some of whom prefer to remain anonymous.

An enormous amount of appreciation goes to all of the clients, lawyers, in-house lawyers, professors, deans, recruiters, librarians, paralegals (including the incomparable Meg Gleason), secretaries, managers, human resources personnel, and, especially, students (particularly Jennifer Catherine), who took the time to talk with me about their experiences, observations, thoughts, and recommendations. Not only did these individuals provide valuable insight that hopefully I have conveyed in this book, but also these people gave me a better appreciation for the practice of law.

Many thanks to an excellent group of colleagues, including my "boss" Joseph Wargo, a superb lawyer who has been teaching me since my first day of work, as well as Michael French, J. Scott Carr, Daniel Kent, and the rest of this fine group of litigators. My gratitude extends to Altman, Kritzer & Levick, P.C. for its continual support of my efforts, and especially to Mark Levick for his insightful and witty commentary on the current state of law practice and the economics underpinning a firm. I would be remiss if I failed to mention Vickie Walker, who for many years has taught me the ropes, learned along with me, and who always provides an excellent common sense perspective to our matters.

I want to thank the people at American Lawyer Media, especially Neil Hirsch, Liz Delfs, and Sara Diamond, for making this experience painless and bringing to fruition something that has been in my heart for many years.

Finally, I give thanks to God for the giving me the words, strength, and inspiration to finally put pen to paper.

Christen Civiletto Carey

## FOREWORD

A few lawyers still remember what it was like to practice law in the old days, the really old days. The days before LSAT exams, bar review, or time-sheets dominated the thoughts of anxiety-ridden students and new lawyers. These lawyers learned their trade through apprenticeship. They literally "read the law" and performed tasks, at times menial ones, for more established lawyers in the hopes of learning their craft. Many lawyers had an accurate picture of the practicalities of practicing law before taking on the enormous responsibility of representing clients. In other words, they were prepared.

Upon graduation, today's new lawyers encounter a world of complex litigation and deal-making that early-American attorneys could scarcely have imagined. Much of our work is performed for sophisticated clients, many of whom are lawyers themselves, against a backdrop of negative perceptions about our character, motivations and billing practices. On average, we work harder and longer hours than our counterparts at any other time in the history of the legal profession in the United States. Our clients make decisions about legal services based on value and firm reputation, not solely on bonds of loyalty forged by long-deceased partners.

Despite the increasingly complex work, more sophisticated clients, and multiple demands on our time, today's lawyers seem less equipped than ever to handle the practical aspects of practicing law. Our law school courses train us to think analytically and write persuasively. Our property classes begin with the reading of cases in the 1600's or sooner; nothing is said all year about how to actually convey that property to someone else or where to record that conveyance. Not a word is said about working with your secretary, managing the conflicting expectations of your partners, or diffusing the temper of difficult opposing counsel. All of this brings me back to the old days. If we can incorporate those positive aspects of attorney apprenticeship and mentoring into present-day lawyer training, perhaps we can better prepare our new lawyers and raise the bar, even just a little.

Law firms are attempting to address this lack of practical preparation by using formal or informal mentoring programs and seminars. These measures, however, are dependent on the commitment level of overworked and, at times, less experienced attorneys. Often, intervention comes too late for a new lawyer as bad habits have formed or the associate's reputation has been damaged. My hope is that this book will supplement those efforts and further bridge the mentoring gap evident in today's law firm environment.

This book has been a long time coming. For years I passed along to law students and new lawyers advice on everything from little-used library resources to the importance of doing time sheets everyday (which I had to learn the hard way). I decided to put my thoughts on paper with the hope that students and new lawyers would find them useful. I talked with hiring partners, practicing attorneys on every level, managers active in attorney recruitment, law school professors, career services directors, and legal recruiters. I also talked to law students.

Much of my research, however, came out of my own experience as an attorney who has been on both sides of the interview and associate review tables. I thought about the things that I wished someone had told me when I was looking for a job as an attorney. Even more important, I thought about the advice (good and bad) that was passed along to me as a new lawyer. I don't profess to have all the answers, but for what its worth to you, the law student or new lawyer, this book is a labor of love born out of experience.

Christen Civiletto Carey
Atlanta, Georgia

# TABLE OF CONTENTS

**CHAPTER 15**

# Chapter 1

# The Big Picture

## The (Sometimes) Harsh Realities of Private Practice

Lawyers love to give advice, especially to new lawyers. By the time a young lawyer shows up for her first day of work, she likely will have received opinions on everything from what to wear to the length of time it takes to make partner. (They make everyone who stays partner, right?) Because a new attorney can be overwhelmed by the day-to-day work of learning to be a lawyer, too often, she never finds the time to sort what's sound advice from what's shaky. Some of the guidance experienced (and not-so-experienced) lawyers offer to new lawyers is important because, just as in life, many of these lessons were learned the hard way. Difficult and time consuming that it may be, a new lawyer should sift through offered recommendations and suggestions, corroborate them if necessary, and ultimately do what makes sense, given the context within which she works.

The thoughts and opinions that follow represent a "collective experience" approach to many of the issues that face new arrivals to the private practice of law, whether they work in small, medium or large firms. Many lawyers were interviewed for this book. The question that seemed to elicit the most emphatic response was "what do you know now that you wish you knew at the *beginning* of your career." The most common response: The "big picture."

So, let's begin with the big picture.

You have left academia and are now in the business world. Try not to overlook this concept because it sounds simplistic or obvious. Without doubt, your graduation effected changes in your life beyond geographical ones, although not all of these changes are immediately apparent. For instance, you just spent three years trying to figure out what your law school teachers expected of you. There was a process by which these professors taught you to think and analyze a certain way. Now, you have to go through that process all over again. Your employer, whether a law firm or a corporation, expects something totally different. Probably no one will tell you that you have to start thinking differently, and probably no one will tell you how to do it. Nonetheless, law firms (and corporations) will expect that you will figure this out.

Think of it this way: law schools get you lost in the forest to find the acorn; legal employers require that you grasp the forest. You must now pull back and broaden your approach to trouble shooting and problem solving. No longer can you spend weeks working on a moot court brief or an entire semester researching and writing a law review note. If you do, you will be of little practical value to your employer, no matter how correct your conclusions. Part of your job as a new lawyer is to figure out how to provide value to your employer and your clients. Value means that you provide a top quality work product for a reasonable price. Price is inextricably bound up in time.

Next, understand that although you have a *juris doctor* degree and maybe some summer clerkship experience, you have little substantive knowledge of the law. Partners at law firms know that you know next-to-nothing. Understand that you are not being paid for your expertise; rather, you are being paid for your time. It follows that you must be prepared to devote time (energy, creativity and commitment are all part of the equation) to the firm. On the surface it is a good match: Firms sell time; time is about all you can supply as an inexperienced lawyer.

Many of you will be uncomfortable with this formulaic analysis of your initial contribution to the law enterprise. You know yourselves to be bright, creative individuals who strive to better the practice of law through the contributions to the profession that you intend to make. You recognize that if being a lawyer were as simple as the time-money/supply and demand characterization implies, far fewer people would leave the practice within their first few years or grapple with disillusionment over the nature of their practice. It is partly because lawyers are individuals that success is not guaranteed, even when the formula is followed. In other words, the economics of supply and demand do not translate into assured success because we are people dealing with other people. None of this changes the fact, however, that since law firms sell time, the most important product that you can supply is your time. New lawyers (and all lawyers, for that matter) are well-advised to interpret events happening in their law firms, as well as factors shaping their careers, in light of that bottom-line orientation.

Here is another sobering thought that most new lawyers do not think about: You are a fungible commodity. You are replaceable during your first, third or even the fifth associate year. You are replaceable at the partner level. It may not be quick or cheap to replace you, and there may be repercussions felt at the firm by your leaving, but you can be replaced. (Later we discuss how more senior lawyers fall into categories of "lawyers the firm does not really want to lose" and "lawyers the firm wants to lose.") Lawyers easily convince themselves that they are necessary or indispensable when firms are busy, the economy is strong and law firms cannot keep associates without increasing salaries to obscene levels. Many lawyers get their first dose of reality when the economy takes a downturn and law firms start firing associates (and unproductive partners). It's also a given that lawyers and partners can be fired even when the economy is strong. Many others who want your job are just as qualified (or perhaps more-so) as you are to research, write and conduct due diligence. Conduct your affairs and keep your demands consistent with the belief that the firm can lose you at any point and still function as a business. We all like to believe that we bring something unique to the workplace. After all, we all have different life experiences and talents that give depth to our technical legal training. The reality, however, is that when it becomes financially or politically necessary, the firm can and will function without you.

The next point is related: A law firm is a business and, for long-term survival, it must be run like a business. As detailed in Chapter 8, your value to the firm is tied in large part to your billable hours. Other things are important, too, like your work quality, ability to get along with others, handling of clients, and level of maturity. But these things become less important if you are not a productive member of the business. Equate productive with billable hours.

Politics will come into play in most any firm of two or more people. The word "politics" is a loose term describing office alliances and relationships that will inevitably impact decisions made by people. These relationships and alliances will also impact your working life. There will be times during your career when you will not understand what is happening to you. For example, you may experience hostility from another attorney or partner that seems unjustified or unprovoked. Perhaps the partner who was mentoring you has left the firm and others are viewing you with suspicion. Perhaps others perceive your practice group as arrogant and insular. Perhaps you rubbed someone the wrong way when you told him that you had too much work to do and could not assist him. Perhaps you went to the wrong school and an attorney is taking a rivalry too far. In any event, endeavor to understand the subtleties (and relationships) at work and consider that information as you progress in your career.

As a lower level associate, you will have three types of clients: (1) partners; (2) senior associates; and (3) firm clients. You will have no firm clients to please if you fail to please the partners and senior associates. As you navigate the tricky waters of attorney development, you might try evaluating yourself and your contributions as a client would: Are you adding value to this project? Are you reliable and trustworthy? Are you a team player? Once you understand that your relationship with your superiors is one of attorney-client, then you must learn to treat the partners and senior associates as clients. Of course, the lessons you learn in that context are fully applicable to the attorney-firm client relationship too. Much of Chapter 9 deals with learning to handle your clients, including partners and associates. Chapter 14 addresses handling the corporation as a client.

Your reputation will be established within the firm and the legal community much sooner than you think. Within the firm, a hard-working associate who produces a consistently superior work product will, depending on the size of the firm, develop a favorable reputation within a year. An associate who gossips, complains, boasts, displays immaturity, lacks judgment, or produces a poor-quality work product will establish a negative reputation in a much shorter time period. Over time, your reputation, good or bad, becomes known among members of the bar.

One large-city firm hired every member of its litigation team by relying foremost on each attorney's reputation in the legal community for producing superior work. Interestingly, some of these attorneys were at the time second-year associates. These associates had already earned a solid reputation in the bar.

One of the reasons that your professional reputation gets around so quickly is that attorneys change jobs frequently. Your entering class of twenty-nine first-year lawyers might be reduced to four lawyers within a few short years. Many of the twenty-five attorneys who left are now practicing in other firms. If you combine those lawyers with opposing counsel, co-counsel on matters handled by you, loose-lipped headhunters, and attorneys in professional organizations in which you are involved, then you can see how a reputation is made or destroyed within a short period of time. Remind yourself that you do not practice in a vacuum; your professional abilities as well as your words, actions and treatment of others will shape your reputation as a lawyer (and a human being). To the extent you have control over those factors, be sure to exercise it early.

You and only you are ultimately responsible for the development of your career. If you are a third-year associate and have never argued a motion or taken a deposition, then you are at least partly responsible for not having had that experience. If you lack substantive knowledge about your area of law, you need to rectify that. One first year attorney wanted to travel out-of-state to defend what would have been her first deposition. She sent her supervising partner a list entitled "Top Ten Reasons Why I Should Defend the Deposition." She then called him to make her case. Ultimately, the partner agreed that both of them would attend the deposition and the firm would write off the associate's time. The partner was persuaded that the value of the experience outweighed the dollar loss to the firm. Once the associate had this experience under her belt, the next deposition opportunity came quickly. (It is a law firm axiom that if you do something once, everyone assumes you are knowledgeable). Her deposition experience was off to an early start.

Another lower-level associate needed practical court experience. She took advantage of a deal made with the local district attorneys' office that allowed law firm associates to try jury cases that were not overly complicated (misdemeanors and the like). Several aspects of this criminal experience were applicable to the civil context, including learning to pick a jury and handling difficult witnesses. Had she not pursued this opportunity, she would merely become a senior associate with no jury experience.

Responsibility for your career carries over into the realm of feedback. It is your responsibility to follow up with the lawyers with whom you work. If they are unavailable or too busy, it is your job to be persistent, without being obtrusive, until they give you feedback. It is up to you to then incorporate into your work those suggestions or comments provided by the reviewing attorney. By pursuing feedback, you can not only improve your work product, but also get some idea of where you stand in the eyes of your client.

It is important that you have at least an idea of why you want to practice law and what you hope to get out of it. You may be in it for a satisfying and challenging career. You may be in it to learn and gain experience and then move on. Or, you may be in it for the money. Whatever your reasons, having a clear understanding will alleviate some amount of stress down the road. You will have a benchmark by which to measure your idea of success. Finally, you can better keep your expectations in check.

Practicing law is a difficult way to make a lot of money. Certainly there are people who have made incredible amounts of money: a plaintiff's lawyer settles a large personal injury case, or a partner shares in the profits of an especially lucrative year. Not every attorney has this experience. The vast majority of lawyers are sole practitioners making far less than $500,000 per year. Moreover, don't rely too heavily on the high salaries offered by large firms as the way to riches. There is a direct correlation between how much you earn and how hard the firm will make you work for it. Sustaining that level of effort and stress is more difficult than you can imagine. If money is your sole motivation, you may want to re-think your career.

As you begin your career, try not to view partnership as the pot at the end of the rainbow. As one large-firm partner suggested, have a "present orientation" and enjoy each day of your career and your life *now*. Try to figure out what aspects of practicing law that you enjoy. Start thinking about the practice areas that interest you. One new associate was concerned about how his handling of a certain minor matter would play out in partnership decisions down the road. The mid-level associate with whom he was talking expressed surprise and pointed out that the chances of him being at that firm eight years down the road were so slim that his worries were unfounded. The new associate could not contain his surprise. Associates should focus first on the factors that make them satisfied, skilled lawyers; partnership issues seem to fall into place from there.

On that note, it will become increasingly clear that partnership decisions are based on a myriad of factors, including (but not limited to) your previous years of penance as a hard-working associate. While this book focuses on some of those partnership factors, it is more about doing the things that will make you a great lawyer and a fulfilled lawyer.

To that end, keep these "big-picture" thoughts in mind as you read the rest of this book and perhaps put some of these thoughts into action. No one, of course, can do all of these suggestions all of the time. Take this information, however, and use it to the extent it works for you, taking into consideration your firm's environment, the group within which you work, and your personality.

# Chapter 2

# Prepare Your Case

## How and Where to Begin
## Your Job Search

Sometimes finding a job is about who you know. Most of the time, however, it's about preparation. Finding a job with a law firm is not much different. A few people find employment easily—they have a connection or the right family name. Maybe they were in the right place at the right time. For most people, however, it takes a lot of hard work.

A law firm job search is much like litigation. A litigator avoids taking action until she has a firm grasp on the facts. Then, using the facts, she develops a strategy. Every angle is researched and the plan adjusted as necessary. Finally, she executes the plan, bringing all her skills, abilities and research to bear. In litigation, as in your job search, ignoring or overlooking any of these steps greatly diminishes your chances of success. Even worse, it leaves you ill-equipped to handle unexpected circumstances, such as when you unintentionally insult the interviewer from the firm at the top of your list.

Advice promoting preparation is nothing new. Successful campaigns of all types, including litigation, come with preparation. What may be new to you, however, is how much similar strategies should be used in getting a job. Words or phrases like "making a case" or "campaigns" are not typically associated with a job search. They should be. The job-seeking process is one of the many times when a methodical, informed, and aggressive approach will yield big rewards down the road. An approach emphasizing preparation increases your chances of not only landing a job, but finding one that is a good fit, which is infinitely more important. Strive to avoid being a fifth-year lawyer trying to figure out what you can do outside of law that will still get your loans paid.

Law students typically do not think in terms of a "good fit." Most weigh the pressing facts—one or two offers, high debt, the need for a job—and accept a position with the law firm that makes an offer, or the one that is in the city at the top of their list of preferred places to live. A lot is at stake for law students when choosing a first law firm. Depending on the length of employment with the firm, an attorney's first firm will have an enormous impact on several aspects of her career. For example, the type of work a lawyer ultimately practices is usually determined in the first few years. One new attorney began helping a firm partner on occasional immigration matters. Soon, more and more immigration cases were being sent his way and eventually (and unexpectedly) he became a full-fledged immigration lawyer. It is not unusual for a new attorney to simply fall into a practice area after handling some initial matters for a partner with whom the young attorney has developed a good relationship. One summer clerk's office was next door to a partner; she became a certain type of lawyer simply by her proximity to someone else.

The first few years of practice are also important because, during that time, you will develop work habits and ways of doing things that will be hard to change later. Your attention to detail or the level to which you research a matter is often shaped by the "way it's done" at a particular firm. One attorney may consider final what another would regard as a draft. Setting standards and when those standards are met, varies from firm to firm.

Your career will also be shaped, in part, by some of the people that you work with during your first few years of practice. This is especially true of the attorneys that started at the firm when you did. Many early colleagues will be a source of your future business. Some colleagues will move on to different jobs, which is the start of a network for future job hunting and referrals. The type and quality of developing opportunities is at least partially tied to the caliber of the attorneys with whom you have established a relationship.

The firm of your initial employment may also have a city-wide reputation and, professionally speaking, you will be painted with that brush as well. One firm may be known for using particularly questionable or aggressive tactics to further its client interests. This reputation can become so entrenched among members of the bar that attorneys from other firms will deal cautiously with these lawyers, believing that they cannot taken at their word, or should not be given the benefit of the doubt.

Some additional examples might demonstrate the importance of choosing your first firm carefully and the impact your choice can have on the rest of your career. After law school, you accept an offer from a large, national firm. After four years with the firm, you determine that big-firm life is not what you want out of practice. You probably will have little difficulty finding another job. The firm name will stay with you for the next several years. People will think that you worked long hours and thus must have a good work ethic, even if you did not or do not. Provided you made a good impression while at the firm, you also have many other lawyers who think highly of you or at least know your work. These lawyers may go on to other firms or obtain employment as in-house counsel with a corporation. You now you have contacts all over the city, and sometimes beyond.

On the negative side, future employers might be concerned about your practical experience. They may assume that the large firm did not give you many opportunities to work directly with clients or handle administrative, agency or court matters. These assumptions (if untrue), however, can be overcome by providing specific information about your experience.

What if your experience was the reverse? Out of law school, you worked for a small insurance defense firm that only handled work from one insurance company (these firms are sometimes known as "capture firms"). You have excellent deposition and trial experience, but now, after three years, you want to handle general litigation matters at a large firm. This is certainly possible, but you have some perception hurdles to overcome. Lawyers at large firms will question why you did not go to work for a large firm right out of law school. Older partners will probably assume that you failed to receive an offer from a large firm and were forced to work for the capture firm. In reality, you wanted early trial experience and thought that insurance defense was a good way to obtain it.

Future employers will also question your research and writing ability. They will assume that you did little substantive brief writing or that you relied heavily on canned briefs. The larger firms may also question whether you can handle the grind of long hours and high stress, because they believe that insurance defense lawyers do not work as hard or long as do the lawyers at large firms. Whether these generalizations are true is not relevant. What is relevant is that you will have to overcome varying perceptions stemming from your first job. These perceptions range in degree and mean the difference between easily being able to switch jobs or being stuck in a position you no longer find suitable. You have a great incentive to early on choose a firm that is a good fit.

So what exactly is a good fit? A good fit means that you are doing work for which you are well suited at a place that roughly matches your long-term goals. You are well suited for your work when there is a convergence between your skills, interests, and aptitudes. For example, if you are a detail-oriented person who enjoys putting together acquisition deals, you may be well-suited for certain corporate work. There are some people who enjoy the firm and the people with whom they work, but detest the type of work they do. This may work for a few years, but at some point serious job dissatisfaction will overtake these attorneys and their performance will suffer or they will leave the firm. The bottom line is that you are not just looking for *a* job, but the *right* job.

Another essential component of a good fit is that your firm will further your long-term career goals. For example, let's say your ultimate goal is to work as an in-house counsel for a large corporation. You need to work at a firm that will not only provide experience servicing these companies, but also will give you access to the decision-makers at the companies. It is not uncommon for a lawyer to leave private practice to go in-house with a client. In this instance, it would fit your long-term goal to choose a firm that provides a natural avenue by which you can make a career change.

Another example might be your goal to ultimately open your own practice. It is imperative that you first work where you will get good mentoring and hands-on experience. The size of the firm is not as important as the experiences available there. Determining whether a particular firm is right for you requires going through an investigation and interview process outlined in the rest of this chapter.

By doing your homework and having at least a basic understanding of your goals, you can stack the deck in your favor for finding a job that is a good fit. In doing so, you will increase the likelihood of staying with the firm, if that is your goal, or providing a smooth transition to a later career. Your level of satisfaction will also be much higher during your time with the firm.

Sometimes your contentment is the difference between simply *making a living* or *practicing law*.

The good news about your job search is that you are in control of most of this process. As with most things, your chances of success increase in direct measure with the amount of preparation you complete. The remainder of this chapter sets forth one approach to researching and finding the right law firm job.

### Step 1—Assessing Yourself

Getting a grasp on the facts is the first and probably most difficult step in finding the right job. The relevant facts at this stage are facts about you: your skills, aptitudes, experiences, interests, goals and needs. Begin with an honest assessment of your skill and aptitude. What do you think you do well? What do you enjoy? Are you a detail person? Are numbers your strong point? Are you patient? Do you have vision or are you a worker bee? Examine your past accomplishments and determine what skills you used or what qualities you possessed to make them successful. Perhaps you helped found a local chapter of a fraternity. Your organizational or management skills surely contributed to that success, as did your leadership qualities.

Begin to record these facts about yourself; this list will be helpful in the preparation of marketing materials such as your resume and cover letter. In addition, maintain a file where this list and all other relevant job search documents are kept. That way, you will never unintentionally apply twice to the same firm, nor will you forget which firm has already sent you a rejection or acceptance letter.

Ask other people, including employers, friends and family, what skills they believe you possess. Do they think you write well? Have good analytical ability? Relate well to business people? Possess good self-management skills? Tolerate conflict? Have a strong work ethic? Do they think you are able to focus on the big picture and not get consumed by small issues? Be sure to ask what you do not do well. Sometimes others see deficiencies that we are not aware of. To quote a borrowed line, "A man's got to know his limitations." Sometimes the way to figure this out is by asking others.

Finding out how skills and aptitudes play out in the careers of practicing attorneys is instructive. One lawyer thinks and operates on an intellectual level far above most people. She is a policy-level thinker. As a result, she experiences frustration when dealing with the day-to-day, down-in-the-trenches work of interviewing witnesses, sorting out facts, and resolving petty discovery disputes. This is an example of how early self-knowledge can be beneficial. Her interests and skills make her better suited for a legislative, appellate, or clerk position.

Next, understand the relevance of your past experience and how that training and knowledge can best be marketed and used in your legal career. Many lawyers use their military background, including their organizational and leadership experience, as the foundation for a successful law career. Another lawyer is a fiction writer. He is able to write persuasively and creatively—a combination that puts him in high demand as a brief writer.

Your interests, goals and needs are other important "self" facts. What do you like to do when you are not studying? Do you enjoy politics? Sports? Math? People tend to do well when they are doing something they enjoy. Lawyers who enjoy writing have a much easier time than those who do not, particularly since most practices involve endless drafting, writing and re-writing. Another lawyer has little tolerance for those who have undergone misfortune, whether or not of their own making. She should (and does) avoid plaintiffs' work. Other lawyers have translated an interest in sports, entertainment or assisting the elderly into legal work tailored around those interests. While it may be difficult to know your area of specialization when you're just out of law school, you do know what you like and should consider making career decisions that are closely aligned with your interests and long-term goals. You will not last long in a job that is contrary to some long-held belief or in which you have little or no interest.

Some of the factors that impel attorneys to seek a law firm job were discussed in Chapter One. Whatever your motivation and whatever it is that you expect to get out of your career, be realistic. You will work hard. Your life will be governed by the expectations of partners and clients, to say nothing of your own pre-conceived notions of what it means to practice law. You will constantly question whether you are really living up to the way in which you have prioritized your life. Finally, you will realize that the choices you make in this context affect virtually every other aspect of your life as well as that of your family. These are important decisions and should be made only after thorough research and careful consideration.

When you are in the job-seeker position, you almost have to remind yourself to factor in your needs. How important is a certain salary level? What about the amount of travel required? Do you have family circumstances that will make it more difficult for you to have an erratic schedule, typically experienced by tax, litigation or securities attorneys? For some reason, usually due to a need for money, some attorneys accept jobs that are a recipe for disaster. One summer clerk, who was seeking a job with a litigation group in a large firm, had a disease that worsened under stressful conditions. If practicing law was her goal, she should have made it her business to find a less stressful, even-keeled practice group. That would certainly not describe litigation.

Once you have gathered the facts about you, including your motivations and expectations, be sure that you can articulate and roughly categorize what you have learned about yourself. There is little point of going through the exercise of gaining self-knowledge if you do not know how to package the information and use it. Some suggested ways to categorize:

(1) technical strengths and weaknesses;

(2) emotional strengths and weaknesses; and

(3) personal and family needs (including salary, lifestyle, location, personal fulfillment, future career goals, etc.).

Add these rough categorizations to your list. This information will become increasingly relevant as you find out more about particular firms and practices.

### Step 2—Determining Location

Narrow down the geographical area within which you want to practice. Start with the obvious regional divisions: west coast, southwest, northeast, etc. You may be able to identify particular cities or towns within which you want to practice. Then, research the regional economic market and legal employers. Understanding the economic backdrop is key; it not only drives hiring decisions, but impacts the type of work you will do and the clients you represent. One attorney's decision to focus on the southeast was driven largely by economic factors. Her home region was in an economic decline, whereas the southeast was flush with pre-Olympic anticipation. Get online and read the major newspapers from the region. Find out what major corporations are located or considering locating in a particular area. Talk with friends, family and family contacts, and anyone else who can give you information on the economic picture in a particular area.

There are other relevant regional factors. What is the nature of work being done the geographic area you are interested in? What is considered a large firm for the area? Practicing in New York, Washington, D.C., or San Francisco, is very different than practicing in Cincinnati, Macon, or Milwaukee. The nature of the work differs, as does the level of sophistication in certain areas. Do not assume, however, that the work is more sophisticated in a larger city; mid-sized or smaller cities, like Charlotte, North Carolina, have very specialized and complex work in particular industries.

The culture of the bar will also differ with the region. While many would like to think of the Atlanta bar as being relatively small, one in which lawyers know most of their colleagues in the city, it is becoming increasingly difficult, with the growth of the bar, to keep track of everyone's reputation. As a result, lawyers are less able to rely on their adversary's reputation and relations are more formal and better documented. Other cities, like Little Rock, have a much smaller bar where you are more likely to know of an attorney by name and reputation.

Understand also that while salaries and benefits in a region may sound high, that might not be the case once you factor in the hours you are expected to work or the cost of living for that area. After an especially busy month, a highly-paid lawyer at a large firm allegedly computed that he made two dollars an hour. This may not be factually true, but at times it will feel like it. In short, until you understand the economic context within which you will work, your salary and benefits will be difficult to evaluate properly.

### Step 3—Researching the Firms

Investigate particular firms within the region. You want information on the firm's reputation, financial stability, and client or industry base. For example, does this firm primarily represent oil companies? Tobacco companies? A single insurance company? Real estate clients? Perhaps the firm represents a consortium of players within a particular industry. These factors are important to the financial stability of the firm. Start with the firm web site, which often includes information about the history of the firm and representative clients. Many firms update their sites with information about where their attorneys are teaching or speaking, as well as matters in which the firm is involved. Chapter 4 deals with additional strategies for getting information about firms and specific employment opportunities.

Use your law school placement department as a resource. Placement directors often deal with the same law firm over a period of years. Not only do they draw their own conclusions about firms or markets, but they also speak to returning students and hear about various experiences at a particular firm. While the placement director may not be forthright about negative information (after all, these directors have a future professional relationship with these firms.), they may provide direction as to information you can explore further.

A city legal newspaper is another good resource. For example, the Atlanta Fulton County Daily Report (www.dailyreportonline.com) or the New York Law Journal (www.nylj.com) will provide a wealth of information about local firms, cases and controversies. Many of these papers are online and available to anyone who has access to a computer.

To a lesser extent, a state bar journal may provide some information about the firms and local practices within the state. The data will probably be more practice or law-oriented, but may contain some information about particular lawyers or firms.

The Martindale-Hubbell directories (www.martindale.com) may also be a valuable source for learning about a particular firm and especially about individual attorneys within a firm. The directories contain facts about the attorney's educational background, as well as activities and clubs in which the attorney is or was involved.

Informational interviews, which are discussed in more detail in Chapter 4, are another good research tool. These are interviews that you conduct with practicing lawyers (or others) about their jobs, often after an introduction or lead by a mutual acquaintance. Do not expect to get called back for an interview after this meeting, although it does occasionally happen. This type of meeting is for informational purposes only and your expectations should be made clear to the person with whom you are speaking. You may want to contact lawyers who graduated from your alma mater. Many attorneys are happy to talk with a fellow graduate. They will tell you if they are too busy or do not have an interest in talking with you. You have lost nothing by trying.

The size of a particular firm with which you seek employment may not be as important as the group within which you work, and more specifically, the particular attorneys for whom you work. These factors will be primary influences on your day-to-day life. In large firms, practice groups operate similarly to those in small firms. In fact, in mid-sized and large firms, aside from a few attorneys with whom you have regular contact, you may not get to know many attorneys outside your group.

It is generally expected that associates keep hours similar to those of firm partners in the same group. In one firm, a specialized group of litigators generally arrived at work late and stayed late. Associates within the group generally followed suit. The general commercial litigators, on the other hand, arrived and left earlier than did the specialized litigators. Again, associates maintained a similar schedule.

In another firm, first-year lawyers were not given the opportunity for direct client contact or court appearances. The group leaders reasoned that over time the attorney will gain experience, prove herself, and then be given additional responsibility. Within the same firm, but in another group, first-year attorneys were thrown in and expected to sink or swim. The difference was in the "culture" of the group, which is set by the group leaders. While these are small examples, they demonstrate the significant differences between practice groups and how those differences directly impact your daily professional life.

The big firm/small firm debate does not have an easy answer, mostly because the generalizations traditionally made about firm size are, to a great extent, no longer true. All large firms do not lock young associates up in the library, sentenced to a life of researching and writing. All small firms do not lack resources and backup. In fact, there are surprising similarities between large and small firms. Technology has helped level the playing field. A large law library is available, sometimes at little or no cost, to anyone with a computer. New regulations, statutes, or cases are published on several different online sources providing easy access to one and all. Specialized temporary staffing agencies and an increase in the amount and availability of independent contractors have diminished the manpower gap that may, in the past, have put small firms at a disadvantage. Further, the pay scale has become so skewed that it is not necessarily true that small firms don't pay as much as big firms.

There are differences, of course. In a large firm, you may not know all of the firm attorneys in your building, let alone in satellite offices around the world. There is a certain collegiality that might be missing on a firmwide level at a large firm. Large firms can also absorb more of the training costs for young associates (which may or may not be an advantage—some smaller firms provide better hands-on experience). For example, the large firm may provide monthly training classes for real estate lawyers.

If you believe it necessary, however, to make some initial assessments about whether you will perform better in a large, small or medium-sized firm, ask yourself these questions: Do you have a strong preference and, if so, why? Is there a prestige factor? Do you have future sources for definite client referrals? Will these clients pay higher rates for your services? Do you have an entrepreneurial spirit that would be better nurtured in a small firm? Are you the type of personality that becomes lost in a crowd? Is it difficult for you to seek out mentoring and training from other lawyers? Do you want access to a certain size or type of client for your future career plans? Not all of the answers will point you to a particular sized firm. These questions should help you develop further and better questions to ask of yourself and of firms.

In choosing your firm, your personality, the firm's clients, and the group within which you work, not so much the size of the firm, will determine whether you will be satisfied.

### Step 4—Developing a Plan

You have gathered information about you, your goals and needs, your target market and employers. Now you need a plan. Just as in litigating a case, you should proceed on several fronts at once.

Here is how one attorney developed her plan. She knew that given her interest in writing, oral advocacy, and strategizing, she wanted to be a litigator. There was nothing about transactional work that excited her. She perceived, rightly or wrongly, that transactional work was devoid of advocacy and that it was made up of staid lawyers who enjoyed endless discussions about the proper language in a contract provision. She was not so concerned with being in a particular city, so long as it was in the eastern half of the United States. She knew that she wanted a larger firm with a reputation for having an aggressive and well-respected litigation department. She had high loans and thus needed to make a respectable salary. She took those facts and started narrowing down her choices. She then developed her plan as follows:

(1) Develop good marketing tools (cover letter, resume, writing sample);

(2) Research the firms interviewing on campus to determine location, litigation department reputation, etc., and narrow down to top choices;

(3) Use contacts for firms that were not interviewing on campus, but ones that nonetheless meet desired criteria;

(4) Write some blind letters and hope for the best.

She followed through on this plan with mixed results, some of which were influenced by the dismal state of the legal market that existed at the time. The blind letters yielded nothing. The contacts were only marginally helpful. As it turned out, her contacts were in an economically depressed city, and a large savings and loan institution—along with its law firm—had just gone under. As a result, scores of lawyers were looking for a job, resulting in a tighter-than-normal market. The on-campus interviews, however, were productive. She interviewed with about twenty firms, all of which she had thoroughly researched, and was called back for an interview by thirteen. Those firms were located in different cities. Her lack of a connection with a particular city did not pose a problem. Location was not paramount to her, and she was able to convince the interviewer of that fact.

This job campaign teaches that it is important to gather information about yourself, the relevant market, and potential employers and use that information in formulating and following through on a solid plan. The next step, discussed in the next chapter, is to prepare persuasive papers.

# Chapter 3

# Draft Persuasive Papers

## Preparing the Cover Letter and Resume;
## Things to Do and Not Do for
## Your Writing Sample

The next step in your job search campaign is to prepare persuasive papers—a resume, cover letter, and a writing sample. The whole point is to back up the interest you may have in a job with the credentials, ability and technical skills required for the position. Law firms look at these papers as examples of the best you have to offer. For example, the resume should set forth your finest educational and professional achievements. Further, it should convey that information in a way that highlights your talents—the ability to write well, use proper grammar, and not make typographical errors. It is much the same with your cover letter and writing sample.

Putting forth your best work requires early preparation and lots of revision and proofing. Here's where some of the self-analysis and information gathering discussed in the last chapter will come into good use. Your resume really is a concise presentation of your skills, abilities and experience. You cannot convey that information properly unless you know first what it is you do well. By this stage, then, you will have gathered all the facts and now it's time to put pen to paper.

### The Resume

You've heard it said that the purpose of a resume is to land the interview. While the goal is clear, achieving it takes some doing. Students often stray from that objective and start pursuing others, like drafting a detailed life history or producing a creative piece of self-congratulatory propaganda. The resume should be an easy to read document that presents your experience in a positive and forceful way. It should contain all of the information that employers want to know and little else. The legal profession is still somewhat conservative when it comes to interviewing and pursuing a law firm job. Knowing what prospective legal employers want and need to know is essential.

Your resume will be reviewed in a matter of minutes by a single hiring partner or recruiting committee members. When a stack of student resumes is sent by the school to a law firm, one or more attorneys will quickly flip through the pile and decide which resumes bear additional review. The additional review will likely not take more than a few minutes. An attorney who graduated from your law school may also review your resume; graduates can often make better assessments about your grades (they know the teachers and the course difficulty level) or the journals for which you write. The attorney or committee members will then compile a list of interviewees.

If your resume was sent directly by you to the firm, a copy will be made and routed to the hiring partner (or group leader) and recruiting coordinator. These resumes are generally kept in a file for a period of time, sometimes as long as two years. The person reviewing your resume will give it at most five minutes. If you pass this initial screening, the reviewing attorney may forward your resume to a partner with an anticipated opening who might be interested in looking at your credentials. Regardless of how your resume is sent, the object is to catch the attention of the reviewing attorneys quickly.

Draft your resume so that it is clear and easy to read. It will likely be sent via facsimile or photocopied several times over. Don't reduce your margins in order to fit in more information. Information at the bottom or top of the resume may get cut-off by sloppy duplicating, or the edges may become blurred when the resume is faxed several times. Even a clean copy looks like too much information when the margins are reduced.

Use indentations and group information so that it can be read easily. Too many indentations, however, will defeat the purpose. As you look at the resume from a distance, it should be uniform and organized.

Be sure that your name is prominently displayed at the top. The type size of your name should be larger than the size used in the rest of the resume. Some employers find it helpful when a student identifies his or her gender (by adding Ms. or Mr., for example), if it cannot be ascertained by your name or because of the use of initials. Your inclusion of that information will save the recruiting coordinator a phone call to determine how to address correspondence to you.

Below or near your name you should list your contact information. If you have a temporary and permanent address, list both, particularly if the permanent address is in the city in which you want to practice. Be sure to include your zip code and telephone number(s).

Many students ask whether an e-mail address should be included. It depends. Omit your e-mail address if it includes words or phrases that are inappropriate in a professional setting. Also, omit your e-mail address if it communicates personal information about you that the firm is probably better off not knowing. Lawyers are fairly conservative, so when they see addresses that include the words "tattoo" or "party" or the numbers "69" or "666," (students do submit these) they will eliminate your resume from the pile. Do not include your email if you do not check it regularly or if you are planning on closing your account. If you don't fall into any of the above categories, you should include your e-mail address. Increasingly, lawyers are using e-mail for follow up communications with students and potential recruits.

It is not recommended that you include an objective on your resume. It is almost impossible for students to narrow a goal for future practice. You don't want to rule out a position that you might otherwise consider. Attorneys are also somewhat skeptical when they see students with little practical experience have such definite aims. Equally unhelpful is a broad objective. These are useless and convey to the reader that you don't know what you are talking about. Striking the right balance is something that only experience in the legal profession will provide. Many times students include language like "My objective is to obtain a position with a law firm practicing litigation, corporate or tax work." These resumes are dismissed out of hand. Attorneys understand that students don't have the particulars about the practice of law to focus on narrow objectives. On the other hand, an objective that includes anything and everything is not a goal at all.

After your name and contact information, present your education and work experience in a workable, coherent format. Most applicants organize this information in reverse chronological order. Employers expect to see your educational experience first, beginning with your present enrollment. List your complete school name and the city and state where the school is located. Include your expected degree and the month and year in which you anticipate receiving that degree.

Listing your grade point average is crucial. You should present your average to at least the 1/100 degree. For example, if your grade point average is 3.407, you should write that as 3.41. Potential employers will have no context in which to evaluate your grades unless they know the grading scale. Thus, you should say 3.41/4.3 or 3.41/4.0. Provide your class rank, but only if your school calculates that figure and you are in the top half. Again, this provides a framework for employers to rate you against other candidates. Employers will assume the worst if you fail to include your grades. If your grades aren't great, which determination depends on the school and what constitutes average, then you should consider leaving them off. You may want to discuss the value of including or omitting your grades with the career services people. They will have an idea of the level at which it's best to be silent.

If your grades are low, you will want to have legitimate reasons available. For example, if during the school year you cared for an ill family member, then that information should be conveyed in the cover letter. Don't state explicitly that "my grades are low because. . ." but find a way to present that information tactfully. For example, you may state on your resume or in your cover letter that during your second year, you spent significant time caring for an ill family member.

Next, include any honors, significant merit-based scholarships or awards that you earned in connection with law school. Give specifics for awards that may not have any meaning to an outsider. It is helpful for the firm to know whether you were elected, selected or picked for the award, and basic information about the qualifications for the award. For example, if to qualify you had to have the highest grade in the class for a particular subject, then state it. You want to give potential employers the tools to assess and analyze your relevant experience and achievements.

Your undergraduate information should follow much the same format, although you need to be more discriminating about the activities you include. Much pre-law school experience is irrelevant at this stage. For both undergraduate and law school, the reader should be able to determine that you were involved in activities and the level of that involvement. If you helped organize a community group that coordinates food drives for the elderly poor, concisely explain your specific involvement. Descriptions of practical, hands-on experience provide concrete examples of leadership, maturity, or organizational ability, which are all things that you want to come across from your resume.

Holding down a job while attending school—whether graduate or undergraduate—is no small achievement and should come across from even a cursory reading of your resume. Identify the average number of hours that you worked and the level of responsibility that you were given.

You may want to divide your work experience into legal, which includes investigation, law enforcement, paralegal work and similar positions, and non-legal categories. List the legal work first. This type of division makes it easier for lawyers to understand your training and background. List the dates of past employment by month and year. Attorneys, somewhat cynical by nature, assume that "2000-2001" on your resume means that you worked somewhere from December 2000 to, at the latest, February 2001. Check that the full company or firm name, as well as the city and state, are on your resume.

Your experience descriptions should be meaningful and contain action words to convey what you did. "Meaningful" means that your experience is not written in a generic fashion that could be found on one hundred resumes. Work at using descriptive language that gives some depth to "drafting memoranda." For example, strong words like conducted, conceived, supported, structured, simplified, expanded, completed, created, or established are all excellent action verbs.

Do not list references on your resume. Doing so takes up valuable space that could be used to better describe your relevant experience. It is best to indicate that references are available upon request. Have a separate sheet with the name, relationship (whether professional, personal, or educational) and contact information already prepared. Be sure that the paper matches that of your resume and cover letter. Produce the list of references only when requested by the potential employer.

List any unique and useful skills that you possess. Fluency in foreign language is a good example;

computer skills, except for exceptional circumstances, are not. It is expected that every lawyer, if hired, will learn the relevant computer system. Computer skills might be relevant if you are seeking to work in a technology-related area and you have a high proficiency with the Internet. This doesn't mean that you can find things more quickly than anyone else. It relates more to your ability to work with and relate to Web developers and computer programmers, all potential firm clients.

Do not include previous salary information or present requirements and do not list your family status or the names and ages of your children. Although this type of information is often found in corporate biographies or resumes (to demonstrate a stable family life, etc.), it is not appropriate in the legal context. Unfortunately, this type of information may be used for exclusionary purposes.

Hobbies and interests are interesting to read, but certainly not required. If you are out of room and have some practical experience that can be fleshed out better, opt for including the experience. Some students go to great lengths to list what they believe are especially interesting or unique interests. While the identified interests may truly be your hobbies, avoid painting a self-portrait of a snob. For example, listing "Gothic architecture, seventeenth century English royalty, and competitive croquet" makes you look like a snob. (People actually list this level of detail and it often becomes the butt of interoffice jokes.)

Do not exceed one page unless your prior experience was lengthy (as in a prior career spanning decades) and significant (as in you were CEO of a publicly traded company for ten years). Your resume will be read quickly and duplicated many times for interviewing attorneys. Use a color paper that photocopies well like white, ivory, or light cream. Your resume, when folded and creased, should not be such a heavy bond that the ink on your paper rubs off easily at the fold.

While there are some careers in which a colorful, creative and catchy resume would work, law is not one of them.

Review your resume for continuity. Look for large or unexplained gaps in your work or educational histories. Eyeball the set-up and ensure that it looks clean and reads smoothly.

Attorneys will get a sense of your writing style from reading your resume. Be sure to use parallel structure when describing your experience, and avoid using tired adjectives found on every law student's resume. Granted, there are some words that are difficult to get around—"drafted" is one of them. But others such as "prepared" are simply worn out.

Lawyers, like most people, form an initial impression about you after reviewing your credentials and activities. You want to avoid drafting a resume that turns you into a stereotype. You want for the attorney to be intrigued enough to take your resume to the next level. For example, attorneys will often see a resume where all of the person's law school activities and some outside interests revolve around assisting prison inmates in advancing legal issues. While there is nothing inherently wrong with that type of work, seeing it on your resume in six different contexts will cause you to be categorized as having a private agenda, when what you want is for the person reading the resume to focus on your skills and abilities. Potential employers may write you off because, whether accurate or not, they may believe you want a certain type of work, which is not what they can provide.

It should go without saying that typographical errors must be eliminated. Even one such error could result in your not being considered by the firm. Employers assume that your resume is an example of the best work that you can do. Your attention to detail will be critically reviewed, as will your ability to use grammatically and contextually correct words and phrases.

Never include false, misleading or inaccurate information about your past experience or education. It will come to light. The repercussions stretch far beyond losing your job and tarnishing your reputation.

Get your resume done in draft form well before the on-campus interviewing season starts. Once you have a draft, take advantage of the professionals in your career services or placement office. They can review your resume for form and content. Take seriously the suggestions they make for improving your presentation and wording. Your final version should also be ready well before the interview season begins. Have plenty of copies made on good quality paper. Spend the money for matching envelopes and extra paper for your cover letters and references. Store copies of your papers at school, if possible, and keep the remainder safely at home. You never know when a new firm will decide to interview on campus, or another copy will be needed by an interviewer. Store the disk on which the resume is saved in a safe place; after all, you don't want to have to go through the initial drafting and formatting process more than once. Your resume will be trotted out and updated several times in the next two years.

### The Writing Sample

The importance of writing well cannot be stressed enough. Few firms will hire an associate without seeing some type of writing sample. You may not get hired solely due to a great writing sample, but you may be eliminated because of a poor one. Writing ability is one of the primary determinants of success in the law firm. Attorneys must be able to rely on less senior associates to present information accurately and concisely or argue a point persuasively. Any lack of ability on the new attorney's part means more work for those who review that person's work. Often, as a first year associate, you will write letters, briefs, and other papers that will be signed by more senior attorneys. These are usually people who won't sign anything until the papers read as if they were the original authors. That's a high expectation for a junior associate. Adding to the pressure is the fact that senior associates, and particularly partners, forget how little training new lawyers have in the art of writing like a lawyer. For all of these reasons, students who write well tend to stand out from the pack. In the hiring context, law firms make determinations about your writing skills by reviewing your writing sample, as well as the written work product prepared over the course of your summer clerkship.

Your writing sample should evidence a strong foundation in all the basics: good grammar, concise and clear writing, and an ability to convey ideas and arguments distinctly and to the point. Do not use client confidential documents if you are using a writing sample from your experience as a summer associate or as a practicing attorney. Even if a document is public, redact the name of the client or opposing party if it appears anywhere within the document.

Most importantly, do not use a document that has been revised or edited heavily by more senior attorneys. Minor changes by someone with more experience are probably acceptable, but anything beyond that, plainly, is not. Attorneys will usually know if you are using a sample revised by someone else. For example, if you, as a student or first or second-year attorney, claim that you wrote an employee agreement that includes restrictive covenants, attorneys will be skeptical. It will be suspected that much of the language was duplicated from a prior agreement drafted by someone else. Moreover, it is more likely than not that the draft went through many revisions by your superiors before being final. Attorneys know that new lawyers are rarely asked to reinvent the wheel.

The writing sample should be brief, but not so brief that readers cannot make a determination as to your writing ability. Aim for about five-to-eight pages of substantive writing. One student submitted a lengthy article on foreign policy, which, while probably interesting, sat on the attorney's desk for a month and then was recycled. It just looked daunting. If possible, submit a writing sample on a subject that is appealing or relevant to the experience of lawyers in general. If you have written for any non-legal publications or for school newsletters, include a copy of the magazine or newsletter with your submission. Throughout your undergraduate and law school experience, you are well advised to procure extra copies of any writing of yours that is published. Submitting an original publication is better than handing over a duplicate. Consider including your name on each page of the writing sample; your paper will be unfastened during copying and may get lost in the shuffle.

Prepare an original writing sample if you do not have a good example from your law school writing projects or from previous work in a law firm. Pick a specific legal question on which to conduct research and write a short memorandum. Explain to your prospective firm that you wrote this document because you did not have a more suitable example of your writing. Bring the writing sample with you when you interview on campus or at the firm.

Because students are increasingly using the Internet to furnish their resume to law firms, it is appropriate to include an attachment containing your writing sample. Be sure that it is in a format that can be read by attorneys at the firm. Although most firms use Microsoft Word or Wordperfect, they may not have the latest versions of the software. Law firms are sometimes behind the technology curve due to the expense of upgrading and training large numbers of people. Consequently, you may want to submit the document in a lower version format of these word processing applications. Consider sending a hard copy of your resume and attachments as well. It might just be the hiring partner who refuses to use e-mail in any way, shape, or form (there's one holdout in virtually every firm).

Throughout your practice, maintain a file of the documents you authored. The file should include briefs filed with the court and memoranda prepared by you for a client or partner. These papers may serve as a writing sample in a future job search. The file as a whole will provide an inventory of the types of matters on which you have worked. This information will be helpful in updating your resume (which you should always do) or for discussion in a future interview. These examples will also be the foundation for your personal form and research files. As discussed in Chapter 9, every associate should be planning ahead and preparing form and research files.

Just as with your resume and cover letter, the writing sample will be read and evaluated in a matter of minutes. The clearer your writing and the better you are able to convey your thoughts concisely, the higher marks you will get.

### The Cover Letter

A well-written cover letter should be helpful to a prospective employer. Be sure that the letter is brief and provides some insight about you that cannot easily be gleaned from a quick review of your resume. For example, you may have prior experience as a non-legal professional. This is good information to bring out in your cover letter, particularly as it relates to your interest in a specific area of law, if you have one. You may also want to draw attention to any practical, relevant work experience acquired before or during law school.

Your cover letter is the appropriate place to state your reasons for moving to a particular city, wanting to be with a certain firm, or practicing in a specific area of law. You must be careful of your wording when addressing these subjects. You will be held to your early representations made to a firm. If they are not entirely true or you don't hold any firm convictions about the type of law you want to practice, then don't put that information in the cover letter. You may rule out a job by narrowing your objective in that manner. Many students look for an angle to distinguish themselves from other applicants. You will not serve your interests when you make representations about matters of which you are not fully apprised.

Use good judgment about the nature of the information you convey in the cover letter. Many students write that they want to move to a particular city because a girlfriend or boyfriend lives there. Without belittling these relationships, this type of information will not carry great weight with law firms and may possibly hurt your credibility. People break up all the time. If the relationship is serious, then simply state in your cover letter that on graduation, you plan to move to the particular city.

Remember that recruiting coordinators talk to their counterparts at other law firms. If you write in your cover letter that firm "A" is the only place you want to be, then you should mean it. It would be embarrassing if you sent a duplicate letter to firm "B" and your name arose in a discussion between two recruiting coordinators. Neither firm will hire you because you are insincere. This example illustrates the danger of making sweeping statements, unless those statements are entirely true.

Your cover letter gives your resume a date and some direction. It should be addressed by name to the hiring partner or recruiting coordinator (some firms will specify which). By naming a particular person, there is a responsibility for someone at the firm to get the resume where it needs to go. For these reasons, a cover letter should always accompany your resume.

As with your resume and writing sample, the cover letter (and any other document you give to a law firm) should be free of errors of any kind. That includes errors in the firm name (students omit the "P.C.," or neglect to list all named partners). Many lawyers will not consider a candidate with a typographical error in a cover letter, resume or writing sample. This may sound harsh, but from the employer's standpoint, if these papers are your best product, they shudder to think what your day-to-day work is like.

You will spend much of your career advancing your clients' interests by presenting information in a clear, persuasive and competent manner. Look at the resume and letter-writing stage as further development of your advocacy skills. In essence, you are the client whose interests are being advanced.

# Chapter 4

# Career Services and Beyond: Creative Job-Hunting Strategies

## Traditional and Non-Traditional Channels for Finding a Law Firm Job, Including Using the Internet, Personal Contacts, Community Involvement, Contract Work, Court Appointments and Headhunters

How you use your law degree is limited only by your imagination and ingenuity. Working in the private sector as a law firm associate is just one of many options. Most people don't realize that the Supreme Court hires lawyers, as do universities, think tanks, and governmental entities. The broad spectrum of opportunity sometimes gets overlooked or ignored as students go through the on-campus interview process (OCI) each fall or spring. The structure and intensity of the OCI process makes it difficult to get a handle on the range of legal opportunities, even those available in the private sector. Students get a skewed picture of private practice because only certain types of firms interview on campus, and those firms are only looking at select students. As a result, graduates-to-be focus on finding a law firm position with a firm similar to those interviewing on campus. These firms are not for everybody, nor do they want just anybody.

The on-campus interview process can be frustrating for students who, in turn, tend to direct their annoyance at the career services office. Why does this happen? How can it be addressed? Is this more of a student problem, a career services problem, or perhaps an institutional problem? This chapter addresses these issues and focuses on surmounting real and perceived impediments to getting a position with the right law firm. The discussion includes working with the law school career services department, using the "OCI+ system" developed by eAttorney, Inc., an online service, and finding the right job outside the career services department.

Most law schools offer a "career placement" or "career services" office. The office may consist of one person who maintains a resource center for students, or it may function with a Dean of Career Services and several assistants, all of whom work diligently to operate (among other things) an on-campus recruiting program. The range and quality of career services offered will vary from school-to-school, and is usually driven by the funding and support available for the services.

Theoretically, the professionals in this office are there to assist all students (and usually alumni too) in securing legal employment, whether that be with public interest organizations, clerkships, law firms, or academia. Due to time constraints, however, many of these offices focus their attention on law firms participating in the OCI program and on students who benefit most by those interviews. Over the course of a typical fall recruiting season, hundreds of firms might visit the campus, thousands of interviews are arranged, and even more resumes are exchanged between the law school and the participating firms. Most of the career services professional's time is dominated by scheduling and coordinating these interviews, as well as overseeing the bid and screening process for the students. These professionals have little time for students who aren't interviewing with the types of firms coming to the campus, nor do they have extra resources to devote to helping students with public interest, academic or clerkship opportunities.

Law firms come to the school for specific reasons. They might be a national or regional firm of influence, recruiting top students from the top twenty law schools. Others are local firms which, in addition to needing warm bodies, support the neighboring law school. (Firms start making their reputation with lawyers when those lawyers are in law school.) These firms are generally full-service or general practice firms that handle commercial disputes. There is not much else in between. As a result, students who go through the traditional OCI process gain only a limited view of the areas of law practice available and the types of firms within which many lawyers work. Students become focused on working for these types of firms. These future lawyers also tend to allow the counseling offered by career professionals and firms participating in the OCI program to shape their view of legal practice.

This is where disillusionment begins to take root. These firms don't want all students; they want the ones in the top half, top tenth or top students, period. Students who do not fall into one of these predefined categories are left out, as are students who do not look or act employable. Moreover, they are unable to secure much of the career placement professional's time and, as a result, become even more frustrated with the job search process. Even worse, many students don't view the OCI program as just one avenue for job hunting, but rather *the* avenue for a job in the legal profession. These issues become obstacles for students looking for the right law firm job.

These issues are addressed individually, followed by a discussion of how to get a job when the on-campus interviews either aren't productive or do not fit with your objective.

### Grades and Ranking

The reality is that many law firms place significant emphasis, if not primary emphasis on grades and class standing. Firms look first to your grades, then your school rank, your rank within the class, and finally such factors as additional degrees you may have earned. We all know that book smarts or high grades do not determine whether you will be a skilled and satisfied lawyer. Yet, the reliance on grade and rank persists. Here's why and here are some strategies for minimizing obstacles presented by your having low grades or attending a lower-tier law school.

In the absence of other objective and reliable data, attorneys believe that grades and ranking are historically accurate predictors of which students can handle the work-load and the intellectual challenge for the next few years. At the very least, attorneys believe that students with high grades have figured out what was expected of them by professors and delivered. They also believe that these students have shown that they can handle the high volume of work and reading required of them for good grades.

The numbers don't exactly bear these assumptions out. The attrition rate for students from large firms with presumably strict hiring criteria is even higher than that at small and mid-sized firms. According to quantitative findings reported in Keeping the Keepers: Strategies for Associate Retention in Times of Attrition, a 1998 study completed by the National Association for Law Placement (NALP) Foundation for Research and Education, lawyers leave firms of 251 or more attorneys at a higher rate at virtually every attorney-year level than firms of smaller size. Unfortunately, aside from grades and rank, there is little other objective information for firms to rely on in the short time available for attorneys to evaluate and review students.

There are other reasons for the emphasis on grades. Law firms want to be able to tell their clients that they employ superior attorneys from top schools. Large firms have to justify the high billable rate charged to clients for a first year associate's time, which in turn allows the firm to continue to pay the new associate a high salary. The economic justifications for the focus on grades will only increase in importance as salaries continue to rise.

Many firms still have old guard attorneys who put more stock in such things as grades and rankings. There is still a certain "I went through it and therefore you should too" mentality that keeps outmoded or unworkable policies in place too long. Moreover, older partners might be comfortable with the firm's traditional reliance on recruiting from certain schools and having specific standards. These ingrained ways of doing things do not disappear overnight. In fact, they generally don't die out until the older partners are retired or firm management takes on a decidedly younger appearance.

In addition, large and mid-sized firms focus on grades and rankings because they can. These firms might travel to, and interview at, twenty or more law schools. They can count on a certain percentage of students accepting their offers, which means that the firm is not disadvantaged by limiting the pool of applicants to a select group.

Throughout this chapter, we will discuss ways to find a job if you are having difficulty, even if you are an unemployed law school graduate. If you are in the top half of your class, there are strategies you can and should be using to improve your chances of getting an offer at a firm in which you will be a good fit. If you are having trouble landing a job because your grades are low or your school does not rank highly, some mental adjustments may be necessary. Start with your expectations. You may have to take a more circuitous route to wind up where you ultimately want to practice. There are certain jobs that enable you to gain relevant experience, which makes grades much less important for subsequent jobs, even in the private sector. For example, clerkship opportunities and positions with a district attorney's office are experiences that afford just such opportunities. Even with borderline grades, there are positions for those with the right connections or those who research the paths to finding them. It may be that once you excel in an environment outside a law firm, you can more easily make the move to private practice. You should not waste your time applying for the jobs that plainly set forth minimum requirements that you do not meet.

You also need to adjust your attitude. Don't label yourself as unmarketable or unemployable because a certain segment of the private practitioner market refuses to interview you. Instead, view yourself as marketable to the practitioners that will value other experiences you bring to the table. Your career is not in trouble, nor are your grades or rank a permanent bar to practicing law.

The next adjustment should be made to your marketing materials. You need to tailor your resume, cover letters, and interview style to emphasize the positive attributes you will bring to the firm. Participation in moot court and other practical education or student clinics is very important, especially if you have been recognized in some way for your advocacy skills or other tangible contributions. You want to give prominence to information like participating in twenty rounds with your moot court brief and placing sixteenth out of 140 in the competition. These are essential skills for any lawyer, especially a litigator. Highlight these achievements and describe them with particularity. Provide all relevant information on your resume so that the employer will have some context within which to evaluate your achievement.

In addition, capitalize on something for which your school is especially known or recognized. For example, if students from your school have a reputation for their knowledge of black-letter law, try to build on that reputation with your own experience. You might state in your cover letter something like, "As you know, our school is noted for preparing students in civil procedure matters, an area in which I have particular interest" (if you do, of course). Be prepared to give specific examples in your academic work (you scored a top grade in civil procedure or evidence). Look for specific ways to differentiate yourself by building on an established institutional reputation.

Market any particular skills or aptitudes that you possess that will help distinguish you from the crowd. You may be very computer literate (as in you have programming or consultant experience—a fact that may help you in growing practice areas). Perhaps you're fluent in Japanese. You need to figure out where your special skills would benefit clients most and focus your job search efforts in that direction. Find out, for example, which firms are trying to establish an office in Tokyo, or attempting to make inroads into the Japanese business community. This information can often be found in regional newspapers or legal or business reporters that track the practice areas of local firms.

Highlight steady improvement from semester to semester and from year to year. Everyone understands that there is a steep learning curve in law school and that sometimes it takes a few exams for things to click. If you have brought your grades up, but are still suffering the effects of a disastrous first semester or year, you need to bring that to the employer's attention in your cover letter. In your interviews, you can iterate what you have already stated in your cover letter, e.g., determination and hard work helped you improve your first to second year GPA by a full point. Be prepared to give specific examples of how you approached things differently and gained good results. These situations are excellent examples of your ability to learn lessons and apply them to your benefit.

Market your prior work or volunteer experience. There are always skills or strengths that are transferable to the legal arena. If you have nursing, teaching or management experience, you have been involved in professions requiring leadership, energy and dedication for success. Your resume and marketing materials need to highlight these aspects of your background. Include brief, but meaningful examples of projects on which you worked or programs that you supervised.

Legitimate reasons for low grades should always be brought to the attention of an employer. Again, the cover letter is the appropriate vehicle for presenting that information. Legitimate reasons include medical emergencies, severe illness of you or a family member, care for a chronically ill relative, or possibly, work in a full time position with a law firm where the benefit of the practical experience had to be weighed against the detriment to your grades. You should have positive references from the law firm to back up your assertions. Provide good examples of the type of work you did and why you took that opportunity instead of focusing on studying. It is not, however, helpful to state that you were juggling many responsibilities which kept you from focusing on your studies. Everyone is busy and if you cannot handle the schedule as a student, you surely won't be able to manage your daily professional responsibilities as a lawyer. Many of these suggestions are dependent on your re-focusing your attitude and marketing materials. No one said that finding a job is easy, and that is especially the case when you have obstacles to overcome, like low grades.

Participate in job fairs. Many of these fairs focus on specialized areas of law or on specific types of students and attorneys. The job fair draws firms interested in a particular area or in attracting a particular type of lawyer. If no fairs are scheduled in your region and you perceive a need for one, find out how you can organize this type of event. Often, law schools, student organizations or local firms or groups with similar interests will help make it happen. The legal market is strong, which means that firms are always looking for paralegals, secretaries and lawyers. A firm might be interested in participating in an event geared towards a particular specialty so that it can widen its pool of applicants. A minority student organization may also be a good place to start. One goal of these groups is to further the interests of its members, and increased representation in the private sector accomplishes that aim.

The bottom line is that the firms interviewing on campus are primarily interested in certain segments of your law school class. Whether you fall within that select group or not, you need to pursue a legal job on many fronts, with the OCI process being just one of them. Everyone should have options, which allows people to make choices more closely aligned with their interests and abilities.

### Employability

Some students will have difficulty getting a job, despite good paper credentials or even excellent grades. There may be a problem with the way these students come across in interviews. They may not look the part, act the part, or behave appropriately in social and professional situations. Common interview problems include extreme nervousness, which can cause the applicant to clam up, give rambling answers, or come across as wooden and inert. Not being prepared is another common problem. Some students' manners need polishing, others are socially inept or are arrogant (which is the fastest way to annoy lawyers with generally large egos).

Some of these deficiencies are curable. Consider taking business etiquette classes or having a third party (even an image consultant) evaluate your interview style. Consultants can be found by word of mouth or through the Internet. Net-etiquette classes, which are free or of minimal cost, are becoming popular. Practicing for the interview will help eliminate your nervous habits or help you relax. Take advantage of a willing roommate or close friend for initial practice interviews. Talk about yourself (out loud) in front of the mirror. Make an appointment with the career services professionals. That's part of their job and they will likely have good suggestions or resources for you to consult. Some students just need to practice listening. This is a basic social convention that for some reason gets left at the door of the interview room by many students. These students think that what they have to say is much more important than what the interviewer has to say, even when it's the interviewer's turn to talk. This is a danger sign to lawyers. People who don't listen miss important information from clients, subtle clues from judges, and they tend to aggravate supervisors and colleagues more so than others. This deficiency can be cured only after a student recognizes that there is a problem, and then addresses it.

### Law School Career Services

A number of law schools have turned to eAttorney, Inc., an online service provider which (among other things) hosts student and employer data for law schools (www.eAttorney.com). The NALP has endorsed eAttorney and law schools are increasingly using its services. Schools subscribing to eAttorney pay all costs associated with its use by students. Students fill out detailed profiles about their experience, extra-curricular activities and interests, and upload their resume. Law firms subscribing to eAttorney have access to the online profiles and resumes from students at the participating law schools. A law firm can also access student profiles from schools where it does not plan on-campus interviews. This means that a student could be contacted by a firm that the student has never considered. Firms can also access the profiles of practicing attorneys looking for employment, but the attorneys' names are not provided to the firm until the attorney gives permission.

Using eAttorney, the law firm and the participating school communicate electronically with respect to all on-campus recruiting activity. All scheduling, bidding and student sign-ups happen over the Internet by using the software eAttorney provides. In essence, these applications help law school career counselors better manage much of the OCI program, which is now called "OCI+." Once a school adopts this program, all students who want to participate in on-campus interviews must use it. Students not using the OCI+ program can also benefit from the research and resume posting aspects of eAttorney.

The benefits of OCI+ are many. Law firms cut down on paperwork because they receive resumes over the Internet, which allows attorneys on the recruiting committee and those interviewing on campus to review one electronic set of resumes. Law firms can store and categorize data electronically, instead of saving hard copies of resumes for two or more years. Firms can search for candidates using a wide variety of criteria, which hopefully will provide additional objective information so that grades and ranking are no longer the paramount factors. The law school also receives a tremendous benefit. Much of the administrative time spent mailing out thousands of resumes and arranging an equal number of interviews is substantially reduced. The career professionals now have more time for actually counseling students and providing guidance on the myriad of other opportunities in private and public practice. Hopefully, increased participation by career counselors will translate into more informed students making better career choices.

Law students at schools using eAttorney must become proficient in the system to take full advantage of it. Set aside time with the eAttorney representative visiting your campus, or attend seminars sponsored by the career services office. As always, preparation and diligence will give you a leg up.

Even with the OCI+ program in place, you still need to be proactive in obtaining the help that you need from the career services office. Take advantage of seminars, talks, videos and library resources offered for the benefit of students. One estimate, based on anecdotal evidence, concluded that less than one-third of students take advantage of these types of programs when offered by career services. Time constraints certainly contribute to low turnout. Your career services office will hopefully be sensitive to heavy exam periods or moot court final rounds. Provide input in order to minimize conflicts.

Schedule an individual appointment with the career services office early in the job-hunting process so that you can discuss grades, information that should or should not be on your resume, and other questions that you may have. Have the representative critique your resume and proposed cover letters. Find out if the office does mock interviews and participate in one or two. Check in with the office from time to time and provide a progress report. This information keeps the office involved in your search and provides data by which they can assess what additional programs might be necessary for your benefit, as well as the benefit of other students.

### Beyond Law School Career Services

All students should pursue alternative strategies for job hunting. Having plans in reserve will provide you with more choices and improve your chances of winding up with a position that is a good fit. The traditional OCI process should be used to the extent it brings to the campus firms in which you are interested. Because you will have done your homework on yourself and on these firms, you should have a good idea early on whether this program is for you. If you know you want to work in the Pacific northwest and your school has fifty firms from the southeast, don't bother wasting your time or theirs by interviewing on campus. On the other hand, if the on-campus program will bring in firms in which you are interested, then pursue that avenue and conduct your own search tailored around your goals, interests and needs.

### Targeting and Contacting Firms

Many students contact firms directly. Be sure to keep within the NALP guidelines for when you may contact a law firm. (The guidlines can be found on the Web at http://www.nalp.org.) Working outside the NALP guidelines will put the firm in an awkward position and will reflect badly on you. Some firms will either discard your too-early inquiry or will notify your law school. You will gain no advantage by jumping the gun.

Blind letters sent indiscriminately to say, every law firm in Orlando, will not work. Letters sent by you directly to a firm have potential only in limited circumstances. One is where you have targeted firms with which you have some type of connection, e.g., there are at the firm several alumni from your undergraduate or law school; or the firm employs people with a degree in biochemistry which you also possess. Any connection of this type should be brought out in a well-written cover letter. Another potential connection is where you have focused on a particular area of practice and can demonstrate to the firm a serious interest in that field. You may have conducted undergraduate or graduate research in environmental issues and now want to pursue that type of practice. Or, you have expertise or training that might make you attractive to this firm's clients, e.g., a nursing degree and you are targeting medical malpractice firms. All of these examples have in common a connection that demonstrates to the firm that you are interested in them, not just a job.

Before you mail anything to the firm, call them and find out to whom your cover letter should be addressed. Be sure to ask for the correct spelling as well. Some firms will ask you to send your materials to the hiring partner, others to the human resources or hiring coordinator. In any event, you want a correctly spelled name on the cover letter. Try not to bypass the established avenues for submitting a resume. It may get lost or never get to the appropriate people. The cover letter should mention the connection or the reason you have targeted this firm. Avoid a cover letter that looks like part of a mass mailing. Form letters are given little, if any, consideration, and you may not even get a rejection letter.

Follow up with the firm in the manner that you state in your letter. Be sure to calendar these follow up dates. For example, if you write "I will call you next Tuesday to further discuss my qualifications," then call next Tuesday.

Make it easy for firms to interview you. Arrange to be in the city where the firm is located and send a follow up letter stating that you are available for an interview and will be there on particular dates. You may get a screening interview, which would not cost the firm much in the way of time or resources.

### Electronic Resources

Increasingly, students are using the Internet to send unsolicited resumes, cover letters or writing samples to law firms. Because business people are generally reluctant to open mail with attachments from someone they don't know, the danger is that your e-mail might get ignored. Moreover, attorneys get enough e-mail and regard unsolicited messages as an intrusion. Remember that not all lawyers know how to use e-mail, even though, like every member of the firm, they have an e-mail account. Many don't even turn on their computers. Keep in mind that when you by-pass the traditional channels for resume intake, you risk getting lost on someone's desk.

Consider calling ahead and asking if you can send your materials to the firm electronically. If you want to send your information to a particular attorney, you may want to send a hard copy and letter, and then follow up with an e-mail that attaches the same information. That way, the attorney has a better chance of recognizing your name and responding. If you do e-mail your resume, make sure that you send it to one firm at a time, or at least prevent the recipient from seeing the other firms to whom you are sending it. As discussed in Chapter 2, your e-mail account name must be suitable for use in a professional setting.

The Internet has had a tremendous impact on searching for a law firm job. Students and graduates need to know what online services are available on the Web and take advantage of these resources as an integral part of their job campaigning.

There are many job search sites offering services for students and J.D's, all with differing degrees of control over the process. Some services charge a subscriber fee; others cost nothing. For law students, there is no real concern about confidentiality and the manner in which your resume is posted. That is not the case for lawyers wishing to make a lateral move, and any site to which such an attorney subscribes or posts a resume should be carefully screened to ensure that confidentiality procedures are in place and followed. The industry-specific sites are probably your best bet, but don't rule out the free job postings at other free sites. For example, at www.4work.com, many attorney jobs are posted, particularly for in-house counsel positions and national legal employers like State Farm.

Some of these sites are used by recruiters to obtain clients or to post jobs available by employers represented by a recruiter.

Many of these sites offer career counseling tips, news on the current state of the legal market, salary surveys, and links to other sites of interest to the job seeker. More than one site claims to be the premier or most used legal job site on the Internet. As with any advice, sift through it, use what you can, and always apply the rule of common sense. What works in New York City may not work in Birmingham, and vice versa. Be aware that regional differences in pay scales and billable hour requirements are significant, so interpret what you read in light of those distinctions. Some helpful sites are:

http://www.legalhire.com

http://www.attorneyjobsonline.com

http://www.findlawjob.com

http://www.legalemploy.com

http://www.washlaw.edu

http://www.lawjobs.com

http://www.eattorney.com

http://www.emplawyernet.com

http://www.4work.com

http://www.abanet.org

http://www.monster.com

http://www.brassring.com (technology legal positions)

http://www.law.com

http://www.iHireLegal.com

http://www.lawschool.com

http://www.lawcentral,com

http://www.lawyersweeklyjobs.com

http://www.legalstaff.com

### Take the Bar Exam and Get Admitted

If you have graduated from law school, take the state bar exam in the state in which you want to practice and get admitted as soon as possible. This is also the time to think about taking the bar exam in states that have reciprocity agreements with other states. You may be able to get admitted in the state where you attended law school and the state where you may want to practice, just by taking one bar exam, or at least one multi-state portion. Find out whether your state requires experience or trial credits before an attorney can practice or sign pleadings. If so, then start obtaining those experiences. The sooner you can hit the ground running, the more attractive a candidate you become. In addition, your actions demonstrate initiative and explain what you have been doing with your time since graduation.

### Write and Get Published

Attempt to have any formal legal writing published and keep your writing skills sharp. Your student status (or recent student status) will qualify you to research and write on many topics, including analysis of recent significant decisions or a split in circuits that hasn't yet been reviewed. You don't have to write a law review article. Instead, focus on monthly special interest newsletters, bar journals, regional legal papers, online legal publications, or even law firm client newsletters (they may be looking for content and/or a person to start one to be issued on a regular basis). A special interest publication might include a quarterly newsletter produced by an in-house counsel association.

Again, the Internet affords a writer unlimited opportunities to have material published. Start with the most respected online legal or business source and review the type of material found there. You can also contact an editor and find out if they are contracting out assignments or looking for articles on particular subjects. Once published, you will boost your credibility with law firms, particularly if you have written in an area in which you are trying to get hired. The income from these articles (if any) may be small, but it will allow you to submit your next piece as an already-published author.

### Move to Where the Job Is and Get Involved

Searching for a job in the city or county where you reside is far easier than doing it from out of town. Even if you have every intention of moving to the locality, until you are there and settled, firms will not take you as seriously. Begin the process of getting involved in the legal community in which you want to practice, even if you do not have legal employment or any immediate prospects of such. You can get involved for the summer, or as a law school graduate.

Join the young lawyers division of the state bar association. Actually attend events and meetings and volunteer for work on committees. Talk with the attorneys with whom you work. They may either have job openings or know of needs within local firms. Most jobs are filled by word of mouth and not posted on the Internet or sought through a headhunter. Lawyers prefer to have personal recommendations, or know first-hand of your connection to the area. The best way to get this information is from local attorneys.

Join groups geared towards serving lawyers in particular practice fields, but only if you have an idea of the area of law in which you want to work. There is bound to be an intellectual property or family law section of the state bar. Again, you must actually be involved if you expect to get any benefit.

Hire yourself out as contract worker or researcher while you're waiting for bar results. Spread the word that you are available for work by talking with local attorneys you've met or know through local organizations. Call small firms and find out if they need help with their current workload. Many small firms don't want to hire a full time attorney, but from time to time use contract workers (if the price is right) to assist during busy times. Be sure to disclose your bar status to the firm before accepting any assignment. Firms will pay you an hourly rate. The going rate varies by locality. (A more detailed discussion of rates can be found in Chapter 12.) A good rule of thumb for attorneys who have experience is to charge half of what your hourly rate would be if you were employed full-time at a firm.

Firms will likely not pay this amount to new lawyers with little or no experience. Small firms will definitely not pay that much. Take less money in the beginning so that you can start earning a reputation for hard work and a solid work product. Make it known to these firms that you are looking for full-time employment or introductions to lawyers who are hiring. Your hard work will pay off—attorneys like to see what you can do before hiring you, or recommending or referring you to someone else. Do a good job with a good attitude and it will happen. Your grades will be less important when they are accompanied by a personal recommendation from someone or backed up by solid legal experience.

Once you have been admitted, there are other excellent ways to get involved in the bar and with local attorneys. Depending on the county or state political organization, some judges will appoint lawyers to handle criminal matters for clients who do not qualify for a public defender. The client will pay a portion of your fee and the state may make up the rest. These cases are a good way to start getting experience, as well as getting to know the attorneys and judges at the courthouse. Although these cases don't pay much, depending on the volume, you may make some money.

### Temporary Agencies

Consider registering with a temporary agency. Many will require that you have passed the bar, but gather information about what you can do before and after passing. This is another good way to get experience and meet local attorneys. Many legal search firms also operate a temporary attorney staffing group. Other companies focus on providing temporary legal help, such as Juris Placement International, Law Match, Ad Hoc Legal Resources or Barrister Referrals, Ltd.

### Volunteer or Intern

Volunteer or apply for an internship with the local district attorney's office. These offices are generally overloaded and will have some type of investigation, trial preparation or general running around that you can do. Volunteering is a financial burden; consider getting a deferment on your loans and working at a non-legal job for extra cash. You must evaluate whether the experience is valuable enough to allow you to do it free. After all, your time spent volunteering is less time spent looking for a paying job.

### Recruiters and Job Search Agencies

Very few recruiters will work with law students or new graduates. Law firms are loath to pay the hefty headhunter fee for a lawyer with no experience and no training. It is unlikely that a recruiter will recoup the time spent on helping you find a job. Law firms turn to recruiters mostly for lateral attorneys at the second to fifth year level, attorneys from out of state, or those with specific training and skills. After the fifth year, most firms will know your reputation in the city and pursue you if there is a need.

A recruiter might work with a law student or recent graduate under limited circumstances or when the recruiter is sure the firm will pay the commission. For example, firms might pay a recruiting commission in practice areas where the demand is high and there is very little legal talent coming in. Or, if the student or new graduate has the potential for significant business (previous career contacts, family business contacts), the recruiter may work with you. In that case, however, you probably could get a job without the recruiter's assistance anyway. If your credentials are that strong, you may want to test the waters with a few firms that have caught your interest, without engaging a recruiter. If you do think having a recruiter would be helpful (perhaps you are looking for a job in a city in which you have as yet no contacts), keep these basics in mind.

Recruiters are paid by on a commission basis. Generally, the fee could be up to 30% of your first year salary—a sizable sum. That means that, ultimately, recruiters work for the law firm and not you. Your interests are secondary to those of the firm. Do not expect that your recruiter will have your career interests at heart. If you are leaving your law firm because you are working too hard, do not expect your recruiter to present only options where there is a clear improvement in your quality of life. Those are decisions that you need to make, anyway. Be sure, however, that your expectations about your recruiters and the role they play are clear.

There are some advantages to using a recruiter. The recruiter can say things about you to a firm that otherwise would be awkward for you to say. The recruiter can assist you in the legwork of finding open positions and gathering information about the group within which there is an opening. A good and experienced recruiter can offer some thoughts on career counseling or alternatives that you may not have considered. The recruiter will likely have some inside information about a firm, particularly if the recruiter is experienced. This could be helpful not only in deciding which firms to talk with, but also in getting information about the attorneys who will be doing the interviewing. The recruiter can give you feedback from firms that interview you, which is something that you normally would never hear. The recruiter can negotiate for you if an offer is to be made.

All recruiters are not equal, however. You will encounter ethical, well-connected recruiters who are genuinely good at what they do. They might give you the straight scoop on a particular partner at a firm or real insight into a specific group. They will keep confidential matters that are confidential. Many times, however, you will encounter recruiters with questionable ethics. Without going into too much detail, these are the recruiters who leak information about your impending move, or who convey information that, for negotiation purposes, should be kept between you and the recruiter. Worse, these recruiters can make you look bad to firms by their own conduct or bad reputation.

Do not hire a recruiter and then set the recruiter loose to find you a job. You must participate in this process, even before you agree to work with a recruiter. Learn about your recruiter and the company for which she works. There might be a difference between the recruiter's reputation and skill level and the reputation of the company. What law firms does this recruiter work with? What type of advertising does this recruiter or the firm do? How does the recruiter develop contacts? How much experience does the recruiter have in career counseling? Does the recruiting firm have a Web site where you can get background information about the company and the individuals employed by it? Ensure that your recruiter has a service-oriented personality and is approachable. This person may be negotiating on your behalf and will be acting as your representative.

Finalize your preparations before working with a recruiter. You must first do some type of self-assessment as to the situation you want or need. Get certified copies of your law school transcript. Have your resume in a final draft before you send it to the recruiter. If you have a professional photograph, you may want to have copies made for the recruiter to give to law firms.

A recruiter will conduct an in-depth interview with you before you begin working together. The interview may take place in person, or over the telephone, but usually from your home if you are already employed at a firm. The interview usually lasts from one and a half to two hours. The interview serves several important functions. The recruiter is essentially pre-screening you for a law firm. They will want to know about your past experience, both legal and non-legal, the type of firm environment you are seeking, salary and benefit requirements. The recruiter will also learn about your personality from the interview, which is what the recruiter will use to help sell you to law firms. You may have to sell yourself to the recruiter if your background is not stellar. This experience will be good preparation as you begin to interview with firms.

This is your time to discuss with the recruiter confidentiality concerns, the logistics of sending out your resume, and the recruiter's experience, philosophy, and professional background. Find out the recruiter's "success rate," which you might define as the ratio between the number of attorneys placed to the number that are still searching one year later.

After talking with you and reviewing your resume, the recruiter may revise your resume or make suggestions. Follow them. You've hired the recruiter for her professional experience and knowledge and to some degree you must make a leap of faith. Many recruiters will reprint your resume into their own format. If that is done, you must proof it before it is ever sent out to a law firm. Recruiters may overlook clerical or proofing mistakes, some of which might not be apparent because it is information about your previous work history or your complete school name. Employers don't debate whether mistakes on resumes are due to the candidate's neglect or the recruiter's carelessness. The bottom line is that these mistakes are your mistakes. Many lawyers will dismiss your application immediately when they spot these types of avoidable errors. Have some sense about the firms in the area in which you are looking. That way, when your recruiter calls you to discuss a firm, you can ask appropriate questions.

You cannot send your resume to most of the firms in the city and then work with a recruiter. If the firm received your resume several months ago, this places the firm and the recruiter in a difficult position with respect to the commission fee. Have a clear understanding of the procedure for sending your resume out. For example, will the recruiter tell you what firm she is submitting the resume to before it goes out?

Likewise, you must be very careful if you have more than one recruiter working for you. Pre-approve all firms that receive your resume, and then keep track of who sent your resume and where. You don't want to have a firm receive your resume from two recruiters who might both seek a commission. The firm will not want to be involved with the situation, which can cost you an offer.

Follow up with your recruiter so that you are both on the same page. If there are changes in your circumstances, either personally or professionally, that the recruiter should know about, be sure to keep him updated. You may have brought a matter to a successful conclusion, which would be excellent anecdotal material for the recruiter to use in talking to firms about you. Or, your family circumstances may have changed, making you less flexible geographically.

Throughout your career, you may receive calls from headhunters. Always return these calls and be courteous to recruiters. You want them to remember you down the road when you may need them. They might also check in with you from time to time and someday, when you are ready to make a move, you will be thankful you were not rude. Don't hesitate to talk to recruiters once you start practicing. It's always good to know what's going on in the marketplace, or to keep tabs on which areas of law are growing the most quickly.

There are numerous database compilations of legal recruiters. Students or lawyers can access the EmplawyerNet database without having to be an EmplawyerNet member (http://www.emplawyer-net.com/recruiter/index.cfm). The excellent Washburn University Law School site offers not only a recruiter directory, but also many other useful links for students and lawyers (www.washlaw.edu). Another database is found at http://legaljournal.net.

Put yourself in the right place at the right time. With a bit of sleuth work, you can figure out the next hot area of practice or a niche area. Start building experience in those areas now through volunteer opportunities, research and seminars. You want to be able to market your "experience" in a burgeoning area because even your limited knowledge may constitute greater capability than a firm has in-house. For example, if public law is a growing area, attend seminars and take third-year classes that deal with public law issues. Save your school materials and search the Internet for recent developments in public law. You will be able to figure out which firms are growing this practice, and then sell your experience and learning to that firm.

Informational interviews are another essential part of your job campaign. These are interviews that you arrange with practicing attorneys or others in the field so that you can learn more about the practice of law and the current market. Inquire about where they believe the practice is headed and what areas are becoming more important in the next five years. All of this information will help you in your job search. You have nothing to lose by asking attorneys for fifteen to twenty minutes of their time. If they say no, you are no further behind than before. If yes, you may learn something. Tell the attorney or other professional that you are not meeting with them in the hopes getting a job with their firm or company. Instead, spell out who you are and what information you are looking for. If there is a connection between you and the other person (similar undergraduate degree, law school), then bring that up as you introduce yourself over the telephone. Attorneys should regard helping out students and recent graduates as part of their responsibility to younger lawyers. Hopefully, you will encounter positive reactions to your requests. Make it as convenient as possible for the attorneys you meet (go to their offices or meet for lunch or coffee near their offices).

A lot of the activity described here falls into the category of networking. A network is comprised of professional contacts, combined with personal acquaintances, law school classmates, neighbors, and parental or family friends. Make sure that people know you are looking for legal employment. Give out some information about the type of work you would like and where. Figure out which contacts are likely to result in an introduction or job lead and focus your efforts on those individuals. Keep an open mind as you go through this process. Remember that you never know where your job lead might come from. Sometimes it is enough to be in the right place at the right time.

*Chapter 5*

# May It Please the Interviewer

## The Informed Student and the On-Campus Interview; How to Ask Good Questions; Frequently Asked Questions

Study groups are forming. Moot court is gearing up. And all the while, in a quiet, behind-the-scenes manner, countless closed-door interviews of law students are taking place. These interviews are your chance, in twenty minutes or less, to distinguish yourself from thirty-nine of your classmates and convince a law firm to give you a second look.

This type of screening is just one step in the interview process for a law student seeking a job with a law firm. These interviews usually last less than a half hour and are conducted by one or two lawyers from the firm. It used to be that a partner and an associate would do the interviewing. But don't be surprised if you see two partners or two associates. Be prepared for an interview by lawyers on any experience level.

These screenings serve an important function for both you and the law firm. From the firm's perspective, recruiting on campus is a traditional method of acquiring new lawyers. From the student's perspective, not only is the interview a chance to clinch the second, or fly-back interview, but also it provides a first live look at a prospective employer.

To make the maximum impression in the screening interview, it is helpful to have a better understanding of its purpose from the law firm's perspective. Lawyers take recruiting seriously. Recruiting is vital to the continued growth of the firm, particularly on the first- and second-year levels. Ideally, a law firm is structured with partners bringing in business and supervising attorneys, senior associates developing that business and handling the work, and mid- and lower-level associates assisting in that work. These are business-driven realities that require a constant influx of young (experience-wise) talent.

Recruiting on campus also helps shape law students' perceptions about the firm, which, of course, impacts the reputation of a firm in the cities where those students ultimately practice. Lawyers call this the image effect. For this reason, law firms take notice when a disgruntled summer associate returns to school and dissuades others from interviewing with the firm. Their reputation is important and is impacted by law students' perceptions.

Recruiting on campus is also important because it screens out applicants who look good on paper, but do not possess the intangible factors lawyers perceive as necessary for success. Your level of maturity will not be readily discernible from your resume, but a skilled interviewer can make some initial judgments in less than twenty minutes.

Lawyers conducting the on-campus interview usually have some interest in interviewing at the particular school. Many are graduates, either of law school or at the undergraduate level. Naturally, these lawyers want to bring top candidates to the firm; when a candidate performs well, it improves the school's reputation for producing prepared lawyers. These lawyers have taken time out of their schedule to travel to the school to interview what may come to over forty candidates a day. Usually, the interviews are held from early morning either through lunch or at lunch as well. One after another, throughout the day, law students walk in, shake hands, answer questions, ask questions, and leave. Given the significant decisions made in a short period of time, your goal at the screening interview is to convince interviewers that you are a standout candidate worthy of a second look. As an aside, be sure to include your picture in the face book, if your law school does one. It enables the interviewer to later connect your resume with your face.

You have a certain amount of control over the interview process. The following are thoughts on steps that you can take to make a favorable impression.

### Do Your Homework

Before you interview with a firm, research information about the firm and its history, clients and reputation. You will impress the interviewer because it shows a real interest in getting to know that particular firm. In addition, given the limited time in an interview, you can focus on the areas that warrant discussion. For example, many firms grew by merging with other firms specializing in a particular field. This is important information to know because interview questions can be geared toward specific issues facing that firm, such as whether there is a difference in firm philosophy that allows one group to run more smoothly than another. You may have read in a newspaper article that a firm partner has left to assume the general counsel position at a Fortune 500 company. This information has a direct impact on the firm's financial picture, and consequently constitutes information you need to explore.

Have some knowledge about the firm's geographical location. Many students spend precious interview minutes asking what it is like to live in a particular city. This information is widely available and students should limit time spent talking about the city and focus more on specifics that are not widely available on line or on the firm's Website. Better questions might be those related to a particular aspect of practicing or living in the city. Ask specific questions that provide useful information and also convey to the interviewer that you have done your homework.

In short, a prepared student will gather as much information as possible before the interview and use that information to formulate good questions.

### Try Not to Interview First with the Firm at the Top of Your List

Interviewing is all about practice and preparation. Avoid having your first interview with the firm that is your top choice. You will be much more comfortable talking about your skills and aptitudes after having discussed them with twenty people in every possible context. Also, you will feel more confident once you have a handle on the logistics of interviewing. Finally, at every interview, you will learn something about the practice of law that will help you ask better questions of your interviewers. For example, you might learn from one interviewer that young employment law attorneys have early and frequent direct contact with clients. That information will provide you with good material to ask about if employment is an area in which you are interested, e.g.: "What are client expectations at your firm with respect to dealing with partners vs. associates?" "What training do new associates get in giving day-to-day legal advice to employers?"

### Your Appearance and Demeanor Should Project Confidence and Competence

Lawyers as a whole are fairly conservative when its comes to appearance. As a result, your appearance should be professional and neat. For men, this means a dark suit, wing-tip shoes and a tie. This is not the time to wear a creative or unusual tie. Nor is it the time for faddish facial hair and earrings. While "creative" or "unusual" might be accepted in some law firms once you are employed as an associate, it is not generally acceptable for the interviewee or summer associate. Attorneys believe that you are putting forward your best, most conservative self during the interview. When you show up to the interview with "creative" or "unusual" their imagination will run away with them about what you will do down the road. You will interview with attorneys from all levels of experience. During the course of your interviewing, you will likely be scrutinized by the "old guard" attorneys, as well as by associates fresh out of law school. Your safest bet, unless you will be visibly uncomfortable, is to project a middle of the road image, one that is not too conservative but also, not too trendy.

Women have a bit more leeway. Consider wearing something other than the standard navy-blue suit. Forty navy blue suits make for one boring day as an interviewer. Instead, wear a well-tailored, moderately conservative suit. Colors in the burgundy, gray, and brown families are appropriate. Red is probably too much. Interviewing lawyers understand that law placement departments make strong recommendations about interview dress, but try not be overly concerned about how conservative your appearance should be. If a cookie-cutter appearance is a deciding factor for the attorneys at a firm, then you probably do not want to work there anyway.

Be sure to have good shoes. They should be free of scuffs and appropriate for the occasion. Women should avoid the extra-high heel. You would not wear those shoes to work every day because they are impractical. It creates the impression that the interview is the only time you dress in your suit (which, as a student, it probably is). If you carry a purse, be sure that it too is professional and not worn out. Many people, attorneys included, make initial assessments about people based on the quality and appearance of shoes and purses.

Practice good posture. This will help you project your voice and exude confidence, even when you do not feel that way. When walking into the interview room, make eye contact, smile, and give a firm handshake. Men, do not shake a female interviewer's hand too firmly; many female attorneys brought this up as something they remember about interviewing students on campus.

There is a fine line between confidence and arrogance. It is appropriate to discuss your qualifications. After all, that is why you are there. It is also appropriate to point out skills or abilities that are not readily apparent from your resume. What is not appropriate, however, is to attempt to turn the tables on the interviewer and ask why you should consider working at this particular firm. One candidate with stellar credentials adopted this approach with her interviewers. She managed to rile them up to the point where she became the subject of an intense cross-examination.

### Convey Enthusiasm

Try to be enthusiastic, engaging and energetic. Interviewers understand that you are juggling moot court competitions, preparing for class and carrying a heavy interview schedule. They also understand that you are suffering from sleep deprivation. (Do not forget that the interviewing attorneys have similar time demands, with the added stress of traveling and being away from our families and work.). All the same, make every effort to muster your energy and make a strong showing. A career in law will only increase the demands on your life, and as with your personal life is probably getting more complicated as the years go by. You must show, even for a brief period, that you have energy and enthusiasm for what you are doing.

Make every attempt to keep the details about your harried life out of the interview. When you are asked, "How are you doing?" avoid saying things like, "Well, you know how it is with moot court, my note due, and I'm behind in my classes." Interviewing attorneys do not want to hear that information. In their minds, they work ten times harder than law students could ever imagine. Nothing you can say about your schedule will be given much credence, so keep it out.

Some lawyers have "tests" for interviewing. For example, lawyers might ask themselves whether they would want to work with you until 2:00 a.m. If you are arrogant, self-absorbed, or devoid of personality, the answer is no and you fail the test. You will not get an offer. Show facets of your personality that have propelled you this far. If you have a sense of humor, let that come through. Attorneys want to work with interesting, motivated people. That is why having varied interests and a resume that reveals a well-rounded background is important.

Another common test is, "Would I leave this person alone with my clients?" Your appearance, confidence and maturity level are some of the important factors here. Attorneys look for people who can relate to business people, whatever the client's job level. In other words, law firms want attorneys who make other people feel comfortable and secure. You will likely fail this test if you come across as too shy or withdrawn, or if you are unable to carry on small talk in the interview setting.

### Know Thyself

Refresh your recollection about facts on your resume and also review your writing sample. An interviewing attorney will have just reviewed one or both of these documents and your experience will be at the forefront of his mind. An interviewer once asked a law student a specific question about her moot court brief. For one agonizing moment, she could not even remember the subject of the brief. When a law student cannot remember important facts about her background, it suggests to the interviewer that the student cannot perform under pressure.

Another attorney asked a candidate about his moot court brief. Even though he had argued both sides of the issues in this brief before a state supreme court, he could not remember the legal issue at all. He then remembered the issue, but changed his mind about the constitutional provision three times during the interview. This looks bad. If you have to guess, stick with it and hope that a new subject is raised.

You should review and memorize, if necessary, important facts about your background.

## Exercise Good Judgment About the Subject Matter of the Interview

This is a bit of dialogue that has happened many times over:

Q: "Why are you interested in a larger firm?"

A: "Because I'm tired of insurance defense work where I have to work with [ambulance-chasing] [insert comment] plaintiff's lawyers on the other side."

Are there some plaintiffs' lawyers who are ambulance chasers? Surely! Is this answer going to offend some attorneys? Yes. You do not know the entire background of the attorney with whom you are talking. You do not know if this attorney is married to a plaintiff's lawyer or formerly practiced as one. Now, if not wanting to work with plaintiff's lawyers really is your reason for wanting to work elsewhere, then state it more diplomatically: "I want to change firms because I'd like to work with attorneys who have training and experience on more complex matters."

Here is where doing your homework and knowing your audience is vital. The bottom line, however, is that you must exercise good judgment in the subjects you bring up.

## Ask Thoughtful or Probing Questions; Avoid Confrontational or Offensive Questions

Law students frequently ask, "What is a good interview question?" A good question is one that is designed to elicit relevant information, but when asked, does not put the interviewer on the defensive or reveal you to be uninformed. Before you can formulate good questions, you need to understand what information is relevant and why you need to know it.

Relevant information can be grouped into several categories. The first is the financial stability of the firm. Because you are (hopefully) looking at a firm for the long haul, knowledge about its financial stability, including its client base, should be one of the main factors on which you base your decision. For example, you need to know whether this firm is so dependent on a particular industry, client or group of clients, that a blip on the radar screen could have huge repercussions for the firm. Also, you need to know information about the firm's largest clients: How long have they been with the firm, did they come over with a partner recently joining the firm? Does the firm provide a wide range of services for that client? The economy will not always be strong. When the real estate market bottoms out, for example, firms with litigation or bankruptcy practices will probably do well. This is information you need to know.

A related, but equally important, category of questions concerns where groups within the firm draw their business. For example, does the litigation practice draw its clients from the corporate side of the firm? Is one person (a rainmaker) solely responsible for all of the employment work? (If so, you should make it your business to know how close that person is to retirement, whether that person has a history of moving around, etc.) Relevant information would include the source of the firm's business, as the source of work for the groups within the firm.

You also need to know the areas within the firm that are growing now and what is projected for future growth. All firms attempt to identify future needs by practice area. Many attorneys are able to give a prediction as to how their practice will do in an economic upturn or down cycle and thus plan accordingly. Perhaps the firm has targeted a particular area for growth. For example, many firms find that having an employment practice makes the firm more desirable to large clients. Establishing or expanding an existing employment practice has been identified as a growth area.

Information relating to the management structure of the firm is extremely important, especially when you are looking at a firm for the long term. For example, if the firm is one of several offices throughout the United States or the world, where are the big decisions made and who makes them? How does that impact the day-to-day workings of the attorneys in the satellite offices? What about hiring decisions on the staff and attorney levels? It may take longer to hire attorneys when those attorneys have to pass muster in the home office in Raleigh or Dallas. These factors will impact your practice down the road.

Information relating to the training and review of attorneys is important. You should have a good understanding of how younger lawyers are trained. Do groups within the firm tend to throw people in and watch them sink or swim? Are younger lawyers mentored? Is there a formal mentoring process in place? Do younger lawyers find it difficult to find a mentor and learn from that person? Some of these are group-specific questions and the interviewer can compare and contrast groups that do these things well.

Some, but not all, issues relating to partnership are important. For example, it is a bit early for you to worry about tiers within the compensation ranks. It is not too early to ask whether the firm hires its associates with an eye towards making all of them partner.

Information relating to the firm's expectations for its young attorneys is important. For example, is it expected that young attorneys are involved in community organizations, pro bono work, or marketing events? While many firms will give standard issue answers, you will occasionally glean some important information from the interviewer. A busy firm may have low expectations with respect to serious marketing by young associates; they would rather you work and work hard servicing existing firm clients. Another firm might have high expectations about your involvement in marketing and community related efforts; this firm expects every associate and member to be productive from a business generation standpoint.

Information relating to the firm's business culture is important. For example, do the litigation and transactional attorneys work hard in cross-selling their clients? Do partners share the credit when a new, large client is brought in to the firm? How are large matters staffed? Does the firm allow groups to borrow associates freely from one another or are partners somewhat proprietary with associates? Few associates ever ask about the interviewer's daily routine. For example, are most of the interviewer's dealings on the phone? Does she work closely with other attorneys? Does she work closely with attorneys in other practice groups?

Now that you know the type of information that is important, use these guidelines in formulating your questions. First, avoid putting your interviewer on the defensive. A number of interviewees have asked interviewers, "Why aren't there more female partners?" Do not ask this question. If this is information that you need to know, then ask the question more diplomatically: "I noticed that an equal number of men and women start out as first year attorneys with the firm, but at the partnership level there is a large disparity. Are there outside factors that might account for this change?" You will get nowhere if you create an "us" versus "them" atmosphere with the interviewer.

Even if the job you are interviewing for is a summer associate position, formulate your questions as if you were asking them from the standpoint of an attorney with the firm. After all, you are looking at these firms for permanent employment and you need information relating to your position as a permanent associate. Information about the summer program is generally available online or from returning second or third year law students. Attorneys get concerned when an interviewee asks questions relating only to the summer program. It demonstrates a lack of foresight. Also, you will have just joined the ranks of hundreds of other forgettable applicants who ask those same thoughtless questions.

Avoid asking questions for the sake of asking questions. Many attorneys can tell when an interviewee really has no interest in the firm and is simply going through the motions. If that is the case, work hard at asking relevant questions that might help you make decisions about other firms in which you are interested. For example, find out what made the interviewer choose her area of law. You might learn something.

One good approach is to frame your questions as if you were actually employed at the firm. For example, "As a first year associate, would I have the opportunity to attend client meetings or argue motions?" "As a mid-level associate, are cases staffed such that I would have the opportunity to work with new attorneys?"

Strive to avoid canned responses. There are some questions that an interviewer will ask that tend to elicit a canned response: Why this city? Why litigation (or tax, or corporate, etc.)? To avoid giving what amounts to a memorized and insincere response, have a number of ways to convey the thoughts you want to convey. Practice saying something in different ways.

As previously mentioned, avoid asking the same, tired questions that everyone else asks. It is disheartening to hear twenty-five people ask "do you like it?" or "tell me about the summer program." Students who exercise some original thought in this area get high marks.

### Be Prepared for Off-the-Wall and Other Unfair Questions

Nobody trains an interviewer on how to interview. As a result, you will get some good interviewers and those who could use some help. Interviewers who ask off-the-wall questions are in the latter category. A law student was once asked, "if you were stranded on a desert island and could have one book, what would it be." She figured out too late that this attorney was looking for a particular answer (the Bible). Her answer ("a long one") did not go over well. So, when you are asked what type of tree, animal, vegetable, etc., most describes you, do not be flippant, but answer the question and move on.

Another favorite question that is patently unfair to ask a law student is, "In what area do you want to practice?" It is perfectly acceptable to say that you do not know; you simply cannot know. Instead, talk about the skills that you have that may incline you towards one area of law over another. For example, if you perform well in an area that has definite answers, you may be inclined towards securities law. On the other hand, if you are comfortable with gray areas, you might do well in commercial litigation.

Occasionally, you will get an interviewer that asks inappropriate questions or makes inappropriate remarks. This is where you must exercise good judgment. Some inappropriate questions or remarks should be handled at the time of the interview. For example, an interviewer may ask one of the "forbidden questions" about your family situation or desire to have children. In that instance, do not answer the question directly. Instead, address the root of the interviewer's concern. An interviewer wanting to know about children and plans for the future is probably concerned about your level of commitment to the firm. Your response might be, "If you are concerned about my level of commitment, I can assure you that my job is a priority." An interviewer who asks these types of questions should raise a red flag in your mind. Consider whether this is indicative of a deeper problem within the firm or with this individual.

There are also situations that you should not attempt to handle at the interview. For example, a male interviewer made reference to the female interviewee's legs, which is plainly inappropriate in any work context, let alone an interview. These types of comments should be handled through the dean of recruiting services or director of that office. Rest assured, the firm will be notified and will take action against the attorney.

## Take Full Advantage of Prior Work Experience

Maturity and experience are excellent selling points and you should be prepared to discuss your experience in detail. Think about the skills that will transfer into the legal world. For example, people with a background in sales tend to do well with clients. Both law and sales are service industries. You may be able to point to specific projects in your former work life that involved organization and planning. These, too, are important aspects of your job as a lawyer. Be prepared to give specific examples of your experience; these examples provide the maximum impact.

Finally, it is important for lawyers to have good business sense. To the extent you can capitalize on your prior experience in this regard, whether that be management, strategizing or analytical skills, it will be worthwhile.

## Look For Areas of Common Ground with Your Interviewer

A law student spent an entire on-campus interview talking about Italy, drawing maps of the country and discussing Italian food with the interviewer. She was not surprised that she received a fly-back to the firm. Years later, as an associate at that firm, the former student and interviewer were still talking about Italy. They connected on some level and enjoyed the interview.

Now, there are instances where the interview becomes a single-subject discussion, which can leave you at a disadvantage when it comes time for the interviewer to review your credentials. If you find that the interview is heading that way, attempt to bring in other information within the context of the discussion. In the previous example, the law student might have mentioned that she not only enjoyed traveling, but also writing. That would provide a natural segue into a discussion about her writing experience.

## Listen

Try not to be so eager to talk about yourself that you miss the opportunity to learn important information about the interviewer or the firm. This information will help you ask better, more focused questions. It will also communicate to the interviewer that you are listening. One partner was irked that after telling the interviewee that she (the partner) had a child, and after looking at pictures of the interviewee's children and talking about them, the interviewee did not ask any questions about the partner's children. In short, it is important to have give-and-take in any conversation, including the interview. You cannot do that unless you are listening.

## Cocktail Parties

Occasionally, a firm will sponsor a cocktail hour at a place near the school and invite a number of candidates. The purpose, of course, is to have more exposure to the candidates in a less formal setting. Make no mistake, this is still an interview and you should conduct yourself accordingly. If you drink, do so moderately. Do not dominate conversations with the firm representatives; they want to talk with as many candidates as possible. Also, be discreet when discussing these parties with other law students. You may have been selected randomly or because of your credentials. You do not want to fuel bad feelings among members of your class who may feel left out. Be sure to thank your hosts for the free food and drinks.

## If Disaster Strikes?

If a complete and utter disaster happens, like you fall off a chair, throw up on the desk, have to run to the bathroom mid-question, ask the interviewer if she is pregnant and she's not (these are all true stories, as you may have guessed) then do not panic. Your reaction to difficult circumstances will often determine whether the disaster is fatal. Maintain your poise and carry on as normally as you can. If the situation is just so bad that you cannot carry on, politely excuse yourself and leave. There is nothing more than you can do at that point.

Are thank you notes necessary after the screening interview? Thank you notes cannot hurt, but must be done promptly if they are to have any value. Often, decisions about whether to bring a candidate back are made within days of the initial interview. Thus, as a gesture, it will have no impact unless it is received in advance of any offer decisions. The notes should be handwritten and legible, of course. Moreover, it is appropriate to send the thank you to one attorney and ask that she extend your gratitude to the other attorneys that may have been present. Thank you notes have more impact if you reference something discussed in an interview. Remember, without specific references, your face will likely get mixed in with the crowd.

The firm will likely ask one or more students back for a second set of interviews at the firm offices. This is known as a fly-back or drive-back interview. If the firm is within driving distance of your law school, more students will be invited for a second interview, partly because the cost is low. Another reason, however, is that local students may be more likely to stay local once they begin practicing.

Always be a gracious loser and refrain from talking negatively about firms. These comments, no matter how innocuous, have a way of getting back to the firm. Also, you never know where you might find yourself interviewing in the future. Statistically, you will change jobs nearly seven times over the course of your career. You do not want firms to rule you out before you even begin practicing.

At the screening interview stage, law firms are looking at both tangible and intangible factors. Interviewers want to see a mature, poised and confident student who is able to articulate solid reasons for interviewing with the firm. Your appearance is important, as is your ability to obtain relevant information about the firm or city where it is located. These factors will also be important as you progress to the next level: the fly-back interview.

### Common Questions Asked By Lawyers in Interviews

Ask me a hard question.

Are you geographically flexible? [This is a legal way of eliciting inappropriate information. For example, "Will your husband move with you?"]

In what size firm do you think you will be a good fit? Why?

Why are you interested in this particular firm?

Tell me what you know about our firm.

We do [insurance defense] [products liability], tell me why you would be interested in that area of law.

What are you looking for in a firm?

Why did you decide to go to law school?

Do you have any early ideas about the area of law in which you want to practice?

Tell me some things about you that would incline you more towards litigation or transactional work.

Tell me about yourself.

Why should I take you back to the firm for more interviews?

Tell me about your moot court brief. What were the contentions on the other side?

Tell me about your law review note. What was the most difficult part about writing this note?

What connection do you have with this geographic area?

What are the main factors on which you will base your decision?

Tell me something about your experience that is not on your resume.

What is your favorite/least favorite law school class? Why?

Why did you choose your major in your undergraduate work?

Did you work as an undergraduate?

Are you working while attending law school?

Where do you see yourself in ten years?

What are some of your weaknesses and how have you tried to address them?

# Chapter 6

# You're Flying Now

## Special Considerations for the Second Interview; Making the Arrangements; Essential and Appropriate Questions; Lunch and Dinner Etiquette

Assuming the initial interview goes well and the firm has room in its summer program, you may get called for a "fly-back" or second interview. The interview guidelines discussed in Chapter 5 are equally applicable in the fly-back context. This chapter focuses on some additional issues that may arise in the fly-back context, as well as some thoughts on the logistics of those interviews.

It may be a very short period between the on-campus interview and the offer from the firm to talk further. Matters are happening quickly on the employer end. The interviewer will return to the firm and discuss, at the next recruiting committee meeting, those students who merit a second look. Then, the attorney with whom you interviewed, or the recruiting coordinator (who might also be the human resources person) will likely call and ask you to come to the firm for a series of interviews. You may get a confirming letter a few days later.

Be sure to have a functioning answering machine. Check it regularly and, if you have roommates, agree on a protocol for recording and reporting messages. Things can get confusing when you are in the process of interviewing with dozens of firms and possibly sending out letters as well. The message you get from the firm will probably be professional and brief.

You should already know whether you want to interview further with a particular firm. If you are no longer interested in the firm, tell the caller that you appreciate the offer, but are pursuing other opportunities. Attorneys will appreciate your candor. It is understandable that students would want to have a "back-up" offer, and thus go on fly-backs with firms they are not seriously considering. You will be doing both the firm and your classmates a favor, however, if you instead turn down the interview offer. You may be the beneficiary of an offer at another firm because a student declined to pursue a job in which she was not interested.

If you are serious about the firm, accept the fly-back offer and schedule your interview as soon as possible. Delay only works to your disadvantage. Positions within the summer class will decrease as more students accept outstanding offers. That means the number of offers of summer employment will be reduced or scaled back. Additionally, the firm may want a broad representation of schools and, if any of your fellow students have already accepted offers of summer employment with that firm, then your chance of getting an offer decreases.

Check in with the recruiting coordinator to finalize or confirm details for your travel arrangements and interview schedule. The firm either will make its travel reimbursement policy available to you or the coordinator will discuss the parameters with you over the telephone. Often, the firm will cover airfare, hotel and taxis to and from the airport. The firm will appreciate any savings that you can arrange, such as flying coach, staying over a Saturday night, or combining a fly-back with another firm so that the cost can be split between them. Your career services office will have sample reimbursement forms, or the firm may have provided them to the office already. Talk with the coordinator if you cannot afford to front the travel expenses. Potential employers understand that students have high expenses and little or no income. There is no need for you to forego an interview opportunity because you lack the finances; something can and should be worked out.

Find out before you leave for your trip exactly where you need to be and at what time. Having the logistics nailed down before you leave will alleviate stress and minimize complications.

The coordinator should have a tentative list of interviewers a few days before the interview. Ask for this information and then research the educational and professional background for each of the attorneys. Once the schedule is finalized, you will have a definite idea of how much time to allocate to the firm. Some students are able to schedule two interviews in one day. If you planning more than one interview, be sure that you first check with the respective coordinators and tell them of your plans. Interviews commonly run over, so leave plenty of time in the event the first interview runs late and for travel contingencies.

Coordinating the recruiting schedule for all of the students interviewed throughout the season is a Herculean effort. Many attorneys participate in the recruiting process and it requires a substantial time commitment. The responsibility for recruiting is in addition to the attorney's daily work demands. Last minute client matters may require that attorneys shuffle interview times or dates, which can create difficulty for already harried recruiting coordinators.

Unless you have a bona fide emergency or urgent circumstances, avoid canceling (unless you are no longer interested in the firm), rescheduling or changing the arrival time for your fly-back. A change of plan on your part creates an additional burden on the recruiting coordinators and will likely evoke the ire of some attorneys.

Bring extra copies of your resume, cover letter, and list of references with you and review the specifics the night before your interviews. As you may have found out during the on-campus interviews, details of your moot court brief or law review note are prime material for interview questions.

Many firms will take you to dinner the night before your interview and to lunch on the day of the interview. It is not unusual for the attorney's spouse or "significant other" to attend the dinner. (When personal or family time is limited, attorneys often include spouses or significant others in firm outings or dinners.) Interviewers often rely on other's perceptions of a candidate. Another set of ears and eyes are always helpful.

One of the purposes of the dinner is to determine how you conduct yourself in public; how you treat the wait-staff at the restaurant, the valet, or anyone else with whom you come into contact. Throughout dinner, your host-attorney will be trying to get a better feel for your personality, interests, maturity, and other qualifications. This is part of the interview. It is not the time to let down your guard, ask borderline questions that you would never think of asking at the firm or divulge information about yourself that will be held against you. This is not the time to drink excessively, even when attorneys drinking on the firm's tab are indulging.

There are several things that you should want to get out of the dinner interview. First, make a good impression. The advice relating to the interview applies equally strongly here. Second, get information about the attorneys with whom you will interview the next day. Ask relevant, work-related questions; do not engage in gossiping, even if the attorneys at the dinner divulge that type of information. Find out as much as you can about your dinner companions' day-to-day practice, lifestyle and interests. You will learn a lot of information about the firm over the course of the evening. The attorneys not at the dinner who will interview you at the firm the next day will have gotten a report about you before you arrive to see them. Make sure your answers are consistent; people will be comparing notes.

You will likely interview with a combination of associates and partners. Firms try to include lower-level and senior associates into the associate mix. At many firms, you can get an indication of the level of the firm's interest in you by the attorneys lined up for the interview. The firm is obviously interested if you are talking with several senior or named partners.

Firms make every effort to include as interviewers lawyers who graduated from your law school. This could be a bonus for you—these attorneys have a strong interest in bringing great candidates to the firm. Interviews with these attorneys will help you in other ways too. Find out how prepared these attorneys felt they were for practice, or ask what elective courses these attorneys found useful. This is how you start learning about the practice of law; use these interviews as a resource.

If you have expressed a strong interest in litigation or another specific group, attorneys from those groups will likely be on your list. Again, this gives you a chance to find out more information about your potential group or partners.

You probably will not interview with the attorney you talked with on campus, although you may see that person as you interview throughout the firm. If not, and time permits, ask to say hello before you leave. It enables the on-campus attorney to reconnect your name with your face.

Other students, perhaps from your school, might interview at the firm on the same date that you do. All of the students who interview on that date might meet with the recruiting coordinator and tour the firm together. Try not to let this throw you off; the competition may look professional and well put together, but all of you are there because you have the credentials and "something else" that the interviewer thought was important.

All of your interactions with firm personnel will be scrutinized. Be polite and professional to the receptionist, recruiting coordinator, and staff, as well as others that you meet on your tour. Try not to let your guard down too much with the recruiting coordinators. These people collect the thoughts of other attorneys, disseminate information about you and others' reactions to you. Hiring partners are busy and rely heavily on the human resources people.

Ask the first person you talk with to go through your interview list and give you some background on the attorneys with whom you will interview. Hopefully, you have already done your homework and remember some basic information about these lawyers. Even if that is the case, be sure to ask about the attorneys' background anyway because you will learn personal information that you might not otherwise discover. This gives you more information on which to establish common ground with your subsequent interviewers.

Be sure to note the physical surroundings of each attorney's office and look for areas of common ground or subjects to ask about. For example, many attorneys have pictures of their children or drawings done by them. In this instance, it is appropriate for an interviewee to ask about ways in which attorneys work together to achieve some type of balance with family and work. While discussions about the attorney's children might sound like idle chit-chat, the information you learn will say a lot about the firm and the attorney's attitude towards her coworkers.

Attorneys within a firm will talk to one another about you, even while you are in the process of interviewing within the building. It is fairly common for attorney X to call attorney Y and say "ask candidate Z about her reasons for wanting to come here; I couldn't get a straight answer." Or, when attorneys believe they've heard a canned response, they tell another person on the list to ask the same question and see if they get the same response. Attorneys do compare answers. A typical question that often gets comparison is your reasons for wanting to practice in this city and at this firm.

The types of interview questions and the subjects you should be exploring were discussed in Chapter 5. Some additional issues often arise during the fly-back. Some students use this opportunity to try the "direct approach." This is where a candidate will state: "I've done my research, I know where I want to practice, and it's at your firm." Don't say this unless you truly mean it, and have a good basis for making such an assertion. Otherwise, it reflects more on your judgment that you think it appropriate to make a career decision and be certain about where you want to be after some research and a series of short interviews.

Never tell the attorneys at the end of your interview schedule that you have no further questions because they've been all answered. This is insulting and short-sighted on the student's part. You could not possibly have asked all the relevant questions of a potential employer. During the interview process, don't be shy about asking the same questions of different lawyers. Be aware of identical answers and be aware of widely differing answers. For example, let's say you ask lower level associates about opportunities for practical experience as a first year. Attorney "A" says that the firm has demonstrated a commitment to helping first year attorneys get experience and his experience has born that out. Attorney "B" says the firm talks about experience, but does not put forth any effort to enable the attorney to get it. You should then ask yourself some questions: (1) Am I getting the straight story from these associates? (2) Is attorney A exaggerating? (3) Are certain groups within this firm more committed to attorney training than others? You should then follow up with other interviewers about attorney A's experience. Ask a more senior associate and partner: "Attorney A seems to have a lot of relevant, practical experience. Is that typical for first year associates within the firm?"

Depending on the answers to this question, you will learn detailed, relevant information about the firm. Refrain from quoting attorney B—it could prove embarrassing for her and for you.

Lawyers will sometimes ask about other firms or other types of firms with whom you are interviewing. Answer the question, but exercise great caution before making any comment about any of those firms. You should be suspicious if an attorney talks negatively about another firm, particularly one with whom you are interviewing. Such behavior is unprofessional and makes a clear statement about that lawyer.

Take a lawyer up on offers to call with any questions. This is your opportunity to clear up conflicting information or impressions about the firm. This is also your opportunity to make a further favorable impression. The attorney will report your conversation to the hiring coordinator or partner and it not only puts your name in front of people again, but also conveys your interest in the firm. Any subsequent calls should be about relevant and important information. Try not to make up something solely for the sake of calling. When the interview with any particular attorney is concluded, have your parting thoughts organized so that you do not end the conversation on an awkward note. For example, thank the attorney for taking the time to talk with you, and perhaps state that you realize what an important decision this is on both ends and you want to make sure that you have all the information you need to make it. Most attorneys extend this offer to candidates; virtually all report that candidates never call back.

Observe how attorneys and support staff interact with one another as you walk the hallways of the firm. Many candidates are able to get a feeling about the culture of the firm from just one day of observing these interactions. Picture yourself working in this environment; does it feel right or is it too conservative and stuffy? Are people friendly and eager to provide assistance with directions to the bathroom or breakroom? These factors will give a context to the specific pros and cons that you identify during decision time.

After your last interview, ask to see the library or other facilities within the firm if you were not shown them before. If time permits, try to get a sense of the area in which the firm is located. Use any time you have before or after the interview to familiarize yourself with city and gathering information about it. Cost of living and the availability of cultural and entertainment events will be among the considerations on which you will make your decision.

Interviewing and talking with attorneys across many disciplines and all experience levels has inherent value, independent of whether you receive an offer. Few people get such an inside glimpse of a law firm at work. As an attorney who will someday be on the other side of the interviewing table, remember the experience and incorporate the positive aspects into your interview style.

# Chapter 7

# The Summer Courtship

**How to Survive the Extended Summer
Interview; Information You Must Get from
the Firm; Managing the Summer Social Calendar**

Practical training as a lawyer begins as a summer associate. The summer associate experience varies greatly, not only from firm to firm, but also from student to student.

Some firms take the approach that they are courting new associates for future employment, and must create an enjoyable, activity-filled summer experience. These are the associates who get to enjoy lengthy lunches and white water rafting trips, and who gain ten pounds over the summer. Other firms try the "realistic approach" and give summer associates a taste of what being a first-year lawyer is like. These associates are expected to bill a certain number of hours and much of their time is billed to clients. Both situations provide practical training, although the summer associate at the first type of firm may be so busy socializing (and eating) she may not realize it.

The extent to which a student gains practical experience is largely self-determined. For some, the clerkship experience is a means to a permanent job. They show up, do their assigned work satisfactorily and, especially in a booming economy, get an offer. Mission accomplished. Others view the experience as the training and apprenticeship program that it should be. The summer clerkship is where you should start learning your craft and understanding some of the subtle aspects of events shaping your career, like the impact of the economy on your practice area, or the importance of a partner who has taken you under his wing. This is where the impact of the culture of a group and the attorneys working within it should start to be impressed on you. You should also during this time be cultivating good work habits and honing research and writing skills. The opportunities exist for discovering, doing or experiencing all of these things, no matter the approach taken by the firm. The trick is to learn how to take advantage of them. Those subjects, as well as the expectations of the law firm for its summer associates and the dos and don'ts for clerks, are discussed in this chapter.

The first thing to understand is why your clerkship experience is not significant. You aren't adding any real value to the law firm for which you are clerking. With very few exceptions, the value the client receives for your work is not commensurate with the amount the client is being billed for your time (if the client is even being billed for your work). Nor will you be learning much substantive law. The value of this experience does not rest on any unique talent or knowledge that you are bringing to the firm as a summer associate. There are always exceptions, but they are truly few and far between.

Here's why the experience is significant. Most obviously, this is an in-depth interview by you of your potential employer. If you investigate properly and know what to look for, just about everything you need to know about what you're getting into is there. Equally, this is the firm's chance to evaluate your potential and get a close look at your skills, personality and interests.

Much of the significance of this experience, however, is less obvious. Your first solid impressions about the practice of law will be formed over the course of your summer clerkship. Many lasting professional and personal relationships will begin to form during this summer. Depending on your experience, you will gain some context for subsequent law school courses and your initial first-year lawyer experiences. In short, recognize that the value of the summer experience (for both the firm and the student) is something beyond payment for services rendered. The value lies in the opportunity for the players to learn more about one another and for the student to learn more about the practice of law.

Your summer clerkship experience will be shaped by the economy. In a seller's market, you are in the driver's seat. Firms tend to notch up their wooing of summer clerks in favorable economic times because they are in need of warm bodies to do the work. One summer program included overnight and weekend trips, concerts, and a city-wide scavenger hunt, all while regularly dining with firm attorneys at their homes and in restaurants. The sooner you understand why you are being treated so well, the better you will be able to focus on the important factors in the interview process.

In a flagging economy or when law school enrollment is high, law firms have less difficulty procuring new lawyers. Competition amongst law students can be tough and firms will spend less money wining and dining summer clerks. Sometimes there is less money to be spent on recruitment. In fact, in weak economic times, the clerk may spend most of her time actually working.

For some reason, the social aspects of a summer program carry great weight with many law students. Summer programs are even rated by associates based on how frequent and entertaining the firm events are. Some students equate enjoyable, activity-filled summer programs with a higher level of care and concern for associates. Don't be fooled. The social activities planned by the firm mean very little in terms of the firm's commitment to its associates. A lackluster summer program does not mean that the firm doesn't care about its associates. The attrition rate for associates is likely to be just as high at the "social" firms than at those with a no-frills summer program. (Although no research has been done on this, the attrition rate could actually be higher at these more "social" firms because students accept these jobs and have high expectations about the care and feeding they will get from the firm as an associate, which of course simply does not happen.) Always remember why law firms plan fun activities for summer associates: to convince students to choose their firm over another; and to allow lawyers a better opportunity to get to know and evaluate summer associates.

With those thoughts in mind, the following are some specific issues for your consideration as a summer clerk.

**You will be nervous your first day; so are all the other summer people**

Your first day as a summer associate may be your first day of professional work. For those who attended law school straight from college, you may be in for a shock. You may not be used to getting up so early or working throughout the day in one setting. Sometimes even the physical surroundings are intimidating—many law firms are designed to daunt and awe visitors to the firm. Nevertheless, just as with any new experience, view it as a challenge and a necessary step towards your ultimate goal of practicing law. Take comfort in knowing that your fellow summer associates probably feel the same way.

Get to know the other summer associates. Introduce yourself at the earliest opportune time and find out one or two pertinent facts about their background—where are they from, do they have a family, etc. Study the facebook, if one is provided, in order to learn some basics about your colleagues. Summer classes quickly develop a collective reputation among the attorneys at a firm. One class established early on that the summer associates were extremely competitive with one another. Another class was relatively quiet and professional, and did not socialize much outside the office.

Some classes establish an early reputation as "partiers." People like to make these generalizations about classes as they come in each year. Do your best to foster a collegial atmosphere with your fellow associates. Avoid becoming associated with the inevitable cliques that form or limiting your interactions to just a few other summer associates. The recruiting committee will be evaluating you on your ability to get along with others, and that includes getting along with your summer colleagues.

It is also important for you to seek out and introduce yourself to firm associates and partners. Firm attorneys—out of embarrassment or laziness—don't often take the initiative when they see a new face in the hallway. They probably have no idea what your name is (and know that they probably should). Introduce yourself first. Remember the attorneys that you have met. If you need to employ some mnemonic devices to remember who is who, do it. These are examples of professionalism that will help distinguish you from your peers.

### The summer program is one long interview by you of the firm

Your summer should be spent gathering information in order to make one of the more important decisions of your career. Figure out where the happy (and unhappy) associates are and find out why they enjoy (or don't enjoy) their job. You need to target associates at various levels (junior and senior) and talk details with them. If you ask general, thoughtless questions like "do you like it" you will get equally thoughtless responses. Just as in the interview stage, you need to focus on specifics and ask questions designed to give you real answers, not the party line.

Ask the permanent associates what they do on a day-to-day basis, what types of clients they work for and how that impacts on their work, what practical experiences they have had and how early they got them, and ask whether it was difficult to obtain those experiences or whether any special factors contributed to their obtaining the experiences. One lower-level associate gained excellent practical experience because a partner in his group withdrew from the firm. There was no one else to do the work and this associate rose to the challenge. His experience was unusual.

Ask how the associate wound up in a particular group. Find out what aspects of that practice the associate enjoys or does not enjoy. Solicit opinions on what skills or personality traits are needed for the type of work the associate performs. By their fourth or fifth year, lawyers should be able to describe the type of personality traits that promote success in a particular practice area. For example, working with certain types of clients might require patience or extreme fortitude. You need to explore these matters and ask detailed questions of these associates. Only then will you begin to get an accurate picture of what associate life is like at a firm.

Consider your source as you ask these questions. You may be getting the party line from some associates. Some don't have the nerve to give you the straight story. They may be up for partner soon and not want to say anything that would put them in a bad light. Be aware that associates recognize that it is to their advantage to bring new blood to the firm and may not want to discourage new associates. More work can be delegated and there are more people to pitch in for the inevitable emergencies.

Don't be above offering to take associates to lunch (put that summer salary to practical use). Many associates are hesitant to ask summer people to lunch because if the firm does not pay, the associate might feel pressure to pick up the bill. Often, given high loan repayments and increased family commitments, associates don't have the extra money. This hesitancy inhibits a lot of meaningful interaction. Find out the firm policy on paying for lunches and plan accordingly. If the firm does not pay for lunches, invite associates to lunch and perhaps jokingly make it clear that this is "dutch" or that you'd like to go somewhere inexpensive to keep within your budget.

Talk with partners as well. Partners love to talk about their work and the clients they represent. Don't hesitate to ask what the partner does on a day-to-day basis. Is she on the phone with clients? Do clients expect immediate, direct advice on particular business matters? Is most of the partner's time spent supervising other lawyers within the group? Does this partner have significant firm responsibilities like recruiting or associate reviews? Why did the partner choose a particular area of law? Importantly, explore the partner's thoughts on the future of her practice area. What will the needs of this practice group be when you graduate? Are there any significant legislative changes that might impact this practice group? From the partner's experience, ask what skills or personality characteristics tend to fare well in the group.

Make it your business to know about the larger firm clients. Where is the most revenue coming from? How solid is that relationship? Are there particular industries or clients that make up more than 10% of the firm's revenue? Much of this information can be learned simply by listening. Lawyers tend to talk about the clients that are dominating their time. For your purposes, this is not just idle talk; it is relevant information for your decision-making process.

You should watch to see how particular partners treat their associates. Do they know their associates well? Do they talk to one another about matters outside of work? Do their actions square with what they tell you when they are trying to sell you on the firm? One partner made an obvious blunder at a firm party where summer associates and non-firm people were present. The partner was talking with a group of people that included a first-year attorney at the firm and a summer associate. He consistently introduced the summer associate to non-firm guests, but not the first year attorney. In fact, he virtually ignored her, which was probably not lost on those present. The young attorney subsequently left the firm, citing lack of training and mentoring among her reasons for leaving.

Observe how the associates and staff treat one another. Some firms have maintained a fairly formal atmosphere where firm employees refer to partners as "Ms." or "Mr." Do lawyers know the staff member's names? Do they introduce employees to clients or visiting attorneys?

Finally, begin to gather additional information about the needs of the firm (and groups within the firm) two or three years from now. Because firms plan ahead with regard to associate needs and client development budgeting, you should be able to get some reliable information.

### The summer program is one long interview of you by the firm

From a recruiting standpoint, the summer clerkship is a great deal for the law firm. Attorneys get an extended opportunity to interview and observe the candidate in a variety of social and professional situations. The attorneys will also have a body of written work from which to review the associate's analytical ability and technical skills. Finally, aspects of the candidate's personality that would not otherwise be manifest in regular interviews will become apparent over the course of the summer.

Law firms have limited expectations of summer associates. There is little prospect that you will be efficient or provide a work product that evinces substantive knowledge of the law. On the other hand, when it comes to legal analysis and writing, there are high expectations that you will turn in grammatically correct and mistake-free work. In fact, this is an absolute requirement. Firms also anticipate that you will be able to hit the major issues and cite the primary authority for any legal memoranda that you prepare. All of the authority you rely on in a memorandum should be checked for accuracy and whether it is still good law. Again, these are minimum expectations. To the extent you can think creatively about an issue or raise tangential issues that perhaps the attorney did not think about is a bonus. It is further expected that you will handle yourself appropriately in front of clients and court personnel. In sum, firms expect that you are putting forth during the summer the best you have to offer. They will generally not consider whether you have the potential to act professional or the potential to pay close attention to detail. They assume that what they see is what you've got.

The associate should think of every day of the summer clerkship as an interview day. Your appearance should always be neat and professional. Firms that have a business casual dress policy might present some challenges for the summer associate who might not know what clothing is appropriate. Having just purchased interview suits for the fall recruiting season, buying casual clothing might strain your student budget. Your best bet is to wear your dressy clothes for the first week and, once you know what people are wearing (and when your first check arrives), buy a few casual outfits.

Aside from looking the part, you must act professional too. That means you must act like a professional in your dealings with firm employees, clients, attorneys from other firms, and especially your peers. Often, summer associates bond with one another and interact socially outside the office. Don't let these casual relationships become too casual at the office. Avoid e-mail communications referencing the previous night's escapades. Continue to treat one another like the colleagues you are. Keep the practical jokes to a minimum.

Professionalism is only part of the recipe for a successful summer. Your attitude toward your work and your colleagues is also important. You are likely being paid a healthy salary for a relatively minimal amount of work. Don't complain about the quality of your work assignments. Learn to handle these issues appropriately through your recruiting coordinator or the attorney assigned to delegate assignments. If you have too much work, again, don't complain (even to your peers), but work with the people designated by the firm to monitor workloads. Gossip about your colleagues or associates will be repeated. Don't engage in it; don't listen to it.

### Be sure to participate in firm activities

Most law firms with a summer program will have lunches and other activities planned for the summer associates. There will be times when you have work to finish or don't feel much like interacting with other associates after working near them all day. It is probably a good idea to stay involved in the activities and participate in the outings. Keep in mind that before you realize it, you will be back at school where you have to pay for everything yourself; at a minimum, take advantage of the free food. An outing may also present a good opportunity to find out information from a partner or associate about their group and experience with the firm. Look at these outings as a way to further your investigation of the firm.

Some associates have family or other non-firm commitments that become strained with the summer associate social agenda. In this case, you may want to bring your concerns to the recruiting coordinator. The recruiting coordinator will help you focus on the events that will get you good exposure to attorneys. It may be that some events involve spouses, significant others or children. You may not feel so overwhelmed once you get more information on the summer schedule.

### Meet and get to know the recruiting committee

The recruiting committee may be comprised of one person or twenty-five. Usually, every few years or so, the make-up of the committee changes. There may be lawyers and non-lawyers working side by side in evaluating the summer associates. It is absolutely essential that you introduce yourself to these people (or this person) and get to know them on a more personal level. They will be making decisions about you based on what others say about you. You need for them to have firsthand knowledge too. These people are also a good resource for information about the firm. Generally, people on the recruiting committee are more aware than the average associate or even some partners about the needs of the firm and what is expected from summer associates.

The people on the recruiting committee, whether attorneys or not, are making a significant time commitment. Depending on the firm, members of the recruiting committee may also act as reviewing attorneys for summer associates. They will read and review all of the work done by a given number of associates. Committee members will try to get a general idea of your writing ability and attorneys' impressions of you.

Members of the recruiting committee regularly attend summer associate functions, talk with the associates on a personal level, and occasionally become supervisors for one or more associates. All of this work is in addition to the billable requirements on the committee members who are attorneys. Recognize that these people are strained to the limit. Focus your questions for them and try not to take up work time with generalized complaints.

### Start deciding whether you prefer litigation or transactional work

During the fall investigation and interview process, you should have started drawing some initial conclusions about the type of work in which you are interested. Hopefully, you asked practicing attorneys what is involved in their day-to-day work, and what aspects they enjoy or don't. Whether you are fairly sure about the work you want to do or completely baffled as to the area that is right for you, the summer program is your time to focus your interest. Over the course of the summer, the major divisions should at least become clearer. Do you prefer litigation or transactional work? Does tax work appeal to you? Do you have any interest in real estate?

### Get out of the office

Seek out opportunities to attend hearings, closings, client meetings or due diligence reviews outside the office. Mention to a few attorneys (perhaps ones whose work you want to know more about) that you would appreciate their thinking of you the next time they leave the office for work purposes. Remind people when you see them. Just as when you are an associate, you must take the initiative to gain certain experience. Seeing attorneys perform in court or handle clients is valuable experience.

### Get to know the recruiting coordinator or human resources person

The human resources or recruiting coordinator's job can sometimes be likened to that of a mother hen. The coordinator has all of these newly hatched "chicks" that look to the coordinator for some of the basics—where to live, how they're doing, what to do when there's a problem, or how to approach attorneys about specific issues. On a professional and sometimes personal level, the recruiting coordinator may be your go-to person. For example, if a family emergency arises out of state, the recruiting coordinator will help you make work arrangements.

From time to time during the summer, you should check in with the coordinator (or assistants, if any). Ask how you are doing in relation to other associates. Ask to review your written work product file so that you can ensure that it includes substantive and solid examples of your writing. You may be responsible for sending a copy of each memo or written work product to the recruiting coordinator so that their file is complete. You want to follow up to ensure that they have received what you sent them. Find out whether they will take care of copying reviewing attorneys on your work.

Avoid becoming too friendly with the coordinators (this includes asking them out on a date, which happens more than it should). Don't confide in the recruiting coordinator with concerns about whether you want to practice law, or whether you will like this firm. At the end of the summer, these people will sit in a room with others and review your strengths, weaknesses, and any other thing that will affect your getting an offer. The recruiting coordinator's opinion will likely be given great weight. Not only has this person's contact with you been regular, but also the coordinator has observed your interactions with non-lawyers and lawyers alike. It's no secret that busy hiring partners and committee members rely heavily on recruiting coordinators. A negative opinion or any reservations that the coordinator might express could put you at a greater disadvantage.

### Avoid letting your guard down with attorneys or staff

Summer associates often form close relationships with firm attorneys or support staff. Don't forget that some of these people will be called on to evaluate you at the end of the summer. Just as with your dealings with recruiting coordinators, never divulge personal information that you do not want the firm to know. Do not, for example, tell firm personnel that you are not sure you want to permanently relocate to the city in which you are clerking. Rest assured, that information will find its way to the recruiting committee. There is a difference between expressing reservations and finding out facts from people in the know. Use discretion in all your dealings, even with newfound friends.

### Avoid getting caught up in "school snobbery"

Small minds and people with not enough work to do get caught up in what can only be termed "school snobbery." This manifests itself in the belief that a student graduating from a first-tier school will be a better lawyer than one who did not. This attitude has a way of playing out in the summer associate ranks and, just as at the associate level, it tends to alienate colleagues and may cause you to underestimate your opposition. No doubt your school rank is significant in certain respects—it might help you get a higher paying job or a better judicial clerkship. There is little correlation, however, between your school rank and your propensity to be a great lawyer. In fact, after a few years (and unless you are changing jobs), few people will care what school you attended. They will be more concerned with your maturity level, technical skills, business sense, and ability to get and keep clients. Those are some of the factors that make great lawyers.

School snobbery works in the reverse, too. Students from national law schools who are working in law firms made up of attorneys who attended a regional law school often perceive animosity directed at them. It's as if the regional school graduate cannot understand why you would leave to attend a national school, only to return to the region and do the same work they are doing. School snobbery in any form is unproductive and theoretically should have no place in a professional setting. Recognize, however, that it exists for some people, and that these attitudes are some of the subtle (and unfortunate) aspects of practicing with other lawyers. For your part, work hard at keeping your pride in your school name or reputation in the proper perspective, and work harder at forming your own solid reputation.

**Avoid doing things that will label you as a trouble maker**

Attorneys have a difficult time remembering who is who in your summer class. That being said, when you complain or when you exercise poor judgment, you quickly develop a reputation that tends to make you stick out in the crowd. Start your schooling in diplomacy now. There will be issues that are not right or that should be addressed by someone in a position of authority. Figure out the appropriate channel (often the recruiting coordinator or your supervising lawyer) and keep the fuss to a minimum. One summer associate was asked to get a partner and a client a cup of coffee. Her overreaction to this request (in front of the client) cost her an offer.

**Prepare a list of the groups or attorneys with whom you want to work**

You will be asked to identify your group or work preferences before you return to school. This is the list that you need to develop all summer. Even before you arrive at the firm, begin compiling information about the work being done by the particular groups in the firm. Expand your list as you gain insight through your interactions with the lawyers. Firm needs often dictate where associates are placed. By having a first, second and third choice you may improve your chances of landing with a group where you will fit in.

**Don't spend all your money**

After months of living on little or borrowed money, law students don't always know what to do with the money they are paid as a summer associate. Depending on the market, salaries can range from $1,000 to $2,600 per week. Save what you can. Use it to pay down school debt. Perhaps you can borrow less than you planned for the upcoming year. Your law school loan repayments generally start within one to six months of graduation and the amount can be staggering. Any payment you make now towards the principal will make a big difference two or three years down the road. Your long-term thinking as a summer associate must extend beyond getting the offer; you must think in terms of your lifestyle as an attorney, too. The financial decisions you make as a law student will have a profound effect later.

### Split summers

Some summer associates split their summer between two or three law firms. They spend fewer weeks with each firm and attempt to pack in a full summer of exposure. Law firms are generally not favorably disposed towards split summers. It forces attorneys to evaluate the associate on less information—less interaction, less written work product—as compared to the summer associate's peers. Split summers also place an additional burden on the firm to ensure that the summer associate has maximum exposure to firm attorneys. This means that there is a shorter period of time within which to schedule dinners, lunches, reviews, etc. Finally, there are some events that the firm believes are important for all summer associates to attend. There might, for example, be a firm retreat where marketing lectures or writing workshops will be given. Associates may miss these events because their time with the firm is up or has not yet started. Every effort to attend these events should be made, even though you may have left for the summer.

One of the few advantages of a split summer is that the associate can make decisions about which law firm will be the best fit, as opposed to accepting the only offer on the table. Although there has been no research on this point, this inures to the benefit of the winning firm because the chances of the associate leaving within the first few years may be lower. On the whole, though, firms don't gain any real advantage when a student decides to split the summer among different firms.

The student considering a split has a number of factors to weigh. The firms involved may have strong preferences about which portion of the summer the associate spends with it or whether the associate should split at all. The firm's position should be consideration number one.

There is generally an advantage for the associate at the first firm. At the beginning of the summer, the student associates are all in the same boat: most don't know the attorneys or one another, and the attorneys don't really know the associates. Over the next several weeks, however, the summer associates will start bonding with one another and many events will be scheduled that will get the attorneys acquainted with the students. When a new person joins the class mid-summer, it is harder to get to know other associates, and the attorneys will have fewer opportunities to meet the newcomer at events. Many attorneys have already devoted all the time that they will spend on recruiting. If possible, schedule the first half of the summer with your first choice firm.

Another consideration is that if you are clerking for two firms in the same city, the respective recruiting coordinators may talk to one another about you, which happens more often than you would think. You cannot be frank with one firm over the other about your preferences because it may jeopardize your offer from the firm that believes you won't accept the offer if made. Also, you have to strike a fine balance between attending "required" firm events while you are clerking for the other firm.

The more limited time period also affects your mid-summer review. If the review is conducted properly, the associate will be told where improvement is needed and whether things are on track. Perceived problems can be addressed and improvements can be shown during the second half of the summer. If you are there for only half the summer, you miss a valuable opportunity for feedback and correction. You can always ask for a mid-point review. Unless you have been particularly prolific, however, there will be little written product on which to evaluate you. In sum, think hard about whether you should split your summer. Unless there is a clear advantage for you, you may want to stick with one firm.

### Reviews

Formal reviews of summer associates are generally given mid-summer and then again at summer's end. The attorneys handling the review will probably have read your written work product and any reviews by the attorneys with whom you have worked. This information should give them an overall picture of how you are doing with respect to your peers. Sometimes summer associate reviews are more focused than permanent attorney reviews because there is a defined body of work to review. Particular comments by reviewing attorneys are also likely be addressed. There will generally be some clues if you are not on track to receive an offer. Occasionally, students are completely surprised when they do not receive an offer. This may be due to a numbers problem or a break down in the review process.

### Offers

You will generally hear at the end of the summer or shortly thereafter whether you will be offered a permanent position by the law firm. If things were handled correctly during the summer, you will hopefully have some idea of whether you will receive one. By the time an offer is made, you should know what your response will be. The time to explore questions or concerns about the firm was while you were there.

Don't panic if you do not receive an offer. First find out why. Perhaps there were some issues with your writing ability or you offended someone with a thoughtless remark. Perhaps it is just a matter of economics. If there have been recent spikes in first-year salaries, the firm may have scaled down first-year recruiting and is instead focusing on second and third-year lateral hires. The firm may not have hired the summer associates with an eye towards being able to offer each of them a permanent position. Whatever the reason, talk to your supervising partner and possibly the recruiting coordinator. If the problem lies with you, you need to address the underlying issues so that you don't find yourself in this position in the future. If the problem is more firm-related, then you can use that to your advantage later as you look for a job.

Next, marshal your resources. Start with the placement or career services office. Talk with them about your summer experience. They might have some experience with this firm that could shed some light on your situation. For example, the placement department might know if this firm routinely overestimates its incoming first-year attorney needs. (If so, hopefully you were already aware of this when you used the placement department to research the firm before accepting the summer associate position.)

If you did not get an offer due to numbers crunching or economics, consider asking the firm to assist you in finding a job. Obviously, the firm will help you only if you did quality work and the reason you did not get an offer has little to do with your abilities. You may get a positive reference from the firm or one that explains why you did not get an offer. Attorneys at the firm may place inquiry calls to colleagues at other firms that do not run a summer program.

Don't burn any bridges with this law firm. You never know down the road what circumstances will arise. You may get an offer next year if the incoming crop of associates is inadequate for the firm's needs. Further, students who have accepted permanent positions occasionally change their minds just before starting. Family situations require that they move, or health factors may arise. Ask to be considered for a permanent position in the event this occurs.

Never bad-mouth a firm where you have had a less than perfect experience or one that did not give you an offer. Professionalism starts as a law student. Learning to use discretion about difficult situations is part of what defines a professional. These types of comments tend to reflect worse on the speaker, particularly when they get back to the law firm. Genuine complaints should have been (or should be) handled through the appropriate channels and at the appropriate time; continued discussion about these matters generally improves nothing. Professionalism extends to the proliferation of the Internet as a free-for-all medium for trashing particular lawyers and law firms. Lawyers and non-lawyers alike visit many of these sites to keep a pulse on the legal community. The reputation of the legal community is not helped by negative and small-minded commentary posted on the Internet by professed law students and practitioners.

Consider having a "plan B" where you pursue clerkships or non-firm legal jobs while continuing to search for law firm employment. It might be late in the game for applying for most judicial clerkships, but positions are always becoming available because judges retire, leave or get appointed throughout the year. Start researching organizations or corporations in which you have an interest. Many, like MTV, offer legal internships (paid or unpaid) that may prove to be interesting and valuable experiences. Your time clerking or interning will buy you some time for finding the right law firm job. In fact, depending on where you clerk or intern, the right job might come to you. In addition, the Internet provides an enormous amount of information about available law jobs and places where you can post your resume for review by potential employers. Chapter 4 contains suggestions for using these resources.

Not getting an offer of permanent employment is scary. Rather than viewing it as a career-killer, categorize it as one of the many obstacles or difficulties that will arise over the years. There are so many options and avenues for defining your legal career that not getting an offer is less of a big deal than it used to be. It will take diligence in discovering available options and, of course, some creativity on your part in handling the practical effects of not having a paid legal position at the end of the year. Be sure to inquire about deferring your loan payments or paying interest-only for six or eight months.

What should you do when you do get an offer? If you haven't already, you should read the National Association for Law Placement's (NALP) Principles and Standards for Law Placement and Recruitment Activities ("NALP Principles and Standards"), as well as the NALP Principles and Standards Interpretations. Part V of the "NALP Principles and Standards," Standards for the Timing of Offers and Decisions, sets forth the important dates for receiving and accepting offers. These documents are available on the Web at http://www.nalp.org. Although law firms generally subscribe to these guidelines, you should double check, especially when dealing with a smaller firm.

From a practical standpoint, it is to your advantage to accept an offer earlier rather than later. The firm always views it as a good sign when a student is excited about an offer and accepts on the spot or very soon after receiving the offer. Having the right attitude is important. When a student does not accept immediately, the firm has to factor this student's possible acceptance into a game of percentages. Law firms generally make a number of offers, but count on a certain percentage of students who will not accept their offer. Forecasting how many will accept or not is difficult and often is affected by real or perceived changes in the economy. Disaster can strike when too many students accept offers from a particular firm, forcing the firm to withdraw or rescind one or more offers. Accepting early provides some certainty for the firm and probably ensures that your offer will not be revoked.

Sometimes law students are unsure about accepting an early offer. These students often opt for interviewing throughout the fall. Your timetable and that of the firm's may not match up. You need to weigh carefully the potential drawbacks to waiting and interviewing, including that the firm will find out that you are looking elsewhere. If you want to pursue this road, interview as early as possible and be up front with the law firm with whom you are interviewing about your situation. Be sure to have plausible reasons for wanting to look elsewhere that do not cast the firm in a bad light.

Law firms make a certain number of offers of permanent employment to students. The number is determined by reviewing several factors, including future practice needs within the firm. There is a certain amount of guesswork involved, particularly when the economy changes. Generally, firms count on about a 40% acceptance rate, meaning that out of every ten offers made about four will be accepted. Occasionally, firms receive more acceptances than there are jobs, forcing them to rescind employment offers.

There are several things that you, as a student, can do if your offer has been rescinded. One option, as previously noted, is to put the firm to work for you. Ask for assistance in finding another job, and follow up on all suggestions or leads. Request a letter explaining the circumstances so that, if necessary, you can show the letter to potential employers during the interview process. Potential employers may not believe that you had an offer in the first place. Check whether the firm will allow individual attorneys to act as a personal reference. Under typical circumstances, firms are reluctant to give out any information about former employees beyond confirmation that you worked there and the dates of your employment. The rescinded offer situation might be an exception to this policy. Inquire whether the firm maintains a "waiting list" in the event other students revoke their acceptance. This is happening with increasing frequency because there is so much competition for top students and law firms are using outrageous signing bonuses, moving stipends, and guaranteed bonuses, to lure first-year students away from other firms.

Work closely with the career services professionals at your school. You may want to employ career services to act as a liaison between you and the firm rescinding the offer. For example, it might be less awkward if career services inquires on your behalf as to whether the firm will provide any financial assistance in the event you do not get a job.

### Choosing a firm

Perhaps you are fortunate enough to have more than one offer. Maybe you are unsure whether you should accept the offer you do have. In either situation, a decision needs to be made. What factors do you use as a basis for your decision? What constitutes a good fit? The following are some of those factors—and some warning signs—that may provide guidance.

Start by examining your identified "needs" discussed in Chapter 2. How many of those needs are truly essential? Does the firm match up with all or most of those needs? Is your salary in the range that can support you and your family, while still allowing you to repay your student loans? Is this a livable and affordable city for that salary? Are the benefits sufficient—good insurance, paid maternity leave, vacation days? What about the billable and non-billable hour requirements? Do you have a health condition that may hinder you from delivering what you promise in terms of sheer volume of work? Do you have major philosophical objections to the kind of work done at this firm or for the clients serviced by the firm?

How many of your "wants" does the firm meet? Has the firm offered you a position in a desirable group? Is this your first or second choice for a practice area? Will this firm further your ultimate goals for your career, whether they are partnership or leaving to work for a client in a legal and business capacity?

Are your skills and aptitudes compatible with the type of work being offered to you? Think about the various personalities in the group within which you will work. Do quieter associates fare well in that group? What about aggressive women? Do they last in this group? Does this group encourage lawyers to learn by experience? Are you comfortable with trial by fire?

Students often cite the firm "quality of life" as a major factor in whether to accept an offer. By this they apparently mean the opportunity to net good pay, but do it by working fewer hours. Keep in mind that quality of life is generally hard for any attorney at any level to achieve. Some attorneys regard it as non-existent for a first year. Your decision whether to accept an offer should turn more on specifics, as in what type of law you will be practicing or in which group you will be doing it, rather than a generalized goal of higher pay, less hours. As discussed throughout this chapter, part of your job as a summer associate is to observe and evaluate those specifics, especially ones that tend to influence your satisfaction level. Are associates well trained? Are there formal and informal mentoring relationships in place? Are most partners divorced? Do they enjoy close relationships with their children? What is the management style of group leaders and of those in charge of the firm? Do senior associates leave at a rate beyond the normal attrition rate? Do senior associates perceive "face-time" as being important at this firm? Is partnership a goal to which mid-level and senior associates aspire? Do attorneys socialize with one another outside the office? Is this a satellite office? What are the drawbacks? How do attorneys talk about one another? Are there political considerations that might affect your career? How do attorneys treat staff and other professionals within the firm? What is the reputation of the firm and particular attorneys within the firm? Remember that people don't become lawyers to have a good quality of life, as many students understand that term today. Unless a firm styles itself a "lifestyle firm" and reduces the salary accordingly, you should not have high expectations about your quality of life as a new lawyer.

There's something to be said for trusting your gut instincts. You will gain an overall impression of the firm, sometimes within a very short period of time. While there is nothing specific you can point to, you may know that the culture is not one in which you would thrive. Or, you may feel genuinely happy while dealing with the attorneys and staff members at a particular firm. The specifics are important, of course, but so too are your instincts. After all, your instincts will play in important role throughout your career in assessing clients, reading judges, and spotting ethical problems. There's no reason you should rule out your strong feelings at the beginning of your career.

Many suggestions in this chapter deal with things to consider doing or not doing, asking or not asking. In a strong economy, going the extra mile will help distinguish you from your peers. In a troubled economy, doing these things are essential and might mean the difference between employment and unemployment. Being a summer associate is not an easy task; there are high expectations placed on you by the firm and often you aren't told what those expectations are. You are expected to make significant and lasting decisions about your career, with very little guidance. Above all, try not to get confused or distracted by the extraneous events taking place around you. Figure out what you need to know and take steps to learn that information. At the same time, you must think on a more prospective level. Pull out of this experience all the practical lessons that you can and use what you can as a new lawyer. You will find that, as with most things, matters tend to fall in place when you arm yourself with knowledge and apply the lessons you learn.

*Chapter 8*

# Law Firm Economics 101

## How to Understand the Economics at Work in a Law Firm and Its Potential Impact on Your Career

Today's lawyer must have a basic knowledge of law firm economics to understand the factors that will influence her career. In a nutshell, your job security hinges on the economics at work in a firm. Any leverage that you may be able to exert in terms of negotiating salary, bonuses, or alternative work arrangements will come from your being aware of the bottom line. Long-term planning for your career and properly evaluating your partnership potential depends on your ability to comprehend the business of the law firm and how it operates.

Having this knowledge is important for lawyers at every level, at any sized firm. The factors that drive firm economics—billable rates, revenue, and overhead—determine whether a firm stays in business. When one of those factors becomes disproportionately high, or low, things happen. Lawyers and staff at every level are affected. The theme can be summed up this way: more than ever before, the bottom line for law firms really is the bottom line.

An understanding of firm economics must start with the basics. Every business has some type of inventory, which may be a service, process or a tangible product. A law firm's inventory is made up of time. Lawyers sell time. Some sell expertise, too, but even that is wrapped up in the amount of time it takes to provide that expertise.

Attorneys capture that time by tracking it and then billing clients at a set rate for work performed within a defined period. Most firms break the day into smaller increments of time and then round off any fragments of billable time to the nearest increment. The firm might use one-tenth or one-twelfth hour increments.

An example might help illustrate how this works. Let's say an associate spends an hour and twenty-six minutes performing due diligence work on behalf of a firm client. The associate's hourly rate is $130. The firm breaks time down into increments of one-tenth of an hour (i.e., every six minutes). On her time sheet, the associate will write down that 1.5 hours of time should be billed to this client. The client will then receive a bill that includes a charge for $195, assuming that all of this associate's time is billed to the client. This dollar figure represents the amount of this associate's time for the identified work.

Usually a "billing partner" or senior associate will handle client billing. The billing partner generally has some interest in the client—she may be the primary contact or have originated the business. The billing partner will review all of the time entered for this client by associates, partners and other billing professionals. The billing partner will see each and every description of work entered by these timekeepers, as well as the amount of time billed for that work. The billing partner may edit the descriptions or write-off time. Time is written-off for a variety of reasons. The associate may have taken too much time for a given project, or the partner may be trying to keep the bill within a certain dollar amount for client-relations purposes. Another example might include partners who routinely write-off very small increments of time, perhaps an entry for .1 hours of billable time. Time that is written-off does not count against the associate or timekeeper who initially billed the time. In the previous example, the associate would still be given "credit" for 1.5 hours, even if .4 hours of her time was written off and not billed to a client.

Before you think lightly about over-billing time with the expectation that it might be written off, don't. Not only are there firm policies and ethical rules prohibiting such a practice, but the time written off by a billing partner is monitored. The ratio between the amount each timekeeper writes down for a client vs. the amount recovered in dollars from the client is known as the "realization rate" or the "billing realization rate." Thus, the more time written off by a billing partner, the lower the partner's realization rate.

It is essential that whoever is entering your time—whether you or a secretary—must spell names and use terms of art correctly. Billing partners get irritated when they have to make grammatical or typographical corrections to a bill, which inevitably makes more work for the billing partner and support staff. Often, a secretary and a billing support person work with the partner in getting the bills out.

Periodically examine your entered time sheets to ensure that the entries and calculations are accurate. Review is essential if you have a temporary or a fill-in secretary, particularly since that person may not be used to your writing or to the unique spellings of words in your field. A client may not see the error in legal analysis that you made on your last memorandum, but rest assured he will spot an error on the bill. The first call the client makes will be to the billing partner (and the next call will be to you).

The client is sent a bill for all services performed in a given period, usually a month or a quarter. The total time spent by all attorneys who worked on the client's case on a particular day will be set forth. Consequently, you shouldn't use phrases like "continued researching matter from yesterday" or "interviewed witness from yesterday in follow-up." The inventory (or your time) is not "sold" until the firm is actually paid for the services provided to a client.

Since attorneys sell their time, keeping an accurate and detailed contemporaneous account of billable time is of the utmost importance. Accurate timekeeping constitutes the basis for billing clients, which is the lifeblood of the firm. It also provides a detailed picture of a firm's "inventory," for lack of a better word. Your recorded time helps partners track the level of work within the group on a monthly, weekly or sometimes daily basis.

The surest way to get on the wrong side of firm partners is to enter or hand in incomplete or late timesheets. You will lose or over-inflate your time when you rely on your memory to fill out time sheets. Your descriptions of work performed will not give sufficient detail and will be open to challenge by clients. You will be hard pressed to provide more descriptive narratives of your time several months down the road. None of these situations will make a partner happy. In short, do your time sheets contemporaneously with the work performed and do them everyday. If your time sheets use a straight chronological format, be sure to add the time yourself so that you can compare it with the amount of time entered by your secretary. You should always have a general idea of the amount of time you have billed on a weekly and then monthly basis. When you are out of town or away from the office, send your timesheets by facsimile or call them in to your secretary.

More and more firms are requiring that associates enter their own time using any number of new software time-keeping packages. Along with the telephone, document retrieval, and word processing systems, you must learn your way around the time-keeping system.

Be aware of and follow the billing partner's rules for billing. Billing partners are notorious for having very specific ways to describe legal work performed for a client. Often these particular ways of doing things are at the request of a client or in response to particular client concerns about billing. For example, a billing attorney or a client may not want to see "conference with" on your time sheet. Some clients will not pay for two or more people to discuss a legal matter. Some attorneys prefer "Ms. Jones" as opposed to "Janet Jones." Others prefer "client" as opposed to a specific name. Lower-level attorneys or staff can help you with these idiosynchracies. If someone else is entering your time, be sure to convey information about making unusual or specific entries to the secretary or other person who enters your time.

New lawyers may want to ask a senior associate for a sample of that associate's time sheets. That way, you can see how legal services are described and the level of detail required. If the associate also works for your billing partner, you will get to see in practice how to accommodate the partner's specific billing preferences.

Billable hours are a constant source of discussion among attorneys. Inevitably, certain attorneys will compare their hours with others in the firm or take pride in a high billable hour month or year. It is best to avoid specific discussions about hours. People should know that you are busy, but avoid excessive complaining about your hours and giving out specific numbers. This information will get around without your input. People notice when you are working hard.

Increasingly, firms are circulating the billable hours of associates and partners within the firm. Despite mixed reaction from associates, managers have found that having a yardstick by which to compare your productivity with that of your peers is motivational. This is peer pressure at its best (or worst). You should review this information if it is available to you even if the only purpose is salary negotiation or merely ascertaining where in the pack you fall.

At some point in your career, you should review the ethical rules and canons dealing with billing. You will feel incredible pressure to churn out billable hours, particularly when salaries are rising faster than associates' potential worth. Attorneys become especially creative in billing during these times. Prior to an explicit prohibition against such a practice, some attorneys were actually billing more than twenty-four hours in a day. They would bill a client for time spent on an airplane on the way to conduct business for the client, and also bill another client for work actually performed on the airplane for the second client. Creativity cannot cross the ethical lines plainly laid out in the rules and canons.

Over the years, and with mixed success, law firms have tried alternative billing methods that do not rely on the hourly rate. Firms may handle a matter for a flat or fixed fee, or it may combine hourly billing with a contingency fee or other billing methods. Some firms are weighing the ethical implications of taking a percentage ownership interest in growing companies in exchange for providing the legal and consulting advice to help those companies grow. Most of these alternatives will not affect the associate or the manner in which the associate bills her time. Firms must know what associates are doing. Firms must also track the amount of time spent on a client matter for evaluation purposes. For the near future, at least, the associate's work life will continue to be dominated by time sheets and billable hours.

A spike in law firm salaries provides an excellent picture of the role economics play in the professional life of the associate. During a period of escalating demand for legal services with a lower supply of available lawyers, heavy increases in compensation rates are the norm. Accompanying this phenomenon is the fact that firms are reeling from reports of dismal attorney retention rates. The higher salaries are a band-aid approach to attract and keep lawyers.

A rise in associate salaries is financed in one of several ways: (1) cut partner profits; (2) raise client billing rates; (3) lower expenses; (4) make people work harder and more efficiently; or (5) a combination of all or some of the above.

High salary rates for first year associates may be bad business planning that can endanger the long-term survival potential of mid and large-sized firms. Young lawyers usually aren't profitable until sometime after their second or third year. Firms (and some clients) recognize that there is a certain amount of inherent inefficiency in the work performed by first and second year lawyers. This inefficiency may be reflected in a lower billing rate, but it is not reflected in a salary commensurate with the associate's experience. In some markets, first-year associates command starting salaries in excess of $100,000. Firms hiring at this rate will probably lose money on first and possibly second year associates. Unless there are compensating factors, few firms can operate with such a significant money drain, particularly when the need for more lawyers shows no sign of slowing. Some firms are going to feel the pinch.

Another complicating factor is that clients will not tolerate large or frequent jumps in the hourly rate they pay for legal services. Most corporate managers or in-house lawyers are trying to reduce the legal budget, and they watch carefully the costs of outside legal services. The billing statement sent to them is actually read and scrutinized. These clients have private law firm experience and understand the power that they can exert over the billable rate charged them. They also recognize when an hourly rate raise is unreasonable. Firms will not be able to finance compensation increases by raising hourly rates.

Reducing the profits per partner is an equally difficult option. While some may view these reductions as a fair "redistribution of wealth," partners certainly don't view it that way. This is particularly the case in firms that are already struggling with lower profits and higher overhead. Partners with significant business may leave and join firms with higher profits per partner. Senior associates may view the prospect of lower profits per partner as a reason to look elsewhere now.

Ultimately, partners may have no choice—some of the associate compensation increase will have to come out of partner profits.

Another option for financing associate compensation increases is to make the associates work harder or more efficiently. In the short term, this option is less painful for the partnership. Associates, particularly ones benefiting from pay hikes, should expect that their stated or unstated billable hour requirement will increase. There will be higher expectations about job performance. A better option focuses on improving associate efficiency through improved mentoring and teaching. This option, however, will take time away from billable work, and thus in the short term will cost more money. Past experience shows that attorneys simply aren't willing to take the time to invest in associates. The mentoring gap and solutions to bridge it are addressed in Chapter 15.

What is clear is that the economic factors surrounding extraordinary pay hikes impact associates on several levels. You will work harder for higher salaries. Expectations about your efficiency will increase, even though you will not be given the tools or the guidance for improving it. Your partnership options at a firm with declining profits per partner may be less attractive, and therefore less of an incentive for you to give up a substantial portion of your life. Finally, there is the possibility that your firm will not survive the economic pressure. What is clear is that you must understand firm economics and how the current market pressures will affect you and your career direction.

# SAMPLE TIME SHEET—FIFTEEN MINUTE INCREMENTS

ATTORNEY: _____    DAY: _____    DATE: _____

7 A.M. _____
.15 _____
.30 _____
.45 _____

8 _____
.15 _____
.30 _____
.45 _____

9 _____
.15 _____
.30 _____
.45 _____

10 _____
.15 _____
.30 _____
.45 _____

11 _____
.15 _____
.30 _____
.45 _____

12 P.M. _____
.15 _____
.30 _____
.45 _____

1 _____
.15 _____
.30 _____
.45 _____

2 _____
.15 _____
.30 _____
.45 _____

3 _____
.15 _____
.30 _____
.45 _____

4 _____
.15 _____
.30 _____
.45 _____

5 _____
.15 _____
.30 _____
.45 _____

## SAMPLE TIME SHEET—SIX MINUTE INCREMENTS

DATE _____

| 7:00 A.M. _____ | 11:00 A.M. _____ | 3:00 P.M. _____ |
|---|---|---|
| 7:18 _____ | 11:18 _____ | 3:18 _____ |
| 7:24 _____ | 11:24 _____ | 3:24 _____ |
| 7:30 _____ | 11:30 _____ | 3:30 _____ |
| 7:36 _____ | 11:36 _____ | 3:36 _____ |
| 7:42 _____ | 11:42 _____ | 3:42 _____ |
| 7:48 _____ | 11:48 _____ | 3:48 _____ |
| 8:00 A.M. _____ | 12:00 P.M. _____ | 4:00 P.M. _____ |
| 8:18 _____ | 12:18 _____ | 4:18 _____ |
| 8:24 _____ | 12:24 _____ | 4:24 _____ |
| 8:30 _____ | 12:30 _____ | 4:30 _____ |
| 8:36 _____ | 12:36 _____ | 4:36 _____ |
| 8:42 _____ | 12:42 _____ | 4:42 _____ |
| 8:48 _____ | 12:48 _____ | 4:48 _____ |
| 9:00 A.M. _____ | 1:00 P.M. _____ | 5:00 P.M. _____ |
| 9:18 _____ | 1:18 _____ | 5:18 _____ |
| 9:24 _____ | 1:24 _____ | 5:24 _____ |
| 9:30 _____ | 1:30 _____ | 5:30 _____ |
| 9:36 _____ | 1:36 _____ | 5:36 _____ |
| 9:42 _____ | 1:42 _____ | 5:42 _____ |
| 9:48 _____ | 1:48 _____ | 5:48 _____ |
| 10:00 A.M. _____ | 2:00 P.M. _____ | 6:00 P.M. _____ |
| 10:18 _____ | 2:18 _____ | 6:18 _____ |
| 10:24 _____ | 2:24 _____ | 6:24 _____ |
| 10:30 _____ | 2:30 _____ | 6:30 _____ |
| 10:36 _____ | 2:36 _____ | 6:36 _____ |
| 10:42 _____ | 2:42 _____ | 6:42 _____ |
| 10:48 _____ | 2:48 _____ | 6:48 _____ |

# Chapter 9

# That's Why They Call It Practice

**Where in the Big Picture You Fit; Practical
Advice About Practicing; How to Handle
Your Partners; Proper Use of Electronic Mail;
Courtroom Decorum; Dating Within the Firm**

Becoming a great lawyer is a process. The length of
time you have practiced, while relevant, is not the
determining factor. Rather, a combination of relevant
experiences, raw talent, and a certain amount of passion
for the law are the most important factors. Everyone
knows that you learn by experiencing and working
through issues and problems. For example, you will
never forget the lesson you learn the first time you get
burned by the federal removal rule. You will never forget the first time you see your partner mishandle and
lose a client. You will never forget the first time a client
writes you a note to tell you that you did a good job.
While experience for its own sake has value, what you
make of it and how you use it is what really counts.
That's where your intellectual ability and common
sense come in to play. It takes a certain amount of ability to apply the lessons and knowledge learned from
past situations to new and different contexts. This application process is critical to becoming a great lawyer.

Passion for your work is also important. When you
enjoy what you do it is easier to maintain the high energy level and stamina necessary to go the distance. The
difficult and stressful times seem to be more tolerable
when you believe that you are being productive and
when you are satisfied with your work. Also, a certain

amount of passion for your area of law keeps you thirsting for more information and knowledge. You care about what you are doing as opposed to just going through the motions. Finally, clients and other attorneys like to work with people who are excited about their work —a result that can only operate to your benefit.

This chapter deals with some of the lessons and experiences that go into the process of becoming a great lawyer. Before we get to some specific suggestions, however, it might be helpful to understand what is expected of associates during their first three or four years, and beyond.

### Litigation Associates

As a first year associate, you should be able to research legal issues and prepare well-written, concise memoranda for use by other lawyers. You might not see every issue, particularly those that are not evident without some experience in the area, but you should be able to hit the big issues and some of the tangential ones. Never rely on the headnotes in a case decision. They are usually supplied by the company publishing the decision, not the judge who wrote it, and are sometimes inaccurate. It is expected that your work will be error-free. This means that there are no typographical mistakes, nor are there glaring mistakes in your analysis of a case. One new lawyer who was asked to provide a portion of a brief, wrote that a case had a certain holding. The case held the opposite. This lawyer lost all credibility (and her job) in that one moment.

It is helpful to have a sense of how your memorandum will be used and by whom. More senior attorneys will use your memorandum to gain familiarity with an issue or an area of law. Your memorandum might be used to clarify how courts or circuits are split on a particular issue. Also, your memorandum might be used to explore the finer points of an area of law about

130

which the senior lawyer is already familiar. Your memorandum might be sent to a client, particularly if the client is a lawyer.

Additionally, as a first year litigation associate, it is expected that you can write basic motions, such as a motion for an extension of time within which to answer a complaint. The first year associate should, with minimal or no supervision, be able to prepare subpoenas and deposition notices, including Rule 30(b)(6) deposition notices that will include categories of information. Moreover, the first year associate should be able to interview witnesses and provide some input as to strategy decisions in the case. The ability to accurately and quickly calendar the time for responses and other important dates in a case is something that a first year associate must know how to do, even if no-one fully relies on the associate to perform that function. Triple-check your calculations and write them down or log them into an electronic calendar system. The first year associate should also be able to take a first crack at preparing a complaint and answer, and preparing and responding to discovery requests. This means that you must have at least general knowledge of discovery objections that can be raised, as well as knowledge about appropriate defenses to be raised in an answer.

It is fully expected that the associate will rely on examples of documents prepared by other attorneys within the firm. For example, if a first year attorney is asked to prepare a complaint setting forth a breach of contract claim, the attorney is encouraged to review other complaints filed by litigators within the firm and revise those examples accordingly.

First year lawyers will find themselves doing chores that a secretary or paralegal could do. There are reasons for your being asked to fill in. Work demands on the support staff may necessitate your being called on. Sometimes you are the closest person to the partner or senior associate when the need arises. But it just may be that the partner or senior associate simply wants you to have certain experiences. You need to know how to do everything that your secretary and paralegal does because there will be times when you are the support staff. You must have the ability, for example, to schedule depositions, contact court reporters, put Bates' numbers on documents or prepare a coherent witness profile and folder. Moreover, you must know how to file papers with the court clerk. It is expected that you know how many copies must be filed with the court and where to file them. In short, along with the challenging assignments, a first year will be asked to do a share of grunt work. Accept that as your lot in life, and look forward to the day that you can delegate some of your less "lawyerly" tasks to a lower-level associate.

Second through fourth year lawyers are expected to have learned all of the responsibilities of a first year associate and be able to perform them more efficiently and with less supervision. Additionally, second through fourth year associates should be able to prepare increasingly complicated motions and supporting memoranda, discuss the legal theories of a case with the client, prepare witnesses and clients for deposition, and prepare a matter for trial. These more senior associates should begin delegating work to first year associates and paralegals. It takes time to understand what can be delegated and also the level of knowledge of less experienced attorneys and paralegals. Many lawyers expect a level of competence out of junior lawyers that is more comparable to a peer.

Finally, second through fourth year lawyers are expected to grasp the nuances of practicing law. These are things that come with experience. For example, understanding that a client must make a business decision with the legal advice provided by you is something that comes with experience. Or, one minute your client is the sworn enemy of the party on the other side and the next they are in partnership together. Another example might be when settlement discussions surface in litigated matters; a more experienced lawyer knows how to pursue alternative courses of action without becoming sidetracked. Perhaps these examples are simply a matter of gaining perspective. In any event, second through fourth year lawyers should begin to develop a much broader way of thinking about their cases and clients.

### Corporate Associates

The term "corporate associate" generally describes a lawyer who handles all manner of transactions, deals, mergers, acquisitions, sales, leases, or financing and lending matters. There are some expectations about the general skill level of any corporate associate, and also specific experiences that the lawyer should have acquired in the first few years of practice.

The corporate associate plays a key role in any transaction. Particularly with respect to a newer associate, sometimes the position is comparatively "non-lawyerly," with functions equivalent to those of a secretary, document manager, or photocopy-checker. On other occasions, the associate's participation is on the strategy or deal-enabling end. In addition to the specifics that the corporate associate is responsible for, there are some larger concepts that are important for a young associate to grasp.

An associate should first try to get her mind around the whole process in which she will take part. What is the purpose of this transaction and what specifically does the client hope to accomplish? What are the fundamental points from which the client will not budge? What constitutes a bargaining chip for your client? What are the areas open for negotiation? You must be able to sift through what's important to your client and what isn't. Understanding that your job is to help bring about the client's objectives and get the deal done will help you in your dealings with counsel for other parties in the transaction. Nothing is served by your stalling the process or making the working relationship so difficult that things don't get accomplished. You should be an effective advocate for your client, but this should be accomplished by negotiating and deal-making, or diplomatically sticking to your bottom-line points. Using brute force of will to win a concession will slow the process and possibly stall or even kill the deal.

Next, the associate should outline the process and the goals of the transaction. Models exist for these outlines, including closing checklists and the like. Use the forms more senior associates have relied on and improved. Do not, however, totally rely on those forms because your deal may have certain particulars, or your supervising partner may do things a bit differently. You must use and analyze the forms in light of these distinctions. All of these items should be reflected on your checklist. A "time and responsibility" checklist is also important. Circulate this list to those working on your team on the deal, and possibly other lawyers for the parties to the transaction. Solicit their input and comments. This list will help clarify your role in a complicated transaction and facilitates the interactions among all lawyers involved.

Another responsibility of the associate is to coordinate periodic status calls with representatives from each of the parties to a transaction. You may want to increase the frequency of these status calls as you get closer to the closing of a transaction. Update your time and responsibility checklist after each status call.

Virtually all "transactions" (in the broadest sense of the term) start with due diligence. Due diligence can be described as a detailed review of information related to a company or of the legal structure of an entity for purposes of ascertaining whether a conflict exists or a problem needs to be addressed before another transaction takes place. For example, in order to evaluate properly the liabilities of company A, company B must know whether senior executives can invoke a golden parachute and retire. The payments that will be made to these executives are factors that affect the company's bottom line. A first year associate must start learning how to conduct due diligence in both simple and complex transactions. Often, a new lawyer will be asked to review documents in connection with a due diligence review. The lawyer must know what he is looking for and how to properly categorize that information. These are basic skills that lawyers should be developing during the first year or so.

Corporate associates also must know how to revise simple agreements so that the terms reflect the particulars of the deal on which the associate is working. Young corporate associates do not do much in the way of original drafting. They must know, however, how to make conforming changes all the way through a document and the legal effect of those changes. Corporate associates really start building (or destroying) their reputations by paying (or failing to pay) attention to detail.

First year associates will likely be asked to draft corporate board resolutions. Again, review good examples from more senior associates and get a feel for the language and level of specificity required. You will develop the ability to draft these quickly and efficiently as you progress in your training.

Another likely assignment will be to prepare schedules associated with various types of contracts. A schedule might include information or exceptions relating to representations and warranties. An associate must read the representations and warranties carefully and correlate this information with the facts learned during the course of due diligence. Moreover, the associate, in order to prepare great schedules, must be able to extract thorough information from the client. Again, accuracy is paramount and associate reputations rise or fall on these schedules being perfect.

Many transactions have a securities component. An associate should be familiar with filling out registration statements and other basic forms, including drafting corporate biographies. The associate should also know how to draft related correspondence (to the relevant agency, for example) and begin to draft comment letters. Identifying these issues well before closing, turning these documents around, and doing them without error are other skills necessary for a corporate associate.

The associate has significant responsibilities for ensuring that the closing process goes smoothly. Even the smallest omission can block a deal on which multiple parties have worked for months. Early organization (again, long before closing) is absolutely crucial. Your organizational efforts will increase the odds of discovering hard to determine information prior to the closing date, and also minimize the chance of your looking completely disorganized in front of your client at the closing. A young associate will probably take a first stab at preparing a detailed closing checklist and the closing documents in connection with transaction. This list, too, should be circulated to your supervising partner and senior associates. They can provide commentary and identify areas that require more specificity. The closing list might be eighty pages long for a complicated transaction.

The associate will have responsibility for arranging conference rooms for the closing, coordinating part-time or overtime secretarial help, ordering lunch, notifying related parties of the logistics, as well as the technical aspects of the closing such as making sure the signature pages are included on all copies and signed properly. Make it your responsibility to see that the consideration for the deal is at the closing and actually exchanged by the parties. Often this is accomplished by a money wire transfer on the day of closing, particularly when you are dealing with banks. Ensure beforehand and again at the closing that all persons with the requisite signing authority and special signature stamps are there and present.

An associate gains much of this experience during

the first few years of practice. The associate should also be compiling a good bank of form files. Most corporate associates will have closing binders from other deals that include a complete set of closing documents. The form files should also include sample merger agreements, stock and asset purchase agreements, employment agreements, which include non-competition, non-solicitation and confidentiality provisions, board resolutions and other documents specific to areas in which you find yourself working with more frequency.

By the time associates are third or fourth year attorneys, they ought to be able to close a moderately-sized deal with minimal supervision. Increasingly, the associate will be asked to handle more advanced drafting. As before, your continued attention to detail and accuracy is critical to your advancement. Your negotiating ability is another skill that should improve as you watch your partners and senior associates in action. With this increased level of responsibility on the drafting and negotiation end, it is almost assumed that you are better able to understand the economics of a transaction. Your advice to clients will frequently stem from your assessments of risk allocation and how best to effectuate your client's goals in that regard. Having the right combination of technical legal skills and good business sense are what make in-house opportunities and corporate officer positions a natural progression for many corporate associates.

The following are specific thoughts on practicing law. Some of these thoughts center on the day-to-day events confronting a new lawyer, some relate to the direction of your career.

### Take Care of Logistics Before You Start Working

Many new attorneys move to the city in which they will be working just days before starting their job. Their first full work week is taken up with unpacking, orchestrating cable and telephone hook-ups, and learning their way around the city. You will have little time left over after being in orientation or training classes all day and then getting to work on your first projects. The fewer household matters that you have to focus on during the first few weeks of work, the better.

Some attorneys are in a precarious financial position as they begin working. Remember that you haven't earned a paycheck until you've worked, and you may have to wait two weeks or possibly a month before getting paid. Some law firms will give an advance to new lawyers (which is paid back out of your first few paychecks); others will help you secure a line of credit with a local bank. By planning ahead and perhaps using some income from your summer associate days, you can avoid a great deal of stress at the start of your job.

### Read the Rules and Relevant Statutes First

Every attorney, including transactional attorneys who have no desire to litigate, should be generally familiar with certain rules and statutes. Make every attempt to read these rules at the beginning of your career. Begin with the Federal Rules of Civil Procedure, the state civil practice rules, and the local court rules. These rules deal with the basics of filing, prosecuting and defending an action. Attorneys must also have at least some working knowledge of state statutes dealing with contracts, including the state's codification of the Uniform Commercial Code, torts and actions for fraud. You should review the table of contents for agency related statutes as well. Litigators, of course, should actually read every one of these provisions because the issues will not only regularly arise in the course of practice, but knowledge of the relevant statutes will help spur creative thinking. Finally, become familiar with the treatises and hornbooks in your field. Knowing their physical location in the library will save time in a crunch.

Once you have a frame of reference, perhaps after six to nine months of practice, you will benefit greatly by again reviewing the appropriate statutes and rules. This sounds time-consuming and it is. Try to think in terms of the benefit to your training and base knowledge level.

Become generally familiar with the library and the resources housed there. It is usually when you are most pressed for time that you will need specific library resources. One litigator was at a firm for two years before she noticed a great deposition series with sample deposition questions. This resource provided a good checklist for attorneys in specific types of civil cases, which would have proved helpful earlier in her career.

While a transactional attorney has less need of familiarity with the local or civil practice rules, or substantive statutes, it is still important to have this background. Clients expect you to have at least passing familiarity with all legal issues confronting them. This means that although you may handle securities work for client X, client X might expect you to have a general idea of the timeline in the sexual harassment case pending against it in federal court, particularly if it could impact the company's financial picture. Also, you may need the ability to spot a problem relating to fraud or breach of contract issues. You cannot refer the matter to an attorney competent to handle such matters unless you understand that there is a problem in the first place. Furthermore, from time to time, your transactional work will involve analyses of claims pending against your client or against a potential acquisition for your client. Again, you need to have some basic knowledge before you can know that another opinion is needed.

This same logic applies to litigators. Every litigator should be able to figure out when there is a bankruptcy, tax, antitrust, or other problem that requires the assistance of a more knowledgeable attorney. These are areas of law fraught with malpractice pitfalls and you need to know when you must consult with someone with the appropriate expertise.

## Have a Basic Understanding of the Court System in the State Within Which You Practice

Lawyers often attended law school in a state other than the one in which they practice. Attempt to gain an early understanding of the civil and criminal court system (including small claims and magistrate courts) of the state in which you practice. For example, New York's system is counter-intuitive: the Supreme Court is the trial court and then there are appellate divisions. You will embarrass yourself if you are a lawyer in New York and do not understand this system. This information, of course, is mandatory for litigators. Transactional lawyers should have some basic knowledge as well.

## Get your Trial Credits in Early; Get Sworn In Immediately

Attorneys in many states must fulfill what are sometimes known as "trial credits" or "trial experiences" before acting as lead or sole counsel in any litigated matter. For example, in Georgia, an attorney must verify under oath that she has completed certain trial experiences in federal and state courts. If your state requires these experiences, do them before you start working for the firm, if possible, or within the first few months. They are good experience. Also, most people find that once they start practicing, they get busy so quickly that these credits get delayed for a year or more. These attorneys learn too late that missing a few days of work in their second year as an associate is much more difficult than missing them in the first year.

The same holds true for getting sworn in to the various state and federal courts. One lawyer put off being admitted to federal court because she was busy working on a large, all-consuming case. She was ten times busier later that year when she had to file an emergency motion in a federal district court and was not sworn in. Her failure to get admitted was an inconvenience, and reflected badly on her. Your partners expect you to hit the ground running and that includes the ability to sign pleadings right away.

### Be Informed

Clients value an informed attorney. An informed attorney is one who has some awareness of and interest in the local business, political and legal climate. To that end, review the daily newspaper headlines. Also, read the local legal paper for business or legal news that might impact your clients or their legal position in a matter. Forward to your partner (not the client) articles that might be of interest to a firm client. Clients appreciate it when the firm looks out for their business interests; partners appreciate it when their associates look out for them.

The Internet affords lawyers an incredible opportunity to stay abreast of developments involving firm clients and their competitors. Sometimes, lawyers know information before employees of the client. One good source for business information is hoovers.com. A subscription to this site will provide daily information on the publicly-traded companies of your choice. In this age, there is no excuse for ignorance about your clients, their competitors, or the industry in which they operate.

### Adjust Your Expectations

Accept that you will not be efficient during your first several months of practice. Simple tasks like drafting a Rule 30(B)(6) notice will take you hours or even days. More senior lawyers recognize that you need more time to do these things and want you to take great care with your first assignments. Learning the mechanics of being a lawyer and gaining an understanding of why certain things are done a certain way are basic skills. Instead of worrying about efficiency, concentrate on doing your work perfectly, with absolutely no errors.

Discussions about efficiency necessarily raise the billable hour issue. Some attorneys will instruct you to bill all of your time. They believe you are too inexperienced to make a judgment call about efficiency and that only a billing partner should decide whether to write off time to a client. Furthermore, they understand that your inefficiency is built into the firm hierarchy and billing rates.

Other attorneys, however, caution new associates not to bill all of their time for certain tasks, even when the partner says that they should. These attorneys warn that partners forget how little first year associates know and thus huge blocks of time devoted to a single task will reflect badly on the associate. They appear inefficient. The simple answer to this dilemma of whether to bill all of your time is that you need to exercise some judgment. If your firm scrutinizes each partner's realization rate, or the time written down for the client compared to the amount the client is actually billed for that time, then use your judgment about billing large amounts of time to a particular project that perhaps took longer than it should. Also, if a matter took longer due to a factor within your control, then use your judgment in that situation as well. For example, there may come a time when you're too tired to focus on a client matter and have to re-do it. Many attorneys do not believe it appropriate to bill all of that time.

### Perception as Reality

An unfortunate truth of law firm life is that too often perception is reality. Sometimes, no matter how hard or how little you work, people will have their own perception of what you are doing. This perception becomes the truth, as understood by the firm. No amount of factual backup will dissuade some people from forming an opinion about you. Your attempts to demonstrate the facts will only result in you being labeled defensive or argumentative. Some lawyers arrive at work late, take a full lunch, break for dinner, and then stay at the firm late. In reality, they may be billing the same amount of hours in a day as a lawyer who gets in early, skips lunch, and leaves at 5:30 p.m. One of these lawyers will be regarded as working harder than the other.

How others perceive you, your commitment level, or the work you are doing, will determine whether you succeed with your firm. This is a frustrating reality, but one that must be understood early on by a new lawyer.

### How to Handle Assignments

Late in the week, your partner calls you on the telephone. She relates that she promised the client a written work product by Monday afternoon and wants to know if you can handle it. Make no mistake, that is a statement, not a question. First, respond with: "I'll be right there." Then consider doing the following: Report to the partner's office with a blank pad of paper and two pens in hand, in case one pen does not work. You must be prepared. Write the date at the top of the paper, along with the client name and billing number, if given. If you are not given the billing number and the opportunity to ask does not present itself, get that information later from the partner's secretary. Listen closely while the attorney talks; do not write down every word, but do take legible notes.

After you have listened to all the partner has to say, ask questions to clarify your understanding of your assignment or to get more background information. Do not be afraid to ask questions. Some attorneys are notorious for omitting relevant background information. Try not to ask simple questions that you can easily answer for yourself, like how to spell the name of the client or contact. When you have a really dumb question, save it for a mid-level associate or other colleague.

Find out what type of tone to adopt if you are drafting a letter, brief or other court paper. Casting your client's claim and maintaining credibility with the reader is partially determined by the attitude you take in your writing. For example, there are times when the equities of a situation are strongly on your side. You are wearing the "white hat" and can take a more aggressive stance in your writing. You may be on the side where your client has done something wrong. A respectful and straightforward tone may be more appropriate.

You may want to ask the partner for suggestions on where to start your research. For example, the partner might know that a particular treatise would be helpful. Also, the partner might know of another attorney who handled a similar matter. If so, talk next with that person or search on the firm computer database for relevant research or documents. This information will give you a head start on your work and will also serve as a checklist to ensure that you have covered the bases.

Ask the partner for a deadline. All projects take longer than an attorney says they will. Many new lawyers use a factor of three: multiply the projected number of hours by three and you will likely have a better approximation of the time it will take. Try to determine whether this is a hard or soft deadline, without asking that question outright. For example, is this a court, client or partner deadline?

Determine exactly the end product being sought by the partner. For example, is she looking for a memorandum, oral report, or an outline? Then, be sure to provide that exact work product to the partner, even if you think it is inadequate or unnecessary. Those are issues you can perhaps address after giving the partner whatever was requested of you.

Resist the urge to give the partner an initial reaction about the law or the assignment. If you have some knowledge about the issue, or remember studying it in law school, use that information to ask more focused questions. When associates draw early conclusions it causes concern to the assigning attorney because it indicates you may have preconceived notions about the project and will miss the nuances.

Some attorneys recommend that you send a brief e-mail or memorandum summarizing your assignment and confirming the end product and due date. This may be overkill, but it certainly does not hurt. For example, if you misunderstood the facts, you can easily avoid looking bad later. Avoid writing e-mail messages that sound like you are trying to cover your bases in the event you have gotten inaccurate or incomplete information (otherwise known as a CYA letter). While self-protection may indeed be the purpose of the message, take care that it does not sound that way.

Try to get a sense of the bigger picture and understand your assignment in that context. For example, you have been given a straightforward evidence issue to research. Make a determination as to the manner in which your client will be affected by the results of that search. You may be that much more creative in your approach if you know you need to find a way to get a piece of evidence excluded. Also, you can make suggestions about other areas of research once you understand the larger context. In addition, your work will become much more meaningful when you see where and how it will be used.

Work hard at keeping your partner (or senior associate) updated on your progress, but do not inundate her with detailed messages. There is a fine line between keeping everyone informed and coming across as not being able to work independently. A more frequent progress report is recommended if you are on a very short deadline. On the other hand, a weekly update might be appropriate when there is no deadline or the work is not pressing. Of course, if the partner or senior associate specifies how she wants to be informed, you must act accordingly.

Follow up if you become confused rather than spending hours of time and significant amounts of client money spinning your wheels. Find out from the attorney if there are any other facts that might help you focus your research. Talk with other lawyers who are familiar with the matter. Often a fresh perspective provides new insight.

If a project is truly and overwhelmingly broad, go back to the assigning attorney and attempt to draw some parameters. Sometimes the assigning attorney is unaware of how much is involved in a particular project until initial research is done. Be prepared to articulate why the project appears broad and have a firm understanding of the basics before talking with the assigning attorney.

There are times when there is no definitive answer. Before you report that conclusion to the assigning attorney, be sure that you have exhausted all resources, including consulting the firm's librarian as well as other attorneys, and searching for law review articles on related subjects. Then, prepare a summary of the research you conducted before returning to the attorney who assigned the project. It always makes an assigning attorney uncomfortable to hear that there is nothing out there. There is usually analogous authority or a law review article on a related issue. Related law review articles are helpful because they generally raise every conceivable issue and sometimes confirm that there is nothing out there.

Keep thorough and neat notes detailing your research. Inevitably, two or three years down the road, someone else will have to review your attorney and research notes. Your background work and the notes you keep will impact your reputation for being thorough. Because handwritten notes can be indecipherable by the time a case goes to trial (even to the person who wrote them), some lawyers suggest dictating a brief memorandum to the file summarizing handwritten notes. You and others will some day appreciate your earlier efforts at organization.

Many first year attorneys write a law review article instead of a memorandum of law on a specific legal issue. For example, they are assigned to research whether under Florida law, the attorney client privilege has been waived by a witness in a deposition. The resulting memorandum should not begin with an historical overview of Florida's treatment of the privilege. Your ability to be concise and provide relevant information is valued highly by partners and clients alike.

Proofread your work several times and then ask your secretary to proof it. One typo is too many. There are many partners and senior associates who will not tolerate avoidable mistakes. One summer associate's review consisted of a single comment by the supervising partner: an "s" was left out of the fifteen-plus letters in the name of the foreign client. He was right, of course, and the associate learned a valuable lesson.

All of this focus on typographical and avoidable errors may seem like overkill. It is not. Assigning attorneys worry about what else an associate has screwed up when the assigning attorney starts seeing avoidable mistakes. Also, because an associate often does limited work for numerous partners and associates, individual attorneys may begin to form an overall impression of the junior associate just from their minimal interaction. Time and again, the reputation of an associate is affected by one attorney's impression from a single episode or interaction. Consequently, because it is inevitable that you will make a mistake, make sure that the avoidable mistakes are not one of them.

Think creatively about the problem or project on which you are working. If the work product requested is a memorandum, include a section on related issues about which further research that might prove fruitful. In addition, if you have suggestions about another way to structure the argument in a motion, talk with the partner. Attorneys value independent and creative thinkers; these associates add real value to a team.

Above all, turn in quality work and do it on time. Absent an emergency, legal or otherwise, you should do everything in your power to meet or beat your deadline. There are times when finalizing an assignment requires you to put in inordinate overtime. Partners expect that you will do whatever it takes, including staying up all night, to get it done. If you have put significant hours in on a project and it still will not be finished on time, then you can legitimately go to the partner, explain the situation, and ask for additional time or support.

Meeting deadlines is an incredibly stressful and difficult part of an associate's day-to-day work life. The reasons are many: work expands (scope creep), additional work is piled on, old projects come back to life, projects take longer than you were told, etc. An associate should be legitimately concerned about meeting any and every deadline, which can lead to a pattern of working too late or staying up all night several nights in a row. How you manage these issues in the context of your career is absolutely critical.

The following guidelines might help handling deadlines generally (a chronic, overwhelming work-load is addressed separately). Above all, do what you say you will do. Reliability is key. Few factors have as much of an impact on an associate's career as reliability, which includes elements of consistency, ethical behavior and credibility. If you commit to a deadline, you must deliver absent a true emergency.

Contact the assigning attorney as soon as possible in the event of a non-work-related emergency. If you do not reach the attorney at the office, then under appropriate circumstances you may need to contact her at home. Obviously, you must use judgment in this situation. If an agency filing or closing might be affected, then you must reach the attorney at home. If a memorandum is at issue that will be used to educate a partner about the legal aspects of a matter, then leave a voice or e-mail message if you do not get in touch with the assigning attorney directly. Earlier in this chapter it was suggested that you try to determine whether there is a "hard" or "soft" deadline for a newly assigned project. This would be an example of how having that information is important. Knowing what will be done with your work and when will help you determine an appropriate response in the event of an emergency. Also, keep in mind that some attorneys do not check e-mail or voicemail directly. It is incumbent on you to make sure that the attorney gets the message you leave.

There are times when a work-related emergency will keep you from meeting other deadlines. For example, you are working on a draft of a brief that a partner wants to review on Tuesday morning. On Monday afternoon, you learn that a motion for a temporary restraining order has been filed against your client in a matter to which you have been assigned. Several of the attorneys in your group are required to drop everything and work until the research and briefs are done. In that situation (a work-related emergency), it is appropriate to ask the senior associate or partner who is pulling you off of your assigned project to call the assigning attorney and clear the way for you to work on the emergency. Make sure this call is made; do not rely on an attorney saying "I'll call her and it will be fine." This is fertile ground for a problem that will only hurt you and your reputation. Attorneys are notorious for getting side-tracked away from personnel or management issues; follow up with the senior associate or partner to ensure that the call was made. If time permits, follow up immediately with the original assigning attorney so that the two of you can reschedule the deadline for the assigned project. If time does not permit, call or see the assigning attorney as soon as possible.

Part of deadline-management involves early assessment. Do not commit to a deadline you cannot possibly meet. One partner advised that attorneys should have one of two responses when being assigned a project: If you can do the assigned work, say "yes" unequivocally and without giving a recitation of other things that you have going on. Often, associates respond with "yes, but I have research projects due for two others, computer training tomorrow afternoon, and . . . ." Such "thinking out loud" or hedging makes assigning attorneys uneasy and they lose confidence in the associate. If you cannot meet the deadline, then in most cases you should say so. At that point, you can ask the partner to talk with your other partners to see about reshuffling projects; or, you can undertake that responsibility on your own and tell the assigning partner that you will get right back to her.

That said, there are certain circumstances when you should never say no, even when you are too busy. You must accept a project assigned by a named partner or the managing partner of the firm. When your billable hours have been low, you will have a hard time justifying your refusal to accept work. In addition, a first year associate will have very few occasions to refuse work. It is better in these situations to accept the assignment and then ask your supervising attorney to help you manage the workload after the fact.

Your hours must back you up if you refuse work because of overload. It is true that there are certain days or weeks that just get out of control making it difficult to accept additional assignments for at least those days or weeks. Your hours, however, should show that over the course of the month you have been extremely busy. Attorneys will never say, "Gee, John refused work today and since his hours are acceptable this month, he must have been overly busy on that day." It will never happen. If you are turning down work, your monthly hours (or few months) need to back up your assertions.

If your monthly hours do not back up your assertions, assigning attorneys will ascribe your refusal to accept work to one of several problems: (1) you are avoiding that particular assigning attorney because you do not like her work; (2) you are just trying to maneuver the best work for yourself and filtering out the rest; or (3) you are lazy. Few people will understand that you genuinely have too much work to do. Thus, say "no" only when it is absolutely the case that you cannot in good conscience take on additional work.

Finally, and it almost sounds too simple to write, but make sure that you have a firm understanding of the deadline for a particular project. The responsibility for a miscommunication will fall squarely on the shoulders of an associate. Thus, view it as your job to gets the facts surrounding your assignment.

### Master the Facts

From time to time, you will be asked to recall information about the procedural posture of a matter, the parties' respective settlement positions, or a relevant date. Make it your business to know this information. Review the pleadings in a litigation matter. Review correspondence in transactional matters so that you can understand the facts relayed to the firm by your client. Record on a calendar all relevant dates and events. It may be appropriate for you to talk with the client directly to learn the facts; seek permission first from the partner. Your mastery of the facts will make you (almost) indispensable on complicated or large matters. Moreover, when you accurately remember specific facts or dates, your credibility increases in the eyes of other attorneys. You will often get calls from the partner asking for basic information, like a telephone number or the name of a judge's clerk. Often this is because someone other than the partner will typically have the file. Some attorneys keep readily accessible a sheet of relevant information about a matter. That way, the information is at your fingertips when a partner or senior associate calls with a question.

### Write and Rewrite

Your ability to write well is of paramount importance in many careers, but is an absolute necessity in the practice law. Writing ability often weeds out those who stay versus those who are asked to leave. Granted, there are some practice areas where writing is not the focus. You will, however, always have to write letters to third parties, as well as clients. Even in these limited situations, your writing ability is critical. For example, the words you use in a letter become your version of the facts in a matter. If you have used imprecise or inappropriate words, you may have locked your client into a position that it never intended to take. Also, your writing will be scrutinized in many cases by your adversary to try to "read between the lines" to get an idea of your client's true position in a matter. As a result, your tone, choice of words, and facts relied on are all extremely important.

Be prepared to write and re-write. Good writers are rarely happy with a first draft, or even a second or third. Take the time to say what you mean exactly the way you want to say it. Leave things and go back after a break when working on a large document. As with any project, being too close to it can impair your ability to evaluate it properly.

Do not be surprised when reviewing attorneys re-write or heavily edit your work. Many reviewing attorneys feel that if their name is on a document, it must go out as if they had written it. You will see attorneys re-write portions of documents that they have previously authored. This is not unusual.

Work hard at taking criticism well. You will not always agree with an attorney about your writing; sometimes differences are a matter of style. Take what you can out of the comments and incorporate those suggestions when they truly improve the final product.

While it is important to show ownership over your work, avoid the "pride in authorship" syndrome. Some attorneys become too wedded to their work or to a particularly clever phrase or word. An attorney's unwillingness to change certain words or phrases leads to an inferior work product.

Ask your secretary to review short letters for clarity and accuracy. Often, secretaries have good training in the rules of grammar and punctuation. As somewhat neutral observers, they may be able to point out things in your writing that do not come across clearly.

### Do Not Assume a Partner Knows What She Is Talking About

In your own mind, at least, question everything. When you get an assignment from a partner or senior associate, do not assume that the attorney knows entirely what she is talking about. Check out information that does not sound accurate. For example, an attorney asks you to prepare a motion to dismiss and suggests citing a contract not referred to in the complaint. During the course of your research, you run across cases holding that a motion to dismiss will be converted to a motion for summary judgment under such circumstances. You need to follow up with the attorney about this information so that a mistake is not made. If you think something is in error or could compromise the client's interests, go to the assigning attorney with your research. When a mistake is made, it will damage your reputation, regardless of whether it was your fault.

### Do Not Rely on Others

At least for your first two years, do not rely on anyone to finalize or complete your work. For example, a staff person may be very knowledgeable about filing requirements with a local court. No matter how convincing this person sounds, you must do your own review of the rules and perhaps call the court clerk yourself to learn what needs to be done. Relying on others is acceptable once you have some experience under your belt. In the beginning, however, when your reputation is on the line, do most everything yourself.

### Do Not Assume that Someone Will Check Your Work

First year attorneys are always surprised when a senior associate or partner reads their work and relies on it to give advice or prepare a document. Even more alarming to the first year attorney is when a partner signs and files a draft motion prepared by the new attorney. These things happen all the time. To avoid situations that may come back to haunt you, any document, paper, or research submitted by you should be in final form, with all of your citations and facts double checked. Never assume that a more senior attorney will check your research and analysis and confirm that you have arrived at the right conclusion.

### Treat Senior Associates and Partners as Though They Are Your Clients

Clients want their attorneys to be reliable, accessible, knowledgeable, and efficient. Partners and senior associates want nothing less from their lower-level associates. In practical terms, this means that you never, ever hand in a draft, even if the attorneys encourage you to do so. No client can read an incomplete draft and not draw conclusions about the writer's abilities or analysis. Always follow through on your representations and promises. If you say that something will be done by Tuesday, get it done by Tuesday. Be prepared to discuss in detail your research and resulting work product. To do this, you must be able to discuss the facts of a case or the regulations relied on in preparing your work. Offer strategies and solutions for the handling of a matter. Follow-up after handing in an assignment, particularly after the assigning attorney has had a chance to review it. This shows interest in and ownership of your work. Learn to think in terms of "client satisfaction."

Like clients, your superiors have particular ways of doing or handling things. For example, one partner dislikes the word "clearly" in any brief. Another partner insists on using "we" and not "I" when referring to the handling of a client's dispute. Another partner dislikes using initials to define a client name. Thus, he would prefer "Acme" instead of "ARS" for Acme Rocket Supplies. Learn these idiosyncrasies by talking with secretaries and other associates and use their tips in your work.

### Form and Research Files

All associates should keep a copy of every written work product they produce. These copies may be organized by type of document and filed with examples of other like documents, or kept in a separate folder at home. You can use these for future reference or research, or individual documents may comprise your writing sample for a future job search. If you decide to strike out on your own someday, you want to have solid examples of certain types of documents. Be sure to keep these documents as they are authored by you. It will be too difficult to compile these papers two or three years down the road. They may be erased from the office computer system or archived by the firm. If disaster strikes and you are asked to leave the firm immediately, you will not have time to retrieve these documents (a good reason to keep them at home). One firm billed an associate for copy charges after he announced he was leaving and wanted to take his form files with him to his new firm.

Consider whether you want to maintain your own written form files, as opposed to relying on the firm's brief or document bank. Many attorneys find that having particularly good examples of certain documents relative to their practice is good to have on hand or on the computer system. Think in terms of quick access and whether you might want to have these examples for your future practice needs.

A research file is another good reference for the young attorney. Ask your secretary to help organize cases dealing with various areas of the law. Some attorneys have complicated research files with a complete numbering and retrieval guide. Others keep on hand significant decisions or statutes in areas relevant to their practice. For example, a lawyer may maintain a folder of all recent restrictive covenant cases, an issue that might frequently arise in the lawyer's practice. Another lawyer might keep handy a notebook containing the entire Federal Arbitration Act.

### Get to Know Your Clients and Their Work

Listen to your clients when they tell you about their company or industry. Find out exactly the product or service your client provides and, if appropriate, ask to see samples. Understand who is who within the corporate structure. Learn what you can about the industry and your client's competitors. You may want to go "off the clock" and tour your client's facilities or offices. Be sure to tell the client beforehand that you are not billing them for your time. All of this information will help you forge a better relationship with your client, and help you serve their interests better as matters arise.

### Use Caution when Discussing Your Clients or Their Cases

Every law firm has a story about a young associate (or partner) who was overheard in an elevator or at a baseball game discussing a client's business. Somehow, clients will hear what you say about them and they will take action. It is best to use caution in any client-related discussion outside your office. Leave out the specifics if you must discuss a client matter.

Similarly, use discretion when discussing client matters in the firm hallway or shouting instructions to your secretary from your office. You never know who is walking down the hall or getting coffee in the break room. Lawyers from other firms may be visiting. Other clients may overhear you talking about your clients and wonder if you talk that way about them.

Telephone conference calls are another area notorious for getting someone in trouble. Two associates were making disparaging comments about another associate's "social life." Unfortunately for all involved, the two associates were unintentionally broadcast over the firm's public address system. Another attorney thought he had hung up the telephone after leaving a voice mail message for his opposing counsel in another city. He proceeded to have an obnoxious conversation about lawyers in that region with a third person who was on the line with him. This attorney realized too late that all of his petty comments were recorded on the voice mail of his opposing counsel. That voice mail was then forwarded all over the city. His subsequent apology, of course, was not. Always hang up after dropping a caller and call the other party back, particularly if the remaining party is your client. This will avoid the inadvertent disclosure of privileged information. It will also prevent you from embarrassing yourself.

### Learn Courtroom Etiquette

Exhibiting proper courtroom decorum takes practice. Sometimes watching other attorneys is a good way to learn what not to do, as well gain tips on things you should do. There are guidelines that are applicable whether you are attending court for a simple calendar call or trying a lengthy case. Always be extremely courteous to court personnel and every employee working in the judge's office. Thank everyone for their assistance, especially if they have gone out of their way to accommodate you. Do not let your frustration with the process or the judge's rulings spill over into your dealings with the judge's secretary, clerks, or other personnel (or, the judge for that matter). These people have day-to-day contact with the judge and will often tell the judge about a particularly good or bad experience with a lawyer. Act in a professional manner from the moment you arrive at the courthouse. Often you will come into contact with jurors, and your behavior will begin to shape their perception of you or the judicial experience in which they are about to participate. Even if you are not at court to select a jury, remember that you are an officer of the court and as such should avoid any unprofessional behavior any time you are within range of the courthouse. Refrain from talking loudly in the hallway, in the courtroom, or anywhere within earshot of jurors (for example, in a restaurant next to the courthouse). Avoid, if at all possible, running through the courthouse.

Once in court, seek out your opposing counsel and introduce yourself. This may be your first opportunity to meet your opponent face-to-face. If you already know the opposing attorney, regardless of any difficult dealings in the past, professionalism requires that you follow basic rules of civility.

Always introduce yourself to the court slowly and clearly and tell the judge who you represent. Usually, the judge will make a note of your name so that she can properly address you as the matter progresses. Introduce the judge to any co-counsel or associates if they are also present in the courtroom. You may want to indicate whether your client is present.

Do not approach the bench or a witness on the stand without prior permission from the judge. While in front of the judge, never direct questions, accusations, or comments directly at opposing counsel unless the court has specifically requested that you talk with one another about a matter. In fact, refrain from even looking at opposing counsel if at all possible. Your questions or concerns about something that opposing counsel is doing should be directed to the court. The same rule applies when the judge calls you and opposing counsel up to the bench for a sidebar conference. Because the discussion is sometimes more informal, lawyers have a tendency to argue or discuss matters directly with opposing counsel. Remember that whatever action is taken by the other side, it was done by the other party, not the lawyer. You don't want to say to the judge that your opposing counsel advanced an argument that she knew to be unfounded. Her client advanced the argument. You may spend so much time outside of court complaining about opposing counsel that it will be hard to switch gears in the courtroom. Be sure that you do.

Do not sigh, complain, or make a face when the judge rules against you. Instead, thank the judge or say "yes, your honor" and, if no exception for the record is needed, move on. Don't argue with the judge, but do take up certain matters in the appropriate context or through the correct procedural channels. For example, it may be appropriate to ask the judge to reconsider a ruling. You can do this out of the hearing of the jury. Exercise the same restraint when a judge rules in your favor.

When a judge asks you a direct question, answer it directly. If you need to explain your response, ask the court for permission to do so. Too many lawyers start off answers to judges with "Well, judge, you see . . . ." This is not what the judge wants to hear.

Never point at opposing counsel, the judge, or a witness. This is rude behavior and will likely not be countenanced by the court.

Your dress must also be appropriate. Men should appear in suits, with their jackets on. Women should a wear suit, skirt and blouse, or an appropriate one-piece dress. Some judges look with disdain at pantsuits on women, so it is safe to assume that a skirt or appropriate dress is required.

Professionalism is required of your client, too, although clients have much more leeway in the way they dress. Nevertheless, it is your responsibility to make sure that your client's outfit is appropriate for the courthouse (no tank tops, revealing shirts or skirts, flip-flops, short shorts, etc.). Appropriate dress may include a uniform (especially if your client is going to work directly from court) or casual dress. Instruct your client on how to address the judge if a question should be asked directly of your client. Be sure to tell your client to refrain from making faces, audible comments, or reacting dramatically to testimony from a witness. Some emotion is inevitable, but the jury will be watching everything your client (and your client's support network in the courtroom) is doing. One jury sent a note to the judge to ask the plaintiff's mother to cease making faces as she listened to the defendant testify. This was embarrassing for the client and attorneys alike.

### Treat Support Staff with the Same Respect You Show the Firm's Partners

Many new lawyers are uncertain of the protocol in dealing with secretaries and other support staff. These relationships are so important that an entire chapter of this book identifies specific ways to make these relationships more effective. In general, however, treat all people with respect, no matter what their position within the firm. What is respect? It is never yelling or raising your voice to someone, even when that person's mistake has made you look incompetent. It is telling them when they have made a mistake, so that they can learn from it. It is a refusal to immediately point fingers and scatter blame when something goes wrong. It is setting reasonable time limits on work or projects assigned by you.

If the Golden Rule is not sufficient reason for you to treat people well, try this one: You will rely on and need the cooperation of every type of support staff person in that firm at some time or another. An attorney had a difficult time with temporary or floating secretaries. He routinely used the subsequent written review for that secretary as an opportunity to criticize the secretary's performance, rather than talking with her in person. Now, this attorney cannot get anyone to volunteer for overtime. The old saying "what goes around, comes around" is fully applicable to the law firm setting.

## When You Make A Mistake, Tell Someone Immediately

There are few mistakes that cannot be fixed, with the possible exception of missing an applicable statute of limitations. Attorneys in the early stages of their careers generally do not have the ability to appreciate fully when a mistake is fixable or what to do to correct a problem. Thus, when you or someone under you has discovered a potential problem, you should get all the facts, including the procedural stage of the matter, and the work that you did. You may want to pull aside a trusted colleague to help you assess the facts or to keep you calm. Then, go to either your supervising partner or the partner with whom you are working on the file. Apprise that attorney of the facts and take whatever steps are necessary to rectify the situation. Learn from your mistake and move on. Every lawyer makes mistakes; good lawyers do not make the same mistake twice.

You should never inform a client about a mistake without first consulting with your supervising partner. Because the partner is ultimately responsible, she may feel that any notice of a mistake to a client is more appropriately made by her.

### Ethical Dilemmas

You will experience ethical dilemmas in your first few years of practice, some serious, some not. For example, as you guide clients through the discovery process and request certain documents, they will ask questions like: "What if I can't find those documents that might be hurtful?" or "Before I give these documents to you, tell me if they hurt or help my case." You may have a client who is experiencing severe mental distress and you question whether you should be relying on that person's instructions. Perhaps confirmation from a doctor that the client is sober is necessary before you should continue representation. Another example might be when opposing counsel has unethically taped a witness in a matter without disclosing to the witness that he is a lawyer or seeking the witness' permission. In one case, lawyers used the cloak of "zealous advocacy" to encourage a client to file a frivolous lawsuit against a lawyer personally. These lawyers had been bested by the defendant/lawyer and were seeking retribution. The suit was baseless (the plaintiffs were forced to dismiss with prejudice), and, as the matter unfolded, the ethical questions were daunting.

You may need some guidance in how to proceed. The instances described are just a few of the ethical dilemmas that you may face as a young lawyer. Your state bar association may have an "ethics hotline" where you can anonymously call for direction from one of the attorneys on staff. Sometimes they can direct you to case law on point, or they may decline to become involved and suggest that you speak with another lawyer to advise you. Another option for the young attorney is to talk with an experienced member of the firm and solicit that person's opinion. In that case, make sure you know the legal parameters of your problem and have looked at some research already. Such information will allow you to give the attorney all the facts and, after discussion, likely arrive at a workable solution or approach.

Ethics is one of those law school classes that people take less seriously than they should. Unfortunately, ethical issues arise all too frequently, and are compounded by the lack of experience of newer attorneys.

### Morale Issues

It may happen that a group of dissatisfied lawyers departs the firm or several associates or partners leave within a relatively short period of time. Generally, as disgruntled lawyers, they will have negative things to say about the firm, or will talk about financial problems on the horizon. Many times, associates begin to believe that the firm is coming apart, only to learn later that the firm is having a banner financial year. The rumor mill feeds much of this speculation and often impacts the overall morale of the associates. If you have a legitimate concern about the financial stability of the firm or whether the firm is splitting, consider getting the facts from the source—the managing partner or a partner with whom you have developed a close relationship. You may not get the straight story, but if the managing partner hears enough concern from the associates, the firm may opt to address the rumor and morale issues head on. In short, don't put too much stock in the grumblings of disgruntled associates. Instead, get the facts and draw your own conclusions.

### *Pro Bono* Work and Billable Hours

Most firms will have a billing number for time that is not billable client work. This might include recruiting, marketing, or legal education time. It may also include *pro bono* work. Make no mistake, no matter how high your non-billable hours are, the only hours that affect the bottom line are the billable ones. Billable hours are the only ones that really count. Some firms encourage associates to handle significant *pro bono* work. It bears repeating that no matter how high your non-billable hours, the only hours that affect the bottom line are the billable ones.

Very few firms (and you will know whether yours is one of them before you bill your first dollar) rate *pro bono* work in the same class as billable work. One associate was asked to work for several months with a non-profit group off-site as part of her *pro bono* work. At her yearly review, the time was then counted against her; the firm expected to make up her billable hours during the remaining months of the year. Another associate was asked to handle a *pro bono* matter that was not expected to take much time. The matter escalated into a lawsuit, full discovery, briefing, trial, and post-trial motions. The associate learned too late that all of this time was expected to be time over and above the minimum billable hour commitment expected of every associate. These expectations are, of course, unreasonable. Nevertheless, they exist with few exceptions.

### Rules of E-Mail

The proper use of e-mail should be a course in law school. This is one of those small things that can have a great impact on your career. Two summer associates thought it would be humorous to send a firm-wide e-mail from an unsuspecting attorney's computer inviting everyone to witness a fellow summer associate as she made her debut at an adult dance club. Of course, this was meant as a harmless joke. The firm viewed it as anything but. Then there was the attorney who sent an e-mail to a colleague but somehow it went to the whole firm, staff included. The content was innocuous, but there was no end to the commentary the attorney received from dozens of people. Can you imagine if the attorney was venting to friends about a partner? Another lawyer received what she believed to be an e-mail from her (male) partner about hotel arrangements for an upcoming business trip. The e-mail mentioned that she should bring along a bathing suit. The message was sent as a joke by a fellow (female) associate. The attorney receiving the message thought nothing of the situation, but found out months later what a problem this had caused for the associate who sent the message.

Virtually every firm has its stories about embarrassing or damaging incidents involving e-mail. Here are some guidelines so that you do not have to learn this lesson the hard way. Try not use e-mail for anything other than work-related or routine communications with attorneys or staff. If friends or family send you e-mail containing questionable content, ask them to stop. Before sending any e-mail, ask yourself if this is something that anyone in the firm can review. Use general references or code names for people or circumstances if you need to communicate sensitive or potentially embarrassing information.

E-mail plays in important role in a law firm. It is a quick and effective way to keep everyone abreast of developments in a matter. If appropriate, copy an attorney's secretary so that the secretary can update the file. It is also a good way to keep a record in the file of your advice or recommendations in a matter (also known as a CYA letter). Finally, e-mail is a good way to keep your partners and senior associates apprised of your workload.

Increasingly, clients rely on e-mail to communicate with the firm. Be sure to check your e-mail regularly and treat every client communication as you would a letter. Print out a copy and file it. All responses from you should be copied to you or your secretary for printing and filing. Double check your spelling if your spell-check does not correct e-mail misspellings.

### Negotiating and Dealing with Opposing Counsel

After the course on the proper use of e-mail, classes in how to deal with opposing counsel should be next. Your relationships with opposing counsel can be very satisfying or can destroy any enjoyment that you would have hoped to get out of your career. For many practices, dealing with opposing counsel is day-to-day work. Your stress level will escalate as soon as relationships with opposing counsel start to get out of hand. One partner recalled how he physically shook with rage whenever he had to talk with opposing counsel in a particular case, a lawyer who would consistently accuse the partner of fraud and other unethical behavior. This was an opponent who would lie about previous happenings between counsel. The opposing lawyer was so inflammatory and insulting that few people could walk away from a conversation with him without an elevation in blood pressure. You will get no satisfaction from working on a case with opposing counsel like this one.

Start with the premise that the legal dispute is between your clients and those on the other side, not you and opposing counsel. That knowledge will help you maintain an objective focus and not personalize disputes. You may need to remind opposing counsel of that fact.

Attorneys will often tell you to act professional in all your dealings with the other side. What exactly constitutes professional behavior is unclear. Here are some guidelines: Before implying that opposing counsel has engaged in incorrect or improper behavior, investigate the facts. On the telephone, use a reasonable tone at all times; there is never a reason to curse or scream. There are times, however, when it is appropriate to allow your indignation, disgust or disbelief to come through in your tone of voice. The trick is to know the difference between those emotions and behavior that crosses the line, and then how to respond appropriately. Anger may be fitting in some dealings with opposing counsel. An attorney, apparently trying to take advantage of a younger, less experienced attorney, began making outrageous speeches on the record at the deposition of the chairman of a large company. The less-experienced attorney appropriately used anger in a controlled manner to not only address the statements on the record, but also to warn opposing counsel that these tactics could not be tolerated. Anger or other strong emotions should never be reactionary; rather they should be controlled and calculated responses to appropriate situations.

If authorized by your client or supervising partner, accede to an extension of time requested by the other side. At some point during litigation, you will need an extension, whether it is due to an emergency, strategy or client-related problems. Your client may be an accountant whose deposition has been noticed for April 14. If you have taken a particularly hard-line with your opposing counsel, you will be forced to go to the court for each and every inch of time or leeway that you need for your client.

While we are on the subject of scheduling depositions, there are some unwritten rules of courtesy that perhaps should be written down. Telephone or write opposing counsel (once) before setting a firm date for depositions or the like. There are several reasons for extending that courtesy. The opposing attorney and her client will be less able to cite business reasons for avoiding the deposition on that date. Likewise, the opposing lawyer will have fewer grounds for complaining about the timing of the deposition. Even though the notice of deposition normally indicates that the proceeding will take place at the deposing attorney's office, they usually occur, as a courtesy, at the deponent's place of business or at the office of the deponent's attorney. You will then be able to insist upon the same courtesy for your client, which is preferable since your client will be more comfortable in familiar surroundings.

Another reason for taking the deposition at the deponent's place of business is that your deponent can easily access papers referred to in the deposition. This, of course, works both ways. Finally, there are some cases when it is a good idea to see where your opposing party operates. You never know what you might learn. In one case, there was some question as to whether two companies were related. The attorney showed up for the deposition at the deponent's place of business and discovered that among other things, the two companies shared physical location, receptionist, and office equipment, facts that later helped his argument that the companies were one and the same. Again, this argument cuts both ways; if having opposing counsel visiting your client's business would compromise your client's position, then have the deposition at your office or a neutral location.

Find ways to work with opposing counsel on logistics. Some clients refuse to accommodate the other party because the dispute is clouding their judgment. In that case, work with opposing counsel in finding alternative locations for meetings, like using another law firm's facilities, having the meeting a local court, or renting space at a hotel.

In your papers, avoid personally attacking opposing counsel and focus on her client's legal or factual position. It is appropriate to criticize the manner in which opposing counsel has treated a proposition of law, although take care that you do not lightly accuse them of doing it deliberately.

Sometimes you will face opposing lawyers who are incompetent or just plain bad. They may fail to provide authority for stated propositions or do other things that shouldn't be done. These attorneys will actually make handling a client's case more time consuming and difficult. In pointing out their mistakes, you will have to go back and recheck the support for your assertions, and then further argue your own position. You, in effect, have to do the research that your opposing counsel should have already done.

There are times when you must deal aggressively with opposing counsel. For example, opposing counsel is employing tactics that he knows will drive up the cost of litigation for both parties. Or, your opposing counsel is incompetent and your client is expending high fees to combat unfounded arguments advanced by the other side. In that case, avoid dealing with these attorneys on their level; they will bring you down and drive up the cost of litigation. Deal only in writing with such lawyers; do not rely on any representation made by these attorneys unless it has been confirmed in writing. Double check everything you do and they do. These steps may increase the cost for your client in the short run, but it will pay off when opposing counsel neglects to dot an "i" or cross a "t." You must adjust your client's expectations about the cost of litigation early. Solicit advice from your partner on how to deal with difficult opposing counsel.

When opposing counsel puts you on the spot and you do not know the answer to a question posed (e.g., an extension is requested, or an inquiry is made into your client's settlement position), have some stock phrases on hand:

- I need to check with my client

- I'd like to think on that and get back to you

- I need to check some facts before I can make that determination

Pretend that every letter you write to opposing counsel is "Exhibit A" at a trial, meaning that you need to be professional in your writing. Never tell opposing counsel that your letters (or theirs will be that "Exhibit A")—that is something opponents should figure out for themselves. Don't give away too much information unless it is in your interest to do so, and always appear to be reasonable, even when holding firm on a position.

Most judges dislike getting involved in disputes between attorneys. There is a time, however, for court intervention. In that case, make sure that you are absolutely correct in your position, that you have exhausted all suggestions for trying to work it out, and that the written record supports your version of the facts.

Finally, keep in mind that a lawyer may be your opposing counsel one day and a judge the next. Try not to get into the mind-set that your opposing counsel is so incompetent, so ethically challenged, so not like a judge, that the chances of her becoming a judge are slim. Some of these positions are popularly elected. You may know your opposing counsel's professional background, but non-lawyers may not.

### Clients Sometimes Do Stupid Things

Many lawyers express rage and frustration when the client says or does something that damages a case. This is unfortunately a huge source of stress for lawyers. Remember, however, that your client's case is your client's case, not yours. Clients do stupid things that damage the case. Ultimately, this is the client's problem, not yours. You take your facts are they are. You cannot change the facts or direct entirely the behavior of your client. Taking a more philosophical approach will eliminate much frustration from your job.

### Handling Witnesses

Young lawyers are often given the job of interviewing witnesses. Interviewing a witness begins when you first contact the witness. Your demeanor, presentation and attitude convey important information that could affect the information you get from the witness. Non-lawyers are sometimes suspicious of you simply because you are an attorney. Other witnesses may be intimidated by lawyers in general. This may not be immediately evident in your communications with witnesses, but understand that you are dealing with a set of preconceived notions and attitudes held by people simply by virtue of the fact of your profession.

Then, you must factor in a myriad of other influences; your gender, race, religious background, if known or evident, and your client's position in the case at hand. For example, you may represent a plaintiff in a personal injury case. Witnesses to the incident may be unwilling to talk with you because they do not believe your client should sue over the incident. You may never get all the facts known by these witnesses.

New lawyers often give witnesses the benefit of the doubt when it comes to providing truthful statements or testimony under oath. While this is certainly a laudable perspective, it will generally not serve your clients' best interest unless you throw in some measure of skepticism. Lawyers often express surprise that witnesses lie; they lie under oath and they lie on the stand. Your own witnesses will lie to you. Sometimes your witnesses will believe they are telling the truth, but their factual recollections are erroneous. Always stop and consider these possibilities before you get too fired up about your client's case. Do not dismiss out of hand your opposing counsel's outrageous factual claims. Investigate them and be prepared (sometimes for your own sake) to rebut them with provable facts. Ask your client directly if they are true or not.

The next step after contacting the witness is actually interviewing the witness. A telephone interview may be appropriate when the witness has little knowledge about the matter or is only peripheral to the case. All other witnesses should be interviewed in person, if feasible. Many times you will find that witnesses are less inclined to lie during a personal interview as opposed to a telephonic discussion. Also, there will be fewer distractions for the witness as you interview him than if you were on the telephone. Another advantage to an in-person interview is that you can be assured of exactly who is in the room with the witness.

Keep in mind that a witness may be recording your conversation without your knowledge. This is legal in most states. It is not always legal or ethical, however, for an attorney to record a witness without that person's knowledge or consent. For example, in some states it is legal to record another person without that witness' permission or consent, so long as one party consents to the recordation. If the person consenting is a lawyer, then the lawyer has an ethical dilemma; the actions are not illegal but strongly discouraged from an ethical standpoint. You should know these rules because you may need to tape record a conversation at the last minute. You will not have time to first conduct research and then press the record button on your dictation equipment. Do not forget to record the witness' assent to being recorded.

Unless the witness is covered under some privilege, your opposing counsel generally can inquire into all information that you divulge to a witness and vice-versa. Thus, use discretion when discussing your case with a witness and watch what you say about opposing counsel. One lawyer was embarrassed when during a deposition of a witness, the witness was asked:

*Attorney A:*   Attorney B talked with you about this case, correct?

*Witness:*   Yes.

*Attorney A:*  What did he say about me?

*Witness:*  That you would try to trick me.

Of course, you may have strategic reasons for leaking certain information about your strategy or your opposing counsel; obviously judgment is required here.

Bring along plenty of paper. Date your notes and ask for a current address and telephone number from the witness. Write in the corner of the page "WWWWWH" to remind yourself to explore the "who, what, when, where, why and how" with this witness. You probably have done a thorough job if you can answer those questions when the interview is over. Do not be afraid of silence; if you need to review your notes or think of the next several questions, take a few moments to do so.

Soon after the interview, dictate your notes in the form of a memorandum to the file. Start a witness folder for each person interviewed. You may want to keep attorney notes, witness statements, or depositions of that witness in folders in the same gusset. A methodical approach will keep you organized and allow others to later rely on your investigation.

### When You Have Too Much Work to Do

Every associate must balance competing work demands while trying to maintain a "normal life." While there is much debate about whether this is possible, there are at least ways to improve your situation for the short term.

Understand, first, that there will be times when you are stretched to the maximum and there is not much that can be done. For example, you will work extremely hard if you are preparing a matter for trial. You can ask your partners to get you some assistance. You can use your paralegals and your secretary as efficiently as possible. But the bottom line is that the work needs to be done accurately and efficiently and it is your responsibility to accomplish those ends.

172

What you can and must manage is your level of work over an extended period of time. Most people can maintain a high volume of work for a month or two, but not many can do it effectively and well on a sustained basis. The dangers are many. You will wear yourself (and your family) out mentally, physically and emotionally. You will not perform at the top level and you will make mistakes. You will disappoint people by missing deadlines, and not turning in perfect work. The reasons are many to use effective strategies to manage your workload.

Understanding your need to manage work levels is different than actually doing it. Begin by managing expectations. Your partners' are a good place to start. Give accurate estimates of your workload and keep them informed. Next, offer solutions instead of generalized complaints about too much work. The solution might be shuffling internal deadlines or enlisting the help of another associate. Then call on your secretary and paralegal. They can help review your work for accuracy and start initial drafts of routine papers. Ultimately, you may need the assistance of your supervising attorney. That person can act as a gatekeeper for future work assignments coming your way.

### Reviews

If your firm provides regular feedback, the review is usually routine and should be given due weight. Occasionally, reviews are used simply as a vehicle for deciding on bonuses. Reviews take on more importance in a firm that gives little or no feedback to its associates. In that case, pay most attention to the reviews from those with whom you work closely. Do not be surprised at some of the seemingly ridiculous comments made in reviews. Remember, you are dealing with other people's perceptions of you. There may be some comments that do not remotely match your assessment of yourself. However, you probably should reevaluate when you hear the same comment from more than one person.

### Older New Attorneys

Attorneys who attended law school later in life or chose law as a second career often feel "different" than the rest of the first year lawyers. While some firms specifically target older lawyers who have a more settled family situation, this is not the norm. These lawyers should draw on their experience and not downplay their age or previous careers. Make every effort to connect with your peers, even though they may be substantially younger than you. If you are not invited to participate in attorney-organized social outings, express an interest. Sometimes younger lawyers believe you wouldn't want to participate and therefore don't ask. As all you move up the ranks, your age will be less of an issue for you and your peers, and will likely continue to be a great benefit to the firm.

### Passing the Bar

In most instances, an associate will have already started a job at a law firm while awaiting bar exam results. Most firms will allow for a failure. However, that does not always hold true in difficult economic times. For example, in an period when law firms are devastated by a decline in the real estate market, many attorneys-to-be may find themselves looking for a job after hearing that they failed the bar exam. For the most part, however, failing a single time is not cause to be too alarmed. Make sure that you pass on the second try.

### Adopting a "Whatever It Takes" Attitude

Your attitude will shape the perceptions of every attorney with whom you work and meet. You want to give the impression that the team's or group's interests are paramount and you will go to great lengths to advance those interests. An attorney once stayed until 2:00 a.m. preparing arbitration notebooks for a case. This work was not complicated or difficult, but it did need to be done right. He did whatever it took to complete the task and did it well.

Also, project a "we" rather than an "I" attitude. For example, whenever you send a letter on behalf of a client, state "We have been engaged to represent Mr. Jones . . . " When sending a letter to the client to report a victory, be sure to say "We received a favorable ruling . . . ," even if you were the only attorney to have drafted a word of the motion. This all part of a "team player" mentality and communicates to the partners that you want the group to look good, not just you individually.

### Creating a Good Filing System Early

You will have some leeway in setting up your client files. Find out how other attorneys handle client files. Talk with secretaries and see what they recommend. From your first week, develop good filing habits and others will take notice.

### Marketing Expectations

As a first or second year associate, expectations are low with regard to marketing. Partners expect that you will stay in touch with law school classmates. Further, they expect you to participate in marketing projects with other attorneys, like assisting in speech writing or article preparation. Absent unusual circumstances, you will lose credibility if you talk about bringing to the firm a Fortune 500 client. A client of that caliber is unlikely to give business to a first or second year associate and your belief that this is possible reflects on your judgment. Concentrate instead on maintaining good relationships with business acquaintances and classmates. Your friends may be in lower-level positions today, but over the years you and they will advance to positions where marketing and hiring decisions are being made.

### Preparing and Following a Budget

Occasionally, a client will request a budget consisting of a written estimation of the type and amount of services that the firm expects to provide for a client in a given matter. The preparation of a budget is a good exercise for lawyers because it forces them to think about the value of their services and provides a yardstick by which to measure that service.

A budget should contain language that it is an estimate or approximation only. Many external factors can enlarge or shrink time and dollar estimates for particular tasks. For example, your opposing counsel may be such a difficult lawyer that court intervention becomes necessary throughout the discovery process. This, of course, drives up the price for all parties in the dispute. In another example, your client may have several adverse rulings that must be appealed during the progression of the underlying case. Your budget should reflect these exigencies and provide adequate notice to the client of their probability.

The client must be informed whether cost and expense estimates, which are separate from legal fees, are included within the budget estimate. Costs and expenses can become a significant factor in the total legal expenses for a matter.

A budget should give estimate ranges rather than exact dollar figures. For example, you may write that the preparation of a motion for summary judgment will cost between $12,000 and $15,000, rather than $13,000. In addition, the budget should reflect that you have done some strategizing on a matter. For example, a budget may indicate that you anticipate taking five depositions in a matter and include the names of those you intend to take.

Someone with experience should always review the budget before it is given to the client. Budgets are all about experience and you may not be in a position to fully appreciate how much preparation will be needed for certain tasks.

Finally, revisit the budget in a matter from time to time. You should have an idea of how much your client is paying for certain services. Also, you should have an idea whether the firm is within the budget. Gross disparities between the amount of time you forecast versus the amount of time actually billed should have some explanation. You need to be able to explain that disparity because you are the associate on the file. Expect that clients will read and monitor your progress on the matter in light of the budget estimates.

### Get Exposure to Many Different Partners

As a young lawyer, it is easy for a single partner to dominate your time. You do not feel that you have much say in the matter and you are probably learning a great deal with this partner. Over the course of time, however, work hard at working with other partners. You may find work that is more rewarding. Moreover, your reputation will not ride on one person's opinion. Finally, you may need the support of other partners when it comes time for partnership decisions. To support you, they must be familiar with your technical abilities and other information that will only be learned by their having worked with you.

### Is Your Career in Trouble?

There are always signs indicating that your career may be in trouble. Unfortunately, lawyers do a terrible job of conveying this information to the young attorney whose job may be on the line. This failure stems in part from a lack of management ability on the part of many supervising attorneys. Also, many people are reluctant to pass along negative information when it impacts a person's career.

Until lawyers become better managers and mentors, you will have to figure out much of this information by yourself. Over the course of a year, evaluate the quality and quantity of work you are being assigned. If you are getting garbage assignments—work that no-one else wants to do or cases that amount to virtually nothing—then you need to find out why. Senior attorneys may perceive you as unreliable or less competent than your peers. It may be that the quality of your work is not being monitored by anyone, which indicates that you are somewhat invisible to those around you.

There comes a point when your lack of experience on quality matters causes irreparable damage to your career. As one indication, you will be evaluated against your peers. If they are getting good practical experience and you are not, then you lose. In addition, in the event you want to make a firm change, you are less marketable when you are a fourth year attorney with the skill set of a second year. Lateral attorneys are scrutinized more closely for this very reason; firms want to make sure that they get what they pay for. Do not allow this problem to continue without being proactive. Talk first with your supervising attorney. It is that person's responsibility to act when these types of experience issues are raised. Ask that attorney if you are being perceived in such a way that more senior attorneys only use you when they have to. If so, you can identify areas where you need to show drastic improvement. If not, then your lack of quality assignments may be a case of falling through the cracks. Again, your supervising attorney is in a position to funnel better work your way.

Find another mentor if you do not have a good relationship with your supervising attorney. It helps if there is another partner for whom you have done substantive, quality work. Begin by asking that attorney for thoughts on the direction in which your career is going. Find someone else if that person does not make time for you or offers advice without any forethought. Either way, keep in mind that early action on your part may save your career.

Firms have made an investment in you and will work to save that investment, unless the problems are ones that training will not change. For example, no amount of training will help if you lack common sense, a willing attitude, or if you are unreliable. On the other hand, if your writing needs improvement or your telephone skills need polishing, a firm will likely make that additional investment in your training. Many attorneys have had the benefit of a "remedial" writing course. These courses are sometimes handled through an outside expert who evaluates your writing and then works with you on correcting perceived problems. Other firms use the library staff as a resource, particularly when a lawyer is on staff with the library. Accept this help when suggested or offered and try not to feel embarrassed. Your willingness to improve your skills, whether or not you believe improvement is needed, is all part of having a willing attitude in the eyes of firm managers.

There are other signs of trouble. If your partner never involves you with clients aside from researching legal issues and writing documents and briefs, and this continues for some period of time, then start taking note. You may have deficient social skills or your appearance needs polishing. Less often, the problem may stem from the partner's attitude towards you. A partner may have some hesitation about involving you with certain clients due to your sex, sexual orientation, or religious beliefs. This type of discrimination is insidious, but observing the manner in which a partner treats you in front of clients may provide insight.

Another sign that your career is in trouble may be that you are hearing consistently similar negative comments in reviews. Of course, a negative review should always be given additional consideration, but when for two years in a row you hear "unreliable" or "not a team player" you need to take action. Your efforts are best directed towards finding another job.

Another warning sign is when partners or the senior associates start reducing to writing negative feedback or sending you written confirmation of routine matters. They may be "papering your file" by providing evidence or back-up for putting you on probation or terminating your employment.

Sometimes an indication that your career is in trouble is when you are never given a chance to work for the partners servicing the largest firm clients. One of the surest ways to increase your staying power at a firm is to become known to, and provide high quality work for, the largest clients and the partners working with them. Here is where an associate can approach the category of someone the firm does not want to lose. Also, performing high quality work for a large firm client is one of the best ways to have your reputation spread among the firm partners. So take note if you are never given the opportunity to work for the largest firm clients. This may be a simple matter of firm needs as weighed against your experience and availability, but at some point you should seek out this opportunity.

There are also internal factors relating to job dissatisfaction that provide an early indication of later career trouble. Serious disillusionment with the practice of law does not generally go away. Attorneys switch firms, go in-house or change areas of practice. Most of the time, however, these practice changes will not address the root of the problem. You may not understand the root of the problem in the first place. You may not know how to translate your legal skills into meaningful legal work. You may have technical or people skills that are not compatible with the practice of law. You may not be cut out for law firm life or for being a lawyer. You may find that many of the difficulties you have with the practice of law are not firm-specific, but rather occur in whatever setting you work. This disillusionment will eventually spill over into your legal work in one form or another. At the risk of sounding pessimistic, you may want to start looking to see what else you can do with your law degree or what career outside of law interests you.

### Can Your Career Be Rescued?

You may have an idea that your career is in trouble, or possibly unequivocal proof that there's a problem.

For example, you may have been put on probation. Whether your career with the firm is salvageable depends on the circumstances. The answer is "probably" if you have had a problem with a particular partner who is known to be difficult. You can switch to another group, or not work with that partner, and work on restoring your reputation with other partners and senior associates. Remember that you will not be given the benefit of the doubt if you have difficulties with the new people to whom you are assigned. Also, your efforts will be undermined if the first partner goes on a campaign to malign you. If you become aware of such tactics, then consider your tenure with that firm to be limited and start looking for a job elsewhere. This person will be a continual thorn in your side and will make every effort to keep you from getting bonuses or elected to partner down the road. If this partner carries enough weight with the firm, she will make it difficult for you to secure good assignments, even from other partners.

You can also regroup from a bad experience if there is another partner who is willing to act as a strong advocate for you. The relative position of this partner is important, and even that may not be enough if the attorney with whom you had the problem is especially vocal about you.

Consider looking for another job if you are having problems or are put on probation because more than one person has given you successive bad reviews. Law firms are notoriously bad at being straightforward and telling people that they lack an essential quality necessary to be elected partner. Instead, firms handle these matters in a somewhat cowardly way and use the review process to gradually discourage people from staying. (Cynical attorneys argue that firms are simply trying to squeeze the last bit of work out of you until you eventually leave.) You don't need to stay in a situation that is so bad that it is adversely affective your personality, homelife or health. Going elsewhere may mean that you have to re-establish your reputation, but will possibly be better than what you've left.

### Dating or Marrying Within the Firm

Attorneys spend so much time at their offices that often the only people they meet to date are firm colleagues or staff members. Some law firms have a specific policy forbidding dating or marital relationships within the firm. Whether these policies are actually enforced varies from firm to firm. Familiarize yourself with the express policy if you are considering dating someone within the firm. Then, make some discreet inquiries as to whether the policy is enforced or largely ignored.

There may be an unexpressed policy as well. Romantic relationships between attorneys or between attorneys and staff are generally cause for some unease among firm management. Most of these relationships do not work out for the long term. You can imagine the difficulties that arise after a break-up. There are also the special concerns that surface when the relationship is between a supervisor and a subordinate. The potential for subsequent claims of sexual harassment increases. Consciously or unconsciously, promotions, reviews, and raises all come under stricter scrutiny, which often unfairly prejudices the person involved in an office affair. It should be no surprise that same-firm romantic relationships are generally discouraged, even in the absence of an express prohibition.

Understand that perception issues will be one of the additional sources of stress on your relationship. Many people, when they see you talking with your significant other, will assume that you are talking about personal matters rather than work-related matters. People will also think that because your relationship is part of the firm, so to speak, they can discuss your relationship with others. Be assured that any outward sign of disharmony will be grist for the gossip mill.

There are ways to alleviate some of these stresses and

concerns when you choose to have a same-firm romantic relationship. Be discrete about the existence of the relationship until you are sure that it is going somewhere. That way, only the two of you will experience discomfort when the relationship is over. It is best to keep it between you and the other party involved if your relationship will probably not survive longer than the firm retreat or business trip where it started. If you are discreet, assigning attorneys will not have to factor in your former relationship as they put together work teams.

Continue to use discretion as the relationship progresses. Keep your personal life absolutely private by avoiding excessive contact with one another. Do not feel, however, that you have to hide a serious relationship. Obviously, limited interaction at work is a way to strengthen your relationship, which hopefully will inure to the benefit of the firm anyway.

There are times when you may consider informing firm management of the relationship, past or present. You would probably want to give the firm management early notice of a romantic relationship if there is a disparity in your and the other person's respective position (partner-associate, attorney-paralegal, partner-secretary, etc.). Any "notice" should be accompanied by assurances of professionalism. You may also want the firm to intervene if you have unsuccessfully tried to handle a difficult break-up that is impacting negatively some aspect of your job. You should always bring to management's attention when a relationship-gone-bad has crossed the line to a harassment or stalking situation.

### Living Below Your Means, at Least Until Your Debt Is Paid Down

Experienced attorneys raise their handling of personal finances as something that they would do differently if they could revisit their early careers. First year attorneys make more money than they did in law school, and sometimes incredibly more. Here is a common scenario: A new lawyer obtains a job at mid-sized firm making a comfortable salary that qualifies for a large home loan. Within two years, she makes large expenditures on the maximum house, a newer car, insurance, and new clothes. Add to this basic services (like drop-off dry cleaning, house cleaning, yard maintenance, and pre-made dinners delivered to the office or home), since she is too busy to do them herself. Soon, the new lawyer is living at or beyond her means. Factor in what sometimes amounts to a staggering law school loan repayment and you can see where the term "golden handcuffs" got its origin.

The odds are if you revisit this lawyer in three to five years, she will be contemplating leaving the practice of law. According to a 1998 study of recruitment and retention completed by the National Association for Law Placement Foundation for Research and Education, 43% of new associates leave their law firm within three years of practice. The attrition rate for lawyers by the fifth year of practice is an astounding 64.6%. The study is contained in a report entitled *Keeping the Keepers: Strategies for Associate Retention in Times of Attrition.* The lawyer in this example, because she still has high debts to repay and a costly standard of living to maintain, cannot leave the practice and expect to make the same amount of money (or have to potential to make large sums of money). This lawyer is stuck and experiencing serious professional dissatisfaction.

Strive to eliminate debt so that you will have choices down the road. Forego the large house, new car and expensive vacations until after you have paid down a substantial portion of your debt. Seek out financial advice from experts or good money managers that you trust. You want to be in a position to make a career change if you absolutely detest private practice. The knowledge that you can walk away from an overly-stressful job with little or no financial strain is a liberating concept that will provide some support during dark days.

Your debt load is leverage for a firm. There is a certain attitude exhibited by an attorney who cannot lose her job without risk of serious financial difficulties or disaster. This leverage is another aspect of the "golden handcuffs." Some firms do financial background checks and run credit reports on attorneys. These firms have a general idea of the financial health of the attorneys working there, most of the time without the attorneys ever knowing that the firm has this information.

### Initial Partnership Issues

Lawyers differ on when an attorney should start thinking seriously about partnership issues. Some say that attorneys should determine whether they want to become partners at the beginning of their careers in private practice. Others say that an attorney should start focusing seriously on partnership issues around the fourth or fifth year of practice. What is certain is that there is no "one approach," but rather some collective wisdom that will help you along the way.

A new lawyer's preoccupation with partnership issues is like wanting to complete a marathon before you can crawl. You first must master crawling, then walking, jogging and finally running. Then you must learn endurance. Completing the marathon should not be the end in and of itself, but rather part of a long process, and only an aspect of that process. Remember, even people who do not complete marathons can run, and are respected for it.

Partnership is much the same way. From a professional standpoint, your thoughts should center on learning what it is that lawyers do. Then, you must practice and do it well. In a perfect world, partnership should not happen until you have the technical skills, the management skills and the judgment in place. Work on these first and partnership-specific issues will likely fall into place.

SAMPLE
COMPANY X V. COMPANY Y BUDGET
ESTIMATE & COMPARISON

| Activity | Best Case Estimate | Worst Case Estimate |
|---|---|---|
| Fees & Expenses Through Dec. 31, 2000 (includes initial investigation & analysis, litigation budget and plan, Complaint, Mandatory Disclosures, Answer to Counterclaim, Initial Interrogatories and Requests to Produce, Early Planning Conference, Preliminary Planning Report and Scheduling Order) | $93,000 | $93,000 |
| Motion to Dismiss Counterclaim and Reply Brief | $2,500 | $2,500 |
| Responding to Interrogatories and Requests for Production of Documents | $10,000 | $15,000 |
| Responding to Additional Written Discovery | $5,000 | $15,000 |
| Reviewing and Analyzing Defendants' Discovery Responses and Documents Produced | $10,000 | $12,000 |
| Propounding Additional Written Discovery | $2,500 | $5,000 |
| Additional Factual Investigation (our witnesses, current and former employees, third party witnesses, Defendants' assets, abuse of corporate form, etc.) | $5,000 | $7,500 |
| Amending Complaint to Allege Personal Liability for Abuse of Corporate Form (piercing the corporate veil) | $7,500 | $7,500 |
| Preparing Witnesses and Defending Depositions | $35,000 | $40,000 |
| Taking Depositions | $35,000 | $50,000 |
| Retaining and Deposing Experts | $30,000 | $45,000 |
| Discovery Disputes & Motions to Compel | $15,000 | $25,000 |
| Miscellaneous Unanticipated Matters & Strategic Planning | $20,000 | $35,000 |
| Summary Judgment Motions | $35,000 | $50,000 |
| Pre-Trial Order (includes voir dire questions) | $3,000 | $5,000 |
| Immediate Trial Preparation (Jury Charges; Trial Briefs; Motions in Limine; Preparation of Witnesses, Witness Examinations, Exhibits, Opening Statement and Closing Argument) | $25,000 | $50,000 |
| Trial | $40,000 | $65,000 |
| Post Trial Matters | $10,000 | $15,000 |
| TOTALS | $383,500.00 | $537,500.00 |

## SAMPLE
## ATTORNEY PERFORMANCE EVALUATION

**Period of Evaluation:**

_____

**Name of Attorney:**                    **Name of Evaluator:**

_____        _____


### I. Nature of Work

1.  Describe the nature and complexity of the work the attorney did under your supervision.

_____

_____

2.  In the course of this work, did you provide the attorney with constructive feedback? Please provide details.

_____

_____


### II. Judgment/Analysis

Describe the extent to which the attorney analyzes problems independently and identifies the issues that are important?

_____

Does the attorney understand the relevant issues, propose solutions and demonstrate the ability to apply the relevant law? Please explain.

_____

If there are shortcomings in the attorney's judgment and analytical abilities, what are they, and do you believe those shortcomings can be overcome with additional experience and training?

_____

_____


### III. Legal Knowledge, Practice Skills and Work Product

1.  Does the attorney have a sound grasp of basic legal principles necessary for the attorney's area of practice?

_____

2.  How does this attorney's legal knowledge compare to that of other attorneys with similar experience in an area of practice?

_____

_____

3.   If legal research is required, is this attorney's work thorough and reliable?

_____

_____

4.   In meetings with you or others in the firm, is the attorney able to convey his or her ideas clearly and to field questions?

_____

5.   If you have observed the attorney in meetings with clients, does the attorney communicate effectively with clients?

_____

6.   If you have observed the attorney in negotiations, was he or she skillful in explaining and advocating the client's position?

_____

_____

7.   Please evaluate the attorney's writing and drafting skills

_____

_____

8.   Does the attorney consistently produce a work product of superior quality?  Please explain.

_____

_____

## IV. Responsibility

1.   Does the attorney consistently demonstrate a "whatever it takes" attitude? _____

Can you count on the attorney to see a project through to timely completion, including work on weekends and evenings when necessary?

_____

2.   Is the attorney able to develop and maintain effective relationships with firm clients?

_____

_____

3.   Do clients call on the attorney directly for advice?

_____

4.   Do you consider this attorney a "go-to" person? Please explain.

_____

_____

### V. Productivity and Efficiency

1. Does the attorney effectively manage his or her workload?

_____

_____

2. Have you had to write off the attorney's time for reasons related to the quality or efficiency of the attorney's work?

_____

If so, have you communicated this fact to the attorney?

_____

_____

### VI. General

1. Is the attorney committed to non-billable activities that benefit the Firm, including pro bono work, writing, speaking and bar association activities and client development?

_____

2. If you are aware, does the attorney participate in the administrative tasks of the firm?

_____

3. Do you have any reason to doubt the attorney's integrity?

_____

4. Does the attorney adhere to high ethical standards in the practice of law?

_____

5. Does the attorney work well with staff, paralegals and attorneys at the firm?

_____

_____

### VII. Overall Evaluation

1. Putting aside economic considerations, is this attorney someone who seems to have or be likely to develop the qualities and skills necessary to become a member of this firm?

_____

_____

2.    Are there any limitations on the kind of work you would assign to this attorney?
If so, what?

_____

_____

3.    Which of the following best characterizes your views of the attorney's overall performance?  (Check One).

Outstanding, with unique skills and qualities
equaled by few attorneys at this level;
extraordinary work product in terms of
quality and efficiency                                              _____

Solid work and reliable performance, producing
superior work that can be distributed outside
the firm with pride, but some room for
improvement, expectations of continuing
improvement and progress                                      _____

Useful contributions to the work of the firm,
without special merit or serious defects;
significant room for improvement,
but evidence of progress                                         _____

Performance below what the firm should expect
of an attorney at this level; significant
improvement needed and possible, but
improbable                                                              _____

Unacceptable performance significantly below
what the firm should expect; very substantial
improvement needed and does not seem
possible                                                                  _____

Overall Comments:

_____

_____

_____

_____

_____

_____

## SAMPLE
## LITIGATION FORM FILES

Client questionnaire

Letter of representation

Cease and desist letters

Eviction notices

Complaints

Answers/Counterclaims

Abusive litigation letters

Attorneys' fees affidavits

Affidavits

Conflict letters

Consent orders

Discovery-state

Discovery-federal

Sample discovery objections

Notices of deposition

Deposition outlines

Protective orders

Motions to quash

Motions to compel

Motions to transfer

Motions for continuance

Motions to dismiss

Motions to strike

Motions for entry/ opening default

Motions for summary judgment

Opening statements

Proposed orders

Pretrial orders-state

Pretrial orders-federal

Proposed findings of fact and law

Requests for admission

Request for filing original discovery

Subpoenas

Dismissal with prejudice

Dismissal without prejudice

Limited release

Settlement agreement/releases

Closing statements

Jury charges

Jury verdict forms

**SAMPLE**
**CLOSING CHECKLIST**

[Client]

Acquisition of Improvements
from XXX's Property Holding Company

CLOSING CHECKLIST

| # | ITEM | RESPONSIBLE PARTY | PARTY EXECUTING | STATUS |
|---|------|-------------------|-----------------|--------|
| 1. | Settlement Statement/ Closing Statement | | | |
| 2. | Quitclaim Deed Executed by Seller | | | |
| 3. | Quitclaim Deed Executed by Tenant | | | |
| 4. | Bill of Sale with a General Warranty of Title Subject Only to Permitted Title Exceptions | | | |
| 5. | Quitclaim Bill of Sale to the Improvements Specifically Excepting Personal Property | | | |
| 6. | Seller's Title Affidavit Executed by Seller | | | |
| 7. | Seller's Title Affidavit Executed by Tenant | | | |
| 8. | Affidavit of Residency (Seller & Tenant) | | | |
| 9. | Sub Ground Lease | | | |
| 10. | Memorandum of Sub Ground Lease | | | |
| 11. | Store Lease | | | |
| 12. | Memorandum of Store Lease | | | |
| 13. | 1099 Certificate | | | |
| 14. | Affidavit of Seller's Net Gain | | | |

| # | ITEM | RESPONSIBLE PARTY | PARTY EXECUTING | STATUS |
|---|------|-------------------|-----------------|--------|
| 15. | Purchaser's Affidavit with regard to Brokers | | | |
| 16. | Seller's Authority Docs for Tenant including Certificate of Existence, Articles of Incorporation and Corporation Resolution | | | |
| 17. | Authority Docs for Tenant including Certificate of Existence, Articles of Incorporation, and Corporation Resolution | | | |
| 18. | Purchaser's Authority Docs including Certificate of Existence, Articles of Incorporation and Corporate Resolution | | | |
| 19. | Estoppel Certificate for Purchase Agreement | | | |
| 20. | Estoppel Certificate for Store Lease | | | |
| 21. | Estoppel Certificate for Sub Ground Lease | | | |
| 22. | SNDA Store Lease | | | |
| 23. | SNDA Ground Lease | | | |
| 24. | Assignment of Purchase Agreement | | | |
| 25. | Title Insurance Policies | | | |
| 26. | Seller's Reconfirmation of Reps/Warranties | | | |
| 27. | Reconfirmation of Reps/Warranties | | | |
| 28. | Lease Termination Store Lease | | | |
| 29. | Lease Termination Sub Ground Lease | | | |

[listed here would be a key to initials and law firm acronyms]

*Chapter 10*

# Work and Play Well with Others

## Getting the Most out of Your Professional Relationship with Your Secretary, Paralegal, Librarian and Other Firm Staff; Interviewing and Reviewing Staff

The assistance of other people has a lot to do with good lawyers becoming great lawyers. The support staff with whom you work are just some of those people. As the practice of law changes to adjust to the challenges of a new economy, other professionals will become a larger part of your daily firm life. All of these people—secretaries, paralegals, librarians, actuaries, billing professionals, computer support and other staff members—can make you look much better than you are or can leave you to wallow in your mistakes (and you will make them) and inexperience.

There are some guidelines about working with others that apply across the board to any staff member or paraprofessional (or colleague, for that matter) and should go without saying. Treat everyone with respect. Everyone is aware that you are a lawyer. Everyone knows that for years, you studied and absorbed all manner of useful and useless information. Most people are aware or believe that you are paid an astronomical amount of money, probably much more than any support person at the firm. None of these facts gives you the right to dismiss the opinions of non-lawyers or treat them as second-class citizens. While most lawyers would agree with that assertion and many do not believe that they would treat people with disrespect, it happens. It happens when lawyers introduce a client to every other lawyer in the hallway, but not the secretary or paralegal in the immediate vicinity. It happens when lawyers fail to ask the court reporter if she needs a lunch or bathroom break during a lengthy deposition. It happens when lawyers gather in lawyer groups in the breakroom and never sit with staff members. It happens when lawyers shake hands with every one except the staff member to whom they are being introduced. In other words, the disrespect that some lawyers show others is subtle, but it exists nonetheless. Thinking in terms of "human beings" rather than professional/staff member/non-lawyer will enhance all your professional working relationships.

Another guideline that applies across the board is to give people as much notice as you can of impending projects or work requests. Staff members and paraprofessionals often support several people, all of whom have workloads that vary by the day or over the longer term. Alerting your support person that a significant request is coming in an hour or even a week will allow that person to manage other deadlines and possibly shift work where needed. Many of the problems between attorneys and support people stem from crisis situations where an attorney needs something immediately, which contributes to the attorney becoming less patient and more demanding, and a support person who is managing several other crises. Advance planning is certainly not easy to do in a law practice, but any notice will help. Try to remember that your emergencies are not necessarily their emergencies, and may not be treated with the urgency you would expect.

It is also a good idea to update certain people on a regular basis of your whereabouts. Secretaries and paralegals should have a general idea where the attorneys for whom they work are on a given day. Others within the firm will expect that your support people have that knowledge and often they are the first stop for inquiries about you. Try not to put your support people in the difficult position of not knowing what to say or needing you and not having access to you.

Periodic reviews of the support people who report to you is an important and necessary part of your job. These reviews are used to determine raises and/or bonuses and can impact job security. These reviews also provide confirmation as to whether the person is on the right track in performing the job. Give praise where praise is due. Many times, your brief or SEC filing would not have happened without the extra effort of support people. Specific examples of circumstances when things went smoothly because of the contribution of this person are important reinforcement for those being reviewed. Compliments on a job well done also indicates that you have not forgotten the times when people reporting to you have gone the extra mile.

Periodic informal reviews give employees an idea of what needs to be improved and what is being done well. It is hard to review people, particularly those that may be older or more experienced than are you. It will become routine as you develop a set way of dealing with people, including reviewing them. Principles of fairness dictate that before a problem is raised in a review, the support person has advance notice that some behavior or action being complained of was problematic. Just as with an associate review, there should be no surprises on a formal review.

Because you are a new lawyer, and probably an inexperienced manager of people, your reviews of subordinates may be discounted by firm management. This is frustrating to young lawyers, particularly since they often have the closest day-to-day working relationship with their support people and believe that their opinions should carry great weight. You can get beyond this bias by providing thoughtful reviews that give specific examples of problematic or praiseworthy behavior. It's hard to argue with facts and your examples can be checked out with the support person during the course of the review conference. Many review forms include a portion where the attorney can check boxes or write in numbers on a scale. Another portion is reserved for written commentary. If you just fill out or check the numbers and leave the rest blank, then the review will be given less weight by management. Likewise, if you simply fill out "9's" across the board, the review will be taken less seriously. Devote some time to these reviews.

Some attorneys maintain a private file for the support staff (and junior attorneys) with whom they work. Throughout the year, a copy of anything noteworthy gets tucked into the folder to be looked at during review time or before an informal review. This allows the attorney to give specifics during a review, which are taken more seriously then generalized statements of "satisfactory" or "working at expected level." A note of caution if you adopt this approach: the support person may discover this file and its existence will cause friction between the two of you. No one likes to think that their every action is being monitored and noted. Take pains to ensure that no one else working at your desk or looking through your files could discover these "personnel" files. This information could damage someone's reputation and its disclosure might constitute a breach of privacy.

An undeservedly negative review will damage your working relationship not only with your support person, but also with others who hear about the review. Supervisors who have a reputation as tough or unfair reviewers do not get the help they need because people are reluctant to work for them. Naturally, people are less inclined to gamble with their job security by working with such an attorney.

As has been stated elsewhere in this book, use extreme care when discussing personnel matters with others. In fact, don't do it unless there is an appropriate and necessary reason to be discussing the actions of a particular employee. Aside from the moral implications of gossiping, as a practical matter, any information that you disclose or intimate will be repeated, causing possibly irreparable damage to your working relationships.

Remember to share the credit. When a complicated deal closes or a lengthy trial concludes, it is likely that a number of hands were involved in bring those matters to conclusion. Your secretary and paralegal can play large roles even in minor matters. In fact, one of the ways you may have kept costs commensurate with the work being performed was by relying more heavily on your support people. Be sure to say "thank-you," and share the credit. Invite people who put forth substantial or significant effort to help you to a victory lunch or celebration.

### The Secretary

New lawyers often don't have a clue as to how to use or work with a secretary. For many, a legal secretary is the first person a new lawyer has ever supervised. There will likely be an age gap, which makes matters even more awkward. All of this uncertainty comes at a time when the new lawyer is literally overwhelmed with meeting new people, renewing acquaintances from the summer clerkship, and remembering how to get to the bathroom. Make it your business to learn how to work with your secretary.

A legal secretary has training and experience beyond that of a regular secretary. Legal secretaries not only have the skills of a regular secretary, like taking dictation, using advanced word processing, or answering the telephone, but also know how to keep client files and where and how to file real estate, litigation, or corporate papers.

Your secretary may have college-level business courses or an undergraduate degree. You should have a complete understanding of your secretary's educational and work background. You need to know how long this person has worked as a legal secretary and in what areas. Does your secretary have any additional training that you should know about? Ask questions to determine what level of knowledge your secretary has with regard to specific matters in your field. For example:

Does your secretary know what to do with original discovery documents?

Does your secretary know how to bind documents for a court or agency filing?

Does your secretary know how to talk to a judge's clerk or secretary?

Does your secretary understand the importance of attorney-client communications?

Does your secretary understand the magnitude of certain deadlines?

One attorney, who's secretary was out, relied on another (experienced) litigation secretary to file an answer. The secretary mailed the answer to the court instead of having it hand-delivered. The answer was late and the client was in default. You can never make assumptions about what your secretary (or another secretary helping out) knows. You must find out.

Take your secretary to lunch in your first week or two. The two of you need to discuss a number of things, including each other's backgrounds and your expectations for one another. Your secretary has worked with other attorneys before you and will have certain expectations, like being informed of your whereabouts when you are out of the office on client matters. You should establish clear and unambiguous ways of handling the following:

**Phone calls:** Should they go directly to you or to your secretary first? Should your secretary inform you first of who is on the telephone before transferring the call to you? Whatever you and your secretary establish may change over time since the answer to these questions depends on your personal preference. For example, your established procedure may change as you get busier and need for your secretary to screen calls.

**Roll-over calls:** Should your secretary pick up calls that you don't answer or should they go directly to voice mail?

**Security codes:** Should your secretary have your password to check e-mail/phone messages? Do you want your secretary to check these messages when you are out of the office?

**Checking mail:** Do you want for your secretary to open and review your mail before you see it, or do you simply want it placed unopened on your desk? Be sure to determine the procedure for handling mail and faxes when you are out of the office.

**Reading file:** Ask your secretary about keeping a "reading file," which includes copies of any letters sent by you to anyone else. This file is in addition to the copy of a letter that will be placed in the correspondence folder of a client file. The reading file serves as a back-up for you, particularly when you need to double check that a letter was actually sent. A reading file ensures that there will always be a copy of a letter if the file copy gets lost.

**Tickler file:** Many secretaries keep a "tickler file," which contains letters to which you are expecting a reply or action; it serves as a follow up mechanism for you. For the tickler file to work, you or your secretary actually need to read what's in the file or possibly calendar dates for responses or actions.

**Time sheets or time entries:** Your firm may have specific policies about who enters your time, or it may have no policy at all. You need to establish with your secretary who is entering your time, the procedure for time entries when you are out of the office, and who is proofing the time entries. Ask your secretary to remind you to enter your time if not doing so will get you fined. This is probably not your secretary's responsibility, but you will be thankful for any reminders that you do get.

**Proofing:** You may want to establish a standing rule that all final drafts of documents of a reasonable length will be automatically spell-checked and proofed by your secretary. To some extent, your work product is a team effort. Mistakes, proofing errors and other technical problems with your work product will reflect badly on the team, but mostly you. At a minimum, you should expect from your secretary that anything she types or prepares (like letters) should be absolutely error-free. Your mistakes are another matter; enlist the help of your secretary to minimize or eliminate these errors, too.

**Signing your name:** sometimes secretaries sign the attorneys' name to transmittal letters or other routine communications. Establish early on whether your secretary should sign your name at all, and if so, whether your secretary should write "by XXXX" after the signature.

**The protocol for informing your secretary of your whereabouts:** Tell your secretary what to expect in terms of hearing from you. For example, if you are not in by 10:00 a.m., arrange to call your secretary so that she knows your whereabouts. Make sure that you tell your secretary when you are leaving for lunch and when you expect to return.

**Working from home protocol:** If you work on an alternative work schedule, or from time-to-time work from home, consider having your secretary check messages at certain times throughout the day and then calling you at set times. That will give you some certainty while you work from home and will lessen the chance of you missing an important message.

**Call-in procedures:** Have your secretary call you at home or at the office directly if the secretary will unexpectedly be absent from work. Otherwise, you may not hear from the human resources person until late morning that your secretary is out. This will save you from leaving multiple voice and email messages for your secretary when you were unaware she would not be in.

**Overtime:** Know in advance your secretary's willingness to stay late or work weekends. Having this information will minimize friction later when you are in a pinch. You can try to plan ahead and get temporary help or give your secretary advance notice that overtime may be needed.

**Home phone number:** Have your secretary's home number and keep it handy regardless of where you are. Many things come up last minute (being called out of town or a family emergency) and your secretary should have advance notice. Don't call your secretary at home about routine work matters, even when you are at the office on a weekend searching for a letter on the system.

**Client copies:** Establish a standing rule about copying clients on matters having to do with the client's case. For example, when letters come in from the other side, or discovery is served, your secretary should have a general idea of whether the documents should be automatically copied to the client. You may not remember to have the client copied in on what you consider to be routine matters but clients will consider important.

**Instructions for temporary secretaries:** Ask your secretary to prepare an instruction sheet for a temporary or fill-in secretary to review. The sheet should contain your complete name and telephone number, and your specific instructions for answering the telephone, checking mail and e-mail, etc. That way, when your secretary is out, a temporary secretary will not have to ask you multiple questions about things as basic as how do you want your telephone answered.

**Filing system:** This is one of the most important jobs you and your secretary have. Letters, documents, pleadings, notices, drafts, research, original discovery, checklists, attorney notes, and email communications are all things that must be filed in a single client file.

Firm partners will expect that at any given moment, a client file is neat, up-to-date and well-organized. It will reflect badly on you if your supervising partner or another secretary goes to look for something that either isn't there or has been misfiled. You will be evaluated on your ability to manage your files and your secretary. The state of your files is a strong indication of how well you do these things.

Start by soliciting your secretary's thoughts on the best filing method. Find out what the secretary does for the other attorneys with whom she has worked. Try to determine what does and doesn't work. As you get more experience, you will want to see certain things done in your files. It is helpful to keep a eye out for how other files are organized. For example, do notebooks work better for your files or do gussets?

You may have some discretion as to a file's physical location. Figure out who needs the most regular access to the file and perhaps make the determination that way. For example, your secretary may be the person in charge of filing for five or six different timekeepers (usually, one person does the filing for a particular client matter). It may be that lodging the file in a place right near your secretary is better than in your or another attorney's office.

Establish your expectations for how soon things will be filed in your client matters. Your secretary may maintain a "to-be-filed pile" or alphabetized accordion folder for papers that need to be placed in a client file. The two of you should have similar ideas about how frequently that folder is emptied and matters are filed. Some secretaries use Friday to catch up on filing. However it is done, you need to know what to expect. It can put you in a difficult position when you grab a file to meet with a client (or worse, go to court) and the file is incomplete. One attorney filed an amended complaint just before trial. On the date of trial, the judge did not receive the docket copy of the complaint, nor the copy hand-delivered to him. The opposing party claimed ignorance and objected to the amendment. The attorney was asked to produce a stamp-filed copy, but could not since the file wasn't properly updated. This caused delay and embarrassment for the attorney. You can avoid these incidents by making clear your expectations for your secretary.

Don't assume that the way the secretary has always done it or does it for a more senior attorney is the right way. You need to look at the rules or policies yourself and ask questions at the beginning about why something is done a certain way. It is your job to make sure that every thing you do is done the right way.

You may ask your secretary to help you with organizational or timesaving measures. One proven idea is to have your secretary prepare two "Client Information" notebooks. One is for you in your office and one is for your secretary. The notebook may have alphabetized tabs. Each client for whom you do work will have a "client contact sheet" placed behind the appropriate tab. Each sheet should contain your client's complete name, address, telephone and fax numbers, e-mail address, and client contact people. The specific information for each individual should be included as well—correct name spelling, title, direct-dial line, e-mail address, and any other specific contact information that you are given by the client. For example, confidential faxes may need to be sent to a particular number. If so, that should be noted. It might save you time to include the firm client billing number on that sheet as well. Have a separate sheet for each matter being handled by you for a specific client.

The field of law in which you practice may determine the remainder of the information found on the sheet. The following are some suggestions for litigators: Include the complete style for the case, as well as the opposing attorney's full name, firm, telephone number, address, fax number, etc. Make sure that it is very clear who is the client and who is opposing counsel. A temporary secretary may rely on this notebook to send out information and you wouldn't want there to be any confusion. List the court in which a matter is pending, as well as the name, address, telephone and fax numbers for the judge, clerk and secretary. Having this information at hand will save you hours over the course of litigation. Some attorneys include a separate checklist or status report behind this contact information.

Transactional lawyers may want to set these sheets up differently. After the client and "other" counsel information, the sheet may contain the address of the specific property under consideration, or the names and addresses of parties involved in a deal. It might be important to simply have a listing that identifies who belongs with whom.

These client information notebooks serve several important purposes. If your secretary is not available, you can send out information to a client without wasting too much time looking for the correct name spelling or the right fax number. Having quick access to the judge's secretary's number and name will also save you time. When your secretary is out, the temporary secretary can use the notebook to send out letters, and attend to other client matters. Perhaps one of the most convenient uses of the notebook is that you will have information at your fingertips when a client, partner or senior associate calls you for the telephone number for the judge, opposing counsel, etc.

Another important use of the client notebook is to refresh your memory about the types of matters that you have handled in the past. This information will be invaluable as you prepare partnership applications or firm biographies and resumes. This information could also be relevant for future job interviews or client meetings. Do not throw these client information sheets away. You will always want to have something with which to freshen your memory.

Use discretion about the type of information that you put in this notebook. Treat everything in your office as if it could be broadcast throughout the firm. Derogatory comments about clients should never, even jokingly, be put into this book. Lawyers often adopt private names for clients or opposing lawyers, often ones that poke fun at a person's personality (or lack of one) or the person's name. Obviously, don't write these down anywhere, and never mistakenly call this person the name to his face. Sometimes you get so used to calling your opposing counsel a derogatory name that it slips out when you are not thinking clearly.

Another helpful item your secretary can prepare is a list of your client file numbers, as well as frequently used firm and non-billable numbers. On one side of the sheet, you may want to have current matters, and on the other, closed or inactive matters. Having those numbers nearby will save you time, particularly when an inactive matter revives which otherwise would require you to spend time searching for the file number.

Secretaries can also prepare notebooks of key documents in a case or statutes upon which you regularly rely. Often, these notebooks will save you search time and also can be used to quickly refresh your memory when dealing with unexpected calls from the client or opposing counsel.

Your secretary may be the first person a client, potential or opposing counsel encounters. Make sure this is not lost on your secretary. Tell your secretary that you expect that she will maintain client confidences. If you are unavailable, clients will use your secretary as a sounding board for their frustration in being involved in legal matters or to find out what is happening in their cases. Again, this is information that should not be broadcast in an elevator or breakroom.

Make sure your secretary understands that you expect information about your personal and professional life will be kept confidential. Your secretary will come to know a lot about you, perhaps because of things you discuss directly, the telephone calls you receive, or discussions she may overhear. Sometimes, depending on which other partners or attorneys your secretary works for, your secretary may know information that even you don't know about your upcoming review or a memorandum to your file. Again, keeping this information confidential is of paramount importance.

A related issue is staying out of your secretary's personal life. Try not to blur the supervisor-employee relationship or it will be even more difficult to properly review and manage your secretary. Your secretary, like many people, will have legal problems that will arise in connection with home purchases, probate matters and the like. While it is not inappropriate to assist your secretary to some degree (like a letter or telephone call), exercise caution about handling legal matters for your secretary. If you feel awkward about turning your secretary down or if your secretary has taken advantage of your advice-giving, remember that the firm may have policies addressing this very issue.

Teach your secretary, if she does not know already, how to handle cold calls from potential clients. The secretary should handle these calls in the same way you do—immediately ask for the names of all parties involved, and after hanging up, run a conflicts check. Be sure that your secretary does not let the caller give details or expect initial thoughts about the merits of a case. Unfortunately, some of these calls are made with the explicit purpose of precluding your firm from representing a company or person involved in the matter. Your secretary should be on the alert when a cold call comes in and should know what to do.

Keep your secretary informed about the matters you are handling. She should have a general idea of where deals stand or the procedural status of a case. With that general knowledge, your secretary will be better able to find things for you in the file or answer questions from a client or partner when you are not around.

Your secretary will probably work for one or two other attorneys or paralegals. Frequently, your urgent request or instructions to your secretary will impinge on work given by someone else. It is not your secretary's job to handle these conflicts. You need to talk with the other attorney or paralegal and figure out which is the greater emergency. It may be that extra help is needed. Your secretary can quickly make those arrangements. Try not to put your secretary in the stressful position of having to arbitrate between you and someone else. If your secretary is chronically overloaded because she works for an especially busy attorney, then talk with the other lawyers about ways to rectify this problem, including one of you getting another secretary.

Many conflicts can be avoided by being sensitive to time. For example, waiting until the last minute to delegate work increases the likelihood that your secretary will have to juggle competing deadlines. Avoid promising your client documents close to quitting time unless you've checked with your secretary first or are prepared to do it yourself.

Do not be afraid to ask your secretary to get extra training in word processing, spreadsheets or anything else that you need. You may ask your secretary to become a notary public, which, depending on your practice could be very helpful.

Talk with your secretary about her willingness or desire to take on additional responsibility. Some secretaries like doing the work they do and do not want to challenge themselves further. They regard getting through the day dealing with lawyers as challenge enough. Others want to learn to prepare basic pleadings and enjoy taking a stab at drafting orders, initial drafts of documents, etc. Know where your secretary falls on this spectrum. The review discussion might be a good place to discuss your secretary's goals for the year.

Do not underestimate your secretary. Once you have some experience, have her take a first crack at drafting routine documents. At the same time, do not overestimate your secretary. Always check your secretary's work and always proofread again after substantive changes have been made to a document by your secretary.

Enlist the help of your secretary for proofing important documents. Your secretary will give you another perspective on your writing and sometimes it is helpful to see if you are conveying concepts clearly. If you are a poor proofreader or have a short attention span for proofing, you secretary can serve as an extra set of eyes for you.

Never talk negatively about your secretary except with people who need to know certain information. When a problem occurs in your relationship, always talk with your secretary first and try to resolve it between the two of you. Follow up and look for improvement—nothing on a secretary's review should be a surprise. Weigh your words carefully. Attorneys get used to dealing bluntly, and sometimes forcefully, with opposing counsel or parties. Try not to let that spill over into your interpersonal relationships with others. Your demeanor and choice of words will have great impact on your support staff. Try not to forget that this job is their livelihood and you are one of the people who will determine whether they stay or go.

There are some problems that can't be rectified. Your secretary may have poor technical skills which, despite additional training, do not improve. Or, you may have personality or attitude issues with your secretary that make it difficult to work together. Some young female associates have a stressful time dealing with older female secretaries who have entrenched ways of dealing with (usually male) lawyers. Lawyers, rather unkindly, refer to these secretaries as "battleaxes." The young female lawyer will probably lose this one; there is little that a new attorney can do to change many years of doing things a certain way. Your best bet if you are experiencing chronic difficulties is to work with human resources and get a new secretary assigned.

This relationship is too important to have doubts about attitude, loyalty and concern for the work.

You may want to keep quiet (outside the review, of course) if your secretary is really good. It would not be the first time that a partner, getting wind of this person's abilities, had you reassigned and chose to work with that secretary. Talented, experienced, and dedicated secretaries are hard to come by. As you gain more experience and watch others work with their secretaries, you will see how much support you get from a great secretary.

Accept responsibility for mistakes and don't blame your secretary, even though it is partially the secretary's fault. Ultimately, you are responsible for what happens on a client file.

Your secretary can make or break your career in its early stages. Try to look at this person as part of your team and accord your secretary the respect that you show your partners. Respect and establishing clear expectations will be the foundation for a long and productive relationship.

### The Paralegal

Much of what has been said about secretaries applies equally to the paralegal-attorney relationship. There are additional matters, however, that should be mentioned. Your paralegal will likely have an undergraduate degree as well as a certificate from paralegal school. At paralegal school, students study legal research, as well as certain substantive areas of law.

Just as with your secretary, you should have a firm understanding of your paralegal's educational and work background. Find out what types of projects your paralegal has worked on and what exactly she did. Talk with others in the group about this paralegal's experience and ability. Get a sense of what you can rely on and what you should be careful about with this particular paralegal.

211

Present your paralegal with interesting and challenging work. It is expected that paralegals can summarize depositions, track witnesses, research corporate status, locate assets, draft subpoenas, prepare witness folders, organize exhibits, appendices or schedules, and assist in trial preparation. If the client file can support it, have the paralegal start pulling relevant statutes and cases for a large research project. Experienced paralegals function at a higher level than first-year attorneys. Do not underestimate the work that a paralegal can do with or for you.

### The Librarian and Assistants

Your law firm may employ a full or part-time librarian. Depending on the size of the firm and library, the librarian may oversee a staff of library professionals. Your interaction with these professionals will begin as a summer associate and continue throughout your tenure with the firm. The library staff is there to service all attorneys and paralegals, not just new ones.

Take advantage of orientation programs, training seminars, or other programs offered by the library. You will always feel like you are too busy to make time, but try anyway. These programs are offered generally in response to a need on the part of the attorneys. Librarians hear many of the same questions and frustrations from lawyers of all levels, and thus gear programs towards addressing these issues before they become a problem.

Librarians generally have an undergraduate degree and a Masters of Library Science degree. Every few years, they attend continuing legal education programs designed to bring them up to speed on the many changes in information technology and research. Some librarians have a law degree, but may or may not have actually practiced. Library staff members may be students working towards a law degree or one in library science, or people with experience working in a library. Some restrict their work to filing and updating books.

Libraries are becoming progressively smaller as law firms turn to technology as a resource. The firm will work with librarians in making this transition, and the librarian will still be a resource for teaching you how to find what you are looking for quickly.

You can do some things to better enable the librarian to help you. Bring your questions and research problems into focus before going to the librarian. Just as clients bring generalized problems to lawyers, and it's the lawyer's job to sort out the legal issues, new lawyers often begin with a legal story that needs to be sorted out. The librarian cannot help you figure out the issues in your case because they do not have the facts, did not meet with the client, or talk with the assigning partner. Once you figure out the nature of the problem, the librarian can help you use on-line and firm resources to research your issues.

Communicate clearly any time limits for the project on which you are requesting assistance. As with any other legal professional, this information will help the librarian prioritize other projects.

Have a rough idea of the amount of money you can spend finding information. For example, books outside the library can be located for you within a few hours or within the week, depending on how much money your client will spend and the urgency of the matter. Ask the supervising partner on the case about any expense that would seem out of the ordinary, given the size of the matter and the type of client for whom it is being performed.

Talk with the librarian about doing substantive research on the Internet where there is no cost. Most librarians are familiar with the on-line legal resources for searching corporate records or assets, or finding legislative materials and statutory law for each state in the union. They can either conduct preliminary research for you or show you where to go.

Develop a good working relationship with your firm's librarians; they sometimes have good practical

213

advice for the new lawyer. New lawyers often vent about partners to the librarian. (Often frustration stemming from the current project is what drove the associate to see the librarian in the first place.) Avoid, however, placing the librarian in a difficult position by telling them more information than they should know. Partners frequently come to librarians to check up on certain associates and to ask about particular deficiencies in skills. Partners are notorious for sweeping the library to see which associates are there. These partners are not above asking the librarians to observe who is working in the library and who isn't. As with anyone else at the firm, be circumspect about the information you divulge and work hard at developing a lasting, professional relationship with the librarian.

### The Non-Attorney Professionals in the Firm

The rules that once prohibited lawyers from closely associating with non-legal professionals are slowly eroding. Clearer guidelines are being issued by individual state bar associations, which have enabled more law firms to enter into these relationships. The implications for the associate are not immediately obvious. Associates are expected to work on legal matters with non-legal professionals like actuaries and accountants. The line between what is legal advice versus accounting or tax advice can become blurred.

The associate, in working with a non-legal professional, should first understand what service the professional provides. If you are working with an actuary employed by the firm, you need to know what an actuary does for a client. Once you know what service the actuary provides, you need to understand how that specifically will apply to the matter on which you are working. An actuary may provide retirement plan consulting, but what does that mean for you as you draft the plan?

Ask the non-legal professional about billing and payment issues. Is this person hired separately by the client? Is this person billing the client at an hourly rate? If so, find out the rate so that you can make better decisions about how often and how much to use this non-legal professional. You may want to clarify with your supervising partner who makes the final call on certain aspects of the joint project. The attorney-client privilege may or may not apply to consultations involving the non-legal professional. There may be another applicable privilege—like the accountant-client privilege—but you need to know what information is protected and under what authority. Having the facts will eliminate misunderstandings as legal and non-legal professionals work together to service the needs of a single client.

You will see common themes throughout this book that highlight respect to others and knowing the facts. Your relationships will probably go more smoothly if you can somehow incorporate these two things into your dealings with others. It's no secret that the quality of your interactions with others at the law firm will ultimately affect your satisfaction with the practice of law.

## SAMPLE
## CLIENT CONTACT SHEET

**<u>Edmond Dantes (a.k.a. Count of Monte Cristo) v. M. de Villefort, Individually and as Deputy Crown Prosecutor;</u>** Civil Action No. 2000CV16839 in the Superior Court of Marseilles, France

| | |
|---|---|
| **File number:** | 8460.00010000 |
| **Client:** | M. Edmond Dantes |
| | Number 30, Champs-Elysees |
| | Paris, France |
| | (555) 555-5555 (home) |

**Opposing counsel:** M. de Chateau-Renaud
1815 Rue de Helder
Paris, France
(555) 555-5555 (office)

**Judge:** King Louis XVIII
(555) 555-5555

**Case Manager:** _____
(555) 555-5555

## SAMPLE STAFF APPRAISAL FORMS
## MEMORANDUM

**To:**     Attorneys and Paralegals
**From:**   Personnel Committee
**Date:**   January 4, 1999
**Re:**     Annual Performance Appraisal (Legal
            Secretary)

As of January 1, 1999 all legal secretaries and administrative staff will be reviewed on the anniversary of the employee's date of hire. Evaluation forms will be distributed 2 weeks before the individual's anniversary date. Please return all forms 1 week prior to the individual's anniversary date, so that we may schedule a review meeting with the secretary on or before the effective date of their pay increase and bonus.

Your appraisal will continue to be used as part of the overall evaluation process to determine compensation and a performance based bonus. The purpose of this review is to provide an opportunity to evaluate job performance; identify outstanding assets and strengths and weaknesses; constructively discuss ways to improve or eliminate problems; and to establish performance goals for the next year.

The evaluation should be an accurate and fair reflection of the individual's performance based on the full year's performance; you should not be influenced by unusual situations that are not typical. It is important to concentrate on one factor at a time, not general impressions.

You are encouraged to review your comments with the staff member; this will maximize the effectiveness of the review.

Please return the completed forms to _____ as soon as possible.

Thank you.

## COMPANY X

*STAFF PERFORMANCE APPRAISAL - 2000*

**Name:**                                    **Hire Date:**

**Position:**

**Appraisal Period: From:**          **To:**

**Purpose:**

The performance appraisal is an ongoing process throughout the year. This formal evaluation is based on the employee's performance over a specified period of time, not just on isolated incidences. It is designed to measure performance and achievement; communicate to employees their development and progress and establish performance goals.

**Instructions:**

A number of traits, abilities and characteristics that are important for successful performance are listed. Please evaluate each category by selecting the rating that best describes performance.

**Levels of Performance**

**EXCEPTIONAL**      (9-10)      Superior; unusually capable; performs well beyond position requirements; shows unusual initiative; outstanding worth to firm for the position

**COMMENDABLE**      (7-8)      Significantly high quality; consistently performs above position requirements; anticipates problems and takes appropriate action; accomplishes more than expected

**COMPETENT**      (5-6)      Solid, fully acceptable; competent and consistent performance; errors are few andseldom repeated

**FAIR**      (3-4)      Does job reasonably well; needs to work under close supervision; performance notconsistent; slightly below average

**MARGINAL**      (1-2)      Consistently inadequate performance; prompt and substantial improvementnecessary; makes repeat errors

| PERFORMANCE RATING FACTORS | 1-2 Marginal | 3-4 Fair | 5-6 Competent | 7-8 Commendable | 9-10 Exceptional |
|---|---|---|---|---|---|
| **WORK HABITS** | | | | | |
| 1. Meets deadlines; uses time effectively. | | | | | |
| 2. Works independently with a minimum amount of direction or supervision. | | | | | |
| 3. Organizes and establishes priorities; focuses on most important work first. | | | | | |
| 4. Understands and follows through on instructions. | | | | | |
| 5. Punctual; conscientious regarding attendance. (daily hours, lunch hours, time off) | | | | | |
| 6. Quality of work; attention to detail, accuracy and completeness of work. | | | | | |
| 7. Quantity of work; amount and rate produced. | | | | | |
| 8. Accepts responsibility. | | | | | |
| **COOPERATION AND ATTITUDE** | | | | | |
| 9. Displays positive attitude. | | | | | |
| 10. Takes initiative; willingness to seek new assignments and expand capabilities. | | | | | |
| 11. Accepts guidance and suggestions willingly; uses to improve performance/work product. | | | | | |
| 12. Willing to do whatever is needed to get the job done. | | | | | |
| 13. Performs well under pressure. | | | | | |
| 14. Complies with established practices and procedures. | | | | | |

| | | | | | | | |
|---|---|---|---|---|---|---|---|
| **ABILITY TO DEAL WITH PEOPLE** | | | | | | | |
| 15. Effective with and projects a professional attitude towards clients. | | | | | | | |
| 16. Ability to cooperate, work and communicate with lawyers and staff throughout the firm. | | | | | | | |
| 17. Shows willingness to assist others; displays "team" approach. | | | | | | | |
| **JUDGMENT** | | | | | | | |
| 18. Demonstrates common sense. | | | | | | | |
| 19. Maintains confidentiality. | | | | | | | |
| 20. Copes effectively with unusual or difficult situations. | | | | | | | |
| **JOB KNOWLEDGE** | | | | | | | |
| 21. Understands requirements of job. | | | | | | | |
| 22. Masters skills and processes information thoroughly and quickly. | | | | | | | |
| 23. Demonstrates creativity; finds new and better ways of doing things | | | | | | | |
| 24. Specific Skills:<br>a. Proofreading<br>b. Formatting documents<br>c. Drafting correspondence<br>d. Filing<br>e.<br>f.<br>g. | | | | | | | |

SPECIFIC COMMENTS (If needed, please attach a separate sheet.)

1. What are the strongest qualities, most outstanding assets and strengths?

_____

_____

_____

2. What should be done to build on these strengths?

_____

_____

_____

3. What are the weaknesses or areas where improvement is desirable?

_____

_____

_____

4. What should be done to improve in these areas?

_____

_____

_____

5. What specific suggestions, performance goals and development actions for 1999-2000 are recommended?

_____

_____

_____

6. Additional comments:

_____

_____

_____


7. OVERALL EVALUATION:

_____ Superior, unusually capable, outstanding in value to the firm.

_____ Among best ever observed; contributions and performance are exceptional in all areas.

_____ Regularly does more than the job calls for; above average performance.

_____ Solid performance at a level that permits firm to function at the desired efficiency; sometimes does more than the job calls for.

_____ Consistent and competent; meets position requirements; does complete and satisfactory job.

_____ Not consistent, results fall short of expected requirements; meets minimal standards, but improvement is necessary.

_____ Performance is below job requirements; results are generally unacceptable, show prompt and substantial improvement to retain.


8. Has this performance review been discussed with the employee? _____ Yes _____ No


Evaluated by: _____  _____
Signature              Date

# Chapter 11

# Focus on Gender in Law Firms

**A Look at the Real and Perceived Differences
Between the Sexes; the Impact of Gender
Perceptions on Your Career, Including Potential
Problem Areas and How to Handle Them**

Doing your job well should be the principal factor driving your advancement at a law firm. After all, beyond getting good results, doing your work competently and efficiently, having a can-do attitude, and working well with others, what else should affect others' perceptions about your work or your success at the firm? Alas, doing well is not good enough. The reality is that many more things will shape your career and your advancement within a firm. Attorneys must deal with the "perception is reality" problem (discussed in Chapter 9), as well as other people's biases and prejudices towards them. Your gender, race, sexual orientation, religious affiliation, nationality, physical appearance, social status, as well as a host of other things, will influence how people treat, evaluate, or deal with you. This chapter discusses gender, just one of those sources for potential bias, and examines some of the gender-related issues that both men and women may face in private practice.

Start with the premise that we all know that men and women are different. Differences—both real and imagined—spill over into professional lives in a myriad of ways.

Your gender may cause others to treat you differently or inappropriately. A client may refuse to work with a female lawyer or call the lead attorney directly for legal advice. A judge smirks at a female lawyer as she argues her case and repeatedly refers to her as "little lady." Your firm and clients may assume that because you are male, you are committed to making partner and any indication that you would prefer an alternative arrangement will be deemed a character flaw. Addressing gender bias is difficult because it is the infrequent case that a lawyer is directly touched, propositioned, or told that due to gender or appearance, the firm will not consider the attorney for partnership. Instead, gender bias or disparate treatment stemming from inaccurate preconceptions about gender is often expressed in subtle ways, but with equally devastating effect.

Gender issues have had an impact on the practice of law in other ways. Perhaps due to the high-publicity sexual harassment accusations prevalent in the 1980's and 1990's, the climate in which men and women professionals work has changed dramatically, and not always for the better. Many male lawyers go to extreme lengths to avoid the appearance of improper behavior. They refuse to travel alone with female attorneys, or compliment female attorneys, and avoid placing themselves in situations where someone could misconstrue their attentions or comments as being inappropriately gender-based. The unwanted side effect is to stifle professional and mentoring relationships between men and women. Much of the mentoring that occurs between experienced lawyers and young associates happens out of the office. The young attorney might observe the experienced lawyer handling depositions, hearings or negotiations, and then discuss these matters on the plane or car ride back to the office. Older attorneys benefit from having better-trained younger attorneys, as well as the opportunity to see how the younger generation of lawyers views issues that arise over the course of handling a matter. Both sexes lose out when attorneys refuse to put themselves in these situations with younger attorneys of the opposite gender.

At the risk of being too general, and therefore falling into the trap of gender bias, it needs to be said that male and female attorneys each bring unique perspectives and abilities to their careers, which adds depth and color to the profession as a whole. They may evaluate matters differently, although both may arrive at the same conclusion, and they generally handle clients, witnesses, and judges in a different manner. Attorneys cite consensus building as a positive attribute that women bring to the profession, particularly when a decision needs to be made that may have consequences for a number of people. Women sometimes listen better and demonstrate an ability to empathize with clients as they struggle through litigation or negotiations. Others point out that women often pursue a just result, rather than exacting a pound of flesh. They may be more precise in their writing or in attention to detail. Women are less easily distracted by having numerous items to tackle; perhaps this is a result of practice juggling domestic and childcare responsibilities with career demands.

Men generally have their own unique qualities that they bring to the profession. They are often better able to dissociate themselves from their clients' problems and view them as exactly that—clients' problems, not their own. They generally keep focused on the issues of the case by maintaining a bottom line orientation that many women don't have. These are generalizations about both sexes, and there are many examples of lawyers of either sex exhibiting all or some of those traits, with no correlation to their gender. The point, however, is that gender will always have an effect on your career, whether due to real personality, physiological, or thought differences, others' biases or preconceptions about your gender, or because people take great care to avoid having gender become an issue.

Differences in treatment, or hostile or unprofessional behavior directed towards you, may have nothing to with your gender. It may happen simply because you are young, inexperienced, from a big city, or in the wrong firm. It may be for no reason having to do with you, but rather the person with whom you are dealing. People occasionally have personal or psychological problems that influence their work performance, causing them to be rude, condescending or hostile towards others. When you experience such treatment, think carefully as to whether it is truly gender-motivated or generated by something else. Do not immediately assume that it stems from discriminatory or illegal forms of bias. Avoid jumping to conclusions, even when suspicious statements are made to you. Work hard at examining facts and other possible motivations for behavior or treatment. Seek out an unbiased opinion from someone for whom you have respect, perhaps another attorney or family member.

Given law school statistics on gender, it is difficult to believe that gender bias exists, or lawyers are treated differently because of their sex. According to the American Bar Association Section of Legal Education and Admissions to the Bar, women are coming close to outnumbering men among incoming law students. Statistics garnered at the end of the twentieth century show that male enrollment is decreasing slightly, while female enrollment is steadily increasing. In the fall of 1999, men totaled 22,144 (a decrease from 22,485 from 1998) and women totaled 21,008 (an increase over the 20,319 from the previous year). These statistics are published in the American Bar Association Guide to Approved Law Schools, 2001 Edition. Statistically, more women are choosing to practice in law firms, although the percentage of such women is still lower than that of male attorneys.

It is hoped that many forms of gender bias will disappear, given the steadily increasing number of female lawyers, as well as the increasing number of women in corporate board rooms and legal departments. Many forms of discrimination or disparate treatment, however, stem from misconceptions or concerns about real differences between the sexes—such as pregnancy and level of domestic responsibility—and the structure of the law firm setting. As long as billable hours are paramount, women who are caretakers or have primary domestic responsibility in the home will be viewed, and sometimes treated, differently. Their commitment level may be questioned, or their alternative arrangements may be the cause of resentment by full-time colleagues. Again, these types of gender issues will not completely change unless and until law firms change their profit and billing structure, which doesn't appear to be happening anytime soon. Despite shifting statistics, gender bias or issues stemming from an attorney's gender will continue to be a part of an attorney's professional life.

### Interview Process

Gender may come into play in the interview and job seeking process. For women, the initial years of your career (and the point when all you have to offer the firm is your time) are the years when you will possibly establish a family, if you haven't already. Many employers believe that just when women are gaining experience and becoming productive and profitable contributors to the group, they leave to devote more time to parenting or aging-parent care. While employer fears are diminishing as more female attorneys are choosing to stay in the workforce, albeit on a reduced work schedule, many employers avoid hiring young females altogether. Other employers may ask illegal questions (disguised as legal ones) to try to discern whether the attorney is one of those women who will likely leave in three years. When faced with this type of questioning, as discussed in Chapter 5, do your best to address the employer's basic concern, impressing on the interviewer that you will be a dedicated member of the team. Many women do this by downplaying their femininity or presenting themselves as "career women" with no thoughts of starting a family. This is unfortunate, particularly since a woman's femininity is something that can be used in the profession to great advantage. It is also unfortunate that when these women eventually do leave, it reinforces employer notion that women aren't worth the investment in training and resources. Others interviewees handle these questions directly by stating their interest in and commitment to their career. Few of these illegal lines of questioning go beyond the interview room. It's up to the candidate to handle them as appropriately as possible, and also decide whether she wants to pursue a position with this firm.

Overtly illegal questions should be brought to someone's attention. Your career services director, or, when you are not interviewing through the on-campus process, the managing partner of the firm, should be made aware of problems with an interviewer. An interviewer's particular biases may not reflect the position embraced by the firm. You will be doing the firm a service by bringing its attention to the views held by the interviewer. A woman may be made to feel that she is the one "creating" a problem by bringing these issues to light, not the attorney asking the illegal questions. Many are hesitant to report these types of problems. Women should carefully weigh the questions asked or comments made and decide whether they merit reporting. Men, on the other hand, report few problems relating to gender bias in the interview setting.

### In the Law Firm

Gender bias takes many forms in a law firm setting. Factors such as the city in which the firm is located, the composition of the partnership, or the type of work and clients served by the firm, influence the likelihood of whether an associate will be on the receiving end of gender bias. Attorneys, particularly female attorneys, may experience hostile, abusive or disparate treatment from opposing counsel, colleagues, supervisors, clients or staff. Illegal or inappropriate treatment is often covert. Examples include women of childbearing age not being assigned to complex legal matters, and given only administrative tasks on large work teams, or not given experiences or opportunities similar to those of male colleagues. In some instances, male colleagues may be informally singled out by the firm and given good work assignments, client development opportunities, high profile committee appointments, and pairing with successful partners. In effect, the firm is making the way smooth for some lawyers that it knows it will keep. These lawyers tend to do well, probably as a result of the higher expectations and opportunities afforded them. On the other hand, a woman in such a firm may be written off as not committed, likely to leave after having children, or not cut out for firm life. As a result, they are virtually ignored, or worse, criticized until they leave.

Misconceptions about female attorneys abound. For example, many lawyers find that it's easy to classify female litigators as either ineffective or overly aggressive. One large-firm partner in a mid-sized, mid-west city, stated that he found female litigators to be "bitchy" or "incompetent." Unfortunately, it takes very little for a woman to be labeled in such a manner. Behavior that in a male attorney would likely be regarded as zealous or confident is regarded as inappropriate for female litigators. Men seem to have more leeway in this regard.

Soft-spoken, feminine, women litigators also find that attorneys make immediate assumptions about their abilities. One female associate was told by her supervising partner that she needed to be more aggressive and forceful in her handling of litigation matters. The associate later asked the partner to review and critique a transcript from a deposition she conducted. He praised it as aggressive and exactly the tone that was needed in her work. Interestingly, during the deposition the associate never changed her voice from her normal soft-spoken tone of speaking. She elicited the same information and served her client's interests best by sticking with her personality.

Women may also experience hostile or disrespectful behavior from staff. Again, female attorneys have less of a margin of acceptable behavior or attitude before they are negatively regarded. The attorney-secretary relationship and the attorney-paralegal relationship, particularly when the staff member is an older female, can be a particularly difficult area for women lawyers. One female, mid-level attorney had a paralegal interrupt her on a conference call twice, demanding an answer to a question. The client on the other end of the conference call (a large, multinational company representative) expressed surprise at the tone of voice and the manner in which the associate was accosted. The paralegal did not back down, even when asked to be quiet. It's possible (even likely) that this wouldn't have happened if the associate were male.

In many cases, the attorney should speak first with the staff member and see whether the behavior continues. In extreme cases, such as the paralegal example, the attorney should first determine whether there were any witnesses to the incident, and then immediately talk with the human resources director or the person who supervises staff. This type of behavior should not be tolerated by the firm.

Female attorneys may experience gender bias from clients or potential clients of the firm. A client may refuse to allow a female attorney to work on an assignment or be the lead attorney on a case. Some clients may not state any objections, but direct legal questions only to the male attorney on the file. The client may scrutinize or criticize a female attorney's work more than what is appropriate. Other instances include assumptions made about the experience level of a female versus male attorney working on a case, simply by virtue of gender. Sometimes female attorneys experience difficulty with clients from a foreign country, where a different view of what is appropriate behavior toward women can increase the chances of misunderstandings or cause outright problems. Although it happens only occasionally, the client may make inappropriate sexual comments to a female lawyer or engage in sexually harassing behavior.

Significant matters involving clients also should be brought to the firm's attention. Firm support for women attorney is critical. In the case of a client's outright refusal to allow a female attorney on the case, the firm should, if the client's concerns cannot be addressed, refuse the representation. Discriminatory attitudes, even when disguised as "strategy calls" should not be tolerated by the firm. The less clear cases when, for example, reservations are expressed about a woman's competence or aggressiveness to handle matters for the client, should be addressed on a case-by-case basis. It may be appropriate for a male partner at the firm to talk to the client about the reasons the attorney was assigned to the matter and the extent of her abilities, experience, and training. Stray comments by a client regarding the female attorney should, for the most part, be first handled by the attorney herself. She may ignore these comments, if they are innocuous, or take action if they increase in frequency or the comments are plainly inappropriate. Some female attorneys talk first with an experienced lawyer at the firm and then handle the matter personally. She may tell the client outright that the comments are inappropriate and that the she would like to continue doing a professional and competent job for the client, but must keep the relationship professional. After all, part of your job is to resolve conflict and advocate your clients' interests. Apply this directive to your own career and perhaps you will feel less apprehension in dealing with certain clients. In every case, the lawyer on the receiving end of the commentary should maintain her professionalism and seek a diplomatic resolution to the problem.

Some large firms have organizations at the firm made up of female attorneys, or other minority groups. Generally, associates as well as partners, many of whom may be on firm management committees, are members of these organizations. This group might periodically report to the firm current issues amongst its members, or it may act as a representative voice when a firm-wide problem is perceived. One firm investigated a complaint that women were not being placed on cases that were expected to last more than a few years before going to trial. The firm investigated the complaint, ultimately determining that there was a gender disparity in how female associates were assigned, but that it did not stem from gender bias. The firm reacted immediately to a concern raised by the women's group.

These groups might be helpful for younger women to find mentors or even to get to know other women at the firm on a more personal level. Some attorneys feel that these groups are divisive because they necessarily exclude a portion of the attorney population. A young woman lawyer's participation in these groups might—accurately or not—contribute to stereotypes about her political activism for feminist issues, or increase the likelihood that attorneys will regard her as a "woman lawyer" first, rather than just another lawyer.

Look at the practical benefits of being involved if you have concerns about whether to participate in these types of groups. Are mentoring relationships actually fostered by the types of meetings or events these lawyers hold? Do they tend to bring about real change or foster a spirit of collegiality with non-members of the firm? Are members of firm management part of the group, which would allow you a direct voice into significant issues faced by management? How are these groups regarded by others in the firm? Do these groups deal only with women's (or minority) issues or do they have a broader perspective that takes into account a minority viewpoint?

Finding a mentor as a woman is sometimes more difficult than it should be. To begin with, there simply aren't that many women in firm leadership positions or women who have successfully balanced a career and family. Many females who are held up as role models carry an extraordinary burden juggling work, home, non-billable, and marketing activities. This leaves little time for mentoring, except by example. Other lawyers have found that some of these women are not particularly supportive, especially when it comes to advising younger associates on balancing children and a legal career. Experienced female lawyers point out that there is a difference in the way they had to manage family versus career, as opposed to the way younger female attorneys are dealing with these issues. When the older females were associates, part-time or alternative arrangements were simply not an option, and many went to extraordinary lengths to maintain the firm's belief that they were committed attorneys in it for the long haul. Many remember keeping discussions about family happenings or their children to a minimum, and they did not bring family pictures or children's drawings to the office. As more women entered the field, and as more men began truly co-parenting with their wives, the attitudes that caused these women toward defensive reactions has steadily changed. The sense of cooperation and support for younger women by more experienced women, however, has not. You may find that as an associate today, your role models will have a different face—perhaps a (male or female) senior associate or an attorney successfully practicing in an alternative work arrangement.

Other firms have tried to head off or address gender issues by implementing mandatory diversity training. Many view these programs as ineffective when dealing with people who aren't willing to be educated or the program is in place simply to protect the firm from greater liability in discrimination lawsuits. These programs may or may not be effective, but one attorney pointed out that they have more efficacy when staff and attorney compliance with them is tied to compensation.

How you should handle disparate, discriminatory or harassing behavior by someone in the firm depends on the situation. You will have an uphill battle even when you strongly suspect (and have some evidence) that you are being treated in an impermissibly discriminatory fashion. People will rarely admit to prejudicial motives when confronted and will undoubtedly point to other reasons, some of which may be plausible. As a result, some matters should either be overlooked or handled by you at the time they occur. Isolated occurrences or stray comments should be handled with due measure. You may want to take a direct approach by telling the person making the statement that his behavior makes you uncomfortable and you'd like to discuss it.

Consider handling more serious incidents or repeat occurrences with the gravity they deserve. First, assess the facts. If relevant, look at the firm partnership: Are there partners who are parents? Are there women? Are they parents? Is there a "profile" of the female partner or litigator? Don't allow one partner or associate to be held up as the "role model," which can have the effect of stifling serious discussion when your circumstances are different from those of the "role model." Are women assigned to large, complex matters that are likely to go to trial? Does the firm hire equal numbers of male and female associates, but six years down the road the numbers are disproportionate? Keep accurate records of your performance reviews, problems, issues, and potential witnesses. Find someone you trust and get an objective opinion, although take care in whom you confide. You will feel a need to talk about your anger, fear, or frustration at not getting results. Talk about these matters with those trained to provide feedback and close confidants with whom your discussions are sure to stay private. Sometimes, after discussing the matter, you may not feel the need to pursue it further.

If you do want to take it to the next level, however, consider using informal channels within the firm first. Perhaps a partner for whom you have worked, or the head of the group where the person under discussion is working. Using diplomatic channels first might go a long way towards resolving the matter more quickly.

For really grievous incidents, you may feel that reporting them to the human resources department is more appropriate. If so, remember that your complaint will be investigated by the firm, and will be taken more seriously. You may also want to talk confidentially with a member on a bar committee related to gender issues or discrimination. These groups sometimes provide a support outlet and other times investigate matters brought to their attention. They also track these complaints and have some expertise in helping attorneys deal with the consequences of gender bias. If after taking these steps, you are still not satisfied, talk with a lawyer about filing a charge with the Equal Employment Opportunity Commission (EEOC) and ultimately a lawsuit against the firm. If this is the path you take, be aware of the tight time limitations imposed by the EEOC. Will this type of a lawsuit affect your career? Absolutely! There are some grievances, however, that are worth the price you will pay in pursuing litigation against the firm. Only you can decide whether the stress and effect on your reputation and career is worth the cost.

Many women report that opposing attorneys often say or do things that appear to be motivated by gender biases. Expect a certain amount of condescension from opposing counsel, which may or may not be driven by gender bias. Such treatment is a tactic to intimidate you and establish the other lawyer as somehow superior. Older male attorneys may prefer having someone they consider a counterpart (in experience, and yes, gender) on the other side of a negotiation, hearing or deposition, and take umbrage when having to deal with a young female attorney. Their frustration may manifest itself in their attitude towards you and they will likely deal with you as little or as roughly as possible.

For a young attorney, and not just female ones, depositions comprise an area especially rife with problems. Expect to be tested early. Your opposing counsel may begin coaching the witness, passing notes to the witness, making lengthy "speaking objections" on the record (where, instead of stating the objection and the grounds therefor, he pontificates on all kinds of issues, generally for the purpose of arguing his case on paper), snickering or making other commentary while the deponent is testifying, or standing over you to make objections. These are all actual examples of what has happened to young attorneys at depositions, male and female.

The best way to deal with this kind of machismo or unethical lawyering is to know the rules inside and out. Establish early your insistence that the rules will be followed; object to opposing counsel's behavior when necessary so that you can create a record for later use; take a break, or terminate the deposition; in extreme examples, involve the court. Always maintain your equanimity and understand that sometimes your professionalism can be used to put pressure on opposing counsel to behave properly. His client may recognize that the lawyer's tactics will do more harm than good, and put a stop to them. Again, try not to assume that these actions are gender-motivated, although some may indeed be. For those situations that are plainly motivated by gender, but not outrageous, there is little you can do outside handling the situation as it arises or using a friendly contact at this attorney's firm to put pressure on this attorney.

Report to the bar or other appropriate body (after discussion with members of your firm) any instances that cross the line of propriety. For example, in a closing argument given by a male attorney, he suggested that the female lawyer on the opposing side inappropriately "contacted" a police officer in order to elicit favorable testimony for her client by rhetorically asking the jury ". . . and how do you think she got his home phone number?" After discussions with her partner, and after seeing the shock on the female judge's face, the woman lawyer decided that this attorney sufficiently embarrassed himself and that no further action was necessary. The jury, however, was very open to suggestion, and, while a favorable decision was rendered in her client's favor, later discussions with jurors revealed that these insinuations should have been addressed immediately. The attorney then considered a complaint to the bar.

Many male lawyers are apt to view a female opposing counsel more harshly than if she were male. For example, a woman's tough stance on behalf of her client will more likely than not be interpreted as her having a "bitchy" or "pushy" attitude or that she is difficult to get along with, rather than tough advocacy. These men will bring with them to hearings, depositions, or negotiations, their own set of prejudices and biases. A female lawyer was taking a deposition where a number of opposing attorneys were present, all of whom were male. Just before the lunch break, a male attorney announced that someone should start making plans for their lunch and all eyes turned to the female attorney in the group (the one taking the deposition). Her reply ("I'll have tuna") was appropriate; this is not overt sexism and could probably be attributable to a number of things, including the intimidation factor. Incidentally, this deposition was being taken down by a male court reporter. The first words spoken by the deponent (the male CEO of a large company) as he looked at the female lawyer was "Oh, you're the lawyer!" Learn to handle these matters with diplomacy, humor, and certainly a reaction commensurate with the comment or action. Use it to your advantage when opposing counsel underestimates you because you are female and/or young. These lawyers will forget to dot their "i's" or cross their "t's", thinking that your inexperience or presumed inability can be used to their advantage.

Client development and marketing activities are another area where perceived ability differences between men and women could have an inappropriate gender basis. Marketing is one of those areas that appears to be easier for some lawyers, but not necessarily for one gender over another. Women who market in environments in which they are comfortable seem to do well. Women who force themselves to participate in activities or attend events in which they have little knowledge or interest may have some difficulty. Try not to feel inadequate because you don't golf or like sports events, if that is the case. Those events are not the only places to meet or take clients. (One firm allows its women attorneys to take female clients to local spas). Increasingly, women are finding that the make up of in-house legal departments, corporate decision-makers and other people who contract for legal services are women.

While it should not be assumed that women prefer women lawyers (because then the converse might be true), it does illustrate how the marketing climate has changed as more women are in the position to hire legal services. Female attorneys should also consider attending seminars or courses that focus on helping women market more productively. A local women's bar association should sponsor these events, or at least gather resources for other women to use. Consider organizing a symposium of women who enjoy marketing activities and perform well in that setting. These events are usually well-attended and well worth the organization time. Finding a female mentor or observing the activities of females who get business is a great way to learn by experience. Don't be discouraged, however, if the women who are truly good marketers don't have a lot of extra time for mentoring. Marketing takes a lot of time, energy and resources, which is something that is in short supply for attorneys (and particularly female attorneys with children). Instead, you may need to follow these women around to client meetings or volunteer your time in committees or causes in which these women are active. Women who are great marketers are always thinking in terms of networking and looking for clients with a need.

A gap in compensation along gender lines continues to be a problem for female lawyers, particularly in smaller firms where compensation is subjective or negotiated by the lawyer. Studies confirm that these gaps are not explainable by unequal hours worked or a disparity in experience. The best way for women to avoid being paid less for the same amount of work is to be proactive. When negotiating your salary, you must know the market rates for your level of experience and at the size firm in which you will be doing it. You should know, as best you can discover, where the firm has historically fallen in the market salary ranges. Then, you should ask for what you are worth.

If you are already at a firm and believe there to be a pay disparity between you and a male colleague, first examine every other possible explanation for the supposed disparity. For example, does that person hold a degree or have experience that you don't? Has that person practiced longer in his respective field, whereas you changed departments early in your career? Is your colleague bringing in business and you aren't? Bring disparities in compensation to the attention of your supervising partner only after you have investigated the matter and cannot find any logical explanation for the gap. Avoid an accusatory tone with your supervising partner, particularly since you cannot know for certain what your colleague makes or receives as benefits.

Men, too, have perceptions to deal with that stem from preconceived notions about their goals and desires. Men, for the most part, are still expected work towards partnership, without allowing childcare or familial responsibilities to interrupt that career. Notions of what constitutes commitment still seem fairly traditional for men: You work hard, stay the course, and take off as little time as possible. Men who, by choice, aren't on the partnership track (if there is a formed "track") or who take advantage of paternity or personal leave policies are relatively few, despite the fact that many firms offer paternity leave. One male associate who took paternity leave from a large, big city firm, felt pressure from clients to return to work in the weeks following the birth of his child. This associate ultimately became a partner at the firm, but noted that from a client perspective, there are limits as to what is appropriate for a father to take. Another partner took paternity leave (the first in this large city to do so) and had a good experience. He was not completely gone from the firm, however, as a female attorney might be. He kept in contact by checking mail regularly, handling discreet matters that did not involve client contact, and attending meetings and firm functions. A large city, mid-sized firm partner expressed shock that any male lawyer would request paternity leave. It appears that while the policies are in place, many men will probably suffer a set-back in their career if they choose to take advantage of these opportunities. Men should remember, however, that just a few years ago, the same type of thinking prevented attorneys from taking advantage of part-time or alternative arrangement policies. These situations are becoming more acceptable, with some attorneys remaining on partnership track (although a longer one) despite being on a reduced hour schedule. As more men request these opportunities and as the traditional law firm climate continues to change, it will become more acceptable for men to reduce or alter their schedule or take advantage of staying home with their children for a short period of time.

Certain practice areas, or certain levels of these practice areas, are dominated by attorneys of one gender or the other. The reasons stem from client identification, client demands, market realities, and the fact that males or females are attracted to certain types of practice due to the hours or the nature of the work. The practical result is that your routine communications might be primarily with one gender. If you are of the sex that is underrepresented in a field, you may have more than your share of inappropriate behavior with which to deal.

As a lawyer in private practice, you will possibly appear before various state and federal judges. Here, too, you may experience various forms of gender bias or treatment inappropriately based on gender. Remember that judges are people first, and as such bring all of their experience, philosophies, prejudices, and inclinations, with them to the bench. Some judges are known for being plainly biased in favor of men. Others, women. One female attorney appeared before a judge and argued her client's case in a bench trial. Her male opposing counsel was given to histrionics. She therefore tried especially hard to maintain a calm and professional demeanor throughout the trial. At the end of the trial, her client (a female chief executive officer) commented that her composed presentation was in nice contrast to that of her opposing counsel. In later conversations between the judge and the female attorney's supervising partner, the judge commented that the female attorney was extremely aggressive, to the point of being too much so. This example is illustrative of the preconceived notions about men and women lawyers that judges bring to the bench.

Again, when a judge is treating you badly because you are male or female, there is very little that you can do about it. Always maintain your professionalism. While you should preserve objections for appeal or reconsideration purposes, never openly challenge the judge's motivations for rulings. Treat the judge with the utmost respect, even when you are not being treated that way. It may be necessary to request to approach the bench and state legal grounds for your concerns out of the hearing of the jury. Some lawyers talk less formally with a judge when having a whispered conference at the bench. If you do this, the same rules apply. If the circumstances are so extreme that your client's interests are being compromised, then after you leave the courtroom discuss with other, more experienced attorneys what course of action you should take. Remember that your firm will be very reluctant to take on a local judge. You may lose your challenge and then members of your firm, including you, will have to practice for many years before a resentful judge. Another route is a formal complaint to a commission that oversees the conduct of judicial officers. This body, comprised of experienced lawyers throughout the state, will investigate complaints filed with it. In matters that so warrant, the commission will decide on a course of action against the judge.

The only thing for certain when it comes to gender issues in private practice is that things are changing. Tight labor conditions will further the influx of women into power positions within law firms. Law firms will become more integrated on a gender level as firms move (slowly) away from traditional definitions of success and notions about partnership material. Members of the bench are increasingly female, as are corporate decision-makers. These happenings will benefit lawyers of both sexes, as they each bring a unique perspective and approach to the profession. By keeping your sense of professionalism and dignity intact, you will find that dealing with gender bias becomes less and less of a hindrance to professional success.

# Chapter 12

# Alternative Work Arrangements

## Various Types of Alternative Arrangements; Who is Eligible and How to Negotiate One

Attorneys are increasingly turning to alternative or flexible work arrangements in order to balance the competing demands of career and other priorities. Mothers with young children may be the original deal makers for many of these types of arrangements, but today single or childless attorneys are also finding personal satisfaction from breaking out of the full-time, full-availability, in-the-office work mode. A strong legal market has encouraged law firms to be more receptive to alternative work schedules and arrangements. Otherwise, the option for attorneys—mostly women—looking for relief is to leave the firm or the practice of law altogether. Law firms cannot afford to lose experienced attorneys, particularly when the attorney is someone the firm doesn't want to lose and when a substantial investment of time and resources has been made in that person. The high cost of finding, hiring, and training new attorneys is a further incentive for firms to keep what they have. Law firms also lose a valuable segment of their attorney work force when experienced practitioners decide to find a different work environment or just stop practicing.

An alternative work arrangement can include any type of reduced, flexible, or non-traditional work schedule. There may be a reduction in hours, or simply a change in venue for part of the week. Whatever changes you negotiate, they will generally involve a compensation adjustment. The salary decrease may be more complicated than simply less money for less hours—it may include less money for increased flexibility.

In this chapter, we discuss various types of alternative arrangements, which attorneys are eligible for them, and how to negotiate such agreements. We also explore some of the overarching considerations for firms and attorneys alike, which apply in virtually every type of arrangement.

For a number of reasons, a firm will not likely consider an alternative work schedule for a first, second, or third year associate. The inexperienced associate must use these years learning how to be a lawyer, not trying to minimize work demands. The associate must also be fully available to the firm to perform the work that is too costly for more experienced (and more expensive) attorneys to handle. Law firms do not have a good gauge on your technical skills and the level of responsibility you can handle unless and until you are faced with a variety of situations. These experiences don't arise in a year, or even two years.

During these first three years, the attorney can lay the groundwork for a later alternative arrangement. This is the time to establish productive and reliable relationships with colleagues. Having people you trust looking out for you, and vice versa, is absolutely key to making a viable alternative work arrangement.

Develop good organizational habits. One of the ways in which you can demonstrate that a non-traditional schedule will be workable is by being systematic and having complete and up-to-date files. Your organizational efforts will minimize time spent looking for documents and allow others to find what they need when you are out of the office. Being able to organize well is something that is learned and developed. The earlier in your career you acquire organizational skills, the better you career will be.

Another goal for the young attorney is to establish credibility with the attorney's partners and firm management. Do what you say you are going to do and do it well. Reliability is a critical element to the success of any alternative work arrangement. Your chances of negotiating a flexible arrangement and making it successful improve significantly when you have good working relationships with others, are known for reliability, and have credibility with management.

Alternative or flexible work arrangements are generally considered by firms to be an accommodation or allowance, rather than a way of practice. Lawyers and law firms still measure success by the billable hour. This mindset is so ingrained in the legal profession that much of management's thinking about firm operations and attorney employment uses the billable hour as a starting point. The measure of full-time employment starts with a certain billable hour target. Bonuses are often tied to yearly billable hours. Billable hours are the first thing a group leader turns to in deciding whether to hire an additional lawyer. When negotiating alternative arrangements with firm managers, you will always be viewed as someone who is trying to make a favorable arrangement at the expense of the firm's bottom line and your peers. The prevailing view is that for you to benefit, the firm and other associates have to lose in some respect. Firms evaluate in terms of lost flexibility, availability, and money. The impact on others in your group will also be a primary consideration. The firm categorizes keeping the attorney and having the benefit of her experience as the "give" in weighing the benefits or detriments or permitting an alternate arrangement.

The firm's position is not surprising given the billable-hour driven state of the profession. Perhaps as firms move towards value-based billing concepts, and employ better and faster technology, the "alternative" schedules won't be so much an accommodation, but one of many career paths for lawyers. Other industries have undergone analogous shifts with little or no loss in perceived professionalism. Until such a sea-change occurs in the legal profession, however, the lawyer considering alternative work arrangements must understand the law firm mindset and handle matters from there.

Some firms have a standard reduced hour or part-time arrangement and there is little or no room for negotiation. For example, some firms will allow you to work 75% of your full-time total billable hour commitment, and make 70% of your full-time salary. The five-percent "penalty" is ostensibly to cover things like your full-time office that must be maintained, and a full-time secretary that answers the phones for you when you are not there. In reality, it discourages attorneys from making part-time arrangements. This extra deduction is becoming less prevalent as firms recognize that 75% time every week is rarely possible for attorneys, and that there must be flexibility on both ends of the arrangement. In addition, an attorney seeking a reduction in hours may view the five-percent deduction as a penalty, and many opt to leave on principle rather than accept such an arrangement. You will probably have little success in getting the firm to change a standard part-time arrangement unless you are a partner or senior associate that the firm really wants to keep.

Be aware of alternative arrangements that have worked in the past and those that didn't. For example, the firm policy may be that part-time attorneys leave earlier five days a week, instead of taking an entire day from the firm. This arrangement may work in some practices, but not others. You need to point to the specific facts supporting your position and take your best shot. When proposing an alternate arrangement you should present your thoughts in a clear and fact-based manner.

Many firms do not have a standard or part-time alternative arrangement policy. Each attorney is required to negotiate an individual deal by either proposing an arrangement or asking to be considered for one decided on by the firm. You will likely be asked to keep all arrangements confidential, particularly since benefits and salary figures may vary by attorney, even within the same firm.

Cost to the firm is probably the most important factor underlying a firm's willingness to negotiate a nontraditional schedule. Start with the assumption that the firm intends to operate as a business driven by the billable hour. Your time is part of its inventory, specifically the billable amount that is charged to a client for your time and the amount of hours you bill. Try to estimate what you cost the firm versus what the firm makes on you by billing clients for your time. Those numbers will change if you alter your schedule or time commitment, but it constitutes information you need to know beforehand. Try estimating the number of hours you bill each year, multiplied by the hourly rate you are billed out at, minus salary, bonus, vacation and medical benefits, insurance, social security taxes, and overhead (which includes your secretary, office equipment and supplies, and space). You may be able to plug in various parts of this equation by talking with accounting or management people at the firm. If you reduce your hours, the equation changes on both ends. Your billable hours may decrease, the gross revenue you bring in declines, but you won't cost as much in overhead, salary and use of office resources. You also provide intangible benefits to the firm in the form of more efficient work, better attitude, and possibly good experience not readily available elsewhere. Your proposal has to allow the firm to make money on you. You cannot expect the firm to agree to a situation where it costs money to keep you (unless you generate substantial business that keeps other attorneys busy). In short, your primary consideration is that the firm must view your proposal as economically feasible.

Have some idea of what is going on in the marketplace. Talk with friends at other firms and with the human resources coordinators or managing partners at other firms that have such arrangements. Conduct "informational interviews" on this specific subject and gather facts and reactions. Be sure to ask bottom-line questions like: Are these situations working? Is the partnership generally in favor of these arrangements? Having confirmation from partners of other firms may allay some fear of the unknown. There are also numerous encouraging statistical surveys that will lend credence to your points to the firm. Be aware of them, particularly as they relate to a firm of your size and caliber.

Money is not the sole consideration. The firm benefits by having a more satisfied lawyer working for it. The benefits include better health, fewer and less costly insurance claims, and a loyal employee who is grateful for the arrangement. These lawyers have no qualms about referring other talented lawyers and staff to apply to the firm, and they tend to engage less in firm bashing or other morale-reducing behavior. The fact that the firm will consider flexible alternatives is also an inducement for other attorneys to stay, thereby lowering the attrition rate. Another benefit is that having the attorney part-time versus not at all is worth the extra efforts by the firm. The lawyer in question may have a good working relationship with clients. If a matter is pending, continuity on the case is a benefit for both client and firm. Studies have also indicated that lawyers on an alternative arrangement often work harder and more efficiently than their peers. There seem to be two basic reasons: a large amount of work must be done in a shorter time frame; and the employee is committed to making the arrangement work. Your negotiations and final proposal must include these intangible factors. Many times, a firm reluctant to attempt a new situation will be swayed by these considerations, which perhaps were not previously considered.

Your practice area is perhaps the next most important factor. Some practice areas lend themselves to alternative arrangements, even on the partner level, and some do not. The situations that seem to work best are those where your work is steady, there are few emergencies, and an outside entity (like the court) is not controlling and dictating absolute deadlines. Any clients that you handle must not be the type that frequently needs an immediate answer or quick turnaround on documents.

In addition, much depends on your experience level and the work product clients require of you. For example, if you are an employment lawyer and your clients constantly call you to check if someone can be fired or to determine if probation is appropriate, you take the call and respond immediately. In this kind of situation, a part-time situation may not work, but a work-at-home arrangement just may be the answer. Your availability to the client does not depend on your being physically present at the firm. It is hard to generalize which practice areas lend themselves to alternative work arrangements and which do not. Some in which flexible hours have proved feasible include trusts and estates, some tax areas, and some real estate specialties (e.g., residential closings, in which preparation is primarily done by experienced paralegals and the timing of the closing is scheduled in advance).

Other areas are simply not conducive to a reduced hour or alternative arrangement. Traditional litigation, securities work, and most employment practices are a few examples. In litigation, your schedule is so volatile that it is difficult to set normal full-time hours, let alone a reduced or flexible schedule. There will be times when you need to be there all night, seven days a week, and then other times when you can merely catch your breath. You may have to accept less fulfilling or challenging work in order to make alternative arrangements. One attorney gave up complex litigation matters to work on smaller matters for one client. This change allowed her to reduce her hours because there were no court deadlines, and other deadlines could be scheduled in advance. The trade-off was necessary; most litigation practices are simply not conducive to working out a regular schedule.

In short, your area of practice must be considered, along with the types of clients you service and the nature of the scheduled demands on your time. The more control you have over when and how much of your work is required, the better able you will be to work out an arrangement. Be prepared to identify to the firm the aspects of your practice that are conducive to the alternative arrangement you are proposing, and have specific solutions to address the aspects that may pose problems.

Fairness considerations are another factor you should consider in negotiating your arrangement. How will your arrangement impact other attorneys? Is there work that can be transferred to a paralegal, which can operate to the paralegal's benefit because it might be more challenging and diverse? The firm will want to address this factor, so be prepared to offer a well reasoned analysis on the amount of work, if any, that will be shifted around. There may be little or no direct impact on your colleagues. Your arrangement may merely allow you more time at home while handling the same workload, or your arrangement may be more technologically efficient and allow you to handle the same amount of work, but do it in fewer hours. You can do things like eliminate lunch breaks and non-billable firm activities and try to compress your work week into a shorter period of time.

Arrangements must be made in advance to compensate you if you work a significant amount over your time commitment. Do not allow yourself to be paid less for the same time commitment your colleagues have made. It is best to have a definite formula for significant "overtime," rather than attempting to make it up over the course of a few months or weeks. Making up lost home time is not only difficult, it may change the perception of others on how hard you are working. Your month of working less to make up for the full-time month when you tried a case will be scrutinized carefully as the hours are circulated. Most of the partners will not realize that you worked over your arrangement last month; they just see where you didn't meet your commitment this month. It is better to get an hourly payment for significant overtime work (calculated on a yearly basis) or work out a bonus structure using a range.

Be sure to agree in advance what non-billable obligations will be expected of you and whether some of those activities should count towards your total billable commitment. For example, recruiting will probably be over and above the hours agreed to in your arrangement, but non-billable legal work performed for the law firm itself, required classes, seminars and certain "serious" client development time should not be. The thirty-hour week can easily become a forty or fifty hour week if these matters are in addition to your billable commitment. Be selective as to what you include in this category. Only by having this worked out in advance will you be able to gauge your time on a monthly or weekly basis accurately. Reduce the arrangement between you and the firm to writing. This is not necessarily a contract, but a note to memorialize some of the terms governing your relationship. You may want to send an e-mail, for example, confirming that certain non-billable work counts towards your total billable hour requirement. At the end of the year or during periodic reviews, it is helpful to refer to these terms to ensure that both sides are living up to their end of the arrangement.

These big-picture considerations for negotiating your arrangement will apply more or less depending on what you want to do. All of them, however, will be factored in as the firm decides whether to accept your proposal.

There are other factors for an attorney considering an alternative arrangement. You will have to deal with perception issues, whether from staff, colleagues or the partners. If what you want is a work at home arrangement, it is often difficult for other attorneys to believe that you are working when you are not in the office. This is especially so when their workload is extremely high. Your colleagues will sometimes view your situation as putting more pressure or work on them, and thus treat you differently. For this reason, building credibility before you make an alternative arrangement is crucial.

Don't under estimate the value of working efficiently. Many younger attorneys do not budget their day because they don't perceive a need to. They take a long lunch, talk with colleagues, eat dinner with colleagues, and then work late into the night. These attorneys may not have other matters that they regard as high of a priority, such as a family, a pet, or an outside interest. Thus, they are not motivated to work as efficiently as you might be.

Informing clients about your alternative arrangement shouldn't pose too much of a concern. Many attorneys find that in-house corporate counsel and business people are supportive of alternative arrangements, particularly when the lawyer made the move for lifestyle reasons. In addition, other professions and industries are comparatively progressive when it comes to working with employees to better manage priorities. Your client may also be grappling with alternative arrangements personally, or company-wide in an effort to improve retention rates. Be frank with your clients about your arrangement, and let them know that you are accessible in the event of an emergency. They should know that you regularly check your messages and frequently communicate with the office. They should be made aware that when an urgent situation arises, you or someone else with whom they are familiar will be there to cover the work. Just as with your partners, do what you say you are going to do: check your messages and call clients back from your home, if necessary. Assure your clients that there is no increased cost to them for your schedule, and in fact they benefit by your increased ability to work more efficiently. Support from firm partners in reassuring clients is critical. The partners need to communicate to the client that they continue to have the same level of faith in your abilities, commitment to the firm, and work product. The real test for your clients is watching how your schedule impacts them in actual practice. For this reason, it is even more important that you or someone on your behalf promptly return telephone calls and take all necessary steps to ensure that client needs are being met.

Lawyers debate about whether to inform opposing counsel of an alternative schedule. As a general rule, it is probably best not to convey that information or at least not the specifics. You don't want for your arrangement to be an advantage that the other side tries to press, nor do you want for opposing counsel to question your commitment level to your client's cause.

Here are some specific types of alternative or flexible arrangements.

### Reduced Hour Arrangement

Lawyers may want a reduced hour schedule to spend more time with their children or to take care of an aging or ill relative. Lawyers with dependents often have a much more difficult time with reduced hour schedules; there is a certain loss of flexibility inherent in having a dependent. Is it possible to work out arrangements that meet the needs of the lawyer, firm and family? The following are some thoughts on working less and making it work.

A reduced hour arrangement can be as varied as working fewer hours each day or taking one or more days off entirely. Attorneys differ as to which situation is better. In reality, it probably depends on your ability to walk out the door on time or the nature of the work you do. Having one whole day at home works well for some people. It allows them to escape (to some extent) the stress of the office and concentrate instead on the reason for the arrangement in the first place.

Nevertheless, the truth is that for an attorney with small children, a reduced hour arrangement can still be very difficult. A career in private practice where traditional notions of profitability and the billable hour dominate, is hard to square with being a committed parent. That is not to say that parents who practice law are not committed. It's just harder, and particularly so when both parents are engaged in a demanding career or have to work for financial reasons. Your ability to juggle many priorities is only the beginning. A reduced hour arrangement certainly will alleviate some of the stress, but it does introduce other elements that weren't there before. For example, other people's perceptions of your commitment to the firm become even more important because it affects the support you get from your colleagues and your advancement opportunity, if that is even still an issue.

Start with the notion that you must be flexible. There will be ups and downs in your schedule. There are times when you will need to be in the office on a "day off" or work a full work week. This is pretty much unavoidable. There are times when you will go into work after your kids are asleep, or you will work from home on days off during a quiet moment. A certain number of calls at home should be expected.

There may come a point when flexibility becomes full-time work for a sustained period of time. You must address this problem with your supervising partners. Too often, attorneys on a reduced schedule and reduced pay, become full-time lawyers with reduced pay. The firm will take as much as you allow. It is up to you not only to discourage this work load, but take affirmative steps to address the root of the problem.

You must also be flexible as to the type of work you handle. It will be difficult for you to be assigned to the high-profile, complicated matters. If you find your work unfulfilling, find ways to remedy that within your practice. Address your case load from a different angle. Find out how upcoming legislation will affect what you are doing. Become knowledgeable about the more subtle or advanced aspects of your work. If you still want additional challenges, periodically ask to be assigned as a second or third attorney on a larger matter and make child care arrangements, if necessary. One attorney handles hearings and depositions for other attorneys when there is a crunch. It keeps her skills sharp and benefits other lawyers by having help when they need it most.

Your colleagues and support people will make the difference as to whether your reduced hours will be suitable. You need people to keep you informed of significant happenings as they occur. Someone in the office should always be responsible for your faxes and incoming mail. Your colleagues should be on the alert for e-mail notices that are time sensitive. The belief of coworkers in your commitment to the firm often shapes the firm's perceptions of whether your arrangement is working.

You should have a fax machine at home and computer with access to the firm's system. Working with your support staff will be immeasurably easier by having these modern communication tools. The danger, however, of having home access to e-mail is that you never will leave the office behind because once you have the ability to check on these client matters, expectations placed on you are higher. There is a fine line between being accessible and being overrun to the point that your arrangement is no arrangement at all.

A reduced hour schedule, especially in certain practice groups, is not easy. It forces you to depend on a lot of other people for support. Having a good working relationship with your colleagues and secretary is a must. So is having a committed spouse or family member.

### Contract Work

Contract work is a type of alternative work arrangement that has been around for a while and gained fairly wide acceptance. Firms and corporations of all sizes use contract lawyers. There is a cost advantage to firms and corporations: low overhead, no benefits, fewer administrative and personnel dealings. Since more attorneys are considering this type of arrangement (and actually prefer contract work to permanent employment), firms have the benefit of the availability of experienced, competent lawyers.

Contract lawyering allows attorneys to have an income while pursuing other interests. Lawyers starting their own firm might do contract work to supplement their income for the first few years. The contract arrangement also allows attorneys who are parents to be at home more, make an income, and still develop their lawyering skills. Contract lawyering is also a good way for a new attorney without a job to establish a reputation for producing a solid work product.

Although contract work as an alternative arrangement is subject to many of the factors previously discussed, it poses some additional concerns with respect to money and responsibility. A rough estimate of the hourly rate to charge should be approximately half your billable rate if you were an associate at a large firm. The legal market in which you practice, however, will have a going rate for the services you can provide and for the firm to whom you are providing them. Smaller firms, for example, will not pay one-half the billable rate for a large firm attorney. Talk with firms about what they are willing to pay contract lawyers and find out what other contract lawyers actually charge. Some firms hire so many contract lawyers that they are brought in at a set amount, with fees calculated on the basis of their experience.

You should also be sure that you and the firm (or company) are clear on what your responsibilities include. The contract attorney should have a specific understanding of the nature of the work and the expectations of the firm. The parties should agree on notification procedures: What advance notice will you be given if your services will be needed (or not needed)? Can you perform contract work for more than one firm? Does one firm have precedence (or a right of first refusal for your time) over other firms? What type of conflict-checking procedures are in place and will working at more than one firm complicate that (you must keep accurate records of the clients for whom you directly perform work)?

Determine who will review your work and whether any type of evaluation will be given. Find out whether there are opportunities to become a full-time employee or associate through your work as a contract lawyer. You will certainly gain insight into the firm or company and can make better-informed decisions.

The nature of work you do as a contract lawyer is necessarily different. Your opportunities to represent clients before administrative or agency officials, in court or at arbitration or mediations is substantially reduced. You may have been hired to do the drudge work that associates at the firm refuse to do. For example, your contract job might be to work with a team of lawyers and conduct a privilege review of two million documents. This assignment could take months or more. The firm knows that its associates will quit if they are assigned to such a project. Your professional development will not be furthered by this type of work, nor will your sanity go untested. Know what you are getting into before you take on the assignment.

You may not get the continued training and mentoring all young lawyers need if you opt to go the contract route. There is often less time to develop strong mentoring relationships or to observe more experienced lawyers in action. This may not be a relevant factor for your situation, particularly if you are using contract lawyering as a way to stay involved in the practice of law.

Attorneys on long-term assignments may feel as if firms treat them as second-class citizens. Lawyers at the firm may perceive contract workers as unable to get a full time job with the firm, or view their credentials as lower than that of regular associates at the firm. The firm culture will dictate the treatment contract lawyers receive. Again, depending on your reasons for accepting the job, you may not care how you are received, as long as you are paid.

### Flexible Work Arrangements

There are various types of work arrangements that fall into the "flexible" work category. You may have discretion as to the time you arrive and leave work, often with certain hours that everyone knows you will be present. For example, you are required to be at the firm between the hours of 11:00 and 4:00, but you have flexibility as to when you arrive and depart. This situation works well when you have a client that needs a quick turnaround on advice-giving and wants for you to work everyday.

Other flexible work arrangements include a full time schedule, but your location varies. You may be in the office three or four days each week, and then work from home one or two days. Over the course of the week, you bill the same amount of time as other lawyers. Give some thought as to whether this arrangement will work for you from a practical standpoint. For example, you may be the type of person who is distracted easily and has difficulty working from home. You may not have a work station that is conducive to concentrating. You may have a child at home who doesn't do well with you working there, even with a caregiver lending assistance.

You and others after you will lose much credibility if the flexible arrangement doesn't work. Expect to be under tight scrutiny for these types of arrangements. One missed telephone call or complaining client could sour the partnership on these types of arrangements for some time.

### Long Term Assignments with Clients

Attorneys at a law firm may be lent out to clients on a short or long term basis. The lawyer essentially becomes in-house counsel or supports other in-house counsel for a given period of time. The lawyer benefits in that the client schedule and atmosphere becomes the new work environment. If the client's lawyers work a full day and then leave at 6:00, the lawyer on assignment generally does too. These assignments provide an excellent opportunity to gain an in-depth understanding of what clients do and how they do it. Hopefully, you will develop a close working relationship with individuals at the client's location and in doing so solidify the client connection.

There are disadvantages to long term assignments. People at the firm may tend to forget about you while you are gone. You don't carry quite the same weight as a true firm client and may not get the support you need back at the firm. Additionally, your client might be more demanding than your firm, taking full advantage of the absence of paying for legal services by the hour.

Understand fully your role and the client's expectations before you agree to go on a long term assignment. Clarify whether the firm wants you to continue handling your firm work, including assignments that come back to life or those that have grown into major time concerns. You must take pains to avoid the situation where you are essentially performing two full time jobs. Check in regularly with the firm and your colleagues. Keep abreast of developments in your area, both internal and external. Perhaps most importantly, this is an excellent opportunity for you to learn to think like a client and thereby improve the level of service you provide as a private practitioner. You will see first-hand how important prompt return calls are, as well as the value of "bottom line" advice.

### Compressed Work Week

In the compressed work week situation, a lawyer works full time hours, but does it in a shorter work week. The lawyer generally eliminates non-billable work, lunches and other unnecessary demands on her time. This situation leaves little time to develop mentoring relationships and spending time with colleagues in non-stressful work situations, but may be worth the drawbacks in the extra time you spend on your other priorities.

### Job Sharing

Job sharing—where two people share one job—is popular in non-legal fields and public legal jobs (e.g., state attorney general offices or legal agencies) but has not gained wide acceptance in the law firm setting. Perhaps it has more to do with the nature of the work, malpractice insurance carrier restrictions, or client considerations. In any event, this is an arrangement to consider when discrete tasks are to be performed by the lawyer and there is little day-to-day contact with a particular client. The attorneys sharing the job may need to be of a similar experience level and have already established a good working relationship. You will need to rely on and trust one another's judgment far more often than do the rest of your colleagues. Work out in advance organizational and communication strategies that will keep you both fully apprised of all shared matters. For example, a notepad may be kept at your desk that details the calls received and made (and by whom), the substance of those calls, as well as a daily or weekly status update on the matters for which the you are both responsible. Extra vigilance is required in this situation; the likelihood of something falling through the cracks is high enough that many firms won't consider this arrangement absent unusual circumstances.

### Extended Leave or Sabbatical

Law firms have discovered that in a booming market, associates need incentives beyond a large paycheck to stay with the firm for the long haul. Partnership in and of itself is not the carrot it used to be. Now, in an effort to improve retention rates and promote increased career satisfaction, many law firms are offering time off. These extended leave opportunities, paid or unpaid, occur in the form of sabbatical leaves at periodic intervals in the attorneys' career. They may include extended maternity or paternity leaves, and the ability to combine accrued vacation weeks into a single firm absence. Lawyers use these opportunities to travel, write, spend time with family, do volunteer work, or simply take time to rest.

If you are considering taking an extended leave or vacation, take pains to ensure that the details are worked out before you leave. The most salient consideration is your work and who will cover your clients and cases while you are gone. Making these arrangements may take months, and clients are generally consulted with respect to the person covering your work. Hopefully, your colleagues will take advantage of the same opportunities down the road and you will be there to cover for them.

Determine in advance whether you will be involved at all with your clients (you may be planning a six-week safari and unavailable for consultation). To the extent you can make a clean break, do it. When that is not possible, accessibility becomes essential. Try setting regular times for checking e-mail, snail mail, and telephone messages. Your voice mail message should state that you are out of the office for an extended period, but checking messages at regular intervals. It may be better if all messages, including voicemail, go through your secretary. That way, priority messages can be addressed by someone else, while all other correspondence waits until you check in. Handle discrete matters if some amount of work is still expected on you. You may want to participate in certain firm events or parties. That way, you'll still be connected with your colleagues and people still think you are committed to the firm.

Alternative work arrangements will get easier as firms become more technology-friendly. Firms will also become more receptive to these arrangements as more attorneys handle them successfully. For now, however, attorneys looking for an alternative to leaving the firm or the profession must take on much of the legwork themselves. They need to determine the relevant facts, present these issues to the firm, affirmatively address the real and perceived drawbacks, and then make good on what they promise.

# Chapter 13

# Evaluating Boutique Firms

## What is a Boutique? The Pros and Cons of Working at One; Considerations for Students or New Lawyers

A boutique firm is usually comprised of a group of experienced lawyers practicing in a specialized area of law. Sometimes the firm is organized around several related legal areas. A boutique, for example, may offer expertise in patent, trademark and other intellectual property services. Less common are boutiques that focus on all the needs of a particular type of client. This type of boutique firm might bill itself as a full-service law firm for landlords or foreign corporations trying to do business in the United States.

While boutique firms tend to have fewer attorneys, small size is not a defining feature. Rather, these firms are characterized by a focus on specialized legal services and a commitment to remain at a manageable size. Boutique firms generally do not try to service all of a client's legal needs. They instead attempt to provide high quality legal services in a niche market, such as entertainment, insurance, immigration, employment or worker's compensation matters, just to name a few types of typical boutique firms. The boutique firm survives by building a reputation for providing expert-level legal services in a particular field beyond that which local law firms can provide.

Some smaller firms that handle many different types of legal matters are calling themselves "boutiques." These firms are trying to bank on the boutique mystique, i.e., a reputation for having highly skilled and knowledgeable lawyers in a particular field. Although these self-styled firms may handle a wide variety of matters, because of their small size, they usually aren't full-service law firm, but neither are they true boutiques. The mere fact that a law firm calls itself a boutique does not make it one.

True boutique firms afford associates many advantages. Senior lawyers and partners at these firms have a high level of expertise in their field. Generally, attorneys achieve some level of success or recognition on the local, state or federal level before deciding to join or form a boutique. Many reach a point in their careers where their expertise and reputation were solid enough to entice large-firm clients to shift a portion of work to them at a new and smaller firm. The associate, who is essentially apprenticing under a recognized expert in the field, benefits in a myriad of ways. Because there are probably few issues in the field that the expert has not encountered, the rate at which associates learn and develop technical skills is high. Associates often cite the superior training at the boutique firm as an advantage over that provided at larger or full-service firms. Boutique firms do not typically hire many inexperienced associates. As a result, training takes on additional importance because a significant investment is made and risk taken with each younger lawyer. As an added motivation to have well-trained associates, the boutique's reputation for providing better quality legal services in a specific field can be destroyed by one associate's mishandling of a matter.

One appeal of the boutique is that all the attorneys in the firm have strong resources in each other. Given the combined years of experience in a particular field, there are few arguments or contentions that have not been previously addressed. A related advantage is that these firms have excellent brief banks and written source material. Less experienced attorneys have a starting point for virtually any legal issue that may arise. Young associates can adapt and improve these models or, in instances where a case has a new wrinkle, use them as a checklist to ensure that the important issues have been addressed.

Expectations are high for each lawyer keeping abreast of the latest developments in the field, which includes monitoring legislation that could affect clients. Clients expect that lawyers at boutique firms have a higher level of knowledge and expertise, and other law firms using the boutique as a consultant or co-counsel expect that the attorneys at the boutique will know more than they could find out by a reasonable amount of research. Associates literally have no choice but to be informed and on top of their game.

Experts tend to gravitate towards boutique firms and slackers tend to leave. Because the caliber of attorneys working within the firm is high, incompetence is not tolerated, particularly since the firm's reputation rides on its expertise. Unlike a general law firm setting, there is less dead weight and less tolerance for attorneys who do not pull their weight intellectually or by work-load.

Boutique firms tend to be less bureaucratic. There may not be established policies on issues traditionally addressed in medium or large law firms, like raises, maternity/paternity leave, or dating within the firm. The lack of guidelines can be a mixed blessing to associates, operating to their benefit or their detriment. On the plus side, a highly-regarded associate may be able to help shape policy in a more progressive manner than might be available elsewhere. On the other hand, with non-standardized policies there is more room for subjectivity in applying them. This sometimes leaves the associate without a benchmark or a guide for judging performance or understanding why different rules apply to different members of the firm.

Nevertheless, a limited bureaucracy means that lawyers can handle large and small clients as they see fit. There aren't the staffing, billing or credit disputes that frequently arise in large firms. Less bureaucracy often results in a faster turn-around time for clients. Clients see this service aspect of a boutique firm as a positive reason to take a portion of work from the full-service firm.

Attorneys at boutique firms tend to enjoy collegial relationships with other members of the bar. In many cases (although it is not an absolute rule), there is little competition among firms for the same clients. An attorney at firm A refers his client to boutique firm B for the handling of certain immigration matters. Firm A has little worry that the boutique firm will take the client because the services offered by the boutique are limited to immigration-related work. The situation works in the reverse, too. Boutique lawyers refer out all work outside the firm's area of expertise. Other attorneys recognize that boutique lawyers are a good source for referrals. The result is that members of the boutique firm enjoy relatively cordial relationships with outside lawyers, without the complications brought about by fears of client-stealing or just serious competition.

Lawyers at boutique firms tend to take their work more seriously. Many are there by choice, and not just because they ended up there or needed to work there for the paycheck. There is less of an inertia factor—where people stay at a firm simply because they don't leave. Other lawyers at the boutique firm are likely to take your work more seriously than would comparable partners at a general practice firm. One immigration attorney noted that while at the general practice firm, immigration work was looked at as a necessity, not a moneymaking part of the firm, and therefore not accorded the respect paid to other groups. After joining an immigration boutique firm, this lawyer noted that immigration is the moneymaking practice for the firm and accorded due respect.

Just as the expectation factor is high for lawyers at boutiques, so too is the credibility factor. Clients, other lawyers, and sometimes judges, expect that boutique attorneys know what they are talking about and are aware of changes and trends in the law in their field of expertise. This is a terrific advantage if indeed you know what you are doing.

Some boutique firms, despite their smaller size, pay at or above market salaries. This may be due to the increased education level or specialized technical training that many boutique firms require of their associates. Some firms require that lawyers be members of particular organizations, such as the patent bar. Others require that the lawyers undertake significant responsibility working with or maintaining involvement in associations or national groups important to their field. The premium salaries also reflect the high demand for experienced lawyers in particular fields, like employment, immigration or patent work. (Many boutique firms have been hit hard by the exodus of lawyers to in-house or .com general counsel positions.) A boutique firm that has a comparatively small number of attorneys may pay more than general practice firms of comparable size.

Some associates at boutique firms believe that the quality of life is higher at a boutique firm. They point to factors such as the smaller firm size, a high level of respect and collegiality among the lawyers, and shared backgrounds or interests in particular areas of study. Several lawyers, for example, might have a background in genetics. This kind of shared expertise leads to relationships that have a dimension often missing from non-boutique firms where the only commonality might be their paycheck or family situation. The associate's overall quality of life, however, still appears to be shaped primarily by the particular group of lawyers with whom the associate works, whether that group is found in a boutique firm or not.

There are disadvantages or potential negatives for an associate to consider. An associate at a boutique firm is less likely to have the opportunity to experience and learn other areas of the law. The associate may be left with some lingering questions about fields of practice that might be more fulfilling. An associate may practice employment defense, but have a strong interest in healthcare. Once at the boutique firm, the associate will have fewer opportunities to combine these interests or explore another area of law entirely. On the other hand, it is not uncommon for an associate at a full-service firm to switch practice groups or gravitate from litigation towards transactional work. This ability to transfer or gradually take on other types of matters is not generally possible at a boutique.

The associate will likely have little experience in other disciplines, which might have provided a more well-rounded base from which to assess tangential issues in a client's legal matter. For example, it is only through experience that an associate might spot a potential antitrust problem in an intellectual property matter. This, however, is an instance where the boutique lawyer can draw on the strong relationships with lawyers outside the firm.

Another downside (depending on how you look at it) is that attorneys who have practiced for the same amount of time are not necessarily paid in lockstep. Prior experience is a factor in the pay scale, as are the other degrees or certifications that the attorney may hold. Again, this introduces a subjectivity factor that is not prevalent in full-service or large law firms (although this too is changing).

The future direction of the specialty practiced by the boutique may also be a drawback. Significant statutory or regulatory changes could eliminate the need for your work or limit the client base. There are some areas that will continue to expand—entertainment, intellectual property, employment, immigration are a few examples. However, history shows that all legal areas do not have the same staying power. When the federal government eliminated the RTC agency, all the work in the field was virtually eliminated. Keeping your eye on trends and understanding the impact of new legislation or case law is mandatory.

Partnership considerations should be evaluated earlier by an associate at a boutique firm. Boutique firms tend to remain focused by managing growth. Many specifically avoid rapid expansion. Because the partner to associate ratio tends to be higher at boutique firms, the associate's chances of becoming a partner are diminished. In addition, factors governing partnership decisions are more nebulous in a boutique firm. It is unlikely that there are written policies on these issues or a significant history of associates making partner, which presents some obstacles for an attorney coming up the ranks.

Law students often ask whether they should interview with a boutique firm after graduation from law school. The answer depends on the student's experience. Boutique firms want lawyers who, in addition to their J.D. degree, have significant work experience or advanced degrees. Many firms actively recruit Ph.D.s or Masters' level graduates. Even students with these credentials are not guaranteed a job with a boutique firm. There simply are not many first year associates at boutiques.

Some students are fairly sure about the area in which they want to practice and the boutique firm may be a good option for them. Before going to law school, one student worked as a human resources director. This person now wants to change the direction of his career and become an employment lawyer. He may have worked with or hired employment lawyers as part of his job and have a realistic view of what employment lawyers do. Scientists working in a corporate laboratory might attend law school and then work for a boutique firm to gain experience. Ultimately, they will be able to serve the corporation in an entirely new capacity. The experience gained at the boutique firm is one step for the scientist or technical expert. These people probably have a better idea than the average law student of what interests them, and the level of satisfaction they will derive from that work.

Aside from the students who have definite career objectives, working for a boutique firm right out of law school may not be advisable. You will never have the opportunity to sample other types of legal work that might be more interesting or fulfilling, and you may feel at a disadvantage as a first year boutique associate because virtually everyone will know a lot more than you do. While the same is true at general practice firms, at those firms there may be several others at your level or just above who also have little or no substantive knowledge. A boutique firm will not generally bring in an entire class of first year or second year lawyers.

Keep in mind that it generally takes a period of time to figure out what you do and do not do well. Your strengths might not be compatible with the work you are doing for the boutique. There is less opportunity for you to change practice groups and stay with the boutique. Although changing your practice field and your firm is always an option, you may not be given full credit by your new firm for the prior boutique experience. Other than choosing right the first time, one way to get around this dilemma is to find a practice area that is complimented by your boutique experience. For example, if you practiced tax work with a boutique, you might want to consider estate planning. You can turn your tax background into an advantage in your new job and negotiate for full credit to be given by the new firm.

A law student, or even an associate considering a move to a boutique, must take into account recent trends in the marketplace. Large firms (including those with a mega-firm mentality) are growing and staying competitive with boutiques by acquiring or merging with successful boutique firms. This move enables the large firm to eliminate strong competition in a particular area, and to heavily market the high level of expertise now existing within the full-service firm. In this situation, the associate loses some of the advantages of working at the boutique. There might be differences in how associates are trained, evaluated, or selected to work in the group. There is less control over the handling of clients. The number of people evaluating the associate for partnership has now increased, with less opportunity for the associate to know these other partners. It is wise to consider the merger potential and to ask questions of the partnership as to future growth and business goals before accepting an offer from a boutique.

Finding a job with a boutique firm requires that you do a few things differently. Remember first that true boutique firms value experience and knowledge and do not hire many first year lawyers. A review of web sites for various boutiques shows that marketing the "lengthy experience" or the "average years of attorney experience" is common. Don't get discouraged if your search takes somewhat longer or requires more legwork than you anticipated. It may also be that the boutique firm is a goal to which you aspire after you have practiced for a few years. If that is your plan, get good experience at a reputable firm and be sure of the area of law in which you want to practice.

That said, many lawyers rely on the boutique firm's reputation in deciding where to apply and interview. Good boutique firms are not plentiful. Lawyers at full-service or medium firms will likely have direct experience or at least knowledge of the big players for a given practice area. You may be interested in working for a plaintiff's labor firm. By asking around, you will likely come up with a short list of the boutique firms that enjoy a good reputation.

Another good way to find and target boutique firms is by using a headhunter. Some headhunting firms specialize in particular areas of law. These people are familiar with who is doing what and where. By talking with more than one headhunter, you may glean information about the reputation, level of satisfaction of

the attorneys, and other intangible benefits or drawbacks of working at a particular boutique. Ask these
headhunters if (and why) many attorneys leave a particular boutique. These headhunters have excellent inside
information that will help you in your decision making.

Once you have narrowed in on a few boutique firms,
focus your research on the firm's founding partners.
They, more than anything else, will dictate the culture
of the firm. Learn about the legal careers of these people. Make discreet inquiries into the temperament and
reputation of these lawyers. The smaller environment
of the boutique means that it is doubly important for
you to respect and tolerate senior attorneys.

Your interview with a boutique firm will focus on
your familiarity with and level of knowledge in the
area of law in which the firm specializes. You must
know what subjects are hot and what people are talking about in this practice field. This would include legislative trends, market trends and popular culture, if
that impacts this area of law. This is especially the case
if you are interviewing for a technology-related boutique. You may want to review industry newsletters or
magazines or search online at sites like vault.com,
which provide channels for finding out what is going
on and where. You also need to have a clear understanding of where you see yourself five and ten years
from now. Remember, people generally join a boutique
for specific career reasons. If you cannot articulate
those reasons in the interview, you will not get the job.

Given trends in law firm mergers, you may want to
inquire of the boutique about immediate or long-term
plans for growing the firm. Find out if limiting growth
is a goal to which the principle partners are committed.

Boutique firms are a good option for some attorneys,
but they are not for everyone. As in any job search, you
must know the facts and what you are about to take on.
Armed with this information, making the move to a
boutique may be a satisfying direction in your career.

# Chapter 14

# In-House Lawyers:
# Opportunity Knocking?

## What Exactly Do In-House Lawyers Do?
## Various Roles Held By In-House Lawyers,
## Including General Counsel of Small Company
## and In-House Lawyers in Legal Department;
## Considerations For Your Future Career In-House

The job description for an in-house lawyer remains an enigma for many law students and practicing attorneys. Most lawyers have at least a general idea of what an in-house lawyer does, but often this perception is so inaccurate or simplistic as to be built up into a "grass must be greener" idealization. Lawyers in private practice (also referred to as "outside counsel") use their limited experience working for in-house lawyers as a source for understanding what the in-house lawyer does. They may also rely on the frequent closed-door discussions with colleagues who are contemplating making the move to "greener pastures." What exactly do these in-house lawyers do? Are the pastures any greener? When should an associate start thinking about or preparing for this type of move?

An in-house legal department can consist of one lawyer or hundreds of lawyers. The *1998 In-House Corporate Attorneys: A Profile of the Profession*, a survey conducted by the American Corporate Counsel Association (ACCA Survey), shows that size ranges for legal departments ranged from one attorney to six hundred-seventeen attorneys. Approximately 21% of those responding to the ACCA Survey report that they are the sole in-house practitioner. About 38% work in a legal department comprised of two- to-five attorneys, 25% in departments employing six-to-twenty attorneys, and 15% in departments of twenty-one plus attorneys.

Ask an in-house lawyer what she does for a living and you will get answers ranging from the serious "we do everything" to the not-so-serious, "saying 'no' and 'I don't think you can do that'" as often as possible. The reality is that, a description of an in-house counsel's duties depends on the size and structure of the legal department, the prevailing corporate culture, and the legal and business roles held by the lawyer. In essence, an in-house lawyer's job is to understand and manage all formal relationships with the outside world for the corporation. Just how lawyers do this and the degree to which they are responsible for particular aspects of risk allocation, depends on the size of the legal department and whether the lawyer is functioning as "general counsel" or an "in-house lawyer."

Virtually all in-house lawyers struggle with certain recurring issues. For example, who is your client? The short answer is that your client is the corporation. To the extent, however, that the corporation operates and functions through the acts of individual people, the practical reality is that these people may also become your clients. Although your first and sole responsibility is to render advice with the corporation's interests paramount, such advice must be given to other individuals as if those individuals are your client. From a practical standpoint, the in-house lawyer answers to many clients, including individual shareholders or directors of a corporation, various departments within the corporation, as well as particular individuals within the corporation who actually wield power.

Sometimes the distinction between your actual client and your *de facto* client becomes an ethical dilemma. You may be asked to provide strictly legal advice with respect to a transaction that ultimately may be detrimental to the corporation from a business standpoint.

On the other hand, you may understand plainly what the business people want to hear, but such advice might be contrary to the best interests of the corporation. In these instances, after weighing the potential impact to the corporation's interests, you might consider expressing some of your concerns to the immediate superior of the person who requested your advice. Ultimately, corporate management may decide to override your objections, but again the company's interests are your first consideration and it is your job to voice your advice in the appropriate context.

Private practitioners generally perceive that in-house lawyers have "fewer" clients, and as a result, their work is less stressful. As mentioned, however, the in-house lawyer actually answers to a number of clients. Those clients are usually right down the hall, or perhaps in a neighboring building. As a result, expectations about response time increase. There is no such thing as avoiding or delaying a meeting with a particularly bothersome client, because the client is always within easy communication distance via phone, e-mail or personal meeting. It is too simplistic to surmise that client relations are less stressful because you practice in-house.

On the other hand, many in-house lawyers enjoy the advantage of having regular and continuing contact with corporate clients. They feel that unlike their experiences in a law firm setting, they are able to forge strong lawyer-client relationships with many individuals, which lasts as long the employment relationship lasts. Many of these individuals are eventually promoted or transferred within the corporation (which is analogous to the law school colleague situation), allowing the in-house lawyer to build a solid client network within the company.

The in-house lawyer's workload is generally high. Legal departments often operate on a limited budget, with few support personnel devoted exclusively to that department. It is the unusual situation to have a legal department overstaffed with lawyers. In-house lawyers report that you should expect to work a solid eight-plus hour day. Some attorneys in corporations report that their hours are similar to those of lawyers in private practice. Most state that while the workday may be shorter than private practice, the pace is more hectic. You may be busy every moment of the day, but you still leave the office at the end of the eight (or nine or ten) hours. You may also have more control over your schedule. You are not directly subject to court or discovery deadlines. You are not the one researching and preparing trial briefs throughout the night before trial (try not to feel too guilty about young associates killing themselves to get work done for you and your client). Instead, you are the one who can set deadlines and hire lawyers based on responsiveness and service. Many in-house lawyers manage their own daily workload and determine how much they can get done in a given day. In-house lawyers do not routinely work weekends or late nights. Just as with private practice, however, there will be times when extraordinary circumstances require enormous amounts of in-house attorney time. For example, a large loan closing or an FTC document request may require the input of the corporate lawyer throughout the entire process. When large matters do go to trial, the in-house lawyer may act as the client representative and attend each day of trial, conferences with the judge, as well as strategy sessions with outside counsel that could last well into the night.

In-house lawyers should understand where they fit within the corporate structure. How they are regarded by the people they represent in the corporation and the manner in which they are used by the corporate client is very important. It may be that the in-house lawyer needs to help others understand the legal department's role in the operations of the company. Everyone should know the capabilities of the legal department, as well as the qualifications and training of its lawyers. Instead of being the bottleneck when deals get shot down, clients need to know that they can work with the legal department to get the deal done the right way. Another aspect of knowing where the legal department fits into the operations of the company is by knowing the legal budget and the amount allocated for resources, training, continuing education seminars for lawyers, as well as anticipated outside legal costs. Having a direct say in the legal budget is valuable, particularly since you will have to meet the client's expectations for quality work within that budget.

In-house lawyers must understand and appreciate the difference between business versus legal advice. All of the advice rendered by an in-house lawyer (as with any lawyer) needs to take into account the business objectives of the corporation. For example, it may be less expensive to breach a contract than for the corporation to fully perform under the contract. In that case, the in-house lawyer is providing a legal opinion (the company's actions may or may not constitute a breach), but is also providing an analysis of the implications of a breach by the company. The lawyer may be asked to provide a strictly legal opinion (which necessarily factors in a certain amount of business knowledge), and omit advice on the course of action that the company should take. One general counsel reported that business executives do not always welcome what they perceive to be "business advice" from the legal department. Instead they want an analysis of the legal implications of an event or course of action, or a stamp of approval from legal so that the project or deal can move forward.

In-house lawyers have to be proactive about the resources available for their use and training. Most business executives are unable to find proper continuing legal education (CLE) seminars for an in-house lawyer to attend, nor may they regard them as necessary. In-house lawyers should seek out appropriate seminars in order to remain current on changes in law affecting the corporation, as well as new technologies that could make the legal department run more efficiently. ACCA, a good resource for in-house lawyers, is an in-house bar association comprised sole-ly of attorneys who practice in the legal departments of corporations and other private sector organizations. ACCA strives to help lawyers with continuing educa-tion matters, improve the understanding of the role of in-house attorneys, and advancements in the standards of corporate legal practice. In-house lawyers also use one another as a resource, probably much more than do lawyers in private practice. Often, the only research into advice rendered on an issue will be the experience of the lawyers in the department. There are also various employment or garnishment handbooks, as well as treatises on specific areas of law that provide at least a general answer for the in-house practitioner. The local courthouse or law school library is always available, and outside counsel will often allow clients to use the firm library.

A specific concern raised by many in-house lawyers is that they cannot fully research issues in order to ren-der advice to the client. Due to time constraints, they often research just enough to believe they have the right answer, and then move on without the additional checking the problem may require. For individuals who cannot operate in this matter, in-house practice is extraordinarily stressful.

Many in-house lawyers manage outside legal counsel or employ outside counsel to handle certain aspects of the company's legal work. For example, all worker compensation issues might be farmed out to an outside lawyer who is managed by the in-house lawyer. The in-house lawyer plays an important role in coordinating litigation on a national scale. She may provide the broad perspective that enables the outside lawyers to formu-late a uniform strategy. Or, because she is active in lobbying efforts or proposing legislation, she may be the person most knowledgeable about legislative changes that may affect the litigation or the company's position in those matters. She may also have experience litigating similar issues in other jurisdictions and can provide both legal and strategy advice to outside counsel. Finally, the in-house lawyer may have her-self litigated these matters while in private practice. In that case, she may opt to take on a more active role in the litigation.

There is significant pressure on the in-house lawyer to manage and control outside legal costs while ensuring that the company is getting solid legal assistance. In-house lawyers evaluate outside counsel on many factors, including value, reputation, responsiveness, and the ability to consider the business needs of the company while rendering legal advice. Simple things like returning telephone calls take on added significance for the in-house lawyer because the in-house practitioner, in turn, responds to various corporate clients who demand a quick answer. The in-house lawyer reviews legal bills and makes certain that they are accurate and reflect work actually performed for the company. When firms are billing high dollars for routine matters (like research regarding removal to federal court), the in-house lawyer should review the work performed and discuss the charges with the outside counsel's billing partner.

Your day-to-day work as inside counsel will vary with the type of position you hold. Many lawyers spend much of their day on the telephone dealing with vendors (or maybe creditors), and customers. Others work solely with marketing and field employees in guiding them through the process of bringing a product to market. Much of their work may be by e-mail or telephone. Some lawyers devote their days to approving contracts and making minor drafting changes to typical agreements used by the company, its vendors or clients. In-house lawyers generally do not track billable hours like law firm attorneys, but are generally expected to account for their time for budgetary purposes. Rather than an absence of billing requirements, there may be a more general manner of tracking your work and services performed for the company.

Not every lawyer is suited for an in-house position. Lawyers unable to manage many discrete tasks at once or daily answer questions on a wide range of issues would probably feel overloaded. Lawyers who feel frustration when they do not have time to find the "right" answer, but instead must rely on a good-enough answer will also have difficulty. Lawyers who cannot balance risk analysis with furthering business objectives will not succeed in the corporate setting. Another important skill is that the lawyer must have a facility in working with people of varying education and experience levels. Your clients might be the public relations people who want a slogan approved for use in marketing materials or assistance drafting a press release. Or, your client might be the vice-president asking you to manage outside counsel in evaluating a potential merger. These issues, as well as those relating to various employee problems or concerns, may all arise in a single day. As opposed to a lawyer in private practice, you may not have other lawyers to delegate to or rely on for assistance.

The financial incentives offered by in-house practice range from less than large-firm private practice to a potential for much greater financial or life-style rewards. Sources of remuneration other than base salary and benefits will likely comprise your financial package. Some corporations offer significant profit-based bonuses, better retirement plans, including contributions by the company, stock options, tuition reimbursement, or car allowances. Use care when evaluating stock options because this form of compensation may never materialize. Over time, however, many of these compensation sources may amount to significant financial incentives to join or stay with a corporation. More so than law firms, there is room for negotiation when it comes to compensation issues. You will find that smaller companies will be willing to discuss restructuring salary versus stock options or make other compensation arrangements. Your experience, of course, will be your number one point for negotiation, followed by your familiarity with a particular industry or type of product.

The opportunity for advancement is present in the in-house counsel role, although it is not as obvious as the associate-partner distinction. Your opportunity may be to move into a lawyer and paralegal management role, or the assistant general counsel or general counsel position. Alternatively, advancement may mean that you are taking on an increasingly larger role in the business affairs of the company, perhaps as vice-president. (Remember that titles mean different things in different corporations.) Another avenue for advancement may be a change in your duties to include a larger geographical area or more specialized legal work that is not farmed out to outside counsel.

Just as in a law firm, there may be varying levels of competition among the lawyers in the department. Some attorneys may angle to work on certain matters, solely for the exposure to top level executives or decision-makers. The same rules that apply to law firm behavior also apply in the corporate setting, e.g., avoid gossip or discussion about your colleagues. Human nature does not change simply because you are outside the law firm setting.

It was previously stated that the size and structure of the legal department, and your role within it, determines much of your daily professional life. Functioning as the general counsel in a small corporation is totally different than being a staff attorney in a large corporate law department. The general counsel's job almost defies exact description. So much depends on who and how many lawyers and paralegals, if any, you are managing. The role of general counsel varies from jack-of-all trades to that of manager. One general counsel referred to himself as "chief risk control officer," in recognition of his ultimate responsibility for managing legal relationships and allocating risk in each business deal undertaken or customer relationship entered into by the company.

The general counsel of a small legal department or one in which she is the legal department has significant business and legal responsibilities. The most important responsibility, as previously discussed, is to manage formal legal relationships of the company by controlling and allocating risk through written contractual agreements entered into by the company.

Another important general counsel function is to manage capital raising transactions. Particularly for small, fast-growing companies, the in-house lawyer might be supervising a "Series B" transaction in which a second round of financing is secured through private investors. A related function is to handle the sale or purchase of a corporation and guide that process until closing. The general counsel may work closely with outside corporate counsel, or may handle the transaction in-house. Either way, the general counsel will put in tremendous hours as these types of matters are brought to a close.

The general counsel will also handle routine and not-so-routine contract negotiation and revision. Many times, the general counsel has to improvise in order to close a deal. There is little time for research and investigation, particularly in a sales or electronic business. It is the general counsel's responsibility to ensure that the basics are covered and that the risk to the company by entering into this contract is worth the benefit the company will likely realize.

It is also the general counsel's job to manage and deal with employee issues. The lawyer will be involved in proposing and finalizing employee policies, and perhaps overseeing the process of preparing an employee handbook. The general counsel will enforce those policies and provide advice to the corporation on the best manner in which to mitigate risk and damage to the company associated with the hiring, firing or disciplining of an employee.

To the extent the company is involved in litigation, the general counsel will manage the process. All strategic decisions, pleadings, substantive motions, briefs, and settlement negotiations will first be approved by in-house counsel. Some in-house lawyers, particularly those with a strong litigation background, take a more active role in the day-to-day aspects of litigation matters. They may review pleadings and other papers—even routine ones—before they are filed with the court or served on opposing counsel. Many of the more involved in-house lawyers offer substantive changes to documents, and may attend or participate in depositions and hearings.

Another important function of the general counsel is to ensure regulatory or licensing compliance. Tracking licenses, permits or other corporate formalities is the responsibility of the general counsel, including maintaining and managing important legal documents (for example, operating agreements, corporate resolutions) for the company.

A corporate legal department with several lawyers can be structured in one of two general ways. The department may be centralized, with attorneys working in a group of lawyers and supervised by either the general counsel or a hierarchy of lawyers in that group. In the second model, the in-house lawyer works in a decentralized office where the lawyers work directly with a business group, and not necessarily in an office with other lawyers. The structure of the legal department, combined with other factors such as the size of the department and type and sophistication of the corporate entity are significant factors that shape your practice as an in-house lawyer.

Generally speaking, interviewing for an in-house position is more challenging and competitive than interviewing for an associate position with a law firm. Like law firms, corporations can be very selective in determining who they will interview. Legal departments are generally small and your ability to get along with others is absolutely essential. Unlike many law firms, there is less of an opportunity to move to a different department if the relationship does not work out. Because corporate legal departments do not suffer from the same level of high attrition common in law firms, and in-house opportunities are generally viewed as a long-term objective, corporations can afford to be more discriminating about their candidates.

Lawyers referred to the corporation through a known reference or attorneys with whom the in-house lawyers have worked will have a considerable advantage over someone blindly applying for an in-house position or one applying through a headhunter. Expect to be screened over the telephone by either a human resources person or a lawyer from the legal department. They generally want to check some facts about your experience and decide whether you can properly and clearly express yourself over the telephone. Because in-house counsel must communicate with so many people on a daily or weekly basis, basic people skills are required for the job. After the screening call, you may have an interview with individuals in the legal department, and then you might meet with non-lawyers in the corporation. The process can be lengthy because the individuals hiring you will want to ensure that you will be a good fit within the legal department and the corporate culture.

You are expected to have substantive knowledge about the area of law in which you practice, as well as a general exposure to matters that routinely arise in the corporate setting. Corporate lawyers have an advantage here. These attorneys routinely deal with the types of documents you will see as in-house counsel and understand corporate form and formalities. Unless the position is litigation-oriented (you will be managing national litigation or in charge of all outsourced legal needs), litigators with little or no corporate drafting, licensing or negotiation experience will have less of a chance of securing an in-house position.

Corporate officers who are not lawyers will have input into whether you are hired. Your interviews may progress from the lawyers in the legal department to the business executives with whom you will likely work. Expect questions from all these people that are geared towards their expectations of you. They will be assessing your ability to grasp a legal issue and provide a timely response, work with non-lawyers in significant business ventures, or have a general working knowledge of several areas of law. You may be given a typical scenario and asked how you would handle it and what advice you would give. You will likely be asked about specific situations in your career where you guided a company through a difficult legal problem. Your interviewers will be looking for a clear description of the facts, an identification of the applicable law, and the application of the law to the facts. Your recognition of the business aspects of your advice and how the company relied on your advice is an important item in assessing you. You may also be asked very specific questions, such as your view of the emerging issues facing corporations or attorneys practicing in your field. Be careful not to disclose or volunteer client confidences. In-house counsel will be especially sensitive to your ability to keep intact the attorney-client relationship.

You may need to adjust your resume and cover letter to reflect the particular requirements of a corporate legal position. For example, you may have both technology experience as well as a general transactional background. A Web development company would be more interested in hearing about your specific drafting, licensing or negotiating experience than about general corporate matters (although those will be important too).

Corporations are increasingly interviewing lawyers out of law school or in their first year of practice, but this is still not the normal route to an in-house career. This trend is driven partly by necessity and partly by current ownership demographics. The shortage of legal talent caused in part by an explosion in technology and dot-com companies (which frequently are owned or operated by younger principals) has not left this employer sector unaffected. For the most part, however, corporations are hiring lawyers for their abilities and training, and they generally look for lawyers with four or more years of private practice experience. There is little opportunity to teach and train new lawyers; corporations are just not staffed or set up that way. Corporations view technical training as the responsibility of law firms. They are reluctant to hire new graduates also because business people can be intimidating, and in-house counsel must have the ability to handle various types of personalities and to say "no"or "you can't do .that" with authority. A young lawyer fresh out of law school will not be taken as seriously as one who has been on both sides of the client table.

If you are pursuing an in-house position as a recent graduate, consider joining a legal department that is larger than five or six lawyers. That way, you will learn from the different styles and perhaps garner some training in the process. Nevertheless, before taking the in-house route, it is wise to take advantage of every opportunity to get practical experience. There really is no substitute for experience and as an in-house lawyer your experience will often be all you have to rely on.

For those younger lawyers who are contemplating an in-house position, use your first few years of practice to learn the substantive law in your area, determine whether your enjoy that work, and observe the in-house clients with whom you currently work. At your expense, you should try to get to know your corporate clients and how they operate. Make a trip out to the client's place of business and observe first-hand its operations. Talk with anyone willing to give you the time; you need to know how various departments work together. Network with other lawyers who ultimately want to practice in-house. You can learn from them as they go through the process and figure out whether you even want this type of practice. Just as with a law firm search, you need to target in-house counsel positions that will fit with your practice philosophy, as well as your skills and abilities. Importantly, work on learning to write clearly and simply. Writing well is an important skill in any legal position, but as an in-house lawyer you will have less time to re-write and edit. Learning techniques for organizing your thoughts before you start your final product will help minimize the need to rewrite. Clear and simple writing will better enable you to communicate with non-lawyers, which you will do virtually every day as an in-house lawyer.

In-house opportunities come in many forms. Making a good decision will require that you analyze numerous factors, some obvious, some not. Start with due diligence on the company. You may already perform work for the company because it is a firm client, so some of this research might be relatively straightforward. Gain an understanding of the company's business. Is the industry growing or is its future shaky as a result of threatened or pending mass litigation? Is this industry one that is increasingly subject to tighter governmental regulation or the object of strong lobby efforts? Is this business influenced by cyclical or seasonal changes? Will that affect your compensation? Are the products the company designs, manufactures or sells becoming obsolete? For example, the market for used equipment like that produced by the potential employer may be bottoming out because better technology is becoming less expensive.

Investigate the background of the principals running the company, especially if it is a dot-com or family run business. These people need to have the vision to move the company forward, but also the ability to accomplish and manage growth. This ability may come in the form of solid credentials or the principals may rely on people like you to manage the growth. The decision-makers of this company will have the greatest affect on your career—whether it is because they impact it directly by hiring or firing you, or because they make good business decisions. A start-up company might have a board of directors with little management experience. In order for this company to secure later rounds of financing or to be bought out, investors will probably want to see management replaced in whole or in part, which will have a significant impact on you. Use available on-line resources to determine whether the principals have past corporate ventures and whether those were successful.

Learning as much as you can about the general counsel is important because this person's management style will tend to trickle downward. How general counsel views the in-house lawyer role will determine how the business people treat the in-house practitioners. Whether the general counsel enjoys a productive and cordial relationship with the business people will also affect you, your compensation, and your job security.

The financial condition of the company may also be an issue. For a dot-com or family run business, ask to speak with an outside accountant about the financial health of the company. Public companies will have filed a Dunn & Bradstreet report, which will identify factors affecting the company's financial picture. Other corporate tax filings are available on-line. Any lawyer contemplating a move to become part of an in-house legal department is well-advised to investigate thoroughly the financials before making a final decision.

As you interview, try to get a feel for how the legal department is regarded by the non-lawyer managers. Ask non-lawyers what the attorneys in the legal department do well. Their perception of how the legal department is used and the importance of its role are important considerations for every candidate. The primary area that will be affected by management is the amount of money budgeted for legal matters, including work sent to outside firms. As firm salaries increase and law firms try to pass those costs onto corporations, the in-house lawyers may be expected to handle more and more matters in-house. The amount of support and administrative help you receive may depend on the value of your department as perceived by corporate decision-makers. Ask what percentage of the budget is devoted to individual attorney continuing legal education. The seminars that would most benefit you in your practice may be nationally oriented seminars which take place in a different city every year. Would the budget allow funds for you to travel for these seminars? Order treatises and updates? Arrange for access to Westlaw or Lexis?

Learn whether the work you will do as an in-house lawyer is related to the core business of the company. The amount of support, both budgetary and otherwise, will sometimes depend on how close you are to the main business. For example, if the corporation is a real estate investment company, there may also be a property management arm to the corporation. You will need to know for which group will you be providing legal services, whether the department is decentralized, and if you are being assigned to the real estate management division.

You should ask about the budgeting and payment for outside legal fees. Are fees paid out of a central legal budget or do business districts pay a portion out of their budget? If the latter, the districts might want more of a say in who is hired. The funding source may also impact your level of authority or accountability.

Every company has a corporate philosophy that guides or informs decisions. While this will be hard to discern in an interview, you can ask questions and conduct research designed to elicit information concerning the company culture or longstanding corporate values. How does the company treat customer complaints? Is there a customer service department that employs well-trained, courteous people (something you can probably determine on your own). Are union workers employed by the company? Will you be expected to deal with union representatives? What is the history of that relationship? If the company operates through various districts nationwide, ask how the legal department supports the managers or heads of those districts. In litigation matters, does the district have authority to move forward or settle the matter? Does the legal department regard its clients as those located in headquarters or also the district managers?

Ask questions of the attorneys in the legal department about resources that are available to you, both in terms of human administrative help, as well as library or computer resources. Ask whether they regard these resources as sufficient for the needs of the department and the likelihood of getting budgetary support if they are not.

Many in-house lawyers are expected to assist in human resources matters, or even handle small employee personal legal problems. These matters can be a significant time drain, and you should know the corporate expectations ahead of time. In addition, pro bono work among in-house attorneys is on the rise. Your corporation may have an unstated policy favoring or discouraging such activities. In either case, you should know the level and extent of your malpractice insurance coverage and ensure that whatever you are being asked to do is covered by the policy.

Consider whether there are any ethical considerations associated with your courting an in-house position while employed with a law firm. Particularly when you are a partner, you should be very careful about pursuing existing firm clients. There may, for example, be confidentiality concerns that would put the client in a difficult position if the firm were to inquire. The firm may have a stated policy or a written partnership agreement that specifically addresses this situation.

Before making the move in-house, ask for a detailed job description and reduce to writing some of the compensation or work-related promises made to you. You may be asked to sign an employment agreement, which may contain restrictive covenants. Make sure that everything you and the company have agreed to is listed in the agreement and that you can live with the effect of any restrictive covenants.

A lawyer new to the corporate organization should first learn the corporate structure and understand who is who. An understanding of the political winds will also help you pinpoint the true decision-makers. Titles can be deceiving and decision-makers may or may not have a title that is appropriate to their responsibilities. Find lawyers you respect to act as mentors. Watch how they handle the client, and learn diplomatic and creative ways to suggest alternative strategies to corporate management when its business behavior is legally problematic.

If you are the first in-house lawyer this company has employed, you will need to educate your client about your role, and how you are to be used. Equally important is for your client to understand what you don't do (personnel performance issues, customer complaints, or routine sales negotiations). Avoid the situation where the scope of your responsibilities is so broad that it would be impossible for you to fully meet the expectations of the CEO. If the company is young or the owners inexperienced, you may encounter some reluctance to share sensitive financial or sales information with you. (One general counsel referred to this as the "paranoid entrepreneur syndrome.") Corporate officers should be made to understand that legal advice is not an exact science and that the lack of information provided to you limits the advice you can give. Explain that it is important that you be made aware of all relevant information so that you can properly safeguard the client's interests. You should spend a few weeks, if necessary, reviewing all sales, employment, vendor and other contracts (including equipment and building leases) to determine those that are valid, obsolete or in need of revision. There may also be specific contractual duties that would fall within your area of responsibility—notice to the landlord of continued occupancy or license renewal dates. Ask whether any oral contracts are in force and determine the specific terms of those agreements.

Use all available resources as you try to get your bearings. Forge relationships with other lawyers in-house, join your local chapter of ACCA, and use upcoming CLE seminars as the learning tools they are meant to be. Making the decision to go in-house is one that should not be made lightly or quickly. So many factors will shape your career, most of which you will have no idea you needed to know about beforehand. Perhaps that makes the in-house move similar to accepting a law firm job—you learn as you go and hopefully through the interview process learn what you need to know to maximize your chances of a good fit.

# Chapter 15

# Raising the Bar

## Lawyers and Their Continuing Responsibility to Train, Teach and Lead; The Importance of the Mentoring Relationship for Instilling the Fundamental Values or Our Profession

The core values underlying the legal profession are not relative. They don't change with shifts in societal tolerance, nor do they apply to some lawyers and not others. Examples that have occurred in the political arena where lawyers point to past public service as "mitigating factors" to forgive their failure to uphold those standards simply aren't consistent with having basic standards governing the legal profession. What exactly are these fundamental values? How do lawyers learn them? Does anyone actually follow them? Does anyone actually care?

A thorough statement of ethical values is found in a work referred to as the MacCrate Report, which in reality has the not very concise title of *Legal Education and Professional Development—An Educational Continuum—Report of the Task Force on Law Schools and the Profession: Narrowing the Gap* (American Bar Association Section of Legal Education and Admission to the Bar 1992). The Report, which addresses the lack of training and competence of law students as they enter the legal profession, identifies the "Fundamental Values of the Profession" as follows: (1) Provision of Competent Representation; (2) Striving to Promote Justice, Fairness, and Morality; (3) Striving to Improve the Profession; and (4) Professional Self-Development.

These values are rarely, if ever, specifically presented, discussed or debated in the nation's law schools. Students study case decisions that might have a public policy element, or an opinion that reveals that the judges struggled with reaching a just result, given a particular fact pattern. Beyond that, few professors present these precepts as part of the duty binding every lawyer. It also doesn't happen enough in law firms. Teaching and mentoring are weighty responsibilities, and they are met with little enthusiasm when attorneys factor in the other demands on their time. When much of the focus is on winning and delivering results to a client, it is difficult to divert attention to something as esoteric as instilling values in a new lawyer. High attrition rates also tend to cause attorneys to be less committed to the development of younger lawyers. Partners and senior associates often invest time only in the superstars in the belief that these are the attorneys who will go the distance, making the investment of time in mentoring worthwhile. In addition, law firms place a high value on lawyers who can hit the ground running, resulting in little time being devoted to teaching the basics underlying responsibilities to the profession, the public, or to one another.

Regardless of whether these values are taught in law school, attorneys at all levels should internalize these precepts and strive to incorporate measures to meet and exceed these standards into their daily professional lives. A great deal of trust is placed in lawyers by clients, the courts, colleagues, and sometimes opposing counsel. Everyone who practices law has the responsibility of "raising the bar" in the sense of measuring up and exceeding the expectations of those who place their trust in a lawyer. Practitioners also have a duty to raise the bar in another sense—providing attention and mentoring to those lawyers around and behind them. This means "raising" them in the sense of guiding and training younger lawyers on how to become great lawyers. That is how lawyers learn the fundamental values underlying the legal profession and visualize ways to incorporate those values into their professional dealings. Mentoring is fundamental to the inculcation of these values into younger lawyers. It is important not only in the formal let-me-review-your-work sense, but also in the sense of being a physical embodiment of what it means—and what it takes—to be a competent lawyer who strives to promote justice, improve the profession, and consistently improve oneself. That's one of the ways younger lawyers learn. They watch their more experienced colleagues, expect to be guided by them, and corrected by them when necessary.

Necessarily, the mentor relationship is the appropriate place to first correct, rebuke or advise those who fail to act in accordance with those values. Part of the responsibility to other lawyers (and the public at large) is to help younger lawyers understand their mistakes and learn how to avoid them in the future. Many of the intangibles—a lack of maturity or inappropriate social behavior—are also matters that should be handled during the mentoring process.

Mentoring is significant for other reasons. Younger lawyers need to know how to interact professionally with other people. Attorneys don't just practice law, they run for office, pursue business careers, or volunteer in the community. Lawyers interact with other professionals, lay people and the public at large. Increasingly, attorneys are getting involved as business partners with clients. The level of trust from these people often determines how smoothly things go. In other words, how the public perceives attorneys affects their day-to-day lives in many respects. The reputation of the bar collectively often shapes others' perceptions about attorney skills, motivations, and their mores when it comes to doing business. Solid mentoring of young lawyers will eventually impact the collective reputation the public holds of attorneys, which will work to the benefit of individual members of the bar.

Much of this book has been devoted to providing straightforward thoughts on the practice of law in firms and corporate legal departments. There have been discussions on written policies, unwritten or unstated requirements, and everything in between. It is hoped that this book will fill a mentoring gap that is evident in the profession. This information can't be repeated too often (except the sections on billing). Some of the subjects addressed, like understanding what information is important as you make significant choices, or understanding the impact of your practice group versus that of the firm, or knowing when to seek out help, are all examples of mentoring advice that will enable students and lawyers to make better choices. A lawyer who has made good choices and works in an environment that is well-suited to his or her personality, skills, interests and training, tends to be a more satisfied lawyer. These thoughts are offered, obviously, in the hope that lawyers who are more satisfied and fulfilled will more likely provide competent legal advice and conduct their professional lives in a manner that will be a credit to the profession. The upshot is that each lawyer, including those new to the practice, has a moral obligation to teach, train and lead younger lawyers. Mentoring takes time. It takes patience.

An attorney who provides teaching, instruction and correction to younger lawyers should be motivated, at least in part, by unselfish reasons. Mentoring for an attorney's own personal interest is appropriate too. Senior attorneys want the lawyers working for them to be knowledgeable and skilled. Younger lawyers will handle firm clients and theoretically constitute the future leadership of the firm. The quality of the work product is directly influenced by those having input into its preparation. A good mentor, however, recognizes that having skilled and knowledgeable lawyers ultimately improves the profession, making everyone's job easier, and improves the bar's collective reputation.

A good mentor is patient with younger lawyers. Some people just don't get the big picture until they see and do things repeatedly. The mentor should take the time to point out why something is important, even for the mundane tasks like reviewing documents for privilege objections.

Another important attribute of a good teacher/mentor is someone who gives the benefit of doubt when it is appropriate. When an apparent mistake or error in judgment is made, the partner should not immediately assume that the associate has missed something. The younger attorney may have considered and disregarded the information. In addition, the supervising attorney should not immediately ascribe negative or immoral motives to actions taken by a subordinate attorney. An example is an associate who has given short treatment to a particular issue of law. Some senior attorneys will assume that the associate is lazy and looking for shortcuts. In reality, the associate may be uncomfortable with a particular argument in light of existing case law.

Good mentors are supportive. They recognize that sometimes more than simple instruction is warranted. Newer attorneys may need encouragement or confirmation that they've made a solid decision or taken the right step. Mentors should be thinking beyond simply marking up a document. Instead, they should focus on ways to improve the associate's overall writing and ability to convey ideas and facts.

Trust and credibility with others is also important. Young attorneys must believe that their foibles and mistakes will not be broadcast firm-wide. Those being taught rely on the mentor's discretion, which fosters a better atmosphere for learning and discussion.

Lawyers should understand that early mentoring from the start of a person's career is important. At many firms, it is the "promising" young lawyers or those perceived as truly talented who receive attention by mentors. The reality is that all new lawyers need this instruction and support, beginning from their first day.

Lawyers must be conscious that their actions, way of handling clients, or research and editing habits will be emulated by others, sometimes by lawyers with whom they have no contact. Often, senior attorneys hear that several younger lawyers look up to them, which comes as a shock to the senior attorneys. A mid- or senior-level associate or partner should always be mindful of the significant responsibilities she has to younger lawyers, even ones with whom she does not work.

Mentors should have a feel for when a younger lawyer needs to learn on his own. Sometimes the answer to a younger lawyer's question is, "Have you looked it up? If not, do so and then tell me what you think." Handling non-emergency questions in this manner is not cruel, but a way of teaching the less experienced that looking to the source first is absolutely essential.

Good teachers recognize that people will occasionally disappoint, and these teachers don't take these disappointments personally. When they feel let-down by an associate, they move on and continue to model suitable behavior and correct in appropriate situations.

A good mentor/teacher does not routinely over or underestimate another's abilities. Doing so only sets that person up for failure. Instead, they have reasonable expectations that take into account the younger attorney's abilities and aptitudes. These expectations may be high, but shouldn't be so high that they are unrealistic.

Attorney mentors must recognize that they too are fallible, that they can benefit from instruction and further learning. It is imperative that lawyers continue to learn themselves so that the level and quality of mentoring they provide is superior.

Knowing appropriate methods for correcting or rebuking subordinates is another hallmark of a good teacher. Mistakes or less-than-competent ways of handling matters should be pointed out in such a ways to prevent their repetition and to avoid similar errors. There's rarely a reason to yell or use unprofessional language. Being straightforward and stating with specificity what was unacceptable and how it could be improved is usually the right way to go. Subtlety is often lost on people; you may need to come straight out and tell the person that there's a problem. Many firms ignore "problem" associates until they go away— by joining another firm or leaving the practice of law altogether. Firms have completely and utterly failed associates who have left in these circumstances. Those responsible for the attorney's development should look on these situations as a direct failure on their part.

Mentors have an obligation to show newer attorneys the range of possibilities open to them, whether developing experience in a niche of the law, or demonstrating how far training and experience can go. The importance of "owning" your field, writing, and teaching others, is something that must be discussed with younger lawyers. This knowledge is not just absorbed, but ingrained and taught.

Opening the lines of communication, while cliched, is also important. The mentor needs to ask the younger attorney in what areas the attorney needs assistance or would like more instruction. On the other hand, the younger attorney needs to communicate to the teacher/mentor the areas in which the attorney has skills that need polish or deficiencies that need to be addressed.

Mentors should make available opportunities for others to see them in action. It may mean that time has to be written off to a client so that two people can attend certain events. Billing attorneys should factor in a certain amount of "lost time" as a trade-off for the investment in the younger attorney's training and development. Writing off time is certainly less expensive than having to pay a headhunter for a replacement after the associate leaves, citing inadequate training and mentoring as the reason for departure.

Practicing law is a privilege. As a lawyer licensed by, in effect, the people, it behooves all attorneys to be worthy of the trust placed in them in conducting the legal affairs of the nation. Practitioners do this by internalizing the fundamental values of our profession and then exemplifying them in our daily professional lives. They also do this by recognizing that each of them has an obligation to teach, train and lead other lawyers— an absolute must if they are to truly raise the bar.

# APPENDICES

# INTRODUCTION TO APPENDICES

The following appendices consist of a corporate legal department directory and a directory of various law firms throughout the United States. Students and attorneys are encouraged to use these directories as a starting point.

As noted in previous text discussions, cold calls or generalized letter writing campaigns are not as effective as sending letters based on your research of a particular group, firm, or attorney. Because information about law firms and corporations tend to go out of date, be sure to verify all firm and corporate information, including whether the relevant names are spelled correctly and that the contact information is still valid.

When it comes to applying for employment in a corporate legal department, the general counsel may not necessarily be the first person you should contact within the company. Take care to conduct some investigation about how recruiting matters are handled within the company in which you are interested. In addition, not all attorneys in a corporate legal department are physically located within the same office or city. In fact, some companies have a legal department, but nevertheless employ lawyers at other business locations in business groups other than legal.

# APPENDIX A
## LAW FIRM DIRECTORY – BY CITY

A city-by-city listing of over 450 law firms and their branch offices. See Appendix B (alphabetical list of law firms) for contact information, including website address, for the main offices of each firm.

## Alabama

*Birmingham*
Balch & Bingham L.L.P.
Bradley, Arant, Rose & White L.L.P.
Burr & Forman L.L.P.
Butzel Long
Maynard Cooper & Gale P.C.Ogletree, Deakins, Nash, Smoak & Stewart P.C.
Sirote & Permutt P.C.

*Huntsville*
Balch & Bingham L.L.P.
Bradley, Arant, Rose & White L.L.P.
Sirote & Permutt P.C.
Balch & Bingham L.L.P.

*Mobile*
Adams and Reese L.L.P.
Sirote & Permutt P.C.

*Montgomery*
Balch & Bingham L.L.P.
Bradley, Arant, Rose & White L.L.P.
Maynard Cooper & Gale P.C.
Sirote & Permutt P.C.

## Alaska

*Anchorage*
Davis Wright Tremaine L.L.P

Foster Pepper & Shefelman P.L.L.C.
Heller Ehrman White & McAuliffe
Keesal, Young & Logan
Lane Powell Spears Lubersky L.L.P.
Patton Boggs L.L.P.
Preston Gates & Ellis L.L.P.

## Arizona

*Nogales*
Fennemore Craig P.C
Peoria
Jennings, Strouss & Salmon, P.L.C.

*Phoenix*
Brown & Bain P.A.
Bryan Cave L.L.P.
Chapman and Cutler
Fennemore Craig P.C.
Gallagher & Kennedy P.A.
Greenberg Traurig P.A.
Hinshaw & Culbertson
Jennings, Strouss & Salmon, P.L.C.
Lewis & Roca L.L.P.
Littler Mendelson P.C.
Meyer, Hendricks, Bivens & Moyes P.A.
Morrison & Hecker L.L.P.
Quarles & Brady L.L.P.
Sherman & Howard L.L.C.
Snell & Wilmer L.L.P.

Squire, Sanders & Dempsey
    L.L.P.
Steptoe & Johnson L.L.P.
Scottsdale
Kutak Rock
Meagher & Geer P.L.L.P.

*Tucson*
Brown & Bain P.A.
Fennemore Craig P.C
Lewis & Roca L.L.P.
Snell & Wilmer L.L.P.

**Arkansas**

*Fayetteville*
Hall, Estill, Hardwick,
    Gable, Golden & Nelson
    P.C.

*Little Rock*
Kutak Rock

**California**

*Bakersfield*
Borton, Petrini & Conron
    L.L.P.
Littler Mendelson P.C.

*Brea*
Richards, Watson and
    Gershon P.C.

*Camarillo*
Burke, Williams & Sorensen
    L.L.P.

*Century City*
Arnold & Porter
Christensen, Miller, Fink,
    Jacobs, Glaser, Weil and
    Shapiro, L.L.P.
Crosby, Heafey, Roach &
    May P.C.
Gibson, Dunn & Crutcher
    L.L.P.

*Cerritos*
Atkinson, Andelson, Loya,
    Ruud & Romo P.C.

*Costa Mesa*
Dorsey & Whitney L.L.P.
Fitzpatrick, Cella, Harper &
    Scinto
Latham & Watkins
Lewis, D'Amato, Brisbois &
    Bisgaard L.L.P.
Lillick & Charles L.L.P.
Musick, Peeler & Garrett
    L.L.P.
Paul, Hastings, Janofsky &
    Walker L.L.P.
Pillsbury Madison & Sutro
    L.L.P.
Robins, Kaplan, Miller &
    Ciresi L.L.P.
Rutan & Tucker L.L.P.
Sheppard, Mullin, Richter &
    Hampton L.L.P.

*Fresno*
Borton, Petrini & Conron
    L.L.P
Littler Mendelson P.C.
Musick, Peeler & Garrett
    L.L.P.

*Indian Wells*
Best, Best & Krieger L.L.P
Quinn Emanuel Urquhart
    Oliver & Hedges L.L.P.

*Irvine*
Allen, Matkins, Leck,
    Gamble & Mallory L.L.P.
Arter & Hadden L.L.P.
Berger, Kahn, Shafton, Moss,
    Figler, Simon &
    Gladstone P.C.
Brobeck, Phleger & Harrison
    L.L.P.
Bryan Cave L.L.P.
Bullivant Houser Bailey P.C.

Burke, Williams & Sorensen L.L.P.

Cox, Castle & Nicholson L.L.P.

Crowell & Moring L.L.P.

Fisher & Phillips L.L.P.

Gibson, Dunn & Crutcher L.L.P.

Jones, Day, Reavis & Pogue

Lyon & Lyon L.L.P.

McDermott, Will & Emery

Morrison & Foerster L.L.P.

Nossaman, Guthner, Knox & Elliott L.L.P.

O'Melveny & Myers L.L.P.

Preston Gates & Ellis L.L.P.

Sedgwick, Detert, Moran & Arnold

Snell & Wilmer L.L.P.

*La Jolla*

Luce, Forward, Hamilton & Scripps L.L.P.

*Long Beach*

Baker & Hostetler L.L.P

*Los Angeles*

Akin, Gump, Strauss, Hauer & Feld L.L.P.

Allen, Matkins, Leck, Gamble & Mallory L.L.P.

Alschuler Grossman Stein & Kahan L.L.P.

Andrews & Kurth L.L.P.

Arnold & Porter

Arter & Hadden L.L.P.

Baker & Hostetler L.L.P

Barger & Wolen

Bingham Dana L.L.P.

Blatt, Hammesfahr & Eaton

Bonne, Bridges, Mueller, O'Keefe & Nichols

Borton, Petrini & Conron L.L.P

Brobeck, Phleger & Harrison L.L.P.

Brown & Wood L.L.P.

Bryan Cave L.L.P.

Buchalter, Nemer, Fields & Younger

Burke, Williams & Sorensen L.L.P.

Carlsmith Ball Wichman Case & Ichiki

Chadbourne & Parke L.L.P.

Coudert Brothers

Cox, Castle & Nicholson L.L.P.

Cozen and O'Connor P.C.

Crosby, Heafey, Roach & May P.C.

Davis Wright Tremaine L.L.P

Dewey Ballantine L.L.P.

Epstein Becker & Green P.C.

Foley & Lardner

Fried, Frank, Harris, Shriver & Jacobson

Fulbright & Jaworski L.L.P.

Gibson, Dunn & Crutcher L.L.P.

Gordon & Rees L.L.P.

Greenberg Glusker Fields Claman & Machtinger L.L.P.

Greenberg Traurig P.A.

Hancock, Rothert & Bunshoft L.L.P.

Harrington, Foxx, Dubrow & Canter

Heller Ehrman White & McAuliffe

Herzfeld & Rubin

Hogan & Hartson L.L.P.

Holland & Knight L.L.P.

Howrey, Simon, Arnold & White

Hughes Hubbard & Reed L.L.P.

Irell & Manella L.L.P.

Jackson Lewis Schnitzler &
Krupman
Jeffer, Mangels, Butler &
Marmaro L.L.P.
Jenkens & Gilchrist P.C.
Jones, Day, Reavis & Pogue
Katten Muchin & Zavis
Kaye, Scholer, Fierman,
Hays & Handler L.L.P.
Kelley Drye & Warren L.L.P.
Kirkland & Ellis
Kirkpatrick & Lockhart
L.L.P.
Knobbe, Martens, Olson &
Bear L.L.P.
La Follette, Johnson, De
Haas, Fesler, Silberberg &
Ames P.C.
Latham & Watkins
LeBoeuf, Lamb, Greene &
MacRae L.L.P.
Lewis, D'Amato, Brisbois &
Bisgaard L.L.P.
Littler Mendelson P.C.
Loeb & Loeb L.L.P.
Long & Levit L.L.P.
Lord, Bissell & Brook
Luce, Forward, Hamilton &
Scripps L.L.P.
Lyon & Lyon L.L.P.
Manatt, Phelps & Phillips
L.L.P.
Mayer, Brown & Platt
McCutchen, Doyle, Brown
& Enersen L.L.P.
McDermott, Will & Emery
McKenna & Cuneo L.L.P.
Mendes & Mount L.L.P.
Milbank, Tweed, Hadley &
McCloy
Milberg Weiss Bershad
Hynes & Lerach L.L.P.
Mitchell, Silberberg &
Knupp L.L.P.
Morgan, Lewis & Bockius

L.L.P.
Morris, Polich & Purdy
L.L.P.
Morrison & Foerster L.L.P.
Munger, Tolles & Olson LLP
Musick, Peeler & Garrett
L.L.P.
Nossaman, Guthner, Knox
& Elliott L.L.P.
O'Melveny & Myers L.L.P.
Oppenheimer Wolff &
Donnelly L.L.P.
Orrick, Herrington &
Sutcliffe L.L.P.
Parker Chapin L.L.P.
Perkins Coie L.L.P.
Peterson & Ross
Pillsbury Madison & Sutro
L.L.P.
Preston Gates & Ellis L.L.P.
Proskauer Rose L.L.P.
Quinn Emanuel Urquhart
Oliver & Hedges L.L.P.
Richards, Watson and
Gershon P.C.
Robins, Kaplan, Miller &
Ciresi L.L.P.
Ropers, Majeski, Kohn &
Bentley
Sedgwick, Detert, Moran &
Arnold
Seyfarth Shaw
ShawPittman
Sheppard, Mullin, Richter &
Hampton L.L.P.
Sidley & Austin
Simpson Thacher & Bartlett
Skadden, Arps, Slate,
Meagher & Flom L.L.P.
Sonnenschein Nath &
Rosenthal
Squire, Sanders & Dempsey
L.L.P.
Steptoe & Johnson L.L.P.
Stroock & Stroock & Lavan

L.L.P.
Thelen Reid & Priest L.L.P.
Tressler, Soderstrom,
   Maloney & Priess
Troop Steuber Pasich
   Reddick & Tobey L.L.P.
White & Case L.L.P.
Wilson, Elser, Moskowitz,
   Edelman & Dicker L.L.P.
Winston & Strawn
Zevnik Horton Guibord
   McGovern Palmer &
   Fognani L.L.P.

*Marina Del Ray*
Berger, Kahn, Shafton, Moss,
   Figler, Simon &
   Gladstone P.C.

*Menlo Park*
Cooley Godward L.L.P.
Davis Polk & Wardwell
Fish & Richardson P.C.
Heller Ehrman White &
   McAuliffe
Howrey, Simon, Arnold &
   White
Latham & Watkins
McDermott, Will & Emery
Orrick, Herrington &
   Sutcliffe L.L.P.
Perkins Coie L.L.P.
Shearman & Sterling
Sughrue Mion, Zinn,
   Macpeak & Seas P.L.L.C.
Weil, Gotshal & Manges
   L.L.P.

*Modesto*
Borton, Petrini & Conron
   L.L.P

*Newport Beach*
Barger & Wolen
Buchalter, Nemer, Fields &
   Younger
Clausen Miller P.C

Irell & Manella L.L.P.
Knobbe, Martens, Olson &
   Bear L.L.P.
Kutak Rock
O'Melveny & Myers L.L.P.
Oppenheimer Wolff &
   Donnelly L.L.P.
Stradling Yocca Carlson &
   Rauth P.C.

*Novato*
Berger, Kahn, Shafton, Moss,
   Figler, Simon &
   Gladstone P.C.

*Oakland*
Burnham & Brown P.C.
Crosby, Heafey, Roach &
   May P.C.
Littler Mendelson P.C.

*Ontario*
Best, Best & Krieger L.L.P

*Orange County*
Howrey, Simon, Arnold &
   White

*Palo Alto*
Baker & McKenzie
Brobeck, Phleger & Harrison
   L.L.P.
Cooley Godward L.L.P.
Coudert Brothers
Fenwick & West L.L.P.
Gibson, Dunn & Crutcher
   L.L.P.
Gray Cary Ware &
   Freidenrich L.L.P.
Heller Ehrman White &
   McAuliffe
Manatt, Phelps & Phillips
   L.L.P.
McCutchen, Doyle, Brown
   & Enersen L.L.P.
Morrison & Foerster L.L.P.
Oppenheimer Wolff &

Donnelly L.L.P.
Orrick, Herrington &
Sutcliffe L.L.P.
Pennie & Edmonds L.L.P.'
Pillsbury Madison & Sutro
L.L.P.
Preston Gates & Ellis L.L.P.
Quinn Emanuel Urquhart
Oliver & Hedges L.L.P.
Simpson Thacher & Bartlett
Skadden, Arps, Slate,
Meagher & Flom L.L.P.
Squire, Sanders & Dempsey
L.L.P.
Townsend and Townsend
and Crew L.L.P.
White & Case L.L.P.
Wilson Sonsini Goodrich &
Rosati

*Palm Desert*
Littler Mendelson P.C.

*Pleasanton*
Atkinson, Andelson, Loya,
Ruud & Romo P.C.

*Redding*
Borton, Petrini & Conron
L.L.P

*Redwood City*
Fisher & Phillips L.L.P.
Ropers, Majeski, Kohn &
Bentley

*Redwood Shores*
Burns, Doane, Swecker &
Mathis L.L.P.

*Riverside*
Atkinson, Andelson, Loya,
Ruud & Romo P.C.
Best, Best & Krieger L.L.P.
Bonne, Bridges, Mueller,
O'Keefe & Nichols
Burke, Williams & Sorensen

L.L.P.
Haight, Brown & Bonesteel
L.L.P.
Knobbe, Martens, Olson &
Bear L.L.P.

*Sacramento*
Arter & Hadden L.L.P.
Atkinson, Andelson, Loya,
Ruud & Romo P.C.
Beveridge & Diamond P.C.
Borton, Petrini & Conron
L.L.P
Bullivant Houser Bailey P.C.
Foley & Lardner
Gray Cary Ware &
Freidenrich L.L.P.
Jackson Lewis Schnitzler &
Krupman
Lewis, D'Amato, Brisbois &
Bisgaard L.L.P.
Littler Mendelson P.C.
Manatt, Phelps & Phillips
L.L.P.
Morrison & Foerster L.L.P.
Nossaman, Guthner, Knox
& Elliott L.L.P.
Orrick, Herrington &
Sutcliffe L.L.P.
Pillsbury Madison & Sutro
L.L.P.
Seyfarth Shaw

*San Bernardino*
Borton, Petrini & Conron
L.L.P
Lewis, D'Amato, Brisbois &
Bisgaard L.L.P.

*San Diego*
Allen, Matkins, Leck,
Gamble & Mallory L.L.P.
Arter & Hadden L.L.P.
Atkinson, Andelson, Loya,
Ruud & Romo P.C.
Baker & McKenzie

Berger, Kahn, Shafton, Moss, Figler, Simon & Gladstone P.C.

Best, Best & Krieger L.L.P

Borton, Petrini & Conron L.L.P

Brobeck, Phleger & Harrison L.L.P.

Cooley Godward L.L.P.

Coudert Brothers

Cozen and O'Connor P.C.

Fish & Richardson P.C.

Fisher & Phillips L.L.P.

Foley & Lardner

Gordon & Rees L.L.P.

Gray Cary Ware & Freidenrich L.L.P.

Haight, Brown & Bonesteel L.L.P.

Heller Ehrman White & McAuliffe

Howrey, Simon, Arnold & White

Knobbe, Martens, Olson & Bear L.L.P.

Latham & Watkins

Lewis, D'Amato, Brisbois & Bisgaard L.L.P.

Littler Mendelson P.C.

Luce, Forward, Hamilton & Scripps L.L.P.

Lyon & Lyon L.L.P.

McKenna & Cuneo L.L.P.

Milberg Weiss Bershad Hynes & Lerach L.L.P.

Morrison & Foerster L.L.P.

Musick, Peeler & Garrett L.L.P.

Pillsbury Madison & Sutro L.L.P.

Sheppard, Mullin, Richter & Hampton L.L.P.

Wilson, Elser, Moskowitz, Edelman & Dicker L.L.P.

Zevnik Horton Guibord

McGovern Palmer & Fognani L.L.P.

*San Francisco*

Allen, Matkins, Leck, Gamble & Mallory L.L.P.

Arter & Hadden L.L.P.

Baker & McKenzie

Barger & Wolen

Beveridge & Diamond P.C.

Bonne, Bridges, Mueller, O'Keefe & Nichols

Borton, Petrini & Conron L.L.P

Brobeck, Phleger & Harrison L.L.P.

Brown & Wood L.L.P.

Buchalter, Nemer, Fields & Younger

Bullivant Houser Bailey P.C.

Cooley Godward L.L.P.

Covington & Burling

Cox, Castle & Nicholson L.L.P.

Crosby, Heafey, Roach & May P.C.

Davis Wright Tremaine L.L.P

Epstein Becker & Green P.C.

Fenwick & West L.L.P.

Foley & Lardner

Gibson, Dunn & Crutcher L.L.P.

Gordon & Rees L.L.P.

Gray Cary Ware & Freidenrich L.L.P.

Haight, Brown & Bonesteel L.L.P.

Hancock, Rothert & Bunshoft L.L.P.

Harris Beach & Wilcox L.L.P.

Heller Ehrman White & McAuliffe

Hinshaw & Culbertson

Holland & Knight L.L.P.

Howard, Rice, Nemerovski, Canady, Falk & Rabkin P.C.

Jackson Lewis Schnitzler & Krupman

Keesal, Young & Logan

Kirkpatrick & Lockhart L.L.P.

Knobbe, Martens, Olson & Bear L.L.P.

Latham & Watkins

LeBoeuf, Lamb, Greene & MacRae L.L.P.

Lewis, D'Amato, Brisbois & Bisgaard L.L.P.

Lillick & Charles L.L.P.

Littler Mendelson P.C.

Long & Levit L.L.P.

Luce, Forward, Hamilton & Scripps L.L.P.

McCutchen, Doyle, Brown & Enersen L.L.P.

McKenna & Cuneo L.L.P.

Milberg Weiss Bershad Hynes & Lerach L.L.P.

Morrison & Foerster L.L.P.

Munger, Tolles & Olson LLP Musick, Peeler & Garrett L.L.P.

Nossaman, Guthner, Knox & Elliott L.L.P.

O'Melveny & Myers L.L.P.

Orrick, Herrington & Sutcliffe L.L.P.

Paul, Hastings, Janofsky & Walker L.L.P.

Perkins Coie L.L.P.

Pillsbury Madison & Sutro L.L.P.

Preston Gates & Ellis L.L.P.

Quinn Emanuel Urquhart Oliver & Hedges L.L.P.

Richards, Watson and

Gershon P.C.

Ropers, Majeski, Kohn & Bentley

Schnader Harrison Segal & Lewis L.L.P.

Sedgwick, Detert, Moran & Arnold

Seyfarth Shaw

Shearman & Sterling

Sheppard, Mullin, Richter & Hampton L.L.P.

Shook, Hardy & Bacon L.L.P.

Sonnenschein Nath & Rosenthal

Squire, Sanders & Dempsey L.L.P.

Stradling Yocca Carlson & Rauth P.C.

Thelen Reid & Priest L.L.P.

Townsend and Townsend and Crew L.L.P.

Wilson, Elser, Moskowitz, Edelman & Dicker L.L.P.

Wilson Sonsini Goodrich & Rosati

Zevnik Horton Guibord McGovern Palmer & Fognani L.L.P.

*San Jose*

Borton, Petrini & Conron L.L.P

Brinks Hofer Gilson & Lione

Coudert Brothers

Kenyon & Kenyon

Littler Mendelson P.C.

Lyon & Lyon L.L.P.

Ropers, Majeski, Kohn & Bentley

Thelen Reid & Priest L.L.P.

*San Luis Obispo*

Bonne, Bridges, Mueller,
O'Keefe & Nichols
Borton, Petrini & Conron
L.L.P

*San Mateo*
Stradley, Ronon, Stevens &
Young, L.L.P.

*Santa Ana*
Bonne, Bridges, Mueller,
O'Keefe & Nichols
Borton, Petrini & Conron
L.L.P
Haight, Brown & Bonesteel
L.L.P.

*Santa Barbara*
Bonne, Bridges, Mueller,
O'Keefe & Nichols
Musick, Peeler & Garrett
L.L.P.
Stradling Yocca Carlson &
Rauth P.C.

*Santa Maria*
Littler Mendelson P.C.

*Santa Monica*
Haight, Brown & Bonesteel
L.L.P.

*Santa Rosa*
Crosby, Heafey, Roach &
May P.C.
Littler Mendelson P.C.

*Stockton*
Littler Mendelson P.C.

*Tahoe City*
Hancock, Rothert &
Bunshoft L.L.P.

*Walnut Creek*
Littler Mendelson P.C.
McCutchen, Doyle, Brown
& Enersen L.L.P.
Morrison & Foerster L.L.P.

*Woodland Hills*
Arter & Hadden L.L.P.
Berger, Kahn, Shafton, Moss,
Figler, Simon &
Gladstone P.C.

*Ventura*
Bonne, Bridges, Mueller,
O'Keefe & Nichols
Borton, Petrini & Conron
L.L.P

## Colorado

*Aspen*
Holland & Hart L.L.P.

*Boulder*
Cooley Godward L.L.P.
Hogan & Hartson L.L.P.
Holland & Hart L.L.P.
Holme Roberts & Owen
L.L.P.

*Colorado Springs*
Hall & Evans, L.L.C.
Hogan & Hartson L.L.P.
Holland & Hart L.L.P.
Holme Roberts & Owen
L.L.P.
Sherman & Howard L.L.C.

*Denver*
Arnold & Porter
Baker & Hostetler L.L.P
Ballard Spahr Andrews &
Ingersoll L.L.P.
Brobeck, Phleger & Harrison
L.L.P.
Cooley Godward L.L.P.
Coudert Brothers
Davis, Graham & Stubbs
L.L.P.
Dorsey & Whitney L.L.P.
Faegre & Benson L.L.P
Foley & Lardner
Gibson, Dunn & Crutcher
L.L.P.

Greenberg Traurig P.A.
Hall & Evans, L.L.C.
Hogan & Hartson L.L.P.
Holland & Hart L.L.P.
Holme Roberts & Owen
L.L.P.
Jackson & Kelly
Kutak Rock
LeBoeuf, Lamb, Greene &
MacRae L.L.P.
Lindquist & Vennum
P.L.L.P.
Littler Mendelson P.C.
McKenna & Cuneo L.L.P.
Merchant, Gould, Smith,
Edell, Welter & Schmidt
P.A.
Morrison & Foerster L.L.P.
Patton Boggs L.L.P.
Perkins Coie L.L.P.
Reinhart, Boerner, Van
Deuren, Norris &
Rieselbach S.C.
Sherman & Howard L.L.C.
Snell & Wilmer L.L.P.
Townsend and Townsend
and Crew L.L.P.
Zevnik Horton Guibord
McGovern Palmer &
Fognani L.L.P.

*Greenwood Village*
Holland & Hart L.L.P.

**Connecticut**

*Greenwich*
Day, Berry & Howard L.L.P.
Robinson & Cole L.L.P.

*Hartford*
Bingham Dana L.L.P.
Brown, Rudnick, Freed &
Gesmer
Day, Berry & Howard L.L.P.
Dechert

LeBoeuf, Lamb, Greene &
MacRae L.L.P.
Morrison, Mahoney &
Miller L.L.P.
Jackson Lewis Schnitzler &
Krupman
Robinson & Cole L.L.P.
Shipman & Goodwin L.L.P.

*Lakeville*
Shipman & Goodwin L.L.P.

*New Haven*
Mintz, Levin, Cohn, Ferris,
Glovsky and Popeo P.C.
Wiggin and Dana

*Stamford*
Cummings & Lockwood
Day, Berry & Howard L.L.P.
Epstein Becker & Green P.C.
Jackson Lewis Schnitzler &
Krupman
Kelley Drye & Warren L.L.P.
Paul, Hastings, Janofsky &
Walker L.L.P
Robinson & Cole L.L.P.
Shipman & Goodwin L.L.P.
Winthrop, Stimson, Putnam
& Roberts

**Delaware**

*Dover*
Hudson, Jones, Jaywork,
Fisher & Liguori
Morris, James, Hitchens &
Williams

*Georgetown*
Hudson, Jones, Jaywork,
Fisher & Liguori

*Rehoboth Beach*
Hudson, Jones, Jaywork,
Fisher & Liguori

*Newark*

Cooch and Taylor

Montgomery, McCracken, Walker & Rhoads L.L.P.

Morris, James, Hitchens & Williams

*Wilmington*
Ashby & Geddes

Blank Rome Comisky & McCauley L.L.P

Biggs and Battaglia

Connolly, Bove, Lodge & Hutz L.L.P.

Cooch and Taylor

Cozen and O'Connor P.C.

Dilworth Paxson Kalish & Kauffman L.L.P.

Fish & Richardson P.C.

Greenberg Traurig P.A.

Klehr Harrison Harvey Branzburg & Ellers

Klett Rooney Lieber & Schorling

Marshall, Dennehey, Warner, Coleman & Goggin

McCarter & English, L.L.P

Morris, James, Hitchens & Williams

Morris, Nichols, Arsht & Tunnell

Obermayer Rebmann Maxwell & Hippel L.L.P.

Pepper Hamilton L.L.P.

Potter Anderson & Corroon L.L.P.

Reed Smith Shaw & McClay L.L.P.

Saul, Ewing, Remick & Saul L.L.P.

Smith, Katzenstein & Furlow L.L.P.

Stradley, Ronon, Stevens & Young, L.L.P.

The Bayard Firm

Tybout, Redfearn & Pell

White and Williams L.L.P.

**Florida**

*Aventura*
Buchanan Ingersoll P.C.

*Boca Raton*
Adorno & Zeder P.A.

Arnstein & Lehr

Becker & Poliakoff P.A.

Blank Rome Comisky & McCauley L.L.P

Bond, Schoeneck & King L.L.P.

Broad and Cassel

Buckingham, Doolittle & Burroughs L.L.P.

Butzel Long

English, McCaughan & O'Bryan P.A.

Greenberg Traurig P.A.

Hodgson, Russ, Andrews, Woods & Goodyear L.L.P.

McCarter & English, L.L.P

Milberg Weiss Bershad Hynes & Lerach L.L.P.

Proskauer Rose L.L.P.

*Bonita Springs*
Bond, Schoeneck & King L.L.P.

Roetzel & Andress L. P. A.

*Bradenton*
Holland & Knight L.L.P.

*Clearwater*
Fowler, White, Gillen, Boggs, Villareal & Banker P.A.

*Coral Gables*
Miller, Kagan, Rodriguez and Silver P.A.

*Fort Lauderdale*
Adorno & Zeder P.A.
Akerman, Senterfitt &
  Eidson, P.A.
Atlas, Pearlman, Trop &
  Borkson P.A.
Becker & Poliakoff P.A.
Broad and Cassel
Eckert Seamans Cherin &
  Mellott L.L.C.
English, McCaughan &
  O'Bryan P.A.
Fisher & Phillips L.L.P.
Greenberg Traurig P.A.
Gunster, Yoakley, Valdes-
  Fauli & Stewart, P.A.
Hinshaw & Culbertson
Holland & Knight L.L.P.
Miller, Kagan, Rodriguez
  and Silver P.A.
Ruden, McClosky, Smith,
  Schuster & Russell PA.
Shutts & Bowen
Stearns Weaver Miller
  Weissler Alhadeff &
  Sitterson P.A.

*Fort Myers*
Becker & Poliakoff P.A.
Fowler, White, Gillen,
  Boggs, Villareal & Banker
  P.A.
Harter, Secrest & Emery
  L.L.P.
Henderson, Franklin,
  Starnes & Holt P.A.
Roetzel & Andress L. P. A.

*Fort Walton Beach*
Becker & Poliakoff P.A.

*Jacksonville*
Akerman, Senterfitt &
  Eidson, P.A.
Foley & Lardner
Hinshaw & Culbertson

Holland & Knight L.L.P.
LeBoeuf, Lamb, Greene &
  MacRae L.L.P.
McGuire, Woods, Battle &
  Boothe L.L.P.
Rogers, Towers, Bailey,
  Jones & Gay P.A.
Squire, Sanders & Dempsey
  L.L.P.

*Lakeland*
Holland & Knight L.L.P.

*Melbourne*
Becker & Poliakoff P.A.

*Miami*
Adorno & Zeder P.A.
Akerman, Senterfitt &
  Eidson, P.A.
Arnstein & Lehr
Baker & McKenzie
Becker & Poliakoff P.A.
Bilzin Sumberg Dunn Price
  & Axelrod L.L.P.
Broad and Cassel
Buchanan Ingersoll P.C.
Carlton, Fields, Ward,
  Emmanuel, Smith &
  Cutler P.A.
Fowler, White, Burnett,
  Hurley, Banick &
  Strickroot P.A.
George, Hartz, Lundeen,
  Flagg & Fulmer
Greenberg Traurig P.A.
Gunster, Yoakley, Valdes-
  Fauli & Stewart, P.A.
Herzfeld & Rubin
Hinshaw & Culbertson
Hogan & Hartson L.L.P.
Holland & Knight L.L.P.
Hughes Hubbard & Reed
  L.L.P.
Hunton & Williams

Jackson Lewis Schnitzler &
  Krupman
Kilpatrick Stockton L.L.P.
Kirkpatrick & Lockhart
  L.L.P.
McDermott, Will & Emery
Morgan, Lewis & Bockius
  L.L.P.
Rice Fowler
Ruden, McClosky, Smith,
  Schuster & Russell PA.
Shook, Hardy & Bacon
  L.L.P.
Shutts & Bowen
Squire, Sanders & Dempsey
  L.L.P.
Stearns Weaver Miller
  Weissler Alhadeff &
  Sitterson P.A.
Verner, Liipfert, Bernhard,
  McPherson and Hand
  Chartered
White & Case L.L.P.
Wicker, Smith, Tutan,
  O'Hara, McCoy, Graham
  & Ford P.A.
Williams, Montgomery and
  John Ltd.
Wilson, Elser, Moskowitz,
  Edelman & Dicker L.L.P.

*Naples*
Becker & Poliakoff P.A.
Bond, Schoeneck & King
  L.L.P.
Buckingham, Doolittle &
  Burroughs L.L.P.
Butzel Long
Harter, Secrest & Emery
  L.L.P.
Porter, Wright, Morris &
  Arthur L.L.P.
Quarles & Brady L.L.P.
Roetzel & Andress L. P. A.
Ruden, McClosky, Smith,
  Schuster & Russell PA.

Stroock & Stroock & Lavan
  L.L.P.

*Orlando*
Akerman, Senterfitt &
  Eidson, P.A.
Baker & Hostetler L.L.P
Becker & Poliakoff P.A.
Broad and Cassel
Carlton, Fields, Ward,
  Emmanuel, Smith &
  Cutler P.A.
Foley & Lardner
Greenberg Traurig P.A.
Jackson Lewis Schnitzler &
  Krupman
Lowndes, Drosdick, Doster,
  Kantor & Reed P.A.
Shutts & Bowen

*Palm Beach*
Butzel Long
Edwards & Angell
Greenberg Traurig P.A.
Gunster, Yoakley, Valdes-
  Fauli & Stewart, P.A.
Hodgson, Russ, Andrews,
  Woods & Goodyear L.L.P.
Thompson Hine & Flory
  L.L.P.
Winthrop, Stimson, Putnam
  & Roberts

*Port Charlotte*
Becker & Poliakoff P.A.

*Port St. Lucie*
Becker & Poliakoff P.A.
Ruden, McClosky, Smith,
  Schuster & Russell PA.

*Sarasota*
Becker & Poliakoff P.A.
Ruden, McClosky, Smith,
  Schuster & Russell PA.

*Stuart*
Gunster, Yoakley, Valdes-
  Fauli & Stewart, P.A.

*St. Augustine*
Rogers, Towers, Bailey,
    Jones & Gay P.A.

*St. Petersburg*
Becker & Poliakoff P.A.
Carlton, Fields, Ward,
    Emmanuel, Smith &
    Cutler P.A.
Fowler, White, Gillen,
    Boggs, Villareal & Banker
    P.A.
Holland & Knight L.L.P.
Ruden, McClosky, Smith,
    Schuster & Russell PA.
Trenam Kemker, Scharf,
    Barkin, Frye O'Neill &
    Mullis P.A.

*Tallahassee*
Akerman, Senterfitt &
    Eidson, P.A.
Becker & Poliakoff P.A.
Broad and Cassel
Carlton, Fields, Ward,
    Emmanuel, Smith &
    Cutler P.A.
Foley & Lardner
Fowler, White, Gillen,
    Boggs, Villareal & Banker
    P.A.
Greenberg Traurig P.A.
Gunster, Yoakley, Valdes-
    Fauli & Stewart, P.A.
Rogers, Towers, Bailey,
    Jones & Gay P.A.
Ruden, McClosky, Smith,
    Schuster & Russell PA.
Shutts & Bowen
Sutherland Asbill & Brennan
    L.L.P.

*Tampa*
Akerman, Senterfitt &
    Eidson, P.A.
Becker & Poliakoff P.A.

Broad and Cassel
Buchanan Ingersoll P.C.
Carlton, Fields, Ward,
    Emmanuel, Smith &
    Cutler P.A.
Foley & Lardner
Fowler, White, Gillen,
    Boggs, Villareal & Banker
    P.A.
Hinshaw & Culbertson
Holland & Knight L.L.P.
Marshall, Dennehey,
    Warner, Coleman &
    Goggin
Ruden, McClosky, Smith,
    Schuster & Russell PA.
Shumaker, Loop & Kendrick
    L.L.P.
Stearns Weaver Miller
    Weissler Alhadeff &
    Sitterson P.A.
Trenam Kemker, Scharf,
    Barkin, Frye O'Neill &
    Mullis P.A.

*Taveres*
Akerman, Senterfitt &
    Eidson, P.A.

*Vero Beach*
Gunster, Yoakley, Valdes-
    Fauli & Stewart, P.A.

*West Palm Beach*
Akerman, Senterfitt &
    Eidson, P.A.
Arnstein & Lehr
Becker & Poliakoff P.A.
Broad and Cassel
Carlton, Fields, Ward,
    Emmanuel, Smith &
    Cutler P.A.
Foley & Lardner
Gunster, Yoakley, Valdes-
    Fauli & Stewart, P.A.
Holland & Knight L.L.P.

Kaye, Scholer, Fierman,
Hays & Handler L.L.P.
Miller, Kagan, Rodriguez
and Silver P.A.
Quarles & Brady L.L.P.
Ruden, McClosky, Smith,
Schuster & Russell PA.
Shutts & Bowen

**Georgia**

*Atlanta*
Alston & Bird L.L.P.
Arnall Golden & Gregory
L.L.P.
Cozen and O'Connor P.C.
Dow, Lohnes & Albertson
Epstein Becker & Green P.C.
Fisher & Phillips L.L.P.
Greenberg Traurig P.A
Holland & Knight L.L.P.
Hunton & Williams
Jackson Lewis Schnitzler &
Krupman
Jones, Day, Reavis & Pogue
Kilpatrick Stockton L.L.P.
King & Spalding
Kutak Rock
Littler Mendelson P.C.
Long Aldridge & Norman
L.L.P.
Lord, Bissell & Brook
McGuire, Woods, Battle &
Boothe L.L.P.
Nelson Mullins Riley &
Scarborough L.L.P.
Ogletree, Deakins, Nash,
Smoak & Stewart P.C.
Paul, Hastings, Janofsky &
Walker L.L.P.
Powell, Goldstein, Frazer &
Murphy L.L.P.
Robins, Kaplan, Miller &
Ciresi L.L.P.
Schnader Harrison Segal &
Lewis L.L.P.

Seyfarth Shaw
Smith, Gambrell & Russell
L.L.P.
Smith Helms Mulliss &
Moore L.L.P.
Stites & Harbison
Sutherland Asbill & Brennan
L.L.P.
Troutman Sanders L.L.P.
Womble Carlyle Sandridge
& Rice P.L.L.C.

*Augusta*
Kilpatrick Stockton L.L.P.

*Macon*
Arnall Golden & Gregory
L.L.P.

**Hawaii**

*Honolulu*
Alston. Hunt, Floyd & Ing
L.C.
Ashford  & Wriston P.L.C.
Cades Schutte Fleming &
Wright
Carlsmith Ball Wichman
Case & Ichiki
Case Bigelow & Lombardi
L.C.
Davis Wright Tremaine
L.L.P
Verner, Liipfert, Bernhard,
McPherson and Hand
Chartered
Watanabe, Ing &
Kawashima P.C.

*Kailua-Kona*
Cades Schutte Fleming &
Wright

*Waimia*
Alston, Hunt, Floyd & Ing
L.C.

## Idaho

*Boise*
Holland & Hart L.L.P.
Perkins Coie L.L.P.
Stoel Rives L.L.P.

*Coeur d'Alene*
Preston Gates & Ellis L.L.P.

## Illinois

*Aurora*
Wildman, Harrold, Allen &
 Dixon

*Belleville*
Greensfelder, Hemker &
 Gale P.C.
Hinshaw & Culbertson
Lewis, Rice & Fingersh L.C.
Thompson Coburn L.L.P.

*Champaign*
Hinshaw & Culbertson

*Chicago*
Altheimer & Gray
Anderson Kill & Olick P.C.
Arnstein & Lehr
Baker & McKenzie
Barnes & Thornburg
Bell, Boyd & Lloyd L.L.C.
Blatt, Hammesfahr & Eaton
Bollinger Ruberry & Garvey
Brinks Hofer Gilson & Lione
Cassiday Schade & Gloor
Chapman and Cutler
Clausen Miller P.C.
D'Ancona & Pflaum
Dykema Gossett P.L.L.C
Epstein Becker & Green P.C.
Fisher & Phillips L.L.P.
Foley & Lardner
Freeborn & Peters
Gardner, Carton & Douglas
Greenberg Traurig P.A.
Hinshaw & Culbertson

Holland & Knight L.L.P.
Hopkins & Sutter
Ice Miller Donadio & Ryan
Jackson Lewis Schnitzler &
 Krupman
Jenkens & Gilchrist P.C.
Jenner & Block
Jones, Day, Reavis & Pogue
Katten Muchin & Zavis
Kelley Drye & Warren L.L.P.
Kirkland & Ellis
Kutak Rock
Latham & Watkins
Littler Mendelson P.C.
Lord, Bissell & Brook
Luce, Forward, Hamilton &
 Scripps L.L.P.
Mayer, Brown & Platt
McDermott, Will & Emery
McGuire, Woods, Battle &
 Boothe L.L.P.
Michael Best & Friedrich
 L.L.P.
Neal, Gerber & Eisenberg
Ogletree, Deakins, Nash,
 Smoak & Stewart P.C.
Peterson & Ross
Pretzel & Stouffer Chartered
Quarles & Brady L.L.P.
Querrey & Harrow Ltd.
Robins, Kaplan, Miller &
 Ciresi L.L.P.
Ross & Hardies
Sachnoff & Weaver Ltd.
Schiff Hardin & Waite
Sedgwick, Detert, Moran &
 Arnold
Seyfarth Shaw
Sidley & Austin
Skadden, Arps, Slate,
 Meagher & Flom L.L.P.
Sonnenschein Nath &
 Rosenthal
Tressler, Soderstrom,
 Maloney & Priess

Vedder, Price, Kaufman &
Kammholz
Wildman, Harrold, Allen &
Dixon
Williams, Montgomery and
John Ltd.
Wilson, Elser, Moskowitz,
Edelman & Dicker L.L.P.
Winston & Strawn
Zevnik Horton Guibord
McGovern Palmer &
Fognani L.L.P.

*Crystal Lake*
Hinshaw & Culbertson
Querrey & Harrow Ltd.

*DeerField*
Bell, Boyd & Lloyd L.L.C.

*Edwardsville*
Blackwell Sanders Peper
Martin L.L.P
Evans & Dixon L.L.C.

*Hoffman Estates*
Arnstein & Lehr

*Joilet*
Hinshaw & Culbertson
Querrey & Harrow Ltd.

*Lake Forest*
Jenner & Block

*Libertyville*
Tressler, Soderstrom,
Maloney & Priess

*Lincolnshire*
Tressler, Soderstrom,
Maloney & Priess

*Lisle*
Hinshaw & Culbertson
Wildman, Harrold, Allen &
Dixon

*Peoria*
Hinshaw & Culbertson

Husch & Eppenberger
L.L.C.

*Rockford*
Hinshaw & Culbertson
Lord, Bissell & Brook

*Springfield*
Altheimer & Gray
Freeborn & Peters
Hinshaw & Culbertson

*Wheaton*
Cassiday Schade & Gloor
Clausen Miller P.C
Querrey & Harrow Ltd.
Tressler, Soderstrom,
Maloney & Priess
Williams, Montgomery and
John Ltd.

*Waukegan*
Cassiday Schade & Gloor
Hinshaw & Culbertson
Querrey & Harrow Ltd.
Tressler, Soderstrom,
Maloney & Priess
Wildman, Harrold, Allen &
Dixon
Williams, Montgomery and
John Ltd.

**Iowa**

*Des Moines*
Dorsey & Whitney L.L.P.
Faegre & Benson L.L.P

**Indiana**

*Elkhart*
Baker & Daniels
Barnes & Thornburg

*Fort Wayne*
Baker & Daniels
Barnes & Thornburg

*Hammond*
Locke Reynolds

*Indianapolis*
Baker & Daniels
Barnes & Thornburg
Bingham Summers Welsh &
    Spillman
Bose McKinney & Evans
    L.L.P.
Brinks Hofer Gilson & Lione
Ice Miller Donadio & Ryan
Locke Reynolds
Ogletree, Deakins, Nash,
    Smoak & Stewart P.C.

*Jeffersonville*
Stites & Harbison

*Merrillville*
Schiff Hardin & Waite

*New Albany*
Brown, Todd & Heyburn
    P.L.L.C.
Wyatt, Tarrant & Combs

*South Bend*
Baker & Daniels
Barnes & Thornburg
Ice Miller Donadio & Ryan

**Kansas**

*Dodge City*
Foulston & Siefkin L.L.P.

*Johnson City*
Bryan Cave L.L.P.

*Leawood*
Evans & Dixon L.L.C.
Lewis, Rice & Fingersh L.C.
Stinson, Mag & Fizzell P.C.

*Mission Hills*
Ice Miller Donadio & Ryan

*Overland Park*
Bond, Schoeneck & King
    L.L.P.
Blackwell Sanders Peper
    Martin L.L.P
Morrison & Hecker L.L.P.
Shook, Hardy & Bacon
    L.L.P.
Polsinelli, White, Vardeman
    & Shalton P.C.

*Topeka*
Foulston & Siefkin L.L.P.
Polsinelli, White, Vardeman
    & Shalton P.C.

*Wichita*
Foulston & Siefkin L.L.P.
Husch & Eppenberger
    L.L.C.
Morrison & Hecker L.L.P.

**Kentucky**

*Covington*
Brown, Todd & Heyburn
    P.L.L.C.
Dinsmore & Shohl L.L.P.
Greenebaum Doll &
    McDonald P.L.L.C
Taft, Stettinius & Hollister

*Florence*
Graydon, Head & Ritchey

*Frankfort*
Greenebaum Doll &
    McDonald P.L.L.C
Stites & Harbison
Stoll, Keenon & Park L.L.P.
Wyatt, Tarrant & Combs

*Henderson*
Stoll, Keenon & Park L.L.P.

*Hyden*
Stites & Harbison

*Lexington*
Bowles Rice McDavid Graff
& Love
Brown, Todd & Heyburn
P.L.L.C.
Buchanan Ingersoll P.C.
Dinsmore & Shohl L.L.P.
Frost & Jacobs L.L.P.
Greenebaum Doll &
McDonald P.L.L.C
Jackson & Kelly
Stites & Harbison
Stoll, Keenon & Park L.L.P.
Wyatt, Tarrant & Combs

*Louisville*
Brown, Todd & Heyburn
P.L.L.C.
Dinsmore & Shohl L.L.P.
Greenebaum Doll &
McDonald P.L.L.C.
Stites & Harbison
Stoll, Keenon & Park L.L.P.
Wyatt, Tarrant & Combs

**Louisiana**

*Baton Rouge*
Adams and Reese L.L.P.
Breazeale, Sachse & Wilson
L.L.P.
Chaffe, McCall, Phillips,
Toler & Sarpy L.L.P
Kean, Miller, Hawthorne,
D'Armond, McCowan &
Jarman L.L.P.
Lemle & Kelleher L.L.P.
McGlinchey Stafford
P.L.L.C.
Jones, Walker, Waechter,
Poitevent, Carrère &
Denègre L.L.P.
Phelps Dunbar L.L.P.

Taylor, Porter, Brooks &
Philips

*Covington*
Breazeale, Sachse & Wilson
L.L.P.
Kean, Miller, Hawthorne,
D'Armond, McCowan &
Jarman L.L.P.

*Lafayette*
Jones, Walker, Waechter,
Poitevent, Carrère &
Denègre L.L.P.
Liskow and Lewis
Onebane, Bernard, Torian,
Diaz, McNamara & Abell

*Lake Charles*
Kean, Miller, Hawthorne,
D'Armond, McCowan &
Jarman L.L.P.

*Lake Providence*
McGlinchey Stafford
P.L.L.C.

*Metairie*
Blue Williams L.L.P.

*Monroe*
McGlinchey Stafford
P.L.L.C.

*New Orleans*
Abbott, Simses, Knister &
Kuchler
Adams and Reese L.L.P.
Blue Williams L.L.P.
Breazeale, Sachse & Wilson
L.L.P.
Chaffe, McCall, Phillips,
Toler & Sarpy L.L.P.
Christovich and Kearney
L.L.P.
Deutsch, Kerrigan & Stiles
L.L.P.
Fisher & Phillips L.L.P.

Frilot, Partridge, Kohnke &
  Clements L.C.
Jones, Walker, Waechter,
  Poitevent, Carrère &
  Denègre L.L.P.
Kean, Miller, Hawthorne,
  D'Armond, McCowan &
  Jarman L.L.P.
King, Leblanc & Bland L.L.P.
Lemle & Kelleher L.L.P.
Liskow and Lewis
Locke Liddell & Sapp L.L.P.
McGlinchey Stafford
  P.L.L.C.
Milling Benson Woodward
  L.L.P.
Montgomery, Barnette,
  Brown, Read, Hammond
  & Mintz
Phelps Dunbar L.L.P.
Porteous, Hanikel, Johnson
  & Sarpy L.L.P
Rice Fowler
Sessions & Fishman L.L.P.
Sher, Garner, Cahill, Richter,
  Klein & McAlister L.L.C.
Simon, Peragine, Smith &
  Redfearn L.L.P.
Taylor, Porter, Brooks &
  Philips
Plaquemine
Kean, Miller, Hawthorne,
  D'Armond, McCowan &
  Jarman L.L.P.

**Maryland**

*Annapolis*
Linowes and Blocher L.L.P.

*Baltimore*
Ballard Spahr Andrews &
  Ingersoll L.L.P.
Beveridge & Diamond P.C.
Blank Rome Comisky &
  McCauley L.L.P

Hogan & Hartson L.L.P.
Littler Mendelson P.C.
McGuire, Woods, Battle &
  Boothe L.L.P.
Miles & Stockbridge P.C.
Ober, Kaler, Grimes &
  Shriver
Piper, Marbury,Rudnick &
  Wolfe L.L.P
Saul, Ewing, Remick & Saul
  L.L.P.
Semmes, Bowen & Semmes
  P.C.
Venable, Baetjer and
  Howard L.L.P.
Whiteford, Taylor & Preston
  L.L.P.
Wilmer, Cutler & Pickering

*Cambridge*
Miles & Stockbridge P.C.

*Columbia*
Linowes and Blocher L.L.P.
Miles & Stockbridge P.C.

*Easton*
Miles & Stockbridge P.C.

*Frederick,*
Linowes and Blocher L.L.P.
Miles & Stockbridge P.C.

*Greenbelt*
Linowes and Blocher L.L.P.
Whiteford, Taylor & Preston
  L.L.P.

*Hagerstown*
Semmes, Bowen & Semmes
  P.C.

*Rockville*
Miles & Stockbridge P.C.
Venable, Baetjer and
  Howard L.L.P.

*Salisbury*
Semmes, Bowen & Semmes
  P.C.

*Silver Spring*
Linowes and Blocher L.L.P.

*Towson*
Miles & Stockbridge P.C.
Semmes, Bowen & Semmes P.C.
Venable, Baetjer and Howard L.L.P.
Whiteford, Taylor & Preston L.L.P.

## Massachusetts

*Boston*
Bingham Dana L.L.P.
Brown, Rudnick, Freed & Gesmer
Burns & Levinson L.L.P.
Choate, Hall & Stewart
Day, Berry & Howard L.L.P.
Dechert
Eckert Seamans Cherin & Mellott L.L.C.
Edwards & Angell
Epstein Becker & Green P.C.
Fish & Richardson P.C.
Foley, Hoag & Eliot L.L.P.
Goodwin, Procter & Hoar L.L.P.
Goulston & Storrs P.C.
Greenberg Traurig P.A.
Hale and Dorr L.L.P.
Hill & Barlow, P.C.
Hinckley, Allen & Snyder
Holland & Knight L.L.P.
Hutchins, Wheeler & Dittmar
Jackson Lewis Schnitzler & Krupman
Kirkpatrick & Lockhart L.L.P.
LeBoeuf, Lamb, Greene & MacRae L.L.P.
McDermott, Will & Emery

Mintz, Levin, Cohn, Ferris, Glovsky and Popeo P.C.
Morrison, Mahoney & Miller L.L.P.
Nixon Peabody L.L.P.
Nutter, McClennen & Fish L.L.P.
Palmer & Dodge L.L.P.
Robins, Kaplan, Miller & Ciresi L.L.P.
Robinson & Cole L.L.P.
Ropes & Gray
Schnader Harrison Segal & Lewis L.L.P.
Seyfarth Shaw
Skadden, Arps, Slate, Meagher & Flom L.L.P.
Sullivan & Worcester L.L.P.
Testa, Hurwitz & Thibeault L.L.P.
Zevnik Horton Guibord McGovern Palmer & Fognani L.L.P.

*Hingham*
Burns & Levinson L.L.P.

*Hyannis*
Nutter, McClennen & Fish L.L.P.

*Springfield*
Morrison, Mahoney & Miller L.L.P.

*Wellesley*
Burns & Levinson L.L.P.
Hale and Dorr L.L.P.

*Worcester*
Morrison, Mahoney & Miller L.L.P.

## Michigan

*Ann Arbor*
Bodman, Longley & Dahling LLP

Brinks Hofer Gilson & Lione
Butzel Long
Dickinson Wright P.L.L.C.
Dykema Gossett P.L.L.C
Miller, Canfield, Paddock
and Stone P.L.C.
Plunkett & Cooney P.C.

*Bloomfield*
Dickinson Wright P.L.L.C.
Dykema Gossett P.L.L.C
Plunkett & Cooney P.C.

*Bloomington*
Larkin, Hoffman, Daly &
Lindgren

*Birmingham*
Clark Hill P.L.C.

*Cheboygan*
Bodman, Longley & Dahling
LLP

*Detroit*
Bodman, Longley & Dahling
LLP
Butzel Long
Clark Hill P.L.C.
Dickinson Wright P.L.L.C.
Dykema Gossett P.L.L.C.
Honigman Miller Schwartz
and Cohn
Jaffe, Raitt, Heuer & Weiss,
P.C.
Miller, Canfield, Paddock
and Stone P.L.C.
Pepper Hamilton L.L.P.
Plunkett & Cooney P.C.
Williams, Mullen, Clark &
Dobbins P.C.

*Flint*
Plunkett & Cooney P.C.

*Gaylord*
Plunkett & Cooney P.C.

Grand Haven
Varnum, Riddering, Schmidt
& Howlett L.L.P.

*Grand Rapids*
Dickinson Wright P.L.L.C.
Dykema Gossett P.L.L.C
Miller, Canfield, Paddock
and Stone P.L.C.
Miller, Johnson, Snell &
Cummiskey P.L.C.
Plunkett & Cooney P.C.
Varnum, Riddering, Schmidt
& Howlett L.L.P.
Waller Lansden Dortch &
Davis P.L.L.C.

*Grosse Point*
Butzel Long

*Holland*
Warner Norcross & Judd
L.L.P.

*Howell*
Miller, Canfield, Paddock
and Stone P.L.C.

*Kalamazoo*
Miller, Canfield, Paddock
and Stone P.L.C.
Miller, Johnson, Snell &
Cummiskey P.L.C.
Plunkett & Cooney P.C.
Varnum, Riddering, Schmidt
& Howlett L.L.P.

*Lansing*
Butzel Long
Clark Hill P.L.C.
Dickinson Wright P.L.L.C.
Dykema Gossett P.L.L.C
Honigman Miller Schwartz
and Cohn
Miller, Canfield, Paddock
and Stone P.L.C.
Plunkett & Cooney P.C.

Varnum, Riddering, Schmidt
& Howlett L.L.P.

*Marquette*
Plunkett & Cooney P.C.

*Monroe*
Miller, Canfield, Paddock
and Stone P.L.C.

*Mount Clemens*
Plunkett & Cooney P.C.

*Muskegon*
Warner Norcross & Judd
L.L.P.

*Petoskey*
Plunkett & Cooney P.C.

*Southfield*
Warner Norcross & Judd
L.L.P.

*Troy*
Bodman, Longley & Dahling
LLP
Miller, Canfield, Paddock
and Stone P.L.C.

**Minnesota**

*Minneapolis*
Briggs and Morgan P.A.
Dorsey & Whitney L.L.P.
Faegre & Benson L.L.P.
Fish & Richardson P.C.
Fredrikson & Byron P.A.
Fulbright & Jaworski L.L.P.
Gray Plant Mooty Mooty &
Bennett P.A.
Hinshaw & Culbertson
Jackson Lewis Schnitzler &
Krupman
Leonard, Street and Deinard
P.A.
Lindquist & Vennum
P.L.L.P.
Littler Mendelson P.C.

Meagher & Geer P.L.L.P.
Merchant, Gould, Smith,
Edell, Welter & Schmidt
P.A.
Oppenheimer Wolff &
Donnelly L.L.P.
Rider, Bennett, Egan &
Arundel L.L.P.
Robins, Kaplan, Miller &
Ciresi L.L.P.

*Mankato*
Leonard, Street and Deinard
P.A.

*Rochester*
Dorsey & Whitney L.L.P.

*Saint Paul*
Briggs and Morgan P.A.
Leonard, Street and Deinard
P.A.
Lindquist & Vennum
P.L.L.P.
Robins, Kaplan, Miller &
Ciresi L.L.P.

**Mississippi**

*Gulfport*
Butler, Snow, O'Mara,
Stevens & Cannada, PLC
Deutsch, Kerrigan & Stiles
L.L.P.

*Jackson*
Adams and Reese L.L.P.
Baker, Donelson, Bearman &
Caldwell P.C.
Butler, Snow, O'Mara,
Stevens & Cannada, PLC
McGlinchey Stafford
P.L.L.C.
Phelps Dunbar L.L.P.

*Tupelo*
Phelps Dunbar L.L.P.

## Missouri

*Jefferson City*
Armstrong Teasdale L.L.P.
Bryan Cave L.L.P.
Husch & Eppenberger
    L.L.C.
Polsinelli, White, Vardeman
    & Shalton P.C.

*Kansas City*
Armstrong Teasdale L.L.P.
Blackwell Sanders Peper
    Martin L.L.P.
Bryan Cave L.L.P.
Evans & Dixon L.L.C.
Husch & Eppenberger
    L.L.C.
Kutak Rock
Lathrop & Gage L.C.
Lewis, Rice & Fingersh L.C.
Morrison & Hecker L.L.P.
Polsinelli, White, Vardeman
    & Shalton P.C.
Shook, Hardy & Bacon
    L.L.P.
Sonnenschein Nath &
    Rosenthal
Stinson, Mag & Fizzell P.C.

*Springfield*
Blackwell Sanders Peper
    Martin L.L.P
Husch & Eppenberger
    L.L.C.

*St. Louis*
Armstrong Teasdale L.L.P.
Blackwell Sanders Peper
    Martin L.L.P
Bryan Cave L.L.P.
Evans & Dixon L.L.C.
Greensfelder, Hemker &
    Gale P.C.
Hinshaw & Culbertson
Husch & Eppenberger
    L.L.C.

Lewis, Rice & Fingersh L.C.
Polsinelli, White, Vardeman
    & Shalton P.C.
Sonnenschein Nath &
    Rosenthal
Stinson, Mag & Fizzell P.C.
Thompson Coburn L.L.P.

## Montana

*Billings*
Crowley, Haughey, Hanson,
    Toole & Dietrich P.L.L.P.
Holland & Hart L.L.P.

*Bozeman*
Crowley, Haughey, Hanson,
    Toole & Dietrich P.L.L.P

*Great Falls*
Dorsey & Whitney L.L.P.

*Helena*
Crowley, Haughey, Hanson,
    Toole & Dietrich P.L.L.P

*Kalispell*
Crowley, Haughey, Hanson,
    Toole & Dietrich P.L.L.P

*Missoula*
Dorsey & Whitney L.L.P.

## Nebraska

*Lincoln*
Kutak Rock

*Omaha*
Blackwell Sanders Peper
    Martin L.L.P
Kutak Rock
Stinson, Mag & Fizzell P.C.

## Nevada

*Las Vegas*
Cozen and O'Connor P.C.
Lewis & Roca L.L.P.

Lionel Sawyer & Collins
Littler Mendelson P.C.
Sherman & Howard L.L.C.
Verner, Liipfert, Bernhard,
McPherson and Hand
Chartered

*Reno*
Lionel Sawyer & Collins
Littler Mendelson P.C.
Sherman & Howard L.L.C.

**New Hampshire**

*Manchester*
Choate, Hall & Stewart

**New Jersey**

*Atlantic City*
Fox, Rothschild, O'Brien &
Frankel, L.L.P.
Sills Cummis Radin
Tischman Epstein &
Gross P.A.

*Camden*
Ballard Spahr Andrews &
Ingersoll L.L.P.
Wolf, Block, Schorr and
Solis-Cohen L.L.P.

*Cherry Hill*
Blank Rome Comisky &
McCauley L.L.P
Cozen and O'Connor P.C.
Dilworth Paxson Kalish &
Kauffman L.L.P.
Klehr Harrison Harvey
Branzburg & Ellers
Klett Rooney Lieber &
Schorling
Marshall, Dennehey,
Warner, Coleman &
Goggin
McCarter & English, L.L.P
Montgomery, McCracken,
Walker & Rhoads L.L.P.

Obermayer Rebmann
Maxwell & Hippel L.L.P.
Pepper Hamilton L.L.P.
Schnader Harrison Segal &
Lewis L.L.P.
Stradley, Ronon, Stevens &
Young, L.L.P.

*Eatontown*
Wilentz, Goldman & Spitzer

*Flemington*
Archer & Greiner

*Florham Park*
Drinker Biddle & Reath
L.L.P.

*Hackensack*
Cole, Schotz, Meisel,
Forman & Leonard, P.C.
Parker Chapin L.L.P.

*Haddonfield*
Archer & Greiner
Eckert Seamans Cherin &
Mellott L.L.C.

*Jersey City*
Thacher Proffitt & Wood

*Lawrenceville*
Fox, Rothschild, O'Brien &
Frankel, L.L.P.
Thorp, Reed & Armstrong

*Livingston*
Marshall, Dennehey,
Warner, Coleman &
Goggin
Vedder, Price, Kaufman &
Kammholz

*Morristown*
Jackson Lewis Schnitzler &
Krupman
Littler Mendelson P.C.
Pitney, Hardin, Kipp &
Szuch L.L.P.

Riker, Danzig, Scherer,
Hyland & Perretti L.L.P.
Thelen Reid & Priest L.L.P.

*Newark*
Anderson Kill & Olick P.C.
Clausen Miller P.C.
Cozen and O'Connor P.C.
Cullen & Dykman
Curtis, Mallet-Prevost, Colt
& Mosle
Epstein Becker & Green P.C.
Gibbons, Del Deo, Dolan,
Griffinger & Vecchione
P.C.
Herzfeld & Rubin
Kirkpatrick & Lockhart
L.L.P.
Latham & Watkins
LeBoeuf, Lamb, Greene &
MacRae L.L.P.
McCarter & English, L.L.P
Mendes & Mount L.L.P.
Proskauer Rose L.L.P.
Reed Smith Shaw & McClay
L.L.P.
Rosenman & Colin L.L.P.
Sills Cummis Radin
Tischman Epstein &
Gross P.A.
Skadden, Arps, Slate,
Meagher & Flom L.L.P.
Tressler, Soderstrom,
Maloney & Priess
Wilson, Elser, Moskowitz,
Edelman & Dicker L.L.P.

*Parsippany*
Kelley Drye & Warren L.L.P.

*Princeton*
Archer & Greiner
Buchanan Ingersoll P.C.
Dechert
Drinker Biddle & Reath L.L.P.
Morgan, Lewis & Bockius
L.L.P.

Reed Smith Shaw & McClay
L.L.P.
Saul, Ewing, Remick & Saul
L.L.P.

*Roseland*
Greenbaum, Rowe, Smith,
Ravin, Davis & Himmel
L.L.P.
Lowenstein Sandler P.C.

*Saddle Brook*
Beveridge & Diamond P.C.

*Short Hills*
Edwards & Angell

*Trenton*
Blank Rome Comisky &
McCauley L.L.P
Riker, Danzig, Scherer,
Hyland & Perretti L.L.P.

*Turnerville*
Dilworth Paxson Kalish &
Kauffman L.L.P.

*Vorhees*
Ballard Spahr Andrews &
Ingersoll L.L.P.
Fox, Rothschild, O'Brien &
Frankel, L.L.P.

*Westmont*
Margolis Edelstein
White and Williams L.L.P.

*Woodbridge*
Greenbaum, Rowe, Smith,
Ravin, Davis & Himmel
L.L.P.
Wilentz, Goldman & Spitzer

*Woodcliff Lake*
Zevnik Horton Guibord
McGovern Palmer &
Fognani L.L.P.

**New Mexico**

*Albuquerque*
Rodey, Dickason, Sloan,
Akin & Robb P.A.

**New York**

*Albany*
Bond, Schoeneck & King
L.L.P.
Harris Beach & Wilcox
L.L.P.
Harter, Secrest & Emery
L.L.P.
Hodgson, Russ, Andrews,
Woods & Goodyear L.L.P.
Hunton & Williams
LeBoeuf, Lamb, Greene &
MacRae L.L.P.
Wilson, Elser, Moskowitz,
Edelman & Dicker L.L.P.

*Brooklyn*
Cullen & Dykman

*Buffalo*
Bond, Schoeneck & King
L.L.P.
Buchanan Ingersoll P.C.
Harris Beach & Wilcox
L.L.P.
Harter, Secrest & Emery
L.L.P.
Hodgson, Russ, Andrews,
Woods & Goodyear L.L.P.
Phillips, Lytle, Hitchcock,
Blaine & Huber L.L.P.
Saperston & Day P.C.

*East Aurora*
Saperston & Day P.C.

*Fredonia*
Phillips, Lytle, Hitchcock,
Blaine & Huber L.L.P.

*Garden City*
Cullen & Dykman

*Great Neck*
Parker Chapin L.L.P.

*Ithaca*
Harris Beach & Wilcox
L.L.P.

*Jamestown*
Phillips, Lytle, Hitchcock,
Blaine & Huber L.L.P.

*New York*
Akin, Gump, Strauss, Hauer
& Feld L.L.P.
Anderson Kill & Olick P.C.
Arent Fox Kintner Plotkin &
Kahn P.L.L.C.
Arnold & Porter
Baer Marks & Upham L.L.P.
Baker & Botts L.L.P
Baker & McKenzie
Barger & Wolen
Beveridge & Diamond P.C.
Bingham Dana L.L.P.
Blank Rome Comisky &
McCauley L.L.P
Blatt, Hammesfahr & Eaton
Brobeck, Phleger & Harrison
L.L.P.
Brown & Wood L.L.P.
Bryan Cave L.L.P.
Buchanan Ingersoll P.C.
Cadwalader, Wickersham &
Taft
Cahill Gordon & Reindel
Carter, Ledyard & Milburn
Chadbourne & Parke L.L.P.
Clausen Miller P.C
Cleary, Gottlieb, Steen &
Hamilton
Clifford Chance Rogers &
Wells L.L.P.
Coudert Brothers
Covington & Burling
Cozen and O'Connor P.C.
Cravath, Swaine & Moore

Curtis, Mallet-Prevost, Colt
   & Mosle
D'Amato & Lynch
Darby & Darby P.C.
Davis Polk & Wardwell
Davis Wright Tremaine
   L.L.P
Debevoise & Plimpton
Dechert
Dewey Ballantine L.L.P.
Dickstein Shapiro Morin &
   Oshinsky L.L.P.
Dorsey & Whitney L.L.P.
Drinker Biddle & Reath
   L.L.P.
Edwards & Angell
Epstein Becker & Green P.C.
Fish & Neave
Fish & Richardson P.C.
Fitzpatrick, Cella, Harper &
   Scinto
Fried, Frank, Harris, Shriver
   & Jacobson
Fulbright & Jaworski L.L.P.
Gibbons, Del Deo, Dolan,
   Griffinger & Vecchione
   P.C.
Gibson, Dunn & Crutcher
   L.L.P.
Goodwin, Procter & Hoar
   L.L.P.
Greenberg Traurig P.A.
Hale and Dorr L.L.P.
Harris Beach & Wilcox
   L.L.P.
Heller Ehrman White &
   McAuliffe
Herzfeld & Rubin
Hodgson, Russ, Andrews,
   Woods & Goodyear L.L.P.
Holland & Knight L.L.P.
Hughes Hubbard & Reed
   L.L.P.
Jackson Lewis Schnitzler &
   Krupman

Jones, Day, Reavis & Pogue
Katten Muchin & Zavis
Kaye, Scholer, Fierman,
   Hays & Handler L.L.P.
Kelley Drye & Warren L.L.P.
Kenyon & Kenyon
King & Spalding
Kirkland & Ellis
Kirkpatrick & Lockhart
   L.L.P.
Kramer Levin Naftalis &
   Frankel L.L.P.
Latham & Watkins
LeBoeuf, Lamb, Greene &
   MacRae L.L.P.
Littler Mendelson P.C.
Loeb & Loeb L.L.P.
Lord, Bissell & Brook
Luce, Forward, Hamilton &
   Scripps L.L.P.
Lyon & Lyon L.L.P.
Mayer, Brown & Platt
McCarter & English, L.L.P
McDermott, Will & Emery
McGuire, Woods, Battle &
   Boothe L.L.P.
Mendes & Mount L.L.P.
Milbank, Tweed, Hadley &
   McCloy
Milberg Weiss Bershad
   Hynes & Lerach L.L.P.
Miller, Canfield, Paddock
   and Stone P.L.C.
Mintz, Levin, Cohn, Ferris,
   Glovsky and Popeo P.C.
Morgan & Finnegan L.L.P.
Morgan, Lewis & Bockius
   L.L.P.
Morrison & Foerster L.L.P.
Morrison, Mahoney &
   Miller L.L.P.
Nixon Peabody L.L.P.
O'Melveny & Myers L.L.P.
Oppenheimer Wolff &
   Donnelly L.L.P.

Orrick, Herrington &
Sutcliffe L.L.P.
Parker Chapin L.L.P.
Patterson, Belknap, Webb &
Tyler L.L.P.
Paul, Hastings, Janofsky &
Walker L.L.P.
Paul, Weiss, Rifkind,
Wharton & Garrison
Pennie & Edmonds L.L.P.
Pepper Hamilton L.L.P.
Peterson & Ross
Phillips, Lytle, Hitchcock,
Blaine & Huber L.L.P.
Pillsbury Madison & Sutro
L.L.P.
Pitney, Hardin, Kipp &
Szuch L.L.P.
Proskauer Rose L.L.P.
Pryor Cashman Sherman &
Flynn L.L.P.
Querrey & Harrow Ltd.
Reed Smith Shaw & McClay
L.L.P.
Riker, Danzig, Scherer,
Hyland & Perretti L.L.P.
Robinson & Cole L.L.P.
Robinson Silverman Pearce
Aronsohn & Berman L.L.P.
Ropers, Majeski, Kohn &
Bentley
Ropes & Gray
Rosenman & Colin L.L.P.
Ross & Hardies
Saul, Ewing, Remick & Saul
L.L.P.
Schiff Hardin & Waite
Schnader Harrison Segal &
Lewis L.L.P.
Schulte Roth & Zabel L.L.P.
Sedgwick, Detert, Moran &
Arnold
Seyfarth Shaw
ShawPittman
Shearman & Sterling

Sidley & Austin
Sills Cummis Radin
Tischman Epstein &
Gross P.A.
Simpson Thacher & Bartlett
Skadden, Arps, Slate,
Meagher & Flom L.L.P.
Sonnenschein Nath &
Rosentha
Squadron, Ellenoff, Plesent
& Sheinfeld L.L.P.
Squire, Sanders & Dempsey
L.L.P.
Stroock & Stroock & Lavan
L.L.P.
Sullivan & Cromwell
Sullivan & Worcester L.L.P.
Sutherland Asbill & Brennan
L.L.P.
Swidler Berlin Shereff
Friedman L.L.P.
Thacher Proffitt & Wood
Thelen Reid & Priest L.L.P.
Vedder, Price, Kaufman &
Kammholz
Vinson & Elkins L.L.P.
Wachtell, Lipton, Rosen &
Katz
Weil, Gotshal & Manges
L.L.P.
White & Case L.L.P.
White and Williams L.L.P.
Wilentz, Goldman & Spitzer
Willkie Farr & Gallagher
Wilmer, Cutler & Pickering
Wilson, Elser, Moskowitz,
Edelman & Dicker L.L.P.
Winston & Strawn
Winthrop, Stimson, Putnam
& Roberts
Wolf, Block, Schorr and
Solis-Cohen L.L.P.
Zevnik Horton Guibord
McGovern Palmer &
Fognani L.L.P.

*Oswego*
Bond, Schoeneck & King
L.L.P.

*Penn Yan*
Saperston & Day P.C.

*Rochester*
Harris Beach & Wilcox
L.L.P.
Harter, Secrest & Emery
L.L.P.
Nixon Peabody L.L.P.
Phillips, Lytle, Hitchcock,
Blaine & Huber L.L.P.
Saperston & Day P.C.

*Saratoga Springs*
Bond, Schoeneck & King
L.L.P.

*Syracuse*
Bond, Schoeneck & King
L.L.P.
Harris Beach & Wilcox
L.L.P.
Saperston & Day P.C.

*Uniondale*
Rivkin, Radler & Kremer
L.L.P

*White Plains*
Jackson Lewis Schnitzler &
Krupman
Thacher Proffitt & Wood
Wilson, Elser, Moskowitz,
Edelman & Dicker L.L.P.

*Williamsville*
Saperston & Day P.C.

*Woodbury*
Jackson Lewis Schnitzler &
Krupman

**North Carolina**

*Charlotte*
Alston & Bird L.L.P.
Cadwalader, Wickersham &
Taft
Cozen and O'Connor P.C.
Hunton & Williams
Kennedy Covington Lobdell
& Hickman L.L.P.
Kilpatrick Stockton L.L.P.
Mayer, Brown & Platt
McGuire, Woods, Battle &
Boothe L.L.P.
Moore & Van Allen P.L.L.C.
Nelson Mullins Riley &
Scarborough L.L.P.
Nexsen Pruet Jacobs &
Pollard, L.L.P.
Rosenman & Colin L.L.P.
Shumaker, Loop & Kendrick
L.L.P.
Smith Helms Mulliss &
Moore L.L.P.
Womble Carlyle Sandridge
& Rice P.L.L.C.

*Durham*
Burns, Doane, Swecker &
Mathis L.L.P.
Moore & Van Allen P.L.L.C.
Womble Carlyle Sandridge
& Rice P.L.L.C.

*Greensboro*
Smith Helms Mulliss &
Moore L.L.P.

*Raleigh*
Hunton & Williams
Kennedy Covington Lobdell
& Hickman L.L.P.
Kilpatrick Stockton L.L.P.
Moore & Van Allen P.L.L.C.
Ogletree, Deakins, Nash,
Smoak & Stewart P.C.
Parker, Poe, Adams &
Bernstein L.L.P.

Smith Helms Mulliss &
   Moore L.L.P.
Womble Carlyle Sandridge
   & Rice P.L.L.C.

*Research Triangle*
Alston & Bird L.L.P.

*Wilmington*
Smith Helms Mulliss &
   Moore L.L.P.

*Winston-Salem*
Kilpatrick Stockton L.L.P.
Womble Carlyle Sandridge
   & Rice P.L.L.C.

**North Dakota**

*Fargo*
Dorsey & Whitney L.L.P.

*Williston*
Crowley, Haughey, Hanson,
   Toole & Dietrich P.L.L.P

**Ohio**

*Akron*
Buckingham, Doolittle &
   Burroughs L.L.P.
Roetzel & Andress L. P. A.

*Canton*
Buckingham, Doolittle &
   Burroughs L.L.P.

*Cincinnati*
Baker & Hostetler L.L.P
Dinsmore & Shohl L.L.P.
Frost & Jacobs L.L.P.
Graydon, Head & Ritchey
Greenebaum Doll &
   McDonald P.L.L.C
Porter, Wright, Morris &
   Arthur L.L.P.
Roetzel & Andress L. P. A.
Schottenstein, Zox & Dunn

Squire, Sanders & Dempsey
   L.L.P.
Taft, Stettinius & Hollister
Thompson Hine & Flory
   L.L.P.
Vorys, Sater, Seymour and
   Pease L.L.P.

*Cleveland*
Arter & Hadden L.L.P.
Baker & Hostetler L.L.P.
Benesch, Friedlander,
   Coplan & Aronoff L.L.P.
Buckingham, Doolittle &
   Burroughs L.L.P.
Calfee, Halter & Griswold
   L.L.P.
Hahn Loeser & Parks L.L.P.
Jones, Day, Reavis & Pogue
Porter, Wright, Morris &
   Arthur L.L.P.
Roetzel & Andress L. P. A.
Schottenstein, Zox & Dunn
Squire, Sanders & Dempsey
   L.L.P.
Taft, Stettinius & Hollister
Thompson Hine & Flory
   L.L.P.
Vorys, Sater, Seymour and
   Pease L.L.P.

*Columbus*
Arter & Hadden L.L.P.
Baker & Hostetler L.L.P
Benesch, Friedlander,
   Coplan & Aronoff L.L.P.
Bricker & Eckler L.L.P.
Buckingham, Doolittle &
   Burroughs L.L.P.
Calfee, Halter & Griswold
   L.L.P.
Dinsmore & Shohl L.L.P.
Frost & Jacobs L.L.P.
Hahn Loeser & Parks L.L.P.
Jones, Day, Reavis & Pogue

Littler Mendelson P.C.
McNees Wallace & Nurick
Porter, Wright, Morris &
    Arthur L.L.P.
Roetzel & Andress L. P. A.
Schottenstein, Zox & Dunn
Shumaker, Loop & Kendrick
    L.L.P.
Simpson Thacher & Bartlett
Squire, Sanders & Dempsey
    L.L.P.
Taft, Stettinius & Hollister
Thompson Hine & Flory
    L.L.P.
Vorys, Sater, Seymour and
    Pease L.L.P.

*Dayton*
Arter & Hadden L.L.P.
Dinsmore & Shohl L.L.P.
Porter, Wright, Morris &
    Arthur L.L.P.
Thompson Hine & Flory
    L.L.P.

*Middletown*
Frost & Jacobs L.L.P.

*Steubenville*
Dickie, McCamey &
    Chilcote P.C.
Marshall, Dennehey,
    Warner, Coleman &
    Goggin

*Toledo*
Roetzel & Andress L. P. A.
Shumaker, Loop & Kendrick
    L.L.P.

**Oklahoma**

*Oklahoma City*
Hall, Estill, Hardwick,
    Gable, Golden & Nelson
    P.C.
Kutak Rock

*Tulsa*
Gardere & Wynne L.L.P.
Hall, Estill, Hardwick,
    Gable, Golden & Nelson
    P.C.

**Oregon**

*Bend*
Schwabe Williamson &
    Wyatt, PC

*Portland*
Bullivant Houser Bailey P.C.
Davis Wright Tremaine
    L.L.P
Foster Pepper & Shefelman
    P.L.L.C.
Heller Ehrman White &
    McAuliffe
Lane Powell Spears
    Lubersky L.L.P.
Miller Nash L.L.P.
Perkins Coie L.L.P.
Preston Gates & Ellis L.L.P.
Schwabe Williamson &
    Wyatt, PC
Stoel Rives L.L.P.

**Pennsylvania**

*Allentown*
Blank Rome Comisky &
    McCauley L.L.P
Post & Schell P.C.
White and Williams L.L.P.

*Berwyn*
Drinker Biddle & Reath
    L.L.P.
Pepper Hamilton L.L.P.
Saul, Ewing, Remick & Saul
    L.L.P.

*Bethlehem*
Marshall, Dennehey,
    Warner, Coleman &
    Goggin

*Bryn Mawr*
Buchanan Ingersoll P.C.

*Camp Hill*
Margolis Edelstein
Post & Schell P.C.

*Doylestown*
Fox, Rothschild, O'Brien &
  Frankel, L.L.P.
Marshall, Dennehey,
  Warner, Coleman &
  Goggin

*Erie*
Marshall, Dennehey,
  Warner, Coleman &
  Goggin

*Exton*
Fox, Rothschild, O'Brien &
  Frankel, L.L.P.

*Harrisburg*
Buchanan Ingersoll P.C.
Dechert
Dilworth Paxson Kalish &
  Kauffman L.L.P.
Eckert Seamans Cherin &
  Mellott L.L.C.
Kirkpatrick & Lockhart
  L.L.P.
Klett Rooney Lieber &
  Schorling
LeBoeuf, Lamb, Greene &
  MacRae L.L.P.
Marshall, Dennehey,
  Warner, Coleman &
  Goggin
McNees Wallace & Nurick
Morgan, Lewis & Bockius
  L.L.P.
Obermayer Rebmann
  Maxwell & Hippel L.L.P.
Pepper Hamilton L.L.P.
Reed Smith Shaw & McClay

L.L.P.
Saul, Ewing, Remick & Saul
  L.L.P.
Schnader Harrison Segal &
  Lewis L.L.P.
Tucker Arensberg P.C.
Wolf, Block, Schorr and
  Solis-Cohen L.L.P.

*Hazleton*
McNees Wallace & Nurick

*Kennet Square*
Cooch and Taylor

*Lancaster*
Post & Schell P.C.

*Lansdale*
Fox, Rothschild, O'Brien &
  Frankel, L.L.P.

*Lawrenceville*
Dickie, McCamey &
  Chilcote P.C.

*Malvern*
Stradley, Ronon, Stevens &
  Young, L.L.P.

*Media*
Blank Rome Comisky &
  McCauley L.L.P

*Moon Township*
Tucker Arensberg P.C.

*Newton Square*
Dilworth Paxson Kalish &
  Kauffman L.L.P.
Marshall, Dennehey,
  Warner, Coleman &
  Goggin

*Norristown*
Marshall, Dennehey,
  Warner, Coleman &
  Goggin

Schnader Harrison Segal &
Lewis L.L.P.
Wolf, Block, Schorr and
Solis-Cohen L.L.P.

*Paoli*
White and Williams L.L.P.

*Philadelphia*
Akin, Gump, Strauss, Hauer
& Feld L.L.P.
Anderson Kill & Olick P.C.
Archer & Greiner
Ballard Spahr Andrews &
Ingersoll L.L.P.
Blank Rome Comisky &
McCauley L.L.P.
Buchanan Ingersoll P.C.
Cozen and O'Connor P.C.
Dechert
Dickie, McCamey &
Chilcote P.C.
Dilworth Paxson Kalish &
Kauffman L.L.P.
Drinker Biddle & Reath
L.L.P.
Duane, Morris & Heckscher
L.L.P.
Eckert Seamans Cherin &
Mellott L.L.C.
Fox, Rothschild, O'Brien &
Frankel, L.L.P.
Greenberg Traurig P.A.
Klehr Harrison Harvey
Branzburg & Ellers
Klett Rooney Lieber &
Schorling
Margolis Edelstein
Marshall, Dennehey,
Warner, Coleman &
Goggin
McCarter & English, L.L.P
Montgomery, McCracken,
Walker & Rhoads L.L.P.

Morgan, Lewis & Bockius
L.L.P.
Obermayer Rebmann
Maxwell & Hippel L.L.P.
Pepper Hamilton L.L.P.
Post & Schell P.C.
Reed Smith Shaw & McClay
L.L.P.
Saul, Ewing, Remick & Saul
L.L.P.
Schnader Harrison Segal &
Lewis L.L.P.
Stradley, Ronon, Stevens &
Young, L.L.P.
Thorp, Reed & Armstrong
White and Williams L.L.P.
Wilson, Elser, Moskowitz,
Edelman & Dicker L.L.P.
Wolf, Block, Schorr and
Solis-Cohen L.L.P.
Zevnik Horton Guibord
McGovern Palmer &
Fognani L.L.P.

*Pittsburgh*
Buchanan Ingersoll P.C.
Dickie, McCamey &
Chilcote P.C.
Eckert Seamans Cherin &
Mellott L.L.C.
Jackson Lewis Schnitzler &
Krupman
Jones, Day, Reavis & Pogue
Kirkpatrick & Lockhart
L.L.P.
Klett Rooney Lieber &
Schorling
LeBoeuf, Lamb, Greene &
MacRae L.L.P.
Margolis Edelstein
Marshall, Dennehey,
Warner, Coleman &
Goggin
McGuire, Woods, Battle &
Boothe L.L.P.

Morgan, Lewis & Bockius
L.L.P.
Obermayer Rebmann
Maxwell & Hippel L.L.P.
Pepper Hamilton L.L.P.
Plunkett & Cooney P.C.
Reed Smith Shaw & McClay
L.L.P.
Schnader Harrison Segal &
Lewis L.L.P.
Thorp, Reed & Armstrong
Tucker Arensberg P.C.
White and Williams L.L.P.

*Reading*
Stevens & Lee

*Scranton*
Margolis Edelstein
Marshall, Dennehey,
Warner, Coleman &
Goggin

*Voorhees*
Post & Schell P.C.

*Washington*
Schnader Harrison Segal &
Lewis L.L.P.

*West Conshohocken*
Cozen and O'Connor P.C.

*Williamsport*
Marshall, Dennehey,
Warner, Coleman &
Goggin

**Rhode Island**

*Newport*
Edwards & Angell

*Providence*
Brown, Rudnick, Freed &
Gesmer
Edwards & Angell
Holland & Knight L.L.P.

Morrison, Mahoney &
Miller L.L.P.
Riker, Danzig, Scherer,
Hyland & Perretti L.L.P.
Ropes & Gray

**South Carolina**

*Charleston*
Haynsworth, Marion,
McKay & Guerard L.L.P.
Moore & Van Allen P.L.L.C.
Nelson Mullins Riley &
Scarborough L.L.P.
Nexsen Pruet Jacobs &
Pollard, L.L.P.
Ogletree, Deakins, Nash,
Smoak & Stewart P.C.

*Columbia*
Haynsworth, Marion,
McKay & Guerard L.L.P.
Nelson Mullins Riley &
Scarborough L.L.P.
Nexsen Pruet Jacobs &
Pollard, L.L.P.
Ogletree, Deakins, Nash,
Smoak & Stewart P.C.
Parker, Poe, Adams &
Bernstein L.L.P.

*Greenville*
Haynsworth, Marion,
McKay & Guerard L.L.P.
Jackson Lewis Schnitzler &
Krupman
Nelson Mullins Riley &
Scarborough L.L.P.
Nexsen Pruet Jacobs &
Pollard, L.L.P.
Ogletree, Deakins, Nash,
Smoak & Stewart P.C.
Womble Carlyle Sandridge
& Rice P.L.L.C.

*Hilton Head*
Nexsen Pruet Jacobs &
    Pollard, L.L.P.

*Myrtle Beach*
Nelson Mullins Riley &
    Scarborough L.L.P.
Nexsen Pruet Jacobs &
    Pollard, L.L.P.

*Spartanburg*
Parker, Poe, Adams &
    Bernstein L.

**Tennessee**

*Chattanooga*
Baker, Donelson, Bearman &
    Caldwell P.C.

*Columbia*
Waller Lansden Dortch &
    Davis P.L.L.C.

*Huntsville*
Baker, Donelson, Bearman &
    Caldwell P.C.

*Knoxville*
Baker, Donelson, Bearman &
    Caldwell P.C.
Bass, Berry & Sims PLC
Hunton & Williams

*Nashville*
Baker, Donelson, Bearman &
    Caldwell P.C.
Bass, Berry & Sims PLC
Boult, Cummings, Conners
    & Berry P.L.C.
Brown, Todd & Heyburn
    P.L.L.C.
Dinsmore & Shohl L.L.P.
Greenebaum Doll &
    McDonald P.L.L.C
Loeb & Loeb L.L.P.
Ogletree, Deakins, Nash,
    Smoak & Stewart P.C.

Wyatt, Tarrant & Combs

*Memphis*
Baker, Donelson, Bearman &
    Caldwell P.C.
Bass, Berry & Sims PLC
Butler, Snow, O'Mara,
    Stevens & Cannada, PLC
Wyatt, Tarrant & Combs

**Texas**

*Austin*
Akin, Gump, Strauss, Hauer
    & Feld L.L.P.
Arter & Hadden L.L.P.
Baker & Botts L.L.P
Bracewell & Patterson L.L.P.
Brobeck, Phleger & Harrison
    L.L.P.
Brown McCarroll & Oaks
    Hartline L.L.P.
Clark, Thomas & Winters
    P.C.
Fulbright & Jaworski L.L.P.
Gardere & Wynne L.L.P.
Gray Cary Ware &
    Freidenrich L.L.P.
Hughes & Luce L.L.P.
Jackson Walker L.L.P.
Jenkens & Gilchrist P.C.
Kelly, Hart & Hallman P.C.
Locke Liddell & Sapp L.L.P
Mayor, Day, Caldwell &
    Keeton L.L.P.
McGinnis, Lochridge &
    Kilgore L.L.P.
Peterson & Ross
Strasburger & Price L.L.P.
Sutherland Asbill & Brennan
    L.L.P.
Thompson & Knight P.C.
Verner, Liipfert, Bernhard,
    McPherson and Hand
    Chartered

Vinson & Elkins L.L.P.
Wilson Sonsini Goodrich &
　Rosati
Winstead Sechrest & Minick
　P.C.

*Corpus Christi*
Bracewell & Patterson L.L.P.
Matthews and Branscomb,
　A Professional Law
　Corporation

*Corrizo Springs*
Matthews and Branscomb,
　A Professional Law
　Corporation

*Dallas*
Akin, Gump, Strauss, Hauer
　& Feld L.L.P.
Andrews & Kurth L.L.P.
Arter & Hadden L.L.P.
Baker & Botts L.L.P
Baker & McKenzie
Bracewell & Patterson L.L.P.
Brobeck, Phleger & Harrison
　L.L.P.
Brown McCarroll & Oaks
　Hartline L.L.P.
Carrington, Coleman,
　Sloman & Blumenthal,
　LLP
Cowles & Thompson P.C.
Epstein Becker & Green P.C.
Fish & Richardson P.C.
Fulbright & Jaworski L.L.P.
Gardere & Wynne L.L.P.
Gibson, Dunn & Crutcher
　L.L.P.
Haynes and Boone L.L.P.
Hughes & Luce L.L.P.
Jackson Lewis Schnitzler &
　Krupman
Jackson Walker L.L.P.
Jenkens & Gilchrist P.C.
Jones, Day, Reavis & Pogue

Littler Mendelson P.C.
Locke Liddell & Sapp L.L.P.
McKenna & Cuneo L.L.P.
Ogletree, Deakins, Nash,
　Smoak & Stewart P.C.
Patton Boggs L.L.P.
Sidley & Austin
Strasburger & Price L.L.P.
Thompson & Knight P.C.
Vial, Hamilton, Koch &
　Knox L.L.P.
Vinson & Elkins L.L.P.
Weil, Gotshal & Manges
　L.L.P.
Wilson, Elser, Moskowitz,
　Edelman & Dicker L.L.P.
Winstead Sechrest & Minick
　P.C.

*Eagle Pass*
Matthews and Branscomb,
　A Professional Law
　Corporation

*Fort Worth*
Bracewell & Patterson L.L.P.
Haynes and Boone L.L.P.
Jackson Walker L.L.P.
Kelly, Hart & Hallman P.C.
Thompson & Knight P.C.
Winstead Sechrest & Minick
　P.C.

*Houston*
Adams & Reese
Akin, Gump, Strauss, Hauer
　& Feld L.L.P.
Andrews & Kurth L.L.P.
Baker & Botts L.L.P.
Baker & Hostetler L.L.P
Baker & McKenzie
Bracewell & Patterson L.L.P.
Brown McCarroll & Oaks
　Hartline L.L.P.
Curtis, Mallet-Prevost, Colt
　& Mosle

Fulbright & Jaworski L.L.P.
Haynes and Boone L.L.P.
Howrey, Simon, Arnold &
　White
Hughes & Luce L.L.P.
Jackson Walker L.L.P.
Jenkens & Gilchrist P.C.
King & Spalding
LeBoeuf, Lamb, Greene &
　MacRae L.L.P.
Littler Mendelson P.C.
Locke Liddell & Sapp L.L.P.
Mayer, Brown & Platt
Mayor, Day, Caldwell &
　Keeton L.L.P.
McGinnis, Lochridge &
　Kilgore L.L.P.
McGlinchey Stafford
　P.L.L.C.
Ogletree, Deakins, Nash,
　Smoak & Stewart P.C.
Phelps Dunbar L.L.P.
Rice Fowler
Seyfarth Shaw
Shook, Hardy & Bacon
　L.L.P.
Skadden, Arps, Slate,
　Meagher & Flom L.L.P.
Squire, Sanders & Dempsey
　L.L.P.
Strasburger & Price L.L.P.
Thompson & Knight P.C.
Verner, Liipfert, Bernhard,
　McPherson and Hand
　Chartered
Vial, Hamilton, Koch &
　Knox L.L.P.
Vinson & Elkins L.L.P.
Weil, Gotshal & Manges
　L.L.P.
Wilson, Elser, Moskowitz,
　Edelman & Dicker L.L.P.
Winstead Sechrest & Minick
　P.C.

*Longview*
Brown McCarroll & Oaks
　Hartline L.L.P.

*McKinney*
Cowles & Thompson P.C.

*Richardson*
Haynes and Boone L.L.P.
Jackson Walker L.L.P.

*Round Rock*
Brown McCarroll & Oaks
　Hartline L.L.P.

*San Angelo*
Jackson Walker L.L.P.

*San Antonio*
Akin, Gump, Strauss, Hauer
　& Feld L.L.P.
Arter & Hadden L.L.P.
Bracewell & Patterson L.L.P.
Fulbright & Jaworski L.L.P.
Haynes and Boone L.L.P.
Jackson Walker L.L.P.
Jenkens & Gilchrist P.C.
Matthews and Branscomb,
　A Professional Law
　Corporation
Strasburger & Price L.L.P.

*The Woodlands*
Andrews & Kurth L.L.P.
Brown McCarroll & Oaks
　Hartline L.L.P.

*Tyler*
Cowles & Thompson P.C.

*Uvalde*
Matthews and Branscomb,
　A Professional Law
　Corporation

**Utah**

*Salt Lake City*
Ballard Spahr Andrews &
   Ingersoll L.L.P.
Chapman and Cutler
Dorsey & Whitney L.L.P.
Holland & Hart L.L.P.
Holme Roberts & Owen
   L.L.P.
LeBoeuf, Lamb, Greene &
   MacRae L.L.P.
Parsons Behle & Latimer
Snell & Wilmer L.L.P.
Stoel Rives L.L.P.

**Virginia**

*Alexandria*
Burns, Doane, Swecker &
   Mathis L.L.P.
Vorys, Sater, Seymour and
   Pease L.L.P.
Whiteford, Taylor & Preston
   L.L.P.

*Arlington*
Brinks Hofer Gilson & Lione

*Charlottesville*
McGuire, Woods, Battle &
   Boothe L.L.P.

*Falls Church*
Holland & Knight L.L.P.
Ober, Kaler, Grimes &
   Shriver

*McLean*
Akin, Gump, Strauss, Hauer
   & Feld L.L.P.
Buchanan Ingersoll P.C.
Hogan & Hartson L.L.P.
Hunton & Williams
Mays & Valentine L.L.P.
McGuire, Woods, Battle &
   Boothe L.L.P.
Miles & Stockbridge P.C.

O'Melveny & Myers L.L.P.
Patton Boggs L.L.P.
Semmes, Bowen & Semmes
   P.C.
ShawPittman
Venable, Baetjer and
   Howard L.L.P.
Verner, Liipfert, Bernhard,
   McPherson and Hand
   Chartered
Williams, Mullen, Clark &
   Dobbins P.C.
Wilson Sonsini Goodrich &
   Rosati

*Newport News*
Williams, Mullen, Clark &
   Dobbins P.C.

*Norfolk*
Hunton & Williams
Mays & Valentine L.L.P.
McGuire, Woods, Battle &
   Boothe L.L.P.
Zevnik Horton Guibord
   McGovern Palmer &
   Fognani L.L.P.

*Reston*
Cooley Godward L.L.P.
Kilpatrick Stockton L.L.P.
Mintz, Levin, Cohn, Ferris,
   Glovsky and Popeo P.C.
Powell, Goldstein, Frazer &
   Murphy L.L.P.

*Richmond*
Hunton & Williams
Kutak Rock
Mays & Valentine L.L.P.
McGuire, Woods, Battle &
   Boothe L.L.P.
Williams, Mullen, Clark &
   Dobbins P.C.

*Tysons Corner*
Greenberg Traurig P.A.

*Vienna*
Pillsbury Madison & Sutro
L.L.P.

*Virginia Beach*
Mays & Valentine L.L.P.
Williams, Mullen, Clark &
Dobbins P.C.

*Winchester*
Bowles Rice McDavid Graff
& Love

**Washington**

*Bellevue*
Davis Wright Tremaine
L.L.P
Perkins Coie L.L.P.

*Kirkland*
Cooley Godward L.L.P.
Wilson Sonsini Goodrich &
Rosati

*Mount Vernon*
Lane Powell Spears
Lubersky L.L.P.

*Olympia*
Lane Powell Spears
Lubersky L.L.P.

*Seattle*
Bullivant Houser Bailey P.C.
Cozen and O'Connor P.C.
Davis Wright Tremaine
L.L.P.
Dorsey & Whitney L.L.P.
Foster Pepper & Shefelman
P.L.L.C.
Garvey, Schubert & Barer
Gordon, Thomas,
Honeywell, Malanca,
Peterson & Daheim
P.L.L.C.
Gray Cary Ware &
Freidenrich L.L.P.

Heller Ehrman White &
McAuliffe
Holland & Knight L.L.P.
Jackson Lewis Schnitzler &
Krupman
Keesal, Young & Logan
Lane Powell Spears
Lubersky L.L.P.
Littler Mendelson P.C.
Merchant, Gould, Smith,
Edell, Welter & Schmidt
P.A.
Miller Nash L.L.P.
Orrick, Herrington &
Sutcliffe L.L.P.
Perkins Coie L.L.P.
Preston Gates & Ellis L.L.P.
Schwabe Williamson &
Wyatt, PC
Sidley & Austin
Stoel Rives L.L.P.
Townsend and Townsend
and Crew L.L.P.
Williams, Kastner & Gibbs
P.L.L.C.

*Spokane*
Foster Pepper & Shefelman
P.L.L.C.
Preston Gates & Ellis L.L.P.

*Tacoma*
Gordon, Thomas,
Honeywell, Malanca,
Peterson & Daheim
P.L.L.C.
Williams, Kastner & Gibbs
P.L.L.C.

*Vancouver*
Bullivant Houser Bailey P.C.
Miller Nash L.L.P.
Schwabe Williamson &
Wyatt, PC
Stoel Rives L.L.P.

*Yakima*
Littler Mendelson P.C.

**Washington DC**

Adams and Reese L.L.P.
Akin, Gump, Strauss, Hauer & Feld L.L.P.
Alston & Bird
Anderson, Kill & Olick P.C.
Andrews & Kurth L.L.P.
Arent Fox Kintner Plotkin & Kahn P.L.L.C.
Armstrong Teasdale L.L.P.
Arnold & Porter
Arter & Hadden L.L.P.
Baker & Botts L.L.P.
Baker & Daniels
Baker, Donelson, Bearman & Caldwell P.C.
Baker & Hostetler L.L.P.
Baker & McKenzie
Balch & Bingham L.L.P.
Ballard Spahr Andrews & Ingersoll L.L.P.
Barnes & Thornburg
Bell, Boyd & Lloyd L.L.C.
Beveridge & Diamond P.C.
Bingham Dana L.L.P.
Blank Rome Comisky & McCauley L.L.P.
Bowles Rice McDavid Graff & Love
Bracewell & Patterson L.L.P.
Bradley, Arant, Rose & White L.L.P.
Brobeck, Phleger & Harrison L.L.P.
Brown & Wood L.L.P.
Bryan Cave L.L.P.
Buchanan Ingersoll P.C.
Cadwalader, Wickersham & Taft
Cahill Gordon & Reindel
Carlsmith Ball Wichman Case & Ichiki

Carter, Ledyard & Milburn
Chadbourne & Parke L.L.P.
Cleary, Gottlieb, Steen & Hamilton
Clifford Chance Rogers & Wells
Collier, Shannon, Rill & Scott, P.L.L.C.
Coudert Brothers
Covington & Burling
Crowell & Moring L.L.P.
Cullen & Dykman
Curtis, Mallet-Prevost, Colt & Mosle
Davis Polk & Wardwell
Davis Wright Tremaine L.L.P.
Debevoise & Plimpton
Dechert
Dewey Ballantine L.L.P.
Dickinson Wright P.L.L.C.
Dickstein Shapiro Morin & Oshinsky L.L.P.
Dorsey & Whitney L.L.P.
Dow, Lohnes & Albertson
Drinker Biddle & Reath L.L.P.
Dykema Gossett P.L.L.C.
Eckert Seamans Cherin & Mellott L.L.C.
Epstein Becker & Green P.C.
Fenwick & West L.L.P.
Finnegan, Henderson, Farabow, Garrett & Dunner L.L.P.
Fish & Richardson P.C.
Fitzpatrick, Cella, Harper & Scinto
Foley, Hoag & Eliot L.L.P.
Foley and Lardner
Fredrikson & Byron P.A.
Fried, Frank, Harris, Shriver & Jacobson
Fulbright & Jaworski L.L.P.
Gardner, Carton & Douglas

Gibson, Dunn & Crutcher L.L.P.

Goodwin, Procter & Hoar L.L.P.

Graham & James L.L.P.

Greenberg Traurig P.A.

Hale & Dorr L.L.P.

Hall, Estill, Hardwick, Gable, Golden & Nelson P.C.

Hall & Evans L.L.C.

Harris Beach & Wilcox L.L.P.

Haynes and Boone L.L.P.

Heller Ehrman White & McAuliffe

Hogan & Hartson L.L.P.

Holland & Knight L.L.P.

Hopkins & Sutter

Howrey, Simon, Arnold & White

Hughes, Hubbard & Reed L.L.P.

Hunton & Williams

Jackson & Kelly

Jackson Lewis Schnitzler & Krupman

Jenkens & Gilchrist P.C.

Jenner & Block

Jones, Day, Reavis & Pogue

Jones, Walker, Waechter, Poitevent, Carrère & Denègre L.L.P.

Katten Muchin & Zavis

Kaye, Scholer, Fierman, Hays & Handler L.L.P.

Keesal, Young & Logan

Kelley Drye & Warren L.L.P.

Kenyon & Kenyon

Kilpatrick Stockton L.L.P.

King & Spalding

Kirkland & Ellis

Kirkpatrick & Lockhart L.L.P.

Kutak Rock

Latham & Watkins

LeBoeuf, Lamb, Greene & MacRae L.L.P.

Lewis, Rice & Fingersh L.C.

Linowes and Blocher L.L.P.

Littler Mendelson P.C.

Long Aldridge & Norman L.L.P.

Lyon & Lyon L.L.P.

Manatt, Phelps & Phillips L.L.P.

Mayer, Brown & Platt

McDermott, Will & Emery

McGuire, Woods, Battle & Boothe L.L.P.

McKenna & Cuneo L.L.P.

McNees Wallace & Nurick

Milbank, Tweed, Hadley & McCloy

Miles & Stockbridge P.C.

Miller, Canfield, Paddock and Stone P.L.C.

Miller & Chevalier, Chartered

Mintz, Levin, Cohn, Ferris, Glovsky and Popeo P.C.

Morgan & Finnegan L.L.P.

Morgan, Lewis & Bockius L.L.P.

Morrison & Foerster L.L.P.

Morrison & Hecker L.L.P.

Nixon Peabody L.L.P.

Nossaman, Guthner, Knox & Elliott L.L.P.

O'Melveny & Myers L.L.P.

Ober, Kaler, Grimes & Shriver

Oppenheimer Wolff & Donnelly L.L.P.

Orrick, Herrington & Sutcliffe L.L.P.

Patton Boggs L.L.P.

Paul, Hastings, Janofsky & Walker L.L.P.

Paul, Weiss, Rifkind, Wharton & Garrison
Pennie & Edmonds L.L.P.
Pepper Hamilton L.L.P.
Perkins Coie L.L.P.
Pillsbury Madison & Sutro L.L.P.
Piper, Marbury, Rudnick & Wolfe L.L.P.
Porter, Wright, Morris & Arthur L.L.P.
Powell, Goldstein, Frazer & Murphy L.L.P.
Preston Gates & Ellis L.L.P.
Proskauer Rose L.L.P.
Reed Smith Shaw & McClay L.L.P.
Robins, Kaplan, Miller & Ciresi L.L.P.
Ropes & Gray
Rosenman & Colin L.L.P.
Ross & Hardies
Schiff Hardin & Waite
Schnader Harrison Segal & Lewis P.A.
Schwabe Williamson & Wyatt PC
Semmes, Bowen & Semmes P.C.
Seyfarth Shaw
ShawPittman
Shearman & Sterling
Shook, Hardy & Bacon L.L.C.
Sidley & Austin
Sills Cummis Radin Tischman Epstein & Gross P.A.
Smith, Gambrell & Russell L.L.P.
Sonneschein Nath & Rosenthal
Squire, Sanders & Dempsey L.L.P.

Steptoe & Johnson L.L.P.
Stites & Harbison
Stoel Rives L.L.P.
Stradley, Ronon, Stevens & Young L.L.P.
Stroock & Stroock & Lavan L.L.P.
Sughrue Mion, Zinn, Macpeak & Seas P.L.L.C.
Sullivan & Worcester L.L.P.
Sutherland Asbill & Brennan L.L.P.
Swidler Berlin Shereff Friedman L.L.P.
Thacher Proffitt & Wood
Thelen Reid & Priest L.L.P.
Thompson Coburn L.L.P.
Thompson Hine & Flory L.L.P.
Verner, Liipfert, Bernhard, McPherson and Hand Chartered
Vinson & Elkins L.L.P.
White & Case L.L.P.
Whiteford, Taylor & Preston L.L.P.
Wiley, Rein & Fielding
Williams & Connolly
Williams, Mullen, Clark & Dobbins P.C.
Wilkie Farr & Gallagher
Wilmer, Cutler & Pickering
Wilson, Elser, Moskowitz, Edelman & Dicker L.L.P.
Winston & Strawn
Winthrop, Stimson, Putnam & Roberts
Womble Carlyle Sandridge & Rice P.L.L.C.
Zevnick Horton Guibord McGovern Palmer & Forgani L.L.P.

## West Virginia

*Charleston*
Bowles Rice McDavid Graff
& Love
Jackson & Kelly
Steptoe & Johnson

*Clarksburg*
Steptoe & Johnson

*Fairmont*
Bowles Rice McDavid Graff
& Love
Jackson & Kelly
Steptoe & Johnson

*Martinsburg*
Bowles Rice McDavid Graff
& Love
Jackson & Kelly
Steptoe & Johnson

*Morgantown*
Bowles Rice McDavid Graff
& Love
Jackson & Kelly
Steptoe & Johnson

*New Martinsville*
Jackson & Kelly

*Parkersburg*
Bowles Rice McDavid Graff
& Love
Jackson & Kelly
Steptoe & Johnson

*Weirton*
Marshall, Dennehey,
Warner, Coleman &
Goggin

*Wheeling*
Dickie, McCamey &
Chilcote P.C.
Jackson & Kelly
Steptoe & Johnson

## Wisconsin

*Appleton*
Godfrey & Kahn, S.C.
Hinshaw & Culbertson

*Green Bay*
Godfrey & Kahn, S.C.

*Madison*
Foley & Lardner
Godfrey & Kahn, S.C.
Michael Best & Friedrich
L.L.P.
Quarles & Brady L.L.P.
Reinhart, Boerner, Van
Deuren, Norris &
Rieselbach S.C.
Whyte Hirschboeck Dudek
S.C.

*Manitowoc*
Michael Best & Friedrich
L.L.P.
Whyte Hirschboeck Dudek
S.C.

*Menomonee*
Whyte Hirschboeck Dudek
S.C.

*Milwaukee*
Arnstein & Lehr
Foley & Lardner
Godfrey & Kahn, S.C.
Hinshaw & Culbertson
Michael Best & Friedrich
L.L.P.
Quarles & Brady L.L.P.
Reinhart, Boerner, Van
Deuren, Norris &
Rieselbach S.C.
Varnum, Riddering, Schmidt
& Howlett L.L.P.
Whyte Hirschboeck Dudek
S.C.

**Wyoming**

*Cheyenne*
Holland & Hart L.L.P.

*Jackson*
Holland & Hart L.L.P.

**International**

Akin, Gump, Strauss, Hauer & Feld L.L.P.
Altheimer & Gray
Arent Fox Kintner Plotkin & Kahn P.L.L.C.
Armstrong Teasdale L.L.P.
Arnold & Porter
Baker & Botts L.L.P.
Baker & Daniels
Becker & Poliakoff P.A.
Bingham Dana L.L.P.
Blackwell Sanders Peper Martin L.L.P.
Blatt, Hammesfahr & Eaton
Bracewell & Patterson L.L.P.
Brobeck, Phleger & Harrison L.L.P.
Brown, Rudnick, Freed & Gesmer
Brown & Wood L.L.P.
Bryan Cave L.L.P.
Buchanan Ingersoll P.C.
Cadwalader, Wickersham & Taft
Cahill Gordon & Reindel
Carlsmith Ball Wichman Case & Ichiki
Chadbourne & Parke L.L.P.
Chaffe, McCall, Phillips, Toler & Sarpy L.L.P.
Clausen Miller P.C.
Cleary, Gottlieb, Steen & Hamilton
Clifford Chance Rogers & Wells
Coudert Brothers

Covington & Burling
Cozen and O'Connor P.C.
Cravath, Swaine & Moore
Crowell & Moring L.L.P.
Curtis, Mallet-Prevost, Colt & Mosle
Davis Polk & Wardwell
Debevoise & Plimpton
Dechert
Dewey Ballantine L.L.P.
Dorsey & Whitney L.L.P.
Dykema Gossett P.L.L.C.
Epstein Becker & Green P.C.
Faegre & Benson L.L.P.
Finnegan, Henderson, Farabow, Garrett & Dunner L.L.P.
Fredrikson & Byron P.A.
Fried, Frank, Harris, Shriver & Jacobson
Fulbright & Jaworski L.L.P.
Gardere & Wynne L.L.P.
Gibson, Dunn & Crutcher L.L.P.
Graham & James L.L.P.
Gray Plant Mooty Mooty & Bennett P.A.
Hale & Dorr L.L.P.
Hancock, Rothert & Bunschoft L.L.P.
Harris Beach & Wilcox L.L.P.
Haynes and Boone L.L.P.
Heller Ehrman White & McAuliffe
Herzfeld & Rubin
Hodgson, Russ, Andrews, Woods & Goodyear L.L.P.
Hogan & Hartson L.L.P.
Holland & Knight L.L.P.
Holme Roberts & Owen L.L.P.
Hughes, Hubbard & Reed L.L.P.
Hunton & Williams

Jones, Day, Reavis & Pogue
Kaye, Scholer, Fierman,
    Hays & Handler L.L.P.
Keesal, Young & Logan
Kelley Drye & Warren L.L.P.
Kenyon & Kenyon
Kilpatrick Stockton L.L.P.
Kirkland & Ellis
Kramer Levin Naftalis &
    Frankel L.L.P.
Kutak Rock
Lane Powell Spears
    Lubersky L.L.P.
Latham & Watkins
LeBoeuf, Lamb, Greene &
    MacRae L.L.P.
Lord, Bissell & Brook
Mayer, Brown & Platt
McCutchen, Doyle, Brown
    & Enersen L.L.P.
McDermott, Will & Emery
McGuire, Woods, Battle &
    Boothe L.L.P.
McKenna & Cuneo L.L.P.
Milbank, Tweed, Hadley &
    McCloy
Miller, Canfield, Paddock
    and Stone P.L.C.
Morgan, Lewis & Bockius
    L.L.P.
Morrison & Foerster L.L.P.
Morrison, Mahoney &
    Miller L.L.P.
Nelson Mullins Riley &
    Scarborough L.L.P.
O'Melveny & Myers L.L.P.
Ogletree, Deakins, Nash,
    Smoak & Stewart P.C.
Oppenheimer Wolff &
    Donnelly L.L.P.
Orrick, Herrington &
    Sutcliffe L.L.P.
Paul, Hastings, Janofsky &
    Walker L.L.P.

Paul, Weiss, Rifkind,
    Wharton & Garrison
Perkins Coie L.L.P.
Peterson & Ross
Phelps Dunbar L.L.P.
Pillsbury Madison & Sutro
    L.L.P.
Powell, Goldstein, Frazer &
    Murphy L.L.P.
Preston Gates & Ellis L.L.P.
Proskauer Rose L.L.P.
Querrey & Harrow Ltd.
Rice Fowler
Ropes & Gray
Schiff Hardin & Waite
Sedgwick, Detert, Moran &
    Arnold
Seyfarth Shaw
ShawPittman
Shearman & Sterling
Shook, Hardy & Bacon
    L.L.C.
Shutts & Bowen
Sidley & Austin
Simpson Thacher & Bartlett
Skadden, Arps, Slate,
    Meagher & Flom L.L.P.
Strasburger & Price L.L.P.
Sughrue Mion, Zinn,
    Macpeak & Seas P.L.L.C.
Sullivan & Cromwell
Thacher Proffitt & Wood
Thompson & Knight P.C.
Troutman Sanders L.L.P.
Vinson & Elkins L.L.P.
Weil, Gotshal & Manges
    L.L.P.
White & Case L.L.P.
Williams, Mullen, Clark &
    Dobbins P.C.
Wilkie Farr & Gallagher
Wilmer, Cutler & Pickering
Wilson, Elser, Moskowitz,
    Edelman & Dicker L.L.P.

Winstead Sechrest & Minick
    P.C.
Winston & Strawn
Winthrop, Stimson, Putnam
    & Roberts
Zevnick Horton Guibord
    McGovern Palmer &
    Fognani L.L.P.

# APPENDIX B

## LAW FIRM DIRECTORY

An alphabetical listing of over 475 law firms. Information for the main office of each firm is listed below, as well as each firms' website address and contact information for the recruiting departments of each firm, if available. For information on the location of the branches of each firm, see Appendix A.

**FIRM NAME**
*ADDRESS*
*PHONE*
*FAX*
*WEBSITE*
*RECRUITING INFORMATION,*
*IF ANY (name, phone, e-mail)*

**Abbott, Simses, Knister & Kuchler**
400 Lafayette St., Suite 200
New Orleans, LA 70130
504-568-9393
504-524-1933 (fax)
http://www.abbott-simses.com

**Adams and Reese L.L.P.**
4500 One Shell Square
New Orleans, LA 70139
504-581-3234
504-566-0210 (fax)
http://www.arlaw.com

**Adorno & Zeder P.A.**
2601 South Bayshore Dr., Ste. 1600
Miami, FL 33133
305-858-5555
305-858-4777 (fax)
http://www.adorno.com
az@adorno.com

**Akerman, Senterfitt & Eidson, P.A.**
One Southeast Third Ave.
SunTrust International Center, 28th Floor
Miami, FL 33131
305-374-5600
305-374-5095 (fax)
http://www.akerman.com

**Akin, Gump, Strauss, Hauer & Feld L.L.P.**
1700 Pacific Avenue, Suite 4100
Dallas, TX 75201
214-969-2800
214-969-4343 (fax)
http://www.akingump.com
Whitney Adams, 214-969-4647, wadams@akingump.com

**Allen, Matkins, Leck, Gamble & Mallory L.L.P.**
515 South Figueroa St., 7th Floor
Los Angeles, CA 90071
213-622-5555
213-620-8816 (fax)
http://www.allenmatkins.com/
Deanna Wilkinson, 213-622-5555

**Altman, Kritzer & Levick, P.C.**
6400 Powers Ferry Rd., NW
Suite 224
Atlanta, Georgia 30339
770-955-3555
770-952-7821 (fax)
http://www.akl.com

**Alschuler Grossman Stein & Kahan L.L.P.**
2049 Century Park East, 39th Fl.
Los Angeles, CA 90067-3213
310-277-1226
310-552-6077 (fax)
http://www.agsk.com
Andrea Hodges, 310-551-9133,
   ahodges@agsk.com

**Alston & Bird L.L.P.**
One Atlantic Center
1201 West Peachtree St.
Atlanta, GA 30309-3424
404-881-7000
404-881-7777 (fax)
http://www.alston.com
Emily C. Shiels, 404-881-7014,
   eshiels@alston.com

**Alston, Hunt, Floyd & Ing L.C.**
1001 Bishop Street
Pacific Tower, 18th Floor
Honolulu, HI 96813-3689
808-524-1800
808-524-4591 (fax)
http://www.ahfi.com
Shelby Anne Floyd, sfloyd@ahfi.com

**Altheimer & Gray**
10 South Wacker Drive, Suite 4000
Chicago, IL 60606-7482
312-715-4000
312-715-4800 (fax)
http://www.altheimer.com
Nancy Verheyen, 312-715-4640,
   verheyenn@altheimer.com

**Anderson Kill & Olick P.C.**
1251 Avenue of the Americas
New York, NY 10020-1182
212-278-1000
212-278-1733 (fax)
http://www.andersonkill.com

**Andrews & Kurth L.L.P.**
Texas Commerce Tower
600 Travis, Suite 4200
Houston, TX 77002
713-220-4200
713-220-4285 (fax)
http://www.andrews-kurth.com
Kim Massingill, 713-220-4378, kim-massingill@andrews-kurth.com

**Archer & Greiner**
One Centennial Square
P.O. Box 3000
Haddonfield, NJ 08033-0968
856-795-2121
856-795-0574 (fax)
http://www.archerlaw.com
Gloria Hyde, ghyde@archerlaw.com

**Arent Fox Kintner Plotkin & Kahn P.L.L.C.**
1050 Connecticut Ave., N.W.
Washington, DC 20036
202-857-6000
202-857-6395 (fax)
http://www.arentfox.com
Colleen O'Hara, 202-857-6443, oharac@arentfox.com

**Armstrong Teasdale L.L.P.**
One Metropolitan Square, Suite 2600
211 North Broadway
St. Louis, MO 63102-2740
314-621-5070
314-621-5065 (fax)
http://www.armstrongteasdale.com
Debra Bollinger, 314-621-5070, dbolling@armstrongteasdale.com

**Arnall Golden & Gregory L.L.P.**
2800 One Atlantic Center
1201 W. Peachtree Street
Atlanta, GA 30309
404-873-8500
404-873-8501 (fax)
http://www.agg.com
Jennifer Harris, 404-870-5717

**Arnold & Porter**
555 12th Streeet, N.W.
Washington DC 20004
202-942-5000
202-942-5999 (fax)
http://www.aporter.com
Lisa Pavia, 202-942-5059, Lisa_Pavia@aporter.com

**Arnstein & Lehr**
120 South Riverside Plaza, Suite 1200
Chicago, IL 60606-3910
312-876-7100
312-876-0288 (fax)
http://www.arnstein.com
Kathleen Hanus, khanus@arnstein.com

**Arter & Hadden L.L.P.**
925 Euclid Avenue
1100 Huntington Building
Cleveland, OH 44115-1475
216-696-1100
216-696-2645 (fax)
http://www.arterhadden.com
Rita Maimbourg, 216-696-1100

**Ashby & Geddes**
One Rodney Square
P.O. Box 1150
Wilmington, DE 19899
302-654-1888
302-654-2067 (fax)
http://www.ashby-geddes.com

**Ashford & Wriston P.L.C.**
Alii Place, Suite 1400
1099 Alakea Street, P.O. Box 131
Honolulu, HI 96810
808-539-0400
808-533-4945 (fax)

**Atkinson, Andelson, Loya, Ruud & Romo P.C.**
17871 Park Plaza Dr, Suite 200
Cerritos, CA 90703
562-653-3200
562-653-3333 (fax)
http://www.aalrr.com

**Atlas, Pearlman, Trop & Borkson P.A.**
New River Center, Suite 1900
200 East Las Olas Boulevard
Fort Lauderdale, FL 33301
954-763-1200
954-766-7800 (fax)
http://www.atlaslaw.com

**Baer Marks & Upham L.L.P.**
805 Third Avenue
New York, NY 10022
212-702-5700
212-702-5941 (fax)
http://www.baermarks.com

B-6

**Baker & Botts L.L.P.**
910 Louisiana St.
One Shell Plaza
Houston, TX 77002
713-229-1234
713-229-1522 (fax)
http://www.bakerbotts.com
Melissa O' Neal, 713-229-1809,
   melissa.o'neal@bakerbotts.com

**Baker & Daniels**
300 Meridian St., Suite 2700
Indianapolis, IN 46204
317-237-0300
317-237-1000 (fax)
http://www.bakerdaniels.com

**Baker, Donelson, Bearman & Caldwell**
   **P.C.**
165 Madison Ave., Suite 2000
Memphis, TN 38103
901-526-2000
901-577-2303 (fax)
http://www.bakerdonelson.com
Sue S. Hunter, 615-726-5600,
   shunter@bdbc.com

**Baker & Hostetler L.L.P.**
1900 East Ninth Street
3200 National City Center
Cleveland, OH 44114-3485
216-621-0200
216-696-0740 (fax)
http://www.bakerlaw.com
Diane Kern, 216-861-7984, dkern@baker-
   law.com

**Baker & McKenzie**
130 E. Randolph Dr., Suite 2500
Chicago, IL 60601
312-861-8000
312-861-2899 (fax)
http://www.bakerinfo.com
Richard Franklin,
   Chicago.Employment@bakernet.com

**Balch & Bingham L.L.P.**
1710 Sixth Avenue North
Birmingham, AL 35203
205-251-8100
205-226-8798 (fax)
http://www.balch.com
Allison Wertheimer,
   AWERTHEI@balch.com

**Ballard Spahr Andrews & Ingersoll L.L.P.**
1735 Market St., 51st Floor
Philadelphia, PA 19103-7599
215-665-8500
215-864-8999 (fax)
http://www.ballardspahr.com
Bonnie Bell, 215-864-8163, bellb@ballardspahr.com

**Barger & Wolen**
515 South Flower Street, 34th Floor
Los Angeles, CA 90071
213-680-2800
213-614-7399 (fax)

**Barnes & Thornburg**
11 S. Meridian St.
Indianapolis, IN 46033
317-236-1313
317-231-7433 (fax)
http://www.btlaw.com
LaNell D. Black, 317-231-7435, lblack@btlaw.com

**Bass, Berry & Sims PLC**
315 Deaderick Street, Suite 2700
Nashville, TN 37238
615-742-6200
615-742-6293 (fax)
http://www.bassberry.com
Diane Marshall, 615-259-6446, dmarshall@bassberry.com

**Becker & Poliakoff P.A.**
3111 Stirling Road
Ft. Lauderdale, FL 33312-6525
954-987-7550
954-985-4176 (fax)
http://www.becker-poliakoff.com
Sandy Murugan, 954-987-7550, smurugan@becker-poliakoff.com

**Bell, Boyd & Lloyd L.L.C.**
Three First National Plaza
70 West Madison Street, St. #3300
Chicago, IL 60602
312-372-1121
312-372-2098 (fax)
http://www.bellboyd.com
Betsy Zukley, 312-338-5092, ezukley@bellboyd.com

**Benesch, Friedlander, Coplan & Aronoff L.L.P.**
2300 BP America Building, 200 Public Square
Cleveland, OH 44114-2378
216-363-4500
216-363-4588 (fax)
http://www.bfca.com
Denise E. Francis, 216-363-4649, dfrancis@bfca.com

**Berger, Kahn, Shafton, Moss, Figler, Simon & Gladstone P.C.**
4215 Glencoe Avenue, Second Floor
Marina del Rey, CA 90292-5634
310-821-9000
310-578-6178 (fax)
http://www.bergerkahn.com

**Best, Best & Krieger L.L.P.**
3750 University Venue
P.O. Box 1028 92502
Riverside, CA 92501
909-686-1450
909-686-3083 (fax)
http://www.bbklaw.com
Patricia Benter, pjbenter@bbkLAW.com

**Beveridge & Diamond P.C.**
1350 I Street N.W., Suite 700
Washington DC 20005-3311
202-789-6000
202-789-6190 (fax)
http://www.beveridgediamond.com
Rosemary Pollard, 202-789-6164, rpollard@bdlaw.com

**Biggs and Battaglia**
1800 Mellon Bank Center
P.O. Box 1489
Wilmington, DE 19899-1489
302-655-9677

**Bilzin Sumberg Dunn Price & Axelrod L.L.P.**
First Union Financial Center
200 South Biscayne Boulevard Ste. 2500
Miami, FL 33131
305-374-7580
305-374-7593 (fax)
http://www.bilzin.com

**Bingham Dana L.L.P.**
150 Federal St.
Boston, MA 02110-1726
617-951-8000
617-951-8736 (fax)
http://www.bingham.com
Maris L. Abbene, Esq., 617-951-8556

**Blue Williams L.L.P.**
3421 North Causeway Boulevard, 9th
  Floor
Metairie, LA 70002
504-831-4091
504-837-1182 (fax)
http://www.bluewilliams.com
Mary K. Peyton

**Bodman, Longley & Dahling LLP**
100 Renaissance Center, 34th Floor
Detroit, MI 48243
313-259-7777
313-393-7579 (fax)
http://www.bodmanlongley.com
Ralph E. McDowell, rmcdowell@bod-
  manlongley.com

**Blank Rome Comisky & McCauley
  L.L.P.**
One Logan Square
Philadelphia, PA 19103-6998
215-569-5500
215-569-5555 (fax)
http://www.blankrome.com
Donna M. Branca, 215-569-5751, bran-
  ca@blankrome.com

**Blatt, Hammesfahr & Eaton**
222 South Riverside Plaza, Suite 1500
Chicago, IL 60606
312-382-3100
312-382-8910 (fax)
http://www.bhelaw.com
Matthew Walsh, 312-382-3108,
  mwalsh@bhelaw.com

**Bingham Summers Welsh & Spillman**
2700 Market Tower Building
10 West Market Street
Indianapolis, IN
46204-2982
317-635-8900
317-236-9907 (fax)
http://www.bsws.com
Sallie Vincino, 317-635-8901 x267, svici-
  no@binghamsummers.com

**Blackwell Sanders Peper Martin L.L.P.**
2300 Main Street, Suite 1000
Kansas City, MO 64108
816-983-8000
816-983-8080 (fax)
http://www.blackwellsanders.com
Erin Waugh Gorny, 816- 983-8909,
  egorny@bspmlaw.com

**Bollinger Ruberry & Garvey**
500 W. Madison St.
Suite 2300
Chicago, IL 60661
312-466-8000
312-466-8001 (fax)

**Bond, Schoeneck & King L.L.P.**
One Lincoln Center
Syracuse, NY 13202-1355
315-422-0121
315-422-3598 (fax)
Ann Perrone, 315-422-0121

**Bonne, Bridges, Mueller, O'Keefe & Nichols**
3699 Wilshire Blvd., 10th floor
Los Angeles, CA 90010-2719
213-480-1900
213-738-5888 (fax)
http://www.bbmon.com
Ann Harvey, 213-738-5802

**Borton, Petrini & Conron L.L.P.**
1600 Truxtun Avenue
Bakersfield, CA 93301
661-322-3051
661-322-4664 (fax)
http://www.bpclaw.com
Mardi Poore, bpc_mpoore@msn.com

**Bose McKinney & Evans L.L.P.**
135 North Pennsylvania Street
Suite 2700
Indianapolis, IN 46204
317-684-5000
317-684-5173 (fax)
http://www.boselaw.com
Dee Doll, 317-684-5000,
    ddoll@boselaw.com

**Boult, Cummings, Conners & Berry P.L.C.**
414 Union Street, Suite 1600
Nashville, TN 37219
615-244-2582
615-252-2380 (fax)
http://www.bccb.com
Tara Boosey, 615-244-2582,
    tboosey@bccb.com

**Bowles Rice McDavid Graff & Love**
600 Quarrier Street
P.O. Box 1386
Charleston, WV 25325-1386
304-347-1100
304-343-2867 (fax)
http://www.bowlesrice.com
Ricklin Brown

**Bracewell & Patterson L.L.P.**
711 Louisiana St., Suite 2900
Houston, TX 77002-2781
713-223-2900
713-221-1212 (fax)
http://www.bracepatt.com
Melanie Beck, 713-221-1296, mbeck@bra-
    cepatt.com

**Bradley, Arant, Rose & White L.L.P.**
2001 Park Place, Suite 1400
Birmingham, AL 35203-2736
205-521-8000
205-521-8800 (fax)
http://www.barw.com
Kristin Denson, 205-521-8445, kden-
    son@barw.com

**Breazeale, Sachse & Wilson L.L.P.**
One American Place, Twenty-Third Floor
P.O. Box 3197
Baton Rouge, LA 70821-3197
225-387-4000
225-381-8029 (fax)
http://www.BSWLLP.com

**Bricker & Eckler L.L.P.**
100 South Third St.
Columbus, OH 43215
614-227-2300
614-227-2390 (fax)
http://www.bricker.com
Jim Flynn, jflynn@bricker.com

**Briggs and Morgan P.A.**
2200 First National Bank Building
332 Minnesota Street
St. Paul, MN 55101
651-223-6600
651-223-6450 (fax)
http://www.briggs.com
Laura Ward- Archbold, 612-334-8479,
    arclau@briggs.com

**Brinks Hofer Gilson & Lione**
455 N. Cityfront Plaza Drive
Suite 3600
Chicago, IL 60611
312-321-4200
312-321-4299 (fax)
http://www.brinkshofer.com
Kathy Early, 312-321-4269

**Broad and Cassel**
390 N. Orange Avenue, Suite 1100
Orlando, FL 32802
407-839-4200
407-425-8377 (fax)
http://www.broadandcassel.com
R. Kim Russell, 407-839-4210,
krussell@broadandcassel.com

**Brobeck, Phleger & Harrison L.L.P.**
One Market, Spear Street Tower, 28th
Floor
San Francisco, CA 94105
415-442-0900
415-442-1010 (fax)
http://www.brobeck.com
Ron Fago, 415-979-2457,
rfago@brobeck.com

**Brown & Bain P.A.**
2901 North Central Ave., Suite 2000
Phoenix, AZ 85012
602-351-8000
602-351-8516 (fax)
http://www.brownbain.com
Dori John, 602-351-8077,
hiringattys@brownbain.com

**Brown McCarroll & Oaks Hartline
L.L.P.**
111 Congress Avenue, Suite 1400
Austin, TX 78701-4043
512-472-5456
512-479-1101 (fax)
http://www.bmoh.com
Donna Daugherty, 512-479-1189

**Brown, Rudnick, Freed & Gesmer**
One Financial Center
Boston, MA 02111
617-856-8200
617-856-8201 (fax)
http://www.brownrudnick.com
Linda Manning, 617-856-8316, lman-
ning@brfg.com

**Brown, Todd & Heyburn P.L.L.C.**
400 W. Market Street, 32nd Fl.
Louisville, KY 40202-3363
502-589-5400
502-581-1087 (fax)
http://www.browntodd.com

**Brown & Wood L.L.P.**
One World Trade Center
New York, NY 10048
212-839-5300
212-839-5834 (fax)
http://www.brownwoodlaw.com
Maureen A. McGovern, 212-839-5406,
recruiting@brownwoodlaw.com

**Bryan Cave L.L.P.**
One Metropolitan Square
211 North Broadway, Suite 3600
St. Louis, MO 63102-2750
314-259-2000
314-259-2020 (fax)
http://www.bryancave.com
Jennifer Sloop, 314-259-2214,
jsloop@bryancavellp.com

**Buchalter, Nemer, Fields & Younger**
601 S. Figueroa Street, Suite 2400
Los Angeles, CA 90017
213-891-0700
213-896-0400 (fax)
http://www.buchalter.com
Kristy Sessions, 213-891-0700, ksessions@buchalter.com

**Buchanan Ingersoll P.C.**
One Oxford Centre, 20th Floor
301 Grant St.
Pittsburgh, PA 15219-1410
412-562-8800
412-562-1041 (fax)
http://www.bipc.com
Frances A. Muracca,
    muraccafa@bipc.com

**Buckingham, Doolittle & Burroughs L.L.P.**
50 S. Main St.
Akron, OH 44309
330-376-5300
330-258-6559 (fax)
http://www.bdblaw.com
Lisa B. Franz, 330-376-5300,
    lfranz@bdblaw.com

**Bullivant Houser Bailey P.C.**
888 SW Fifth Ave., Suite 300
Portland, OR 97204
503-228-6351
503-295-0915 (fax)
http://www.bullivant.com
Jill Baker, recruiting@bullivant.com

**Burke, Williams & Sorensen L.L.P.**
611 West Sixth Street, Suite 2500
Los Angeles, CA 90017
213-236-0600
213-236-2700 (fax)
http://www.bwslaw.com
Jack P. Lipton, jlipton@bwslaw.com

**Burnham & Brown P.C.**
1901 Harrison Street, 11th Floor
Oakland, CA 94612
510-444-6800
510-835-6666 (fax)
http://www.burnhambrown.com

**Burns, Doane, Swecker & Mathis L.L.P.**
1737 King Street, Suite 500
Alexandria, VA 22314
703-836-6620
703-836-2021 (fax)
http://www.burnsdoane.com
Janeanne Carlton, 703-838-6696, janean-
nc@burnsdoane.com

**Burns & Levinson L.L.P.**
125 Summer Street
Boston, MA 02110
617-345-3000
617-345-3299 (fax)
http://www.b-l.com
Allison B. Cunningham,
ACunningham@B-L.com

**Burr & Forman L.L.P.**
420 20th Street N. #3100
Birmingham, AL 35203
205-458-5121
205-458-5100 (fax)
http://www.burr.com

**Butler, Snow, O'Mara, Stevens &
    Cannada, PLC**
17th Floor, Deposit Guaranty Plaza
210 East Capitol St.
Post Office Box 22567
Jackson, MS 39225
601-948-5711
601-949-4555 (fax)
http://www.bsosc.com

**Butzel Long**
150 W. Jefferson, Suite 900
Detroit, MI 48226
313-225-7000
313-225-7080 (fax)
http://www.butzel.com
Terry Vadovski, vadovski@butzel.com

**Cades Schutte Fleming & Wright**
1000 Bishop Street
Honolulu, HI 96808
808-521-9200
808-521-9210 (fax)
http://www.cades.com
Sheree L.F. Belshe, sbelshe@cades.com

**Cadwalader, Wickersham & Taft**
100 Maiden Lane
New York, NY 10038
212-504-6000
212-504-6666 (fax)
http://www.cadwalader.com
Virginia Quinn, 212-504-6290,
    vquinn@cwt.com

**Cahill Gordon & Reindel**
80 Pine St.
New York, NY 10005-1702
212-701-3000
212-269-5420 (fax)
http://www.cahill.com

**Calfee, Halter & Griswold L.L.P.**
1400 McDonald Investment Center
800 Superior Ave.
Cleveland, 44114-2688
216-622-8200
216-241-0816 (fax)
http://www.calfee.com
Catherine A. Davis, 216-622-8200,
    cdavis@calfee.com

**Carlsmith Ball Wichman Case & Ichiki**
Suite 2200, Pacific Tower
1001 Bishop Street, P.O. Box 656
Honolulu, HI 96813
808-523-2500
808-523-0842 (fax)
http://www.carlsmith.com
execdirector@carlsmith.com

**Chadbourne & Parke L.L.P.**
30 Rockefeller Plaza
New York, NY 10112
212-408-5100
212-541-5369 (fax)
http://www.chadbourne.com
Bernadette L. Miles, 212-408-5338

**Chaffe, McCall, Phillips, Toler & Sarpy L.L.P.**
2300 Energy Centre
1100 Poydras Street
New Orleans, LA 70163-2300
504-585-7000
504-585-7075 (fax)
http://www.chaffe.com

**Carter, Ledyard & Milburn**
2 Wall Street
New York, NY 10005
212-732-3200
212-732-3232 (fax)
http://www.clm.com

**Case Bigelow & Lombardi L.C.**
2600 Grosvenor Center, Mauka Tower
737 Bishop Street
Honolulu, HI 96813
808-547-5400
808-523-1888 (fax)

**Cassiday Schade & Gloor**
20 N. Wacker Dr. Ste 1040
Chicago, IL 60606
312-641-3100
312-444-1669 (fax)
http://www.cassiday.com
Joseph A. Giannelli, 312-444-2487,
   JAG@cs-g.com

**Carlton, Fields, Ward, Emmanuel, Smith & Cutler P.A.**
One Harbour Place
777S Harbour Plaza
Tampa, FL 33602-5730
813-223-7000
813-229-4133 (fax)
http://www.carltonfields.com
Elizabeth B. Zabak, 813-223-7000,
   ezaba@carltonfields.com

**Carrington, Coleman, Sloman & Blumenthal, LLP**
200 Crescent Court #1500
Dallas, TX 75201
214-855-3000
214-855-1333 (fax)
http://www.carringtoncoleman.com
Kim Liptak, 214-855-3536,
   recruit@ccsb.com

**Chapman and Cutler**
111 West Monroe St.
Chicago, IL 60603
312-845-3000
312-701-2361 (fax)
http://www.chapman.com
Ann Rainhart

**Choate, Hall & Stewart**
Exchange Place
Boston, MA 02109
617-248-5000
617-248-4000 (fax)
http://www.choate.com
Robin Carbone, 617-248-5000

**Christensen, Miller, Fink, Jacobs, Glaser, Weil and Shapiro, L.L.P.**
2121 Avenue of the Stars, 18th Floor
Century City, CA 90067
310-553-3000
310-556-2920 (fax)
http://www.chrismill.com
Nancy Venturine, 310-553-3000,
 info@chrismill.com

**Christovich and Kearney L.L.P.**
Suite 2300 Pan American Life Center
601 Poydras Street
New Orleans, LA 70130-6078
504-561-5700
504-561-5743 (fax)

**Clark Hill P.L.C.**
500 Woodward Ave., Suite 3500
Detroit, MI 48226-3435
313-965-8300
313-965-8252 (fax)
http://www.clarkhill.com
Elizabeth A. Claes, (313-965-8253),
 eclaes@clarkhill.com

**Clark, Thomas & Winters P.C.**
12th Fl, Texas Commerce Bank Bldg.
700 Lavaca Street, P.O. Box 1148
Austin, TX 78767
512-472-8800
512-474-1129 (fax)
http://www.ctw.com

**Clausen Miller P.C.**
10 South LaSalle Street
Chicago, IL 60603-1098
312-855-1010
312-606-7777 (fax)
http://www.clausen.com
Linda Phillips, 312-606-7816

**Cleary, Gottlieb, Steen & Hamilton**
1 Liberty Plaza
New York, NY 10006
212-225-2000
212-225-3999 (fax)
http://www.cgsh.com
Norma F. Cirincione,
  NYRecruit@CGSH.com

**Clifford Chance Rogers & Wells L.L.P.**
200 Park Avenue
New York, NY 10166-0153
212-878-8000
212-878-8375 (fax)
http://www.cliffordchance.com
Carolyn Older, 212-878-8439,
  carolyn.older@cliffordchance.com

**Cole, Schotz, Meisel, Forman &**
  **Leonard, P.C.**
Court Plaza North, 25 Main Street
Hackensack, NJ 07602-0800
201-489-3000
201-489-1536 (fax)
hhtp://www.coleschotz.com
Gayle P. Englert, 201-525-6307, gen-
  glert@coleschotz.com

**Collier, Shannon, Rill & Scott, P.L.L.C.**
3050 K Street, N.W., Suite 400
Washington DC 20007
202-342-8400
202-342-8451 (fax)
http://www.colshan.com

**Connolly, Bove, Lodge & Hutz L.L.P.**
1220 Market Street PO Box 2207
Wilmington, DE 19899-2207
302-658-9141
302-658-5614 (fax)
http://www.cblhlaw.com
Joann Winterle, jmw@cblhlaw.com

**Cooch and Taylor**
824 Market Street Mall, Suite 1000
Wilmington, DE 19899
302-652-3641
302-652-5379 (fax)

**Cooley Godward L.L.P.**
5 Palo Alto Square
3000 El Camino Real
Palo Alto, CA 94306-2155
650-843-5000
650-857-0663 (fax)
http://www.cooley.com
Jo Ann Larson, 650-843-5000,
larsonja@cooley.com

**Coudert Brothers**
1114 Avenue of the Americas
New York, NY 10036
212-626-4400
212-626-4120 (fax)
http://www.coudert.com
Mary Simpson, 212-626-4400, simpsonm@coudert.com

**Covington & Burling**
1201 Pennsylvania Ave., NW
Washington DC 20004-2401
202-662-6000
202-662-6291 (fax)
http://www.cov.com
Lorraine L. Brown, 202-662-6000, legalrecruiting@cov.com

**Cowles & Thompson P.C.**
901 Main St., Ste. 4000
Dallas, TX 75202
214-672-2000
214-672-2020 (fax)
http://www.cowlesthompson.com

**Cox, Castle & Nicholson L.L.P.**
2049 Century Park East, 28th Floor
Los Angeles, CA 90067-3284
310-277-4222
310-277-7889 (fax)
http://www.ccnlaw.com
Kelly Ryan, 310- 284-2257, kryan@ccn-law.com

**Cozen and O'Connor P.C.**
1900 Market St.
Philadelphia, PA 19103
215-665-2000
215-665-2013 (fax)
http://www.cozen.com
Lori C. Rosenberg, Esq., 215-665-4178

**Cravath, Swaine & Moore**
Worldwide Plaza
825 Eighth Avenue
New York, NY 10019-7475
212-474-1000
212-474-3700 (fax)
http://www.cravath.com
Lisa A. Kalen, 212-474-3215

**Crosby, Heafey, Roach & May P.C.**
1999 Harrison Street
Oakland, CA 94604-2084
510-763-2000
510-273-8832 (fax)
http://www.crosbyheafey.com
Janice E Moore, 510- 763-2000,
  jmoore@chrm.com

**Crowell & Moring L.L.P.**
1001Pennsylvania Avenue, N.W.
Washington DC 20004-2595
202-624-2500
202-628-5116 (fax)
http://www.crowellmoring.com
Anneli Werner, 202-624-2500

**Crowley, Haughey, Hanson, Toole &**
   **Dietrich P.L.L.P.**
500 Transwestern II
490 North 31st St.
P.O.Box 2529
Billings, MT 59103-2529
406-252-3441
406-256-8526 (fax)
http://crowleylaw.com

**Cullen & Dykman**
177 Montague Street
Brooklyn, NY 11201-3611
(718) 855-9000
(718) 855-4282 (fax)
http://www.cullenanddykman.com

**Cummings & Lockwood**
Four Stamford Plaza
PO Box 120
Stamford, CT 06904-0120
203-327-1700
203-351-4532 (fax)
http://www.cl-law.com

**Curtis, Mallet-Prevost, Colt & Mosle**
101 Park Ave
New York, NY 10178-0061
212-696-6000
212-697-1559 (fax)
http://www.cm-p.com
Alberta Baigent, 212-696-6049,
  abaigent@cm-p.com

**D'Amato & Lynch**
70 Pine Street, 44th Floor
New York, NY 10270
212-269-0927
212-269-3559 (fax)

**D'Ancona & Pflaum**
111 E. Wacker Drive #2800
Chicago, IL 60601
312-602-2000
312-602-0923 (fax)
http://www.dancona.com/buzz
Dalene Bryl, 312-602-2000, dbryl@dancona.com

**Darby & Darby P.C.**
805 Third Avenue
New York, NY 10022-7513
212-527-7700
212-753-6237 (fax)
http://www.darbylaw.com
Patricia M. Scanlon

**Davis, Graham & Stubbs L.L.P.**
1550 Seventeenth St., Suite 500
Denver, CO 80202
303-892-9400
303-893-1379 (fax)
http://www.dgslaw.com
Candace Whitaker, (303) 892-7544, candace.whitaker@dgslaw.com

**Davis Polk & Wardwell**
450 Lexington Ave.
New York, NY 10017
212-450-4000
212-450-3800 (fax)
http://www.davispolk.com
Bonnie Hurry, 212-450-4144, hurry@dpw.com

**Davis Wright Tremaine L.L.P.**
2600 Century Square
1501 Fourth Avenue
Seattle, WA 98101-1688
206-662-3150
206-628-7699 (fax)
http://www.dwt.com
Carol Yuly, 206-662-3150

**Day, Berry & Howard L.L.P.**
City Place I
185 Asylum St.
Hartford, CT 06103-3499
860-275-0100
860-275-0343 (fax)
http://www.dbh.com
Barbara Boisclair, 860- 275-0307, bboisclair@dbh.com

**Dickie, McCamey & Chilcote P.C.**
Two PPG Place, Suite 400
Pittsburgh, PA 15222-5402
412-281-7272
412-392-5367 (fax)
http://www.dmclaw.com

**Dickinson Wright P.L.L.C.**
500 Woodward, Suite 4000
Detroit, MI 48226-3425
313-223-3500
313-223-3598 (fax)
http://www.dickinsonwright.com
Tom McNeill, 313-223-3500,
    tmcneill@dickinson-wright.com

**Deutsch, Kerrigan & Stiles L.L.P.**
755 Magazine Street
New Orleans, LA 70130-3672
504-581-5141
504-566-1201 (fax)
http://www.dkslaw.com
Judy L. Burnthorn, 504-581-5141, jburn-
    thorn@dksno.com

**Dewey Ballantine L.L.P.**
1301 Avenue of the Americas
New York, NY 10019-6092
212-259-8000
212-259-6333 (fax)
http://www.deweyballantine.com
William H. Davis, 212-259-7328, nyre-
    cruiting@deweyballantine.com

**Debevoise & Plimpton**
875 Third Avenue, Floor 23
New York, NY 10022
212-909-6000
212-909-6836 (fax)
http://www.debevoise.com

**Dechert**
4000 Bell Atlantic Tower
1717 Arch St.
Philadelphia, PA 19103-2793
215-994-4000
215-994-2222 (fax)
http://www.dechert.com
Carol S. Miller, 215-994-2147,
    carol.miller@dechert.com

**Dickstein Shapiro Morin & Oshinsky L.L.P.**
2101 L Street, N.W.
Washington DC 20037-1526
202-785-9700
202-887-0689 (fax)
http://www.dsmo.com
careers@dsmo.com

**Dilworth Paxson Kalish & Kauffman L.L.P.**
3200 Mellon Bank Center
1735 Market St.
Philadelphia, PA 19103
215-575-7000
215-575-7200 (fax)
http://www.dpkk.com
Linda L. Parthemer, 215- 575-7208, partheml@dilworthlaw.com

**Dinsmore & Shohl L.L.P.**
1900 Chemed Center
255 East Fifth St.
Cincinnati, OH 45202
513-977-8200
513-977-8141 (fax)
http://www.dinslaw.com
Patricia C. Ventress, 513-977-8200

**Dorsey & Whitney L.L.P.**
220 South Sixth Street
Minneapolis, MN 55402-1498
612-340-2600
612-340-2868 (fax)
http://www.dorseylaw.com
Melissa Starkey, starkey.melissa@dorsey-law.com

**Dow, Lohnes & Albertson**
1200 New Hampshire Ave, N.W.,
Suite 800
Washington DC 20036-6802
202-776-2000
202-776-2222 (fax)
http://www.dlalaw.com
Nanette Marton, 202-776-2000, nmar-ton@dlalaw.com

**Drinker Biddle & Reath L.L.P.**
One Logan Square
18th and Cherry Streets
Philadelphia, PA 19103-6996
215-988-2700
215-988-2757 (fax)
http://www.dbr.com
Maryellen Wyrille, 215-988-2700

**Duane, Morris & Heckscher L.L.P.**
One Liberty Place
1650 Market Street
Philadelphia, PA 19103-7396
215-979-1000
215-979-1020 (fax)
http://www.duanemorris.com

**Dykema Gossett P.L.L.C.**
400 Renaissance Center
Detroit, MI 48243-1668
313-568-6800
313-568-6893 (fax)
http://www.dykema.com
Kimberly Amodeo, 313-568-6800,
kamodeo@dykema.com

**Eckert Seamans Cherin & Mellott
L.L.C.**
600 Grant Street - 44th Floor
Pittsburgh, PA 15219
412-566-6000
412-566-6099 (fax)
http://www.escm.com
Kristin J. Gaydosh, 412-566-6000

**Edwards & Angell**
One Bank Boston Plaza
Providence, RI 02903
401-274-9200
401-276-6611 (fax)
http://www.EALaw.com
Julie A. Nassaney, jnassaney@ealaw.com

**English, McCaughan & O'Bryan P.A.**
First Fort Lauderdale Place
100 N.E. 3rd Ave, Ste. 1100
Fort Lauderdale, FL 33301-1146
954-462-3300
954-763-2439 (fax)
http://www.emo-law.com

**Epstein Becker & Green P.C.**
250 Park Ave.
New York, NY 10177-0077
212-351-4500
212-661-0989 (fax)
http://www.ebglaw.com
Linda Altschul, 212-351-4500,
laltschu@ebglaw.com

**Fish & Richardson P.C.**
225 Franklin St.
Boston, MA 02110-2804
617-542-5070
617-542-8906 (fax)
http://www.fr.com
Jill E. McDonald, 617-542-5070,
jobs@fr.com

**Fisher & Phillips L.L.P.**
1500 Resurgens Plaza
945 E. Paces Ferry Rd.
Atlanta, GA 30326
404-231-1400
404-240-4249 (fax)
http://www.laborlawyers.com

**Fitzpatrick, Cella, Harper & Scinto**
30 Rockefeller Plaza
New York, NY 10112-3801
212-218-2100
212-218-2200 (fax)
http://www.fchs.com

**Fenwick & West L.L.P.**
Two Palo Alto Square
Palo Alto, CA 94306
650-494-0600
650-494-1417 (fax)
http://www.fenwick.com
Karen Amatangelo-Block, kamatange-
lo@fenwick.com

**Finnegan, Henderson, Farabow, Garrett & Dunner L.L.P.**
1300 I Street, NW
Washington DC 20005-3315
202-408-4000
202-408-4400 (fax)
http://www.finnegan.com

**Fish & Neave**
1251 Avenue of the Americas
New York, NY 10020
212-596-9000
212-596-9090 (fax)
http://www.fishneave.com

**Evans & Dixon L.L.C.**
1200 Saint Louis Place
200 North Broadway
St. Louis, MO 63102-2730
314-621-7755
314-621-3136 (fax)
http://www.evans-dixon.com

**Faegre & Benson L.L.P.**
2200 Norwest Center
90 South Seventh Street
Minneapolis, MN 55402-3901
612-336-3000
612-336-3026 (fax)
http://www.faegre.com

**Fennemore Craig P.C.**
3003 North Central Ave. #2600
Phoenix, AZ 85012-2913
602-916-5000
602-916-5999 (fax)
http://www.fclaw.com
Laura Zilmer, 888-916-5272

**Foley, Hoag & Eliot L.L.P.**
One Post Office Square
Boston, MA 02109
617-832-1000
617-832-7000 (fax)
http://www.fhe.com
Dina M. Wreede, 617-832-7060,
dwreede@fhe.com

**Foley & Lardner**
777 E. Wisconsin Ave.
Milwaukee, WI 53202
414-271-2400
414-297-4900 (fax)
http://www.foleylardner.com
Alice Hanson-Drew, 414-271-2400, ahan-
sondrew@foleylaw.com

**Foster Pepper & Shefelman P.L.L.C.**
1111 Third Avenue, Suite 3400
Seattle, WA 98101
206-447-4400
206-447-9700 (fax)
http://www.foster.com
Lisa Muller, 206-447-4400,
mulle@foster.com

**Foulston & Siefkin L.L.P.**
Bank of America Center
100 N. Broadway
Witchita, KS 67202
316-267-6371
316-267-6345 (fax)
http://www.foulston.com
Wyatt Hoch, 316-291-9769, whoch@foul-
ston.com

**Fowler, White, Burnett, Hurley, Banick
& Strickroot P.A.**
Bank of America Tower ,17th floor
100 S.E. Second Street
Miami, FL 33131
305-789-9200
305-789-9201 (fax)
http://www.fowler-white.com

**Fowler, White, Gillen, Boggs, Villareal
& Banker P.A.**
501 E. Kennedy Blvd, Suite 1700
Tampa, FL 33602
813-228-7411
813-229-8313 (fax)
http://www.fowlerwhite.com
Amy M. Polonsky, 813-228-7411, polon-
sky@fowlerwhite.com

**Fox, Rothschild, O'Brien & Frankel, L.L.P.**
2000 Market Street, 10th Floor
Philadelphia, PA 19103-3291
215-299-2000
215-299-2150 (fax)
http://www.frof.com
Jean A. Durling, 215-299-2808

**Fredrikson & Byron P.A.**
1100 International Centre
900 Second Ave South
Minneapolis, MN 55402-3397
612-347-7000
612-347-7077 (fax)
http://www.fredlaw.com
Greta Larson, glarson@fredlaw.com

**Freeborn & Peters**
311 S. Wacker Drive, Suite 3000
Chicago, IL 60606-6677
312-360-6000
312-360-6520 (fax)
http://www.freebornpeters.com
Julie Yedinak, 312- 360-6532,
jyedinak@freebornpeters.com

**Fried, Frank, Harris, Shriver & Jacobson**
One New York Plaza
New York, NY 10004-1980
212-859-8000
212-859-4000 (fax)
http://www.ffhsj.com

**Frilot, Partridge, Kohnke & Clements L.C.**
3600 Energy Centre
1100 Poydras Street
New Orleans, LA 70163-3600
504-599-8000
504-599-8100 (fax)
http://www.fpkc.com
Peter Sperling, 504-599-8015,
pes@fpkc.com

**Frost & Jacobs L.L.P.**
2500 PNC Center,
201 East Fifth Street
Cincinnati, OH 45202-5715
513-651-6800
513-651-6981 (fax)
http://www.frojac.com
Karen Laymance, 513-651-6875, klay-
mance@frojac.com

**Fulbright & Jaworski L.L.P.**
1301 McKinney, Suite 5100
Houston, TX 77010-3095
713-651-5151
713-651-5246 (fax)
http://www.fulbright.com
Leslie Rice, 713-651-5151, lstiver@fulbright.com

**Gallagher & Kennedy P.A.**
2575 E Camelback Rd
Phoenix, AZ 85016-9225
602-530-8000
602-530-8500 (fax)
http://www.gknet.com
Mike Kennedy, 602-530-8000, gk@gknet.com

**Gardere & Wynne L.L.P.**
Thanksgiving Tower, Suite 3000
1601 Elm St.
Dallas, TX 75201
214-999-3000
214-999-4667 (fax)
http://www.gardere-law.com
De Lyla Alexander, dalexander@gardere.com

**Gardner, Carton & Douglas**
Suite 3400 Quaker Tower
321 N.Clark St.
Chicago, IL 60610
312-644-3000
312-644-3381 (fax)
http://www.gcd.com
Lisa A. McLafferty, lmclafferty@gcd.com

**Garvey, Schubert & Barer**
1191 2nd Avenue, 18th Floor
Seattle, WA 98101-2939
206-464-3939
206-464-0125 (fax)
http://www.gsblaw.com

**George, Hartz, Lundeen, Flagg & Fulmer**
4800 LeJeune Road
Miami, FL 33146
305-662-4800
305-667-8015 (fax)

**Gibbons, Del Deo, Dolan, Griffinger & Vecchione P.C.**
One Riverfront Plaza
Newark, NJ 07102-5497
973-596-4500
973-596-0545 (fax)
http://www.gibbonslaw.com

**Gibson, Dunn & Crutcher L.L.P.**
333 South Grand Ave.
Los Angeles, CA 90071-3197
213-229-7000
213-229-7520 (fax)
http://www.gdclaw.com

**Godfrey & Kahn, S.C.**
780 North Water Street
Milwaukee, WI 53202-3590
414-273-3500
414-273-5198 (fax)
http://www.gklaw.com
Kelly Kirk

**Goodwin, Procter & Hoar L.L.P.**
Exchange Place
Boston, MA
02109
617-570-1000
617-523-1231 (fax)
http://www.gph.com
Maureen A. Shea

**Gordon & Rees L.L.P.**
275 Battery Street, Suite 2000
San Francisco, CA 94111
415-986-5900
415-986-8054 (fax)
http://www.gordonrees.com
Susan Roe, sumrec@gordonrees.com

**Gordon, Thomas, Honeywell, Malanca, Peterson & Daheim P.L.L.C.**
2200 Wells Fargo Plaza
Tacoma, WA 98401
253-572-5050
253-620-6565 (fax)
http://www.gth-law.com

**Goulston & Storrs P.C.**
400 Atlantic Avenue
Boston, MA 02110-3333
617-482-1776
617-574-4112 (fax)
http://www.goulstonstorrs.com

**Graham & James L.L.P. One Maritime Plaza, Suite 300**
San Francisco, CA 94117-3492
415-954-0200
415-391-2493 (fax)
http://www.gj.com
Esther Sprague, resumes-sf@gj.com

**Gray Cary Ware & Freidenrich L.L.P.**
400 Hamilton Avenue
Palo Alto, CA 94301
650-833-2000
650-327-3699 (fax)
http://www.graycary.com
Leslie Colvin (N.Cal.), 650-833-2133,
Roberta Shrimpton (S. Cal.), 619-699-3478

**Gray Plant Mooty Mooty & Bennett P.A.**
3400 City Center, 33 South 6th St.
Minneapolis, MN 55402-3796
612-343-2800
612-333-0066 (fax)
http://www.gpmlaw.com
Linda M. Spotts, 612-343-2946, linda.spotts@gpmlaw.com

**Graydon, Head & Ritchey**
1900 Fifth Third Center
511 Walnut St.
Cincinnati, OH 45202
513-621-6464
513-651-3836 (fax)
http://www.graydon.com
Emily Cole, 513-621-6464, ecole@gray-don.com

**Greenbaum, Rowe, Smith, Ravin, Davis & Himmel L.L.P.**
P.O. Box 5600
Woodbridge, NJ 07095
732-549-5600
732-549-1881 (fax)
http://www.greenbaumlaw.com
Susan Lehner

**Greenberg Glusker Fields Claman & Machtinger L.L.P.**
21st Floor, 1900 Avenue of the Stars
Los Angeles, CA 90067
310-553-3610
310-553-0687 (fax)
http://www.ggfcm.com
Patricia Patrick, 310-201-7431, ppatrick@ggfcm.com

**Greenberg Traurig P.A.**
1221 Brickell Avenue
Miami, FL 33131
305-579-0500
305-579-0717 (fax)
http://www.gtlaw.com
Janet MeKeegan, 305-579-0855, recruit@gtlaw.com

**Greenebaum Doll & McDonald P.L.L.C.**
3300 National City Tower
101 South Fifth Street
Louisville, KY 40202
502-589-4200
502-587-3695 (fax)
http://www.gdm.com
Jeffery McKenzie, 502-587-3594, jam@gdm.com

**Greensfelder, Hemker & Gale P.C.**
2000 Equitable Building
10 South Broadway
St. Louis, MO 63102
314-241-9090
314-241-8624 (fax)
http://www.greensfelder.com
Lisa Nielsen, 314-241-8624, ghg@greens-felder.com

**Gunster, Yoakley, Valdes-Fauli & Stewart, P.A.**
777 South Flagler Drive, Suite 500
West Palm Beach, FL 33401
561-655-1980
561-655-5677 (fax)
http://www.gunster.com
Nora Miller, 561-650-0783, nmiller@gunster.com

**Hahn Loeser & Parks L.L.P.**
3300 BP America Building
200 Public Square
Cleveland, OH 44114-2301
216-621-0150
216-241-2824 (fax)
http://www.hahnlaw.com
Terri-Lynn Smiles, 614-233-5130, tbsmiles@hahnlaw.com

**Haight, Brown & Bonesteel L.L.P.**
1620 26th St., Suite 4000N
Santa Monica, CA 90404-4013
310-449-6000
310-829-5117 (fax)
http://www.hbblaw.com
Julie S. Lantz, 310-449-6000, lantzj@hbblaw.com

**Hale and Dorr L.L.P.**
60 State Street
Boston, MA 02109
617-526-6000
617-526-5000 (fax)
http://www.haledorr.com
Lizet Garcia, 617-526-6000

**Hall, Estill, Hardwick, Gable, Golden & Nelson P.C.**
320 South Boston Avenue, Suite 400
Tulsa, OK 74103-3708
918-594-0400
918-594-0499 (fax)
http://www.hallestill.com

**Hall & Evans, L.L.C.**
1200 Seventeenth Street, Suite 1700
Denver, CO 80202
303-628-3300
303-628-3368 (fax)
http://www.hallevans.com

**Hancock, Rothert & Bunshoft L.L.P.**
4 Embarcadero Center
Suite 300
San Francisco, CA  94111-4168
415-981-5550
415-955-2599 (fax)
http://www.hrblaw.com
Catherine Christ, 415-981-5550

**Harrington, Foxx, Dubrow & Canter**
Thirtieth Floor, 611 West Sixth
Los Angeles, CA  90017
213-489-3222
213-623-7929 (fax)

**Harris Beach & Wilcox L.L.P.**
130 E. Main Street
Rochester, NY  14604
716-232-4440
716-232-6925 (fax)
http://www.harrisbeach.com
Beth Fredrickson, 716-232-4440

**Harter, Secrest & Emery L.L.P.**
700 Midtown Tower
Rochester, NY  14604-2070
716-232-6500
716-232-2152 (fax)
http://www.hartersecrest.com
Ann B. Austin, 716-231-1292,
   aaustin@hselaw.com

**Haynes and Boone L.L.P.**
901 Main Street, Suite 3100
Dallas, TX  75202-3789
214-651-5000
214-651-5940 (fax)
http://www.hayboo.com
Marina O'Con, 214-651-5720,
   oconm@haynesboone.com

**Haynsworth, Marion, McKay &**
   **Guerard L.L.P.**
Two Liberty Square, 11th Flr.
75 Beattie Place
Greenville, SC  29601
864-240-3200
(864-240-3300) (fax)
http://www.hmmg.com
mgmcdonald@hmmg.com

**Heller Ehrman White & McAuliffe**
333 Bush Street
San Francisco, CA  94104-2878
415-772-6000
415-772-6268 (fax)
http://www.hewm.com
Melissa Katz

**Henderson, Franklin, Starnes & Holt P.A.**
1715 Monroe Street
P.O. Box 280
Fort Myers, FL 33902-0280
941-334-4121
941-334-4100 (fax)
http://henlaw.com
info@henlaw.com

**Herzfeld & Rubin**
40 Wall St.
New York, NY 10005
212-344-5500
212-344-3333 (fax)
http://www.hr.ro.com

**Hill & Barlow, P.C.**
One International Place
Boston, MA 02110-2607
617-428-3000
617-428-3500 (fax)
http://www.hillbarlow.com
Karen Mondell, 617-428-3580, kmon-
   dell@hillbarlow.com

**Hinckley, Allen & Snyder**
28 State Street
Boston, MA 02109
617-345-9000
617-345-9020 (fax)
http://www.haslaw.com

**Hinshaw & Culbertson**
222 N. LaSalle Street, Suite 300
Chicago, IL 60601-1081
312-704-3000
312-704-3001 (fax)
http://www.hinshawculbertson.com
Anne Connor, 312-704-3000,
   aconnor@hinshawlaw.com

**Hodgson, Russ, Andrews, Woods &**
   **Goodyear L.L.P.**
One M&T Plaza, Suite 2000
Buffalo, NY 14203
716-856-4000
716-849-0349 (fax)
http://www.hodgsonruss.com
Mary Kelkenberg, mkelkenb@hodgson-
   russ.com

**Hopkins & Sutter**
Three First National Plaza
Chicago, IL 60602-4305
312-558-6600
312-558-6538 (fax)
http://www.hopsut.com
Jamie L. Bailey, 312-558-6567,
  jbailey@hopsut.com

**Howard, Rice, Nemerovski, Canady,
  Falk & Rabkin P.C.**
7th Floor, Three Embarcadero Center
San Francisco, CA 94111-4065
415-434-1600
415-217-5910
http://www.howardrice.com
Naomi Smith, 415-765-4693,
  recruit@hrice.com

**Holme Roberts & Owen L.L.P.**
1700 Lincoln St., #4100
Denver, CO 80203-4541
303-861-7000
303-866-0200 (fax)
http://www.hro.com
Cindy Hyman, 303-866-0626

**Honigman Miller Schwartz and Cohn**
660 Woodward Avenue
2290 First National Building
Detroit, MI 48226
313-465-7000
313-465-8000 (fax)
http://law.honigman.com
Julie M. Ankers, 313-465-7064,
  jmp@honigman.com

**Hogan & Hartson L.L.P.**
555 13th Street, N.W.
Washington DC 20004
202-637-5600
202-637-5910 (fax)
http://www.hhlaw.com

**Holland & Hart L.L.P.**
555 17th Street, Suite 3200
Denver, CO 80202-3979
303-295-8000
303-295-8261 (fax)
http://www.hollandhart.com.
Julie Carroll, jcarroll@hollandhart.com

**Holland & Knight L.L.P.**
400 North Ashley Dr., Suite 2300
Tampa, FL 33602
813-227-8500
813-229-0134 (fax)
http://www.hklaw.com

**Hunton & Williams**
Riverfront Plaza, East Tower
951 East Byrd St.
Richmond, VA 23219
804-788-8200
804-788-8218 (fax)
http://www.hunton.com
Myrna L. Banaszak, 804-788-8527,
   mbanaszak@hunton.com

**Husch & Eppenberger L.L.C.**
100 North Broadway, Suite 1300
St. Louis, MO 63102
314-421-4800
314-421-0239 (fax)
http://www.husch.com
Belinda Ramsbottom, 314-421-4800,
   belinda.ramsbottom@husch.com

**Hughes Hubbard & Reed L.L.P.**
One Battery Park Plaza
New York, NY 10004-1482
212-837-6000
212-837-4726 (fax)
http://www.hugheshubbard.com
Joann M. Byrne, 212-837-6486,
   byrne@hugheshubbard.com

**Hughes & Luce L.L.P.**
1717 Main Street, Ste. 2800
Dallas, TX 75201
214-939-5500
214-939-5849 (fax)
http://www.hughesluce.com
Nancy E. Louden, 214-939-5517, nan-
   cyk@hughesluce.com

**Howrey, Simon, Arnold & White**
1299 Pennsylvania Ave., N.W.
Washington DC 20004
202-783-0800
202-383-6610 (fax)
http://www.howrey.com
Sarah Ford, 202-383-7358

**Hudson, Jones, Jaywork, Fisher &
   Liguori**
225 South State Street
Dover, DE 19901
302-734-7401
302-734-5532 (fax)
http://www.delawarelaw.com

**Hutchins, Wheeler & Dittmar**
101 Federal Street
Boston, MA 02110
617-951-6600
617-951-1295 (fax)
http://www.hutch.com
Stacey M. Pappas, 617-951-6955,
  sps@hutch.com

**Ice Miller Donadio & Ryan**
One American Square Box 82001
Indianapolis, IN 46282-0002
317-236-2100
317-236-2219 (fax)
http://www.imdr.com
Lisa Watson, watson@icemiller.com

**Irell & Manella L.L.P.**
1800 Avenue of the Stars, Suite 900
Los Angeles, CA 90067-4276
310-277-1010
310-203-7199 (fax)
http://www.irell.com
Robyn Steele, 800-421-4502

**Jackson & Kelly**
Suite 1600 Laidley Tower
P.O. Box 553
Charleston, WV 25322
304-340-1000
(304-340-1130) (fax)
http://www.jacksonkelly.com
Robert G. McLusky, 304-340-1381,
  rmclusky@jacksonkelly.com

**Jackson Lewis Schnitzler & Krupman**
One North Broadway, 15th Flr.
White Plains, NY 10601
914-328-0404
914-328-1882 (fax)
http://www.jacksonlewis.com

**Jackson Walker L.L.P.**
901 Main St., Suite 6000
Dallas, TX 75202
214-953-6000
214-953-5822 (fax)
http://www.jw.com
Lindsay Cagan, 214-953-6029,
  lcagan@jw.com

**Jaffe, Raitt, Heuer & Weiss, P.C.**
One Woodward, Suite 2400
Detroit, MI 48226
313-961-8380
313-961-8358 (fax)
www.jafferaitt.com
recruiting@jafferaitt.com

**Jeffer, Mangels, Butler & Marmaro L.L.P.**
2121 Avenue of the Stars, Tenth Floor
Los Angeles, CA 90067
310-201-3551
310-203-0567 (fax)
http://www.davidconn.com

**Jenkens & Gilchrist P.C.**
1445 Ross Avenue, Suite 3200
Dallas, TX 75202-2799
214-855-4500
214-855-4300 (fax)
http://www.jenkens.com
Lauren Sager, 214-855-4833

**Jenner & Block**
One IBM Plaza
Chicago, IL 60611-3608
312-222-9350
312-527-0484 (fax)
http://www.jenner.com
legalrecruiting@jenner.com

**Jennings, Strouss & Salmon, P.L.C.**
One Renaissance Square
Two North Central Avenue, Suite 1600
Phoenix, AZ 85004-2393
602-262-5911
602-253-3255 (fax)
http://www.jsslaw.com
Janice K. Baker, 602-262-5910, jbaker@jss-law.com

**Jones, Day, Reavis & Pogue**
North Point, 901 Lakeside Avenue
Cleveland, OH 44114
216-586-3939
216-579-0212 (fax)
http://www.jonesday.com

**Jones, Walker, Waechter, Poitevent, Carrère & Denègre L.L.P.**
201 St. Charles Avenue
New Orleans, LA 70170
504-582-8000
504-582-8010 (fax)
http://www.jwlaw.com
recruiting@joneswalker.com

**Katten Muchin & Zavis**
525 West Monroe St., Suite 1600
Chicago, IL 60661-3693
312-902-5200
312-902-1061 (fax)
http://www.kmz.com

**Katz, Barron, Squitero & Faust P.A.**
2699 South Bayshore Dr., 7th Floor
Miami, FL 33133-5408
305-856-2444
305-285-9227 (fax)
http://www.katzbarron.com

**Kaye, Scholer, Fierman, Hays &**
**Handler L.L.P.**
425 Park Avenue
New York, NY 10022
212-836-8000
212-836-8689 (fax)
http://www.kayescholer.com

**Kean, Miller, Hawthorne, D'Armond,**
**McCowan & Jarman L.L.P.**
22nd Floor, One American Place
P.O. Box 3513
Baton Rouge, LA 70821
225-387-0999
225-388-9133 (fax)
http://www.KMLAW.COM
Kelly Johannessen, kellyj@kmlaw.com

**Keesal, Young & Logan**
400 Oceangate
P.O. Box 1730
Long Beach, CA 90801-1730
562-436-2000
562-436-7416 (fax)
http://www.kyl.com
recruiting@kyl.com

**Kelley Drye & Warren L.L.P.**
101 Park Avenue
New York, NY 10178
212-808-7897
212-808-7898 (fax)
http://www.kelleydrye.com
Megan Clouden, 212-808-7510

**Kelly, Hart & Hallman P.C.**
201 Main St., Suite 2500
Fort Worth, TX 76102
817-332-2500
817-878-9280 (fax)
www.khh.com

**Kennedy Covington Lobdell &**
**Hickman L.L.P.**
Bank of America Corporate Center
100 North Tryon Street, Suite 4200
Charlotte, NC 28202-4006
704-331-7400
704-331-7598 (fax)
www.kennedycovington.com
Courtney Myers

**Kenyon & Kenyon**
One Broadway
New York, NY 10004-1050
212-425-7200
212-425-5288 (fax)
http://www.kenyon.com
Kathleen Lynn, 212-908-6177,
klynn@kenyon.com

**Klehr Harrison Harvey Branzburg & Ellers**
260 South Broad Street
Philadelphia, PA 19102-5003
215-568-6060
215-568-6603 (fax)
http://www.klehr.com
Barry Siegel

**Klett Rooney Lieber & Schorling**
One Oxford Centre, 40th Floor
Pittsburgh, PA 15219-6498
412-392-2000
412-392-2000 (fax)
http://www.klettrooney.com

**Knobbe, Martens, Olson & Bear L.L.P.**
620 Newport Center Drive, 16th Floor
Newport Beach, CA 92660
949-760-0404
949-760-9502 (fax)
http://www.kmob.com

**Kirkland & Ellis**
200 E. Randolph Drive
Chicago, IL 60601
312-861-2000
312-861-2200 (fax)
http://www.kirkland.com
Kimberly J. Klein, 312-861-8785, kimber-ley_klein@chicago.kirkland.com

**Kirkpatrick & Lockhart L.L.P.**
Henry W. Oliver Building
535 Smithfield Street
Pittsburgh, PA 15222
412-355-6500
412-355-6501 (fax)
http://www.kl.com
Michele Bendekovic

**Kilpatrick Stockton L.L.P.**
3737 Glenwood Avenue, Suite 400
Raleigh, NC 27612
919-420-1700
919-420-1800 (fax)
http://www.kilstock.com
Kim Dechiara, 404-815-6407

**King, Leblanc & Bland L.L.P.**
3800 Bank One Center
201 St. Charles Avenue
New Orleans, LA 70170
504-582-3800
504-582-1233 (fax)
http://www.klb-law.com

**King & Spalding**
191 Peachtree St.
Atlanta, GA 30303-1763
404-572-4600
404-572-5100 (fax)
http://www.kslaw.com
Rebecca M. Newton, 404-572-3395

**Kramer Levin Naftalis & Frankel L.L.P.**
919 Third Avenue
New York, NY 10022-3852
212-715-9100
212-715-8000 (fax)
http://www.kramer-levin.com
Michelle Fracasso, 212-715-9212, mfra-
cass@kramerlevin.com

**Kutak Rock**
The Omaha Building
1650 Farnam Street
Omaha, NE 68102-2186
402-346-6000
402-346-1148 (fax)
http://www.kutakrock.com
Jeanne Salerno, 402-346-6000,
jeanne.salerno@kutakrock.com

**La Follette, Johnson, De Haas, Fesler,
Silberberg & Ames P.C.**
865 South Figueroa Street, Ste. 3100
Los Angeles, CA 90017-2543
213-426-3600
213-426-3650 (fax)

**Lane Powell Spears Lubersky L.L.P.**
1420 Fifth Avenue, Suite 4100
Seattle, WA 98101-2338
206-223-7000
206-223-7107 (fax)
http://www.lanepowell.com
Len Roden, 206-223-6123,
roden@lanepowell.com

**Larkin, Hoffman, Daly & Lindgren**
1500 Norwest Financial Center
7900 Xerxes Avenue South
Bloomington, MI 55431
952-835-3800
952-896-3333 (fax)
http://www.lhdl.com
recruitptnr@lhdl.com

**Latham & Watkins**
633 West 5th St., Suite 4000
Los Angeles, CA 90071-2007
213-485-1234
213-891-8763 (fax)
http://www.lw.com
Jamie Frick, jamie.frick@lw.com

**Lewis, D'Amato, Brisbois & Bisgaard L.L.P.**
221 North Figueroa St., Suite 1200
Los Angeles, CA 90012
213-250-1800
213-250-7900 (fax)
http://www.ldbb.com

**Lewis, Rice & Fingersh L.C.**
500 N. Broadway, Suite 2000
St. Louis, MO 63102
314-444-7600
314-241-6056 (fax)
http://www.lrf.com
Julia J. Lilly, 314-444-7817, jlilly@lewis-rice.com

**Lemle & Kelleher L.L.P.**
Pan-American Life Center
601 Poydras Street, 21 Flr.
New Orleans, LA 70130
504-586-1241
504-584-9142 (fax)
http://www.lemle.com
Maureen Perry, 504-586-1241, mperry@lemle.com

**Leonard, Street and Deinard P.A.**
150 South Fifth Street, Suite 2300
Minneapolis, MN 55402
612-335-1500
612-335-1657 (fax)
http://www.leonard.com
Dianne Dimond, 612-335-1529

**Lathrop & Gage L.C.**
2345 Grand Blvd., Suite 2500 Kansas City, MI 64108-2684
816-292-2000
816-292-2001 (fax)
http://www.lathropgage.com
Cheri Dwyer, 816-292-2000

**LeBoeuf, Lamb, Greene & MacRae L.L.P.**
125 West 55th Street
New York, NY 10019-5389
212-424-8000
212-424-8500 (fax)
http://www.llgm.com
recruiting@llgm.com

**Lewis & Roca L.L.P.**
Two Renaissance Square
40 N. Central Ave.
Phoenix, AZ 85004
602-262-5311
602-262-5747 (fax)
http://lrlaw.com
Julie Moy, 602-262-0844, jmoy@lrlaw.com

**Lillick & Charles L.L.P.**
Two Embarcadero Center
San Francisco, CA 94111-3996
415-984-8200
415-984-8300 (fax)
http://www.lillick.com
Krissy Austin, atty_recruit@lillick.com

**Lindquist & Vennum P.L.L.P.**
4200 IDS Center
Minneapolis, MN 55402
612-371-3211
612-371-3207 (fax)
http://www.lindquist.com
Lisanne M. Thalhuber,
    lthalhuber@lindquist.com

**Linowes and Blocher L.L.P.**
1010 Wayne Ave., Suite 1000
Silver Spring, MD 20910-5600
301-588-8580
301-495-9044 (fax)
http://www.linowes-law.com
John L. Hollingshead, jlh@linowes-
    law.com

**Lionel Sawyer & Collins**
1700 Bank America Plaza
300 S. Fourth Street
Las Vegas, NV 89101
702-383-8888
702-383-8845 (fax)
http://www.lionelsawyer.com
Margie Bowman, 702-383-8877, mbow-
    man@lionelsawyer.com

**Liskow and Lewis**
One Shell Square
701 Poydras Street, Suite 5000
New Orleans, LA 70139-5099
504-581-7979
504-556-4108 (fax)
http://www.liscow.com
Beverly P. Murphy, 504-581-7979, bpmur-
    phy.ll@mcimail.com

**Littler Mendelson P.C.**
650 California Street, 20th Flr.
San Francisco, CA 94108-2693
415-433-1940
415-399-8490 (fax)
http://www.littler.com
lawrecruit@littler.com

**Locke Liddell & Sapp L.L.P.**
600 Travis St. #3400
Houston, TX 77002
713-226-1200
713-226-1200 (fax)
http://www.lockeliddell.com

**Locke Reynolds**
201 N. Illinois St., Suite 1000
P.O. Box 44961
Indianapolis, IN 46244-0961
317-237-3800
317-237-3900 (fax)
http://www.locke.com
Eric A. Riegner, 317-237-3821,
   eriegner@locke.com

**Loeb & Loeb L.L.P.**
1000 Wilshire Blvd., Suite 1800
Los Angeles, CA 90017-2475
213-688-3400
213-688-3460 (fax)
http://www.Loeb.com
Cecilia Toll, 213-688-3512, ctoll@loeb.com

**Long Aldridge & Norman L.L.P.**
303 Peachtree St., Suite 5300
Atlanta, GA 30308
404-527-4000
404-527-4198 (fax)
http://www.lanlaw.com
Aimee Black, ablack@lanlaw.com

**Long & Levit L.L.P.**
601 Montgomery Street, Suite 900
San Francisco, CA 94411
415-397-2222
415-397-6392 (fax)
http://www.longlevit.com

**Lord, Bissell & Brook**
115 S. LaSalle Street
Chicago, IL 60603
312-443-0700
312-443-0336 (fax)
http://www.lordbissell.com
Kerry Jahnsen, kjahnsen@lordbissell.com

**Lowenstein Sandler P.C.**
65 Livingston Avenue
Roseland, NJ 07068-1791
973-597-2500
973-597-2400 (fax)
http://www.lowenstein.com
Jane Thieberger, jthieberger@lowenstein.com

**Lowndes, Drosdick, Doster, Kantor & Reed P.A.**
215 North Eola Drive
P.O. Box 2809
Orlando, FL 32801
407-843-4600
407-843-4444 (fax)
http://www.lowndes-law.com
H. G. McNeill, mcneillhg@lowndes-law.com

**Luce, Forward, Hamilton & Scripps L.L.P.**
600 West Broadway, Suite 2600
San Diego, CA 92101
619-236-1414
619-232-8311 (fax)
http://www.luce.com
Kathryn Karpinski, kkarpinski@luce.com

**Lyon & Lyon L.L.P.**
633 West Fifth Street
Suite 4700
Los Angeles, CA 90071
213-489-1600
213-955-0440 (fax)
http://www.lyonlyon.com

**Manatt, Phelps & Phillips L.L.P.**
11355 West Olympic Boulevard
Los Angeles, CA 90064
310-312-4000
310-312-4224 (fax)
http://www.manatt.com
Kimberly Firment,
   recruiting@manatt.com

**Margolis Edelstein**
The Curtis Center, 4th floor
Independence Square West
Philadelphia, PA 19106-3304
215-922-1100
215-922-1772 (fax)
http://www.harmonie.org/margolnj

**Marshall, Dennehey, Warner, Coleman & Goggin**
1845 Walnut St.
Philadelphia, PA  19103-4707
215-575-2600
http://www.mdwcg.com
Craig Hudson, chudson@mdwcg.com

**Matthews and Branscomb, A Professional Law Corporation**
112 East Pecan
San Antonio, TX  78205
210-357-9300
210-226-0521 (fax)

**Mayer, Brown & Platt**
190 South LaSalle
Chicago, IL  60603
312-782-0600
312-701-7711 (fax)
http://www.mayerbrown.com
Kelly B. Koster, 312-701-7002, mbpre-
  cruiting@mayerbrown.com

**Maynard Cooper & Gale P.C.**
2400 Amsouth/Harbert Plaza
1901 Sixth Avenue, North
Birmingham, AL  35203-2618
205-254-1000
205-254-1999 (fax)
http://www.mcglaw.com

**Mayor, Day, Caldwell & Keeton L.L.P.**
700 Louisiana Street
Suite 1900
Houston, TX  77002-2778
713-225-7000
713-225-7047 (fax)
http://www.mdcklaw.com
Lauren Talbert, ltalbert@mdck.com

**Mays & Valentine L.L.P.**
1111 East Main Street
P.O. Box 1122
Richmond, VA  23218-1122
804-697-1200
804-697-1339 (fax)
http://www.maysval.com
Linda M. Haudricourt, 804-697-1370,
  lawyer_recruit@maysval.com

**McCarter & English, L.L.P**
100 Mulberry St.
Newark, NJ  07102
973-622-4444
973-622-7070 (fax)
http://www.mccarter.com
Andi A. Jones, ajones@mccarter.com

**McCutchen, Doyle, Brown & Enersen L.L.P.**
Three Embarcadero Center
San Francisco, CA 94111
415-393-2000
415-393-2286 (fax)
http://www.mccutchen.com
Beth Harris, bharris@mdbe.com

**McDermott, Will & Emery**
227 W. Monroe St.
Chicago, IL 60606-5096
312-372-2000
312-984-7700 (fax)
http://www.mwe.com
Karen Mortell, kmortell@mwe.com

**McGinnis, Lochridge & Kilgore L.L.P.**
1300 Capitol Center
919 Congress Avenue
Austin, TX 78701
512-495-6000
512-495-6093 (fax)
http://www.mcginnislaw.com

**McGlinchey Stafford P.L.L.C.**
643 Magazine St.
New Orleans, LA 70130
504-586-1200
504-596-2800 (fax)
http://www.mcglinchey.com

**McGuire, Woods, Battle & Boothe L.L.P.**
One James Center
901 East Cary St.
Richmond, VA 23219-4030
804-775-1000
804-775-1061 (fax)
http://www.mwbb.com
Pamela S. Malone, 202-857-1732,
    pmalone@mcquirewoods.com

**McKenna & Cuneo L.L.P.**
1900 K Street, N.W.
Washington DC 20006-1108
202-496-7500
202-496-7756 (fax)
http://www.mckennacuneo.com
Jennifer Semelsberger, jennifer_seme
    lsberger@mckennacuneo.com

**McNees Wallace & Nurick**
100 Pine Street
Harrisburg, PA 17108
717-232-8000
717-237-5300 (fax)
http://www.mwn.com
Kathi Lipinsky

**Meagher & Geer P.L.L.P.**
4200 Multifoods Tower
33 South 6th Street
Minneapolis, MN 55402-3788
612-338-0661
612-338-8384 (fax)
http://www.meagher.com

**Mendes & Mount L.L.P.**
750 Seventh Avenue
New York, NY 10019-6829
212-261-8000
212-261-8750 (fax)
http://www.mendes.com

**Merchant, Gould, Smith, Edell, Welter & Schmidt P.A.**
90 S. 7th St., Suite 3100
Minneapolis, MN 55402-4131
612-332-5300
612-332-9081 (fax)
http://www.merchant-gould.com
recruiting@merchant-gould.com

**Meyer, Hendricks, Bivens & Moyes P.A.**
3003 N. Central Avenue, Suite 1200
Phoenix, AR 85012
602-604-2200
602-263-5333 (fax)

**Michael Best & Friedrich L.L.P.**
100 East Wisconsin Avenue
Suite 3300
Milwaukee, WI 53202
414-271-6560
414-277-0656 (fax)
http://www.mbf-law.com
Joyce M. Nordman, 414-271-6560

**Milbank, Tweed, Hadley & McCloy**
1 Chase Manhattan Plaza
New York, NY 10005
212-530-5000
212-530-5219 (fax)
http://www.milbank.com
Christine Wagner, 212-530-5112

**Milberg Weiss Bershad Hynes & Lerach L.L.P.**
One Pennsylvania Plaza
New York, NY 10119-0165
212-594-5300
212-868-1229 (fax)
http://www.milberg.com

**Miles & Stockbridge P.C.**
10 Light St.
Baltimore, MD 21202-1487
410-727-6464
410-385-3700 (fax)
http://www.milesstockbridge.com
Randi Lewis, 410-385-3563,
    rlewis@milesstockbridge.com

**Miller, Canfield, Paddock and Stone P.L.C.**
150 West Jefferson, Suite 2500
Detroit, MI 48226-4415
313-963-6420
313-496-7500 (fax)
http://www.millercanfield.com
Deborah W. Thompson, (313-963-6420)

**Miller & Chevalier, Chartered**
655 Fifteenth Street, NW, Suite 900
Washington DC 20005-5701
202-626-5800
202-628-0858 (fax)
http://www.millerchevalier.com
Richild Stewart, 202-626-6012

**Miller, Johnson, Snell & Cummiskey P.L.C.**
Calder Plaza Building
250 Monroe Avenue NW, Suite 800
Grand Rapids, MI 49503-2250
616-831-1700
616-831-1701 (fax)
http://www.millerjohnson.com
Michelle Smith, webattorneyrecruit-
    ing@mjsc.com

**Miller, Kagan, Rodriguez and Silver P.A.**
75 Valencia Avenue
Suite 800
Coral Gables, FL 33134-6135
305-446-5228
305-446-7088 (fax)

**Miller Nash L.L.P.**
3500 U.S. Bancorp Tower
111 S.W. Fifth Avenue
Portland, OR 97204-3699
503-224-5858
503-224-0155 (fax)
http://www.millernash.com
JoJo Hall, 503-205-2404, hallj@miller-
    nash.com

**Milling Benson Woodward L.L.P.**
909 Poydras St., Suite 2300
New Orleans, LA 70112-1017
504-569-7000
504-569-7001 (fax)
http://millinglaw.com

**Mintz, Levin, Cohn, Ferris, Glovsky and Popeo P.C.**
One Financial Center
Boston, MA 02111
617-542-6000
617-542-2241 (fax)
http://www.mintz.com
Julie Zammuto, jezammuto@mintz.com

**Mitchell, Silberberg & Knupp L.L.P.**
11377 W. Olympic Boulevard
Los Angeles, CA 90064-1683
310-312-2000
310-312-3100 (fax)
http://www.msk.com
Constance E. Norton, 310-312-3203, cen@msk.com

**Montgomery, Barnette, Brown, Read, Hammond & Mintz**
3200 Energy Centre
1100 Poydras Street
New Orleans, LA 70163-3200
504-585-3200
504-585-7688 (fax)
http://www.monbar.com

**Montgomery, McCracken, Walker & Rhoads L.L.P.**
123 S. Broad St.
Philadelphia, PA 19109-1099
215-772-1500
215-772-7620 (fax)
www.mmwr.com

**Moore & Van Allen P.L.L.C.**
100 North Tryon Street
Suite 4700
Charlotte, NC 28202-4003
704-331-1000
704-331-1159 (fax)
http://www.mvalaw.com
Patti J. Oswald, 704-331-1140

**Morgan & Finnegan L.L.P.**
345 Park Avenue
New York, NY 10154-0053
212-758-4800
212-751-6849 (fax)
http://morganfinnegan.com
Maryanne Purtill, mpurtill@morgan-
    finnegan.com

**Morgan, Lewis & Bockius L.L.P.**
1701 Market Street
Philadelphia, PA 19103-2921
215-963-5000
215-963-5299 (fax)
http://www.morganlewis.com
Caroline M. Olson, olson5680@morgan-
    lewis.com

**Morris, James, Hitchens & Williams**
222 Delaware Avenue
10th Flr. P.O. Box 2306
Wilmington, DE 19899-2306
302-888-6800
302-571-1750 (fax)
http://www.morrisjames.com
Barbara Normille, 302-888-6800,
    bnormille@morrisjames.com

**Morris, Nichols, Arsht & Tunnell**
1201 North Market Street
P.O. Box 1347
Wilmington, DE 19899
302-658-9200
302-658-3989 (fax)
http://www.mnat.com
Terry V. Derr, 302-658-9200,
    tderr@mnat.com

**Morris, Polich & Purdy L.L.P.**
1055 West Seventh Street Suite 2400 Los
Angeles, CA 90017
213-891-9100
213-488-1178 (fax)

**Morrison & Foerster L.L.P.**
425 Market Street
San Francisco, CA 94105-2482
415-268-7000
415-268-7522 (fax)
http://www.mofo.com

**Morrison & Hecker L.L.P.**
2600 Grand Ave.
Kansas City, MO 64108
816-691-2600
816-474-4208 (fax)
http://www.moheck.com
Tamra Wilson-Setser, 816-691-2600,
    twilsonsetser@moheck.com

**Morrison, Mahoney & Miller L.L.P.**
250 Summer St.
Boston, MA 02210
617-439-7500
617-439-7590 (fax)
http://www.MM-M.com
Dana Harding, 617-439-7500

**Munger, Tolles & Olson LLP**
355 S. Grand Avenue, 35th Floor
Los Angeles, CA 90071-1560
213-683-9100
213-687-3702 (fax)
http://www.mto.com
Kevinn C. Villard

**Musick, Peeler & Garrett L.L.P.**
One Wilshire Boulevard
Los Angeles, CA 90017
213-629-7600
213-624-1376 (fax)
Beverly J. Donatone, 213-629-7758

**Neal, Gerber & Eisenberg**
Two North La Salle St., Ste. 2200
Chicago, IL 60602
312-269-8000
312-269-1747
www.ngelaw.com

**Nelson Mullins Riley & Scarborough L.L.P.**
Keenan Building, Third Floor
1330 Lady Street
Columbia, SC 29201-3332
803-799-2000
803-256-7500 (fax)
http://www.nmrs.com

**Nexsen Pruet Jacobs & Pollard, L.L.P.**
1441 Main Street, 15th floor
P.O. Drawer 2426
Columbia, SC 29201
803-771-8900
803-253-8277 (fax)
http://www.NPJP.COM
Jay Hennig, 803-771-8900

**Nixon Peabody L.L.P.**
Clinton Square, Box 31051
Rochester, NY 14603
716-263-1000
716-263-1600 (fax)
http://www.nixonpeabody.com
Monique Melara, 716-263-1294, mme-
    lara@nixonpeabody.com

**Nossaman, Guthner, Knox & Elliott L.L.P.**
Thirty-First Floor, Union Bank Square
445 South Figueroa Street
Los Angeles, CA 90071
213-612-7800
213-612-7801 (fax)
http://www.ngke.com
Karen Wilmans, 213-612-7816, kwilmans@nossaman.com

**Nutter, McClennen & Fish L.L.P.**
One International Place
Boston, MA 02110-2699
617-439-2000
617-973-9748 (fax)
http://www.nutter.com
Terese Campos, 617-439-2351, tmc@nutter.com

**O'Melveny & Myers L.L.P.**
400 South Hope St.
Los Angeles, CA 90071-2899
213-430-6000
213-430-6407 (fax)
http://www.omm.com
David Watts, 213-430-6000, dwatts@omm.com

**Ober, Kaler, Grimes & Shriver**
120 East Baltimore St.
Baltimore, MD 21202-1643
410-685-1120
410-547-0699 (fax)
http://www.ober.com
Melissa Allison Warren

**Obermayer Rebmann Maxwell & Hippel L.L.P.**
One Penn Center, 19th Floor
1617 John F. Kennedy Blvd.
Philadelphia, PA 19103-1895
215-665-3000
215-665-3165 (fax)
http://www.obermayer.com
R.P. Perry, 215-665-3000, rrp@obermayer.com

**Ogletree, Deakins, Nash, Smoak & Stewart P.C.**
300 North Main Street
Greenville, SC 29602
864-271-1300
864-235-8806 (fax)
http://www.ogletreedeakins.com

**Parker Chapin L.L.P.**
The Chrysler Building
405 Lexington Ave.
New York, NY 10074
212-704-6000
212-704-6288 (fax)
www.parkerchapin.com

**Parker, Poe, Adams & Bernstein L.L.P.**
401 South Tryon, Suite 3000
Charlotte, NC 28202
704-372-9000
704-334-4706 (fax)
http://www.parkerpoe.com
Caryn A. Tuttle, 704-372-9000,
    CAT@ParkerPoe.com

**Orrick, Herrington & Sutcliffe L.L.P.** 400
Sansome St.
San Francisco, CA 94111
415-392-1122
415-773-5759 (fax)
http://www.orrick.com
recruiting@orrick.com

**Palmer & Dodge L.L.P.**
One Beacon St.
Boston, MA 02108
617-573-0100
617-227-4420 (fax)
http://www.palmerdodge.com
Katharine von Mohren, 617-573-0100,
pdhiring@palmerdodge.com

**Onebane, Bernard, Torian, Diaz,**
    **McNamara & Abell**
Suite 600, Versailles Centre
102 Versailles Boulevard
Lafayette, LA 70502
318-237-2660
318-266-1232 (fax)

**Oppenheimer Wolff & Donnelly L.L.P.**
45 S. Seventh St
Suite 3400
Minneapolis, MN 55402
612-607-7000
612-607-7100 (fax)
http://www.oppenheimer.com
Jacalyn Gunstand, 612-607-7000

**Parsons Behle & Latimer**
201 S. Main Street
Salt Lake City, UT  84111
801-532-1234
801-536-6111 (fax)
http://www.pblutah.com
Darcie Koski, dkoski@pblutah.com

**Patterson, Belknap, Webb & Tyler L.L.P.**
1133 Ave of Americas, 22nd floor
New York, NY  10036-6710
212-336-2000
212-336-2222 (fax)
http://www.pbwt.com
Angela Eliane, 212-336-2796,
    aeliane@pbwt.com

**Patton Boggs L.L.P.**
2550 M Street, N.W.
Washington DC  20037-1350
202-457-6000
202-457-6315 (fax)
Kara Reidy, 202-457-6342, kreidy@pat-
    tonboggs.com

**Paul, Hastings, Janofsky & Walker L.L.P.**
555 South Flower Street , 23rd Fl.    Los
Angeles, CA  90071-2371
213-683-6000
213-627-0705 (fax)
http://www.phjw.com
213-683-6000, recruit@phjw.com

**Paul, Weiss, Rifkind, Wharton &
    Garrison**
1285 Avenue of the Americas
New York, NY  10019-6064
212-373-3000
212-757-3990 (fax)
http://www.paulweiss.com
Patricia M. Morrissy, 212-373-2481,
    pmorrissy@paulweiss.com

**Pennie & Edmonds L.L.P.**
1155 Ave. of Americas
New York, NY  10036
212-790-9090
212-869-8864 (fax)
http://www.pennie.com
Patricia Stacey, 212-790-2908

**Pepper Hamilton L.L.P.**
3000 Two Logan Square
18th and Arch Streets
Philadelphia, PA 19103-2799
215-981-4000
215-981-4750 (fax)
http://www.pepperlaw.com
Meg Urbanski, 215-981-4000, urban-skim@pepperlaw.com

**Perkins Coie L.L.P.**
1201 Third Ave
Suite 4800
Seattle, WA 98101-3099
206-583-8888
206-583-8500 (fax)
http://www.perkinscoie.com
Stacie Hollowell, 206-583-8888, holls@perkinscoie.com

**Peterson & Ross**
200 E. Randolph Drive, Suite 7300
Chicago, IL 60601
312-861-1400
213-625-0210 (fax)
http://www.petersonross.com
Dina Zullo, 312-861-1400, dzullo@peter-sonross.com

**Phelps Dunbar L.L.P.**
Canal Place, 365 Canal St., Suite 2000
New Orleans, LA 70130-6534
504-566-1311
504-568-9130 (fax)
http://www.phelpsdunbar.com
Tory Nieset, 504-584-9235, georget@phelps.com

**Phillips, Lytle, Hitchcock, Blaine & Huber L.L.P.**
3400 HSBC Center
Buffalo, NY 14203
716-847-8400
716-852-6100 (fax)
http://www.phillipslytle.com
Maribeth Mroziak, 716-847-5424, MMroziak@PhillipsLytle.com

**Pillsbury Madison & Sutro L.L.P.**
50 Fremont Street
San Francisco, CA 94105
415-983-1000
415-983-1200 (fax)
http://www.pillsburylaw.com
Pillsburyrecruit_SF@pillsburylaw.com

**Piper, Marbury, Rudnick & Wolfe L.L.P**
6225 Smith Ave
Baltimore, MD 21209-3600
410-539-2530
410-580-3001 (fax)
http://www.piperrudnick.com

**Pitney, Hardin, Kipp & Szuch L.L.P.**
P.O. Box 1945
Morristown, N.J. 07962-1945
973-966-6300
973-966-1550 (fax)
http://www.phks.com
Marilyn Olivo, 973-966-3600

**Plunkett & Cooney P.C.**
243 West Congress, Suite 800
Detroit, MI 48226
313-965-3900
313-983-4350 (fax)
http://www.plunkettlaw.com

**Polsinelli, White, Vardeman & Shalton P.C.**
6201 College Blvd Suite 500
Overland Park, KS 66211
913-451-8788
913-451-6205 (fax)
http://www.pwvs.com
John Healy, 913-451-8788

**Porteous, Hanikel, Johnson & Sarpy L.L.P**
704 Carondelet Street
New Orleans, LA 70130-3774
504-581-3838
504-581-4069 (fax)

**Porter, Wright, Morris & Arthur L.L.P.**
41 South High St.
Columbus, OH 43215
614-227-2000
614-227-2100 (fax)
http://www.porterwright.com
David G. Zimmerman, 614-227-1907,
dzimmerman@porterwright.com

**Post & Schell P.C.**
1800 John F. Kennedy Blvd.
Philadelphia, PA 19103-7480
215-587-1000
215-587-1444 (fax)
http://www.postschell.com
Kathleen Nichol, 215-587-1000, kmcni-
chol@postschell.com

**Potter Anderson & Corroon L.L.P.**
Hercules Plaza
1313 N. Market St.
P.O. Box 951
Wilmington, DE 19899
302-984-6000
302-658-1192 (fax)
http://PACDELAWARE.COM

**Powell, Goldstein, Frazer & Murphy L.L.P.**
16th Floor, 191 Peachtree St., N.E.
Atlanta, GA 30303
404-572-6600
404-572-6999 (fax)
http://www.pgfm.com
Jessica Fields, 404-572-6600,
jfields@pgfm.com

**Preston Gates & Ellis L.L.P.**
701 Fifth Avenue, Suite 5000
Seattle, WA 98104-7078
206-623-7580
206-623-7022 (fax)
http://www.prestongates.com
Kristine Immordino, 206-623-7580,
attyrecruit@prestongates.com

**Pretzel & Stouffer Chartered**
One South Wacker Drive, Suite 2500
Chicago, IL 60606
312-346-1973
312-346-8242 (fax)
http://www.pretzel-stouffer.com

**Proskauer Rose L.L.P.**
1585 Broadway
New York, NY 10036-8299
212-969-3000
212-969-2900 (fax)
http://www.proskauer.com
Diane Kolnik, 212-969-3000,
dkolnik@proskauer.com

**Pryor Cashman Sherman & Flynn L.L.P.**
410 Park Avenue, 10th Floor
New York, NY 10022-4441
212-421-4100
212-326-0806 (fax)
http://www.pryorcashman.com

**Quarles & Brady L.L.P.**
411 E. Wisconsin Avenue
Milwaukee, WI 53202
414-277-5000
414-277-3552 (fax)
http://www.quarles.com
Bridget Kesner, 414-277-5207,
  BMK@quarles.com

**Querrey & Harrow Ltd.**
175 West Jackson Blvd, Suite 1600
Chicago, IL 60604-2827
312-540-7000
312-540-0578 (fax)
http://www.querrey.com
Nicholas Anaclerio,
  nanaclerio@querrey.com

**Quinn Emanuel Urquhart Oliver &
  Hedges L.L.P.**
865 South Figueroa Street, 10th Floor
Los Angeles, CA 90017
213-624-7707
213-624-0643 (fax)
http://www.quinnemanuel.com
Gina Clavel, (213) 624-7707, gc@quinne-
  manuel.com

**Reed Smith Shaw & McClay L.L.P.**
435 Sixth Avenue
Pittsburgh, PA 15219
412-288-3131
412-288-3063 (fax)
http://www.rssm.com
Lonnie Nelson, 412-288-3131,
  ibnelson@rssm.com

**Reinhart, Boerner, Van Deuren, Norris
  & Rieselbach S.C.**
1000 North Water Street, Suite 2100
Milwaukee, WI 53202
414-298-1000
414-298-8097 (fax)
http://www.reinhartlaw.com
Sandra Faull, 414-298-1000, sfaull@rein-
  hartlaw.com

**Rice Fowler**
201 St. Charles Ave., 36th floor
New Orleans, LA 70170
504-523-2600
504-523-2705 (fax)
http://www.ricefowler.com

**Richards, Watson and Gershon P.C.**
333 South Hope Street, 38th Floor
Los Angeles, CA 90071
213-626-8484
213-626-0078 (fax)
http://www.rwglaw.com
Susan Guebely, 213-626-8484,
Sguebely@rwglaw.com

**Rider, Bennett, Egan & Arundel L.L.P.**
333 South Seventh Street, Suite 2000
Minneapolis, MN 55402
612-340-7951
612-340-7900 (fax)
http://www.riderlaw.com
recruiting@riderlaw.com

**Riker, Danzig, Scherer, Hyland &**
  **Perretti L.L.P.**
Headquarters Plaza
One Speedwell Ave.
Morristown, NJ 07962-1981
973-538-0800
973-538-1984 (fax)
http://www.riker.com
Alison M. Feldman, 973-538-0800,
  Afeldman@riker.com

**Rivkin, Radler & Kremer L.L.P**
EAB Plaza
Uniondale, NY 11556-0111
516-357-3000
516-357-3333 (fax)
http://www.rivkinradler.com

**Robins, Kaplan, Miller & Ciresi L.L.P.**
2800 LaSalle Plaza
800 LaSalle Ave.
Minneapolis, MN 55402
612-349-8500
612-339-4181 (fax)
http://www.rkmc.com
Cheryl Nelson, 612-349-8500

**Robinson & Cole L.L.P.**
280 Trumbull St.
Hartford, CT 06103-3597
860-275-8200
860-275-8299 (fax)
http://www.rc.com
Sharon Abrams, 860-275-8200

Robinson Silverman Pearce Aronsohn
& Berman L.L.P.
1290 Avenue of the Americas
New York, NY 10104-0053
212-541-2000
212-541-4630 (fax)
http://www.robinsonsilverman.com
Elizabeth Breslow, 212-541-2000,
 recruit@rspab.com

Rodey, Dickason, Sloan, Akin & Robb
P.A.
201 Third Street NW
Suite 2200
Albuquerque, NM 87102
505-765-5900
505-768-7395 (fax)

Roetzel & Andress L. P. A.
222 South Main St ste 400
Akron, OH 44308
330-376-2700
330-376-4577 (fax)
http://www.ralaw.com

Rogers, Towers, Bailey, Jones & Gay
P.A.
1301 Riverplace Blvd., Ste. 1500
Jacksonville, FL 32207-9020
904-398-3911
904-396-0663 (fax)
http://www.rtlaw.com
Kristy Nelson, 904-398-3911,
 KNelson@rtlaw.com

Ropers, Majeski, Kohn & Bentley
1001 Marshall Street
Redwood City, CA 94063
650-364-8200
650-367-0997 (fax)
http://www.ropers.com
Carman Callahan, 650-364-8200

Ropes & Gray
One International Place
Boston, MA 02110-2624
617-951-7000
617-951-7050 (fax)
http://www.ropesgray.com
Joanna White, 617-951-7000,
 jwhite@ropesgray.com

**Rosenman & Colin L.L.P.**
575 Madison Ave.
New York, NY 10022
212-940-8800
212-940-8776 (fax)
http://www.rosenman.com
Edmar J. Petterson, 212-940-7009, ejpetterson@rosenman.com

**Ross & Hardies**
150 N. Michigan Ave, Suite 2500
Chicago, IL 60601
312-558-1000
312-750-8600 (fax)
http://www.rosshardies.com
John McCabe, 312-558-1000,
john.mccabe@rosshardies.com

**Ruden, McClosky, Smith, Schuster & Russell PA.**
200 East Broward Blvd., Suite 1500
Ft. Lauderdale, FL 33301
954-764-6660
954-764-4996 (fax)
http://www.ruden.com
Richard Joblonski, 954-764-6600,
rjj@ruden.com

**Rutan & Tucker L.L.P.**
611 Anton Blvd., Suite 1400
Costa Mesa, CA 92626-1998
714-641-5100
714-546-9035 (fax)
http://www.rutan.com
recruiter@rutan.com.

**Sachnoff & Weaver Ltd.**
30 South Wacker Drive, 29th Floor
Chicago, IL 60606
312-207-1000
312-207-6400 (fax)
http://www.sachnoff.com
Nikki Silvio, 312-207-1000, nsilvio@sachnoff.com

**Saperston & Day P.C.**
1100 M&T Center
3 Fountain Plaza
Buffalo, NY 14203-1486
716-856-5400
716-856-0139 (fax)
http://www.saperstonday.com

**Saul, Ewing, Remick & Saul L.L.P.**
Centre Square West
1500 Market St., 38th Floor
Philadelphia, PA 19102
215-972-7777
215-972-7725 (fax)
http://www.saul.com
Donna J. Nolan, 215-972-7991,
    dnolan@saul.com

**Schiff Hardin & Waite**
6600 Sears Tower
Chicago, IL 60606-6473
312-258-5500
312-258-5700 (fax)
http://www.schiffhardin.com
Tom Grewe, 312-258-5500
tgrewe@schiffhardin.com

**Schnader Harrison Segal & Lewis L.L.P.**
1600 Market Street, Suite 3600
Philadelphia, PA 19103
215-751-2000
215-751-2205 (fax)
http://www.schnader.com
Jamie O'Brien, 215-751-2225,
    jo'brien@schnader.com

**Schottenstein, Zox & Dunn**
41 South High Street, Suite 2600
Columbus, OH 43215
614-462-2700
614-462-5135 (fax)
http://www.szd.com
Kathy Smith, 614-462-2215,
    ksmith@szd.com

**Schulte Roth & Zabel L.L.P.**
900 Third Ave
New York, NY 10022
212-756-2000
212-593-5955 (fax)
http://www.srz.com
Amber Graves, 212-756-2000,
    amber.graves@srz.com

**Schwabe Williamson & Wyatt, PC**
1211 SW 5th Avenue,
Suites 1600–1800
Portland, OR 97204
503-222-9981
503-796-2900 (fax)
http://schwabe.com
Alyson Gilbertson, 503-222-9981,
    agilbertson@schwabe.com

**Sedgwick, Detert, Moran & Arnold**
One Embarcadero Center, 16th Floor
San Francisco, CA  94111
415-781-7900
415-781-2635 (fax)
http://www.sdma.com

**Semmes, Bowen & Semmes P.C.**
250 West Pratt St.
Baltimore, MD  21201
410-539-5040
410-539-5223 (fax)
http://www.semmes.com
Bonita F. Penfield, 410-576-4806, bpen-field@mail.semmes.com

**Sessions & Fishman L.L.P.**
First NBC Center
201 St. Charles Avenue, Suite 3500
New Orleans, LA  70170-3500
504-582-1500
504-582-1555 (fax)

**Seyfarth Shaw**
55 East Monroe Street, Suite 4200
Chicago, IL  60603
312-346-8000
312-269-8869 (fax)
http://www.seyfarth.com
Carol M. Hogan, 312-739-6458, Chogan@seyfarth.com

**Shaw Pittman**
2300 N Street, NW
Washington DC  20037
202-663-8000
202-663-8007 (fax)
http://www.shawpittman.com

**Shearman & Sterling**
599 Lexington Ave.
New York, NY  10022
212-848-4000
212-848-7179 (fax)
http://www.shearman.com
Stephen T. Fishbein, Esq., 212-848-4424, sfishbein@shearman.com

**Sheppard, Mullin, Richter & Hampton L.L.P.**
333 S. Hope Street, 48th Floor
Los Angeles, CA  90071
213-620-1780
213-620-1398 (fax)
http://www.smrh.com

**Sher, Garner, Cahill, Richter, Klein & McAlister L.L.C.**
909 Poydras St., 28th floor
New Orleans, LA  70112
504-299-2100
504-299-2300 (fax)
http://www.shergarner.com

**Sherman & Howard L.L.C.**
633 17th Street, Suite 3000
Denver, CO  80202
303-297-2900
303-298-0940 (fax)
http://www.sah.com
Kimberly Coey, 303-299-8030,
   recruit_legal@sah.com

**Shipman & Goodwin L.L.P.**
One American Row
Hartford, CT  06103-2819
860-251-5000
860-251-5099 (fax)
http://www.shipman-goodwin.com
Deborah Hewey, 860-251-5626,
   dhewey@goodwin.com

**Shook, Hardy & Bacon L.L.P.**
1200 Main St.
Kansas City, MO  64105
816-474-6550
816-421-5547 (fax)
http://www.shb.com
Jessica Baker, 816-474-6550,
   jbaker@shb.com.

**Shumaker, Loop & Kendrick L.L.P.**
North Courthouse Square
1000 Jackson
Toledo, OH  43624-1573
419-241-9000
419-241-6894 (fax)
http://www.slk-law.com

**Shutts & Bowen**
1500 Miami Center
201 S. Biscayne Blvd.
Miami, FL  33131
305-358-6300
305-381-9982 (fax)
http://www.shutts-law.com
Mary Ann Connors, 305-358-6300

**Sidley & Austin**
Bank One Plaza
10 South Dearborn St.
Chicago, IL 60603
312-853-7000
312-853-7036 (fax)
http://www.sidley.com
Jenny Hernandez, 312-853-7000, jherna01@sidley.com

**Sills Cummis Radin Tischman Epstein & Gross P.A.**
One Riverfront Plaza
Newark, NJ 07102
973-643-7000
973-643-6500 (fax)
http://www.sillscummis.com
Dina Cappuccio, 973-643-7000

**Simon, Peragine, Smith & Redfearn L.L.P.**
1100 Poydras St. Suite 3000
New Orleans, LA 70163-3000
504-569-2030
504-569-2999 (fax)
http://www.spsr-law.com

**Simpson Thacher & Bartlett**
425 Lexington Avenue
New York, NY 10017-3954
212-455-2000
212-455-2502 (fax)
http://www.simpsonthacher.com

**Sirote & Permutt P.C.**
2311 Highland Ave
Birmingham, AL 35205
205-930-5100
205-930-5101 (fax)
http://www.sirote.com
Robert Baugh, 205-930-5307

**Skadden, Arps, Slate, Meagher & Flom L.L.P.**
Four Times Square
New York, NY 10036
212-735-3000
212-735-2000 (fax)
http://www.sasmf.com
Carol Lee Sprague, 212-735-3815

**Smith, Gambrell & Russell L.L.P.**
1230 Peachtree Street, N.E.
Suite 3100
Atlanta, GA 30309
404-815-3500
404-815-3509 (fax)
http://www.sgrlaw.com
Sherri M. Knight, 404-815-3523, sknight@sgratl.com

**Smith Helms Mulliss & Moore L.L.P.**
300 N. Greene St.
Greensboro, NC 27401
336-378-5200
336-379-5400 (fax)
http://www.shmm.com
Ashley Smith, 704-343-2065,
    Ashley_Smith@shmm.com

**Smith, Katzenstein & Furlow L.L.P.**
The Corporate Plaza
800 Delaware Ave.. P.O. Box 410
Wilmington, DE 19899
302-652-8400
302-652-8405 (fax)
http://www.SKFDelaware.com

**Snell & Wilmer L.L.P.**
One Arizona Center
Phoenix, AZ 85004-2202
602-382-6000
602-382-6070 (fax)
http://www.swlaw.com
Bonnie Lang, 602-382-6014

**Sonnenschein Nath & Rosenthal**
8000 Sears Tower
Chicago, IL 60606
312-876-3183
312-876-7934 (fax)
http://www.sonnenschein.com
Jennifer Malfas, 312-876-8112
jaa@sonnenschein.com

**Squadron, Ellenoff, Plesent &
    Sheinfeld L.L.P.**
551 5th Avenue
New York, NY 10176
212-661-6500
212-697-6686 (fax)
http://www.squadronlaw.com

**Squire, Sanders & Dempsey L.L.P.**
127 Public Square
4900 Key Tower
Cleveland, OH 44114-1304
216-479-8500
216-479-8780 (fax)
http://www.ssd.com
Sandra Hickle, 216-687-3468,
    shickle@ssd.com

**Stearns Weaver Miller Weissler Alhadeff & Sitterson P.A.**
Suite 2200 Museum Tower
150 West Flagler Street
Miami, FL 33130
305-789-3200
305-789-3395 (fax)
http://stearnsweaver.com

**Steel Hector & Davis L.L.P.**
200 S. Biscayne Blvd.
Miami, FL 33131-2398
305-577-7000
305-577-7001 (fax)
http://www.steelhector.com

**Steptoe & Johnson**
PO Box 2190
Bank One Center, 6th floor
Clarksburg, WV 26302-2190
304-624-8000
304-624-8183 (fax)
http://www.steptoelaw.com
W. Henry Lawrence IV, 304-624-8186,
lawrenwh@steptoe-johnson.com

**Steptoe & Johnson L.L.P.**
1330 Connecticut Ave, N.W.
Washington DC 20036
202-429-3000
202-429-3902 (fax)
http://www.steptoe.com
Rosemary K. Morgan, 202-429-3000,
legal_recruiting@steptoe.com

**Stevens & Lee**
111 North Sixth Street
P.O. Box 679
Reading, PA 19603-0679
610-478-2000
610-376-5610 (fax)

**Stinson, Mag & Fizzell P.C.**
1201 Walnut, Suite 2800
Kansas City, MO 64106
816-842-8600
816-691-3495 (fax)
http://www.stinson.com
Julie Thornton, 816-842-8600

**Stites & Harbison**
400 West Market St., Suite 1800
Louisville, KY 40202-3352
502-587-3400
502-587-6391 (fax)
http://www.stites.com

**Strasburger & Price L.L.P.**
901 Main Street, Suite 4300
Dallas, TX 75202
214-651-4300
214-651-4330 (fax)
http://www.strasburger.com
Karen Mixon, 214-651-4300,
    KMixon@strasburger.com

**Stroock & Stroock & Lavan L.L.P.**
180 Maiden Lane
New York, NY 10038
212-806-5400
212-806-6006 (fax)
http://www.stroock.com
Diane A. Cohen, 212-806-5406,
    dcohen@stroock.com

**Stradley, Ronon, Stevens & Young, L.L.P.**
2600 One Commerce Square
Philadelphia, PA 19103-7098
215-564-8000
215-564-8120 (fax)
http://www.stradley.com
Deirdre M. Mullen, 215-564-8000, atty-
    hire@stradley.com

**Stradling Yocca Carlson & Rauth P.C.**
660 Newport Center Dr., Ste. 1600
Newport Beach, CA 92660-6441
949-725-4000
949-725-4100 (fax)
http://www.sycr.com
Lee Ann Dennis, 949-725-4064, recruit-
    ing@sycr.com

**Stoel Rives L.L.P.**
900 SW Fifth Avenue, Suite 2600
Portland, OR 97204-1268
503-224-3380
503-220-2480 (fax)
http://www.stoel.com
Kara Jordan, 503-224-9539,
    kajordan@stoel.com

**Stoll, Keenon & Park L.L.P.**
201 E. Main St. Ste 1000
Lexington, KY 40507-1380
606-231-3000
606-253-1093 (fax)
http://www.skp.com

**Sughrue Mion, Zinn, Macpeak & Seas P.L.L.C.**
2100 Pennsylvania Avenue, N.W., Suite 800
Washington D.C. 20037-3213
202-293-7060
202-293-7860 (fax)
http://www.sughrue.com
Alicia Dray, 202-293-7060,
    ADRAY@SUGHRUE.COM

**Sullivan & Cromwell**
125 Broad St.
New York, NY 10004
212-558-4000
212-558-3588 (fax)
http://www.sullcrom.com

**Sullivan & Worcester L.L.P.**
One Post Office Square
Boston, MA 02109
617-338-2800
617-338-2880 (fax)
http://www.sandw.com
Natalie Monroe, 617-338-2800, nmon-
    roe@sandw.com

**Sutherland Asbill & Brennan L.L.P.**
999 Peachtree Street NE
Atlanta, GA 30309
404-853-8000
404-853-8806 (fax)
http://www.sablaw.com
Victoria D. Tate, 404-853-8000,
    vdtate@sablaw.com

**Swidler Berlin Shereff Friedman L.L.P.**
3000 K Street N.W.
Suite 300
Washington DC 20007
202-424-7500
202-424-7643 (fax)
http://www.swidlaw.com
Katherine White, 202-424-7500,
    kmwhite@swidlaw.com

**Taft, Stettinius & Hollister**
1800 First Star Tower
425 Walnut Street
Cincinnati, OH 45202-3957
513-381-2838
513-381-0205 (fax)
http://www.taftlaw.com
Shannon K. Fullen, 513-381-2838

**Thompson Hine & Flory L.L.P.**
3900 Key Center
127 Public Square
Cleveland, OH 44114-1216
216-566-5500
216-566-5800 (fax)
http://www.thf.com

**Thompson & Knight P.C.**
1700 Pacific Avenue
Suite 3300
Dallas, TX 75201
214-969-1700
214-969-1751 (fax)
http://www.tklaw.com

**Thorp, Reed & Armstrong**
One Riverfront Center
20 Stanwix Street
Pittsburgh, PA 15222-4895
412-394-7711
412-394-2555 (fax)
http://www.thorpreed.com

**The Bayard Firm**
222 Delaware Ave. Suite 900
P.O. Box 25130
Wilmington, DE 19899
302-655-5000
302-658-6395 (fax)

**Thelen Reid & Priest L.L.P.**
40 West 57th Street
New York, NY 10019
212-603-2000
212-603-2001 (fax)
http://www.thelenreid.com

**Thompson Coburn L.L.P.**
One Firstar Plaza
St. Louis, MO 63110
314-552-6000
314-552-7000 (fax)
http://www.thompsoncoburn.com
Nicole Reid Gore,314-552-6000

**Taylor, Porter, Brooks & Philips**
Bank One Centre, 8th Floor
451 Florida Street
Baton Rouge, LA 70821
225-387-3221
225-346-8049 (fax)

**Testa, Hurwitz & Thibeault L.L.P.**
High Street Tower
125 High Street
Boston, MA 02110
617-248-7000
617-248-7100 (fax)
http://www.tht.com

**Thacher Proffitt & Wood**
Two World Trade Center
New York, NY 10048
212-912-7400
212-912-7751 (fax)
http://thacherproffitt.com
Sarah Fraley, 212-912-7710

**Townsend and Townsend and Crew L.L.P.**
2 Embarcadero Center, 8th Floor
San Francisco, CA 94111-3834
415-576-0200
415-576-0300 (fax)
http://www.townsend.com
inquire@townsend.com
Palo Alto, CA; Seattle, WA; Denver, CO

**Trenam Kemker, Scharf, Barkin, Frye O'Neill & Mullis P.A.**
2700 Barnett Plaza
101 E. Kennedy Blvd., P.O. Box 1102
Tampa, FL 33602
813-223-7474
813-229-6553 (fax)

**Tressler, Soderstrom, Maloney & Priess**
233 South Wacker Drive
Sears Tower
22nd Floor
Chicago, IL 60606-6308
312-627-4000
312-627-1717 (fax)
http://www.tsmp.com

**Troop Steuber Pasich Reddick & Tobey L.L.P.**
2029 Century Park East, 24th Fl.
Los Angeles, CA 90067
310-728-3000
310-728-2739 (fax)
http://www.trooplaw.com
Dottie Miller, 310-728-3738

**Troutman Sanders L.L.P.**
600 Peachtree Street NE
Suite 5200
Atlanta, GA 30308-2216
404-885-3000
404-885-3900 (fax)
http://www.troutmansanders.com
Jodie Zerega

**Tucker Arensberg P.C.**
1500 One PPG Place
Pittsburgh, PA 15222-5401
412-566-1212
412-594-5619 (fax)
http://www.tuckerlaw.com
Pamela J. Maxson

**Tybout, Redfearn & Pell**
300 Delaware Avenue, Suite 1100
Wilmington, DE 19899-2092
302-658-6901
302-658-4018 (fax)

**Varnum, Riddering, Schmidt & Howlett L.L.P.**
Bridgewater Place
333 Bridgewater Street NW
Grand Rapids, MI 49501
616-336-6000
616-336-7000 (fax)
http://www.vrsh.com
Kevin Rynbrandt, 616-336-6000, karyn-brandt@vrsh.com

**Vedder, Price, Kaufman & Kammholz**
222 N. LaSalle St., Suite 2600
Chicago, IL 60601
312-609-7500
312-609-5005 (fax)
http://www.vedderprice.com
Eileen Neis

**Venable, Baetjer and Howard L.L.P.**
1800 Mercantile Bank and Trust Bldg.
2 Hopkins Plaza
Baltimore, MD 21201-2978
410-244-7400
410-244-7742 (fax)
http://www.venable.com

**Verner, Liipfert, Bernhard, McPherson and Hand Chartered**
901 15th St., N.W.
Washington DC 20005
202-371-6000
202-371-6279 (fax)
http://www.verner.com
Diane Ross, 202-371-6077

**Vial, Hamilton, Koch & Knox L.L.P.**
1717 Main St., Suite 4400
Dallas, TX 75201
214-712-4400
214-712-4402 (fax)
http://www.vialaw.com
Kimberly Clayton, kclayton@vialaw.com

**Vinson & Elkins L.L.P.**
1001 Fannin
2300 First City Tower
Houston, TX 77002-6760
713-758-2222
713-758-2346 (fax)
http://www.vinson-elkins.com
Patty Calabrese

**Vorys, Sater, Seymour and Pease L.L.P.**
52 East Gay Street
Columbus, OH 43215-1008
614 464-6400
614 464-6350 (fax)
http://www.vssp.com

**White and Williams L.L.P.**
1800 One Liberty Place
Philadelphia, PA 19103-7395
215-864-7000
215-864-7123 (fax)
http://www.whitewms.com

**White & Case L.L.P.**
1155 Avenue of the Americas
New York, NY 10036-2787
212-819-8200
212-354-8113 (fax)
http://www.whitecase.com

**Whiteford, Taylor & Preston L.L.P.**
Seven Saint Paul Street
Baltimore, MD 21202-1626
410-347-8700
410-752-7092 (fax)
http://wtplaw.com

**Warner Norcross & Judd L.L.P.**
111 Lyon St., N.W.
900 Old Kent Building
Grand Rapids, MI 49503
616-752-2000
616-752-2500 (fax)
http://www.wnj.com
Cathleen M. Meriwether

**Watanabe, Ing & Kawashima P.C.**
First Hawaiian Center
999 Bishop Street, 23rd Floor
Honolulu, HI 96813
808-544-8300
808-544-8399 (fax)

**Weil, Gotshal & Manges L.L.P.**
767 Fifth Avenue
New York, NY 10153
212-310-8000
212-310-8007 (fax)
http://www.weil.com
Donna Lang

**Wachtell, Lipton, Rosen & Katz**
51 West 52nd Street
New York, NY 10019
212-403-1000
212-403-2000 (fax)
http://www.wlrk.com
Ruth Ivey

**Waller Lansden Dortch & Davis P.L.L.C.**
Nashville City Center
511 Union St., Ste. 2100
Nashville, TN 37219
615-244-6380
615-244-6804 (fax)
http://www.wallerlaw.com
Tracie Hogan

**Whyte Hirschboeck Dudek S.C.**
111 E. Wisconsin Avenue
Suite 2100
Milwaukee, WI 53202
414-273-2100
414-223-5000 (fax)
http://www.whdlaw.com
Traci A Mortenson, 414-224-5855
tam@whdlaw.com

**Wicker, Smith, Tutan, O'Hara, McCoy, Graham & Ford P.A.**
2900 SW 28th Terrace, 5th Floor
Miami, FL 33133
305-448-3939

**Wiggin and Dana**
One Century Tower
New Haven, CT 06510
203-498-4400
203-782-2889 (fax)
http://www.wiggin.com

**Wildman, Harrold, Allen & Dixon**
225 W. Wacker Drive
Chicago, IL 60606-1229
312-201-2000
312-201-2555 (fax)
http://www.whad.com
Susan A. Cicero, 312-201-2574,
cicero@whad.com

**Wilentz, Goldman & Spitzer**
90 Woodbridge Center Drive
Woodbridge, NJ 07095
732-636-8000
732-855-6117 (fax)
http://www.newjerseylaw.com
Kimberly Curtis, 732-855-6176,
curtik@wilentz.com

**Wiley, Rein & Fielding**
1776 K Street, N.W.
Washington DC 20006
202-719-7000
202-719-7207 (fax)
http://www.wrf.com

**Williams & Connolly**
725 12th Street, N.W.
Washington DC 20005
202-434-5000
202-434-5029 (fax)
Nancey Svites

**Williams, Kastner & Gibbs P.L.L.C.**
Two Union Square, 601 Union Street,
Suite 4100 P.O.Box 21926
Seattle, WA 98111-3926
206-628-6600
206-628-6611 (fax)
http://www.wkg.com

**Williams, Montgomery and John Ltd.**
20 North Wacker Drive
Suite 2100
Chicago, IL 60606
312-443-3200
312-443-1323 (fax)
http://www.willmont.com
Jeffrey H. Lipe

**Williams, Mullen, Clark & Dobbins P.C.**
Two James Center, 1021 E. Cary St.
Richmond, VA 23219
804-643-1991
804-783-6507 (fax)
http://www.wmcd.com
Terri L. Stimis, 804-783-6505
tstimis@wmcd.com

**Willkie Farr & Gallagher**
787 Seventh Avenue
New York, NY 10019
212-728-8000
212-728-8111 (fax)
http://www.wilkie.com

**Wilmer, Cutler & Pickering**
2445 M Street, N.W.
Washington DC 20037
202-663-6000
202-663-6363 (fax)
http://www.wilmer.com
Cheryl B. Shigo

**Wilson, Elser, Moskowitz, Edelman & Dicker L.L.P.**
150 East 42nd St.
New York, NY 10017
212-490-3000
212-490-3038 (fax)
http://www.wemed.com

**Wilson Sonsini Goodrich & Rosati**
650 Page Mill Road
Palo Alto, CA 94304-1050
650-493-9300
650-493-6811 (fax)
http://www.wsgr.com/

**Winstead Sechrest & Minick P.C.**
1201 Elm St., 5400 Renaissance Tower
Dallas, TX 75270-2199
214-745-5400
214-745-5390 (fax)
http://www.winstead.com
Dominique Anderson

**Winston & Strawn**
35 West Wacker Drive
Chicago, IL 60601
312-558-5600
312-558-5700 (fax)
http://www.winston.com
Paul H. Hensel, phensel@winston.com

**Winthrop, Stimson, Putnam & Roberts**
One Battery Park Plaza
New York, NY  10004-1490
212-858-1000
212-858-1500 (fax)
http://www.winstim.com
careers@winstim.com

**Wolf, Block, Schorr and Solis-Cohen L.L.P.**
1650 Arch Street
Philadelphia, PA  19103
215-977-2000
215-977-2334 (fax)
http://www.wolfblock.com
Eileen McMahon, 215-977-2362

**Womble Carlyle Sandridge & Rice P.L.L.C.**
200 West Second Street
Post Office Drawer 84
Winston-Salem, NC  27102
336-721-3600
336-721-3660 (fax)
http://www.wcsr.com

**Wyatt, Tarrant & Combs**
2800 Citizens Plaza
Louisville, KY  40202-2898
502-589-5235
502-589-0309 (fax)
http://www.wyattfirm.com

**Zevnik Horton Guibord McGovern Palmer & Fognani L.L.P.**
1299 Penn Ave. N.W., 9th Floor
Washington DC  20004
1-800-941-2007
202-824-0955 (fax)
http://www.zevnik.com

# APPENDIX C

## CORPORATE COUNSEL DIRECTORY

An alphabetical listing of over 450 corporate law departments.

*COMPANY NAME*
*ADDRESS*
*PHONE*
*FAX*
*WEBSITE*
*RECRUITING INFORMATION,*
  *IF ANY (name, phone, e-mail)*
*APPROX. SIZE*

**AAA Michigan/Wisconsin**
1 Auto Club Drive
Dearborn, Michigan 48126-2607
Telephone: (313) 336-1284
Fax: (313) 336-1245
http://www.aaamich.com
General Counsel: Richard Thomas White
Approx. size: 5-10

**ABM Industries Incorporated**
160 Pacific Avenue, Suite 222
San Francisco, California 94111
Telephone: (415) 733-4013
Fax: (415) 733-5123
http://www.abm.com
General Counsel: Harry H. Kahn
Approx. size: 5-10

**AIM Management Group Inc.**
11 Greenway Plaza, Suite 100
Houston, Texas 77046
Telephone: (713) 626-1919
Fax: (713) 993-9185
http://www.aimfunds.com
General Counsel: Carol F. Relihan
Approx. size: 10-15

**Abbott Laboratories**
100 Abbott Park Road D-364, AP6D
(Abbott Park)
North Chicago, Illinois 60064
Telephone: (847) 937-8905
http://www.abbott.com
General Counsel: Jose M. De Lasa
Approx. size: 20-25

**ABN AMRO Incorporated**
208 South Lasalle Street, Suite 200
Chicago, Illinois 60604
Telephone: (312) 855-7600
Fax: (312) 553-6801
http://www.abnamro.com
General Counsel: John M. Kramer
Approx. size: 5-10

**Acceptance Insurance Companies Inc.**
222 South 15th Street, Suite 600 N
Omaha, Nebraska 68102
Telephone: (712) 329-3640
Fax: (712) 329-3815
http://www.aicins.com
General Counsel: Peter Knolla
Approx. size: < 5

**Acme Metals Incorporated**
13500 South Perry Avenue
Riverdale, Illinois 60827-1182
Telephone: (708) 849-2500
Fax: (708) 841-6010
http://www.acme-metals.com
General counsel: Edward P. Weber, Jr.
Approx. size: < 5

**ACNielsen Corporation**
177 Broad Street
Stamford, Connecticut 06901
Telephone: (203) 961-3000
Fax: (203) 961-3190
http://www.acnielsen.com
General Counsel: Earl H. Doppelt
Approx. size: 5-10

**Adidas America, Inc.**
9605 Southwest Nimbus Avenue
Beaverton, Oregon 97008
Telephone: (503) 736-5896
Fax: (503) 797-4420
http://www.adidas.com
General Counsel: Susheela Jayapal
Approx. size: < 5

**Administaff, Inc.**
19001 Crescent Springs Drive
Kingwood, Texas 77339-3802
Telephone: (281) 358-8986
Fax: (281) 358-6492
http://www.administaff.com
General Counsel: John Spurgin, II
Approx. size: 5-10

**Advanced Micro Devices, Inc.**
One AMD Place
P.O.Box 3453
Sunnyvale, California 94088
Telephone: (408) 732-2400
Fax: (408) 774-7002
http://www.amd.com
General Counsel: Thomas M. McCoy
Approx. size: 15-20

**Advantica Restaurant Group, Inc.**
203 East Main Street
Spartanburg, South Carolina 29319-9725
Telephone: (864) 597-8000
Fax: (864) 597-8950
http://www.advantica-dine.com
General counsel: Rhonda J. Parish
Approx. size: 5-10

**Aegon USA, Inc.**
4333 Edgewood Road, N. E.
Cedar Rapids, Iowa 52499
Telephone: (319) 398-8622
Fax: (319) 369-2206
http://www.aegon.com
General counsel: Craig D. Vermie
Approx. size: 10-15

**The Aerospace Corporation**
2350 East El Segundo Boulevard
El Segundo, California 90245
Telephone: (310) 336-5000
Fax: (310) 336-0285
http://www.aero.org
General counsel: Gordon J. Louttit
Approx. size: < 5

**Aetna Inc.**
151 Farmington Avenue
Hartford, Connecticut 06156-3124
Telephone: (860) 273-4303
Fax: (860) 273-8340
http://www.aetnafinancial.com
General Counsel: L. Edward Shaw, Jr.
Approx. size: 45-50

**Aetna U.S. Healthcare Inc.**
980 Jolly Road
P.O. Box 1180
Blue Bell, Pennsylvannia 19422-0407
Telephone: (215) 775-6460
Fax: (215) 775-6401
http://www.aetnaushc.com
Chief Legal and Regulatory Affairs
Officer: David F. Simon
Approx. size: 45-50

**AFC Enterprises, Inc.**
Six Concourse Parkway, Suite 1700
Atlanta, Georgia 30328
Telephone: (770) 391-9500
Fax: (800) 628-5109
http://www.afcc.com
General Counsel: Samuel N. Frankel
Approx. size: 5-10

**Affiliated Computer Services, Inc.**
2828 North Haskell
Dallas, Texas 75204
Telephone: (214) 841-6152
Fax: (214) 823-5746
http://www.affiliatedinc.net
General Counsel: David W. Black
Approx. size: 5-10

**AGCO Corporation**
4205 River Green Parkway
Duluth, Georgia 30096-2568
Telephone: (770) 813-9200
Fax: (770) 813-6158
http://www.agcocorp.com
General counsel: C.S.D. Lupton
Approx. size: < 5

**AGFA Corporation**
100 Challenger Road
Ridgefield Park, New Jersey 07660
Telephone: (201) 440-0111
Fax: (201) 440-4056
http://www.agfa.com
General Counsel: Frederick J. Salek
Approx. size: 5-10

**Agilent Technologies, Inc.**
(Subsidiary Hewlett-Packard Company)
3000 Hanover Street Mail Stop 20BQ
Palo Alto, California 94304
Telephone: (650) 857-1501
http://www.agilent.com
future address: 395 Page Mill Road, Palo
Alto, California 94306
General Counsel: D. Craig Nordlund
Approx. size: 35-40

**AgrEvo USA Company**
2711 Centerville Road
Wilmington, Delaware 19808
Telephone: (302) 892-3000
http://www.agrevo.com
General Counsel: Kenneth D. Morris
Approx. size: < 5

**Agway, Inc.**
Post Office Box 4933
Syracuse, New York 13221-4933
Telephone: (315) 449-6436
Fax: (315) 449-6253
http://www.agway.com
General counsel: David M. Hayes
Approx. size: < 5

**Air Liquide America Corporation**
Post Office Box 460229
2700 Post Oak Boulevard
Suite 1800
Houston, Texas 77056
Telephone: (713) 624-8000
http://www.airliquide.com/us
Approx. size: < 5

**Air Products and Chemicals, Inc.**
7201 Hamilton Boulevard
Allentown, Pennsylvania 18195
Telephone: (610) 481-7351
Fax: (610) 481-8223
http://www.airproducts.com
General Counsel: W. Douglas Brown
Approx. size: 20-25

**AKZO Nobel Inc.**
7 Livingston Avenue
Dobbs Ferry, New York 10522-3408
Telephone: (914) 674-5183
http://www.akzonobel.com
General Counsel: M. Kennith Frank, III
Approx. size: 15-20

**Alcan Aluminum Corporation**
6060 Parkland Boulevard
Mayfield Heights, Ohio 44124-4185
Telephone: (216) 423-6600
Fax: (216) 423-6663
http://www.alcan.com
General counsel: William H. Jairrels
Approx. size: 5-10

**Alcon Laboratories, Inc.**
6201 South Freeway
Fort Worth, Texas 76134
Telephone: (817) 293-0450
Fax: (817) 568-7197
http://www.alconlabs.com
Associate General Counsel: Kathleen A. Knight
Approx. size: 15-20

**Alexander & Baldwin, Inc.**
822 Bishop Street
P.O. Box 3440
Honolulu, Hawaii 96801
Telephone: (808) 525-6611
Fax: (808) 525-6678
http://www.alexanderbaldwin.com
General Counsel: Michael J. Marks
Approx. size: < 5

**ALFA Insurance Companies**
Post Office Box 11000
2108 East South Boulevard
Montgomery, Alabama 36191
Telephone: (334) 288-3900
Fax: (334) 288-0905
http://www.alfains.com
General counsel: H. Al Scott
Approx. size: < 5

**Allegheny Technologies Incorporated**
1000 Six PPG Place
Pittsburgh, Pennsylvania 15222
Telephone: (412) 394-2800
Fax: (412) 394-2805
http://www.alleghenytechnologies.com
General Counsel: Jon D. Walton
Approx. size: 5-10

**Allegiance Healthcare Corporation**
1430 Waukegan Road MPKB-A3
(McGaw Park)
Waukegan, Illinois 60085
Telephone: (847) 578-4440
Facsimile: (847) 578-4448
http://www.allegiance.net
General Counsel: William L. Feather
Approx. size: 10-15

**Alliance Capital Management L.P.**
1345 Avenue of the Americas
New York, New York 10105
Telephone: (212) 969-1000
http://www.alliancecapital.com
General counsel: David R. Brewer, Jr.
Approx. size: 10-15

**Alliant Techsystems Inc.**
600 Second Street, N. E.
Hopkins, Minnesota 55343
Telephone: (612) 931-6000
Fax: (612) 931-5518
http://www.allianttech.com
General counsel: Daryl L. Zimmer
Approx. size: 5-10

**Allianz Life Insurance Company of
North America**
1705 Hennepin Avenue
Minneapolis, Minnesota 55403-2195
Telephone: (612) 347-6500
http://www.allianzlife.com
Approx. size: 5-10

**AlliedSignal Inc.**
101 Columbia Road
Morristown, New Jersey 07962
Telephone: (973) 455-2000
http://www.alliedsignal.com
General Counsel: Peter M. Kreindler
Approx. size: >50

**Allied Van Lines, Inc.**
215 West Diehl Road
Naperville, Illinois 60563
Telephone: (630) 717-3573
Fax: (630) 717-3390
http://www.alliedvan.com
General counsel: Robert J. Henry
Approx. size: < 5

**Allstate Insurance Company**
2775 Sanders Road, A2
Northbrook, Illinois 60062-7127
Telephone: (847) 402-5000
http://www.allstate.com
General Counsel: Robert W. Pike
Approx. size: 100+

**Altera Corporation**
101 Innovation Drive
San Jose, California 95134
Telephone: (408) 544-8009
Fax: (408) 544-8000
http://www.altera.com
General Counsel: C. Wendell Bergere, Jr.
Approx. size: < 5

**Aluminum Company of America**
201 Isabella Street , 6th Floor
Pittsburgh, Pennsylvania 15212-5858
Telephone: (412) 553-4243
Fax: (412) 553-3606
http://www.alcoa.com
General Counsel: Lawrence R. Purtell
Approx size: 45-50

**Alyeska Pipeline Service Company**
1835 South Bragaw Street
Anchorage, Alaska 99512
Telephone: (907) 787-1611
Fax: (907) 787-8586
http://www.alyeska-pipeline.com
Deputy General Counsel: Lawrence R.
    Trotter
Approx size: 5-10

**American Automobile Association**
1000 AAA Drive
Heathrow, Florida 32746-5063
Telephone: (407) 444-7990
Fax: (407) 444-7997
http://www.aaa.com
Executive Vice President: Richard D.
Rinner
Approx size: < 5

**American Bankers Association**
1120 Connecticut Avenue, N. W.
Washington, D.C. 20036
Telephone: (202) 663-5026
Fax: (202) 828-4548
http://www.aba.com
General counsel: John J. Gill
Approx. size: 5-10

**America Online, Inc.**
22000 AOL Way
Dulles, Virginia 20166-9323
Telephone: (703) 265-1000
Fax: (703) 265-2208
http://www.aol.com
General Counsel: Paul T. Cappuccio
Approx size: 50-55

**American Arbitration Association**
335 Madison Avenue, 10th Floor
New York, New York 10017-4605
Telephone: (212) 716-5800
Fax: (212) 716-5902
http://www.adr.org
General Counsel: Michael F. Hoellering
Approx size: < 5

**AMBAC Financial Group, Inc.**
One State Street Plaza
New York, New York 10004
Telephone: (212) 668-0340
Fax: (212) 344-5297
http://www.ambac.com
General counsel: Joseph V. Salzano
Approx. size: 10-15

**Amerada Hess Corporation**
1185 Avenue of the Americas
New York, New York 10036
Telephone: (212) 997-8500
Fax: (212) 536-8390
http://www.hess.com
General Counsel: J. Barclay Collins, II
Approx size: 10-15

**American Council of Life Insurers**
1001 Pennsylvania Avenue, N. W.
Suite: ACLI Research Library
Washington, D.C. 20004-2599
Telephone: (202) 624-2000
http://www.acli.com
General counsel: Gary E. Hughes
Approx. size: 5-10

**American Electric Power Service Corp.**
1 Riverside Plaza
Columbus, Ohio 43215-2373
Telephone: (614) 223-1000
Fax: (614) 223-1687
http://www.aep.com
General Counsel: Susan Tomasky
Approx. size: 30-35

**American Express Company**
American Express Tower
200 Vesey Street
New York, New York 10285-4900
Telephone: (212) 640-2000
Fax: (212) 619-7099
http://www.americanexpress.com
General Counsel: Louise Marie Parent
Approx. size: 35-40

**American Express Financial Advisors**
IDS Tower 10, T27/52
Minneapolis, Minnesota 55440
Telephone: (212) 640-3804
Fax: (212) 619-8942
http://www.americanexpress.com
General counsel: Gordon L. Eid
Approx. size: 15-20

**American Family Insurance Group**
6000 American Parkway
Madison, Wisconsin 53783-0001
Telephone: (608) 249-2111
Fax: (608) 243-4917
http://www.amfam.com
Executive Vice President, Corporate
   Legal Department – James F. Eldridge
Approx. size: 110-120

**American Family Life Assurance
   Company of Columbus (AFLAC)**
1932 Wynnton Road
Columbus, Georgia 31999
Telephone: (706) 323-3431
Fax: (706) 596-3577
http://www.aflac.com
General counsel: Joey M. Loudermilk
Approx. size: 5-10

**American Financial Group, Inc.**
One East Fourth Street
Cincinnati, Ohio 45202
Telephone: (513) 579-2121
Fax: (513) 579-2113
http://www.amfnl.com
General counsel: James E. Evans
Approx. size: 5-10

**American Greetings Corporation**
One American Road
Cleveland, Ohio 44144
Telephone: (216) 252-7300
Fax: (216) 252-6741
http://www.corporate.americangreet-
  ings.com
General counsel: Jon Groetzinger, Jr.
Approx. size: < 5

**American Home Products Corporation**
5 Giralda Farms
Madison, New Jersey 07940
Telephone: (973) 660-5000
Fax: (973) 660-6030
http://www.ahp.com
General Counsel: Louis L. Hoynes, Jr.
Approx. size: 45-50

**American Insurance Association**
1130 Connecticut Avenue, N. W.
Suite 1000
Washington, D.C. 20036
Telephone: (202) 828-7100
http://www.aiadc.org
General counsel: Craig A. Berrington
Approx. size: 10-15

**American International Group, Inc.**
70 Pine Street
28th Floor
New York, New York 10270
Telephone: (212) 770-7000
http://www.aig.com
General counsel: Ernest T. Patrikis
Approx. size: 85-90

**American National Red Cross**
National Headquarters
430 17th Street, N.W.
Washington, D.C. 20006-5307
Telephone: (202) 639-3268
Fax: (202) 639-3700
http://www.redcross.org
General Counsel: Richard L. Dashefsky
Approx. size: 10-15

**American Pioneer Title Insurance Company**
493 East Semoran Boulevard
Casselberry, Florida 32707
Telephone: (407) 260-8080
Fax: (407) 260-1952
http://www.aptic.com
General counsel: George P. Daniels
Approx. size: 5-10

**American Re-Insurance Company**
555 College Road East
Princeton, New Jersey 08543-5241
Telephone: (609) 243-4200
Fax: (609) 243-4992
http://www.amre.com
General counsel: Robert K. Burgess
Approx. size: 5-10

**American Society of Composers, Authors and Publishers (ASCAP)**
One Lincoln Plaza
New York, New York 10023
Telephone: (212) 621-6000
Fax: (212) 787-1381
http://www.ascap.com
Vice President Legal Services: Richard H. Reimer
Approx size: 5-10

**American Standard Companies Inc.**
One Centennial Avenue
Post Office Box 6820
Piscataway, New Jersey 08855-6820
Telephone: (732) 980-6000
Fax: (732) 980-6118
http://www.americanstandard.com
General counsel: Richard A. Kalaher
Approx. size: 20-25

**American Stock Exchange, LLC**
86 Trinity Place
New York, New York 10006
Telephone: (212) 306-1000
http://www.amex.com
Associate General Counsel: J. Bruce Ferguson
Approx. size: < 5

**American Suzuki Motor Corporation**
3251 East Imperial Highway
Brea, California 92822-1100
Telephone: (714) 996-7040
Fax: (714) 996-3144
http://www.suzuki.com
General counsel: None designated
Approx. size: < 5

**American United Life Insurance Company**
One American Square
Post Office Box 368
Indianapolis, Indiana 46206
Telephone: (317) 263-1877
http://www.aul.com
General counsel: William R. Brown
Approx. size: 5-10

**American Water Works Company, Inc.**
1025 Laurel Oak Road
Post Office Box 1770
Voorhees, New Jersey 08043
Telephone: (609) 346-8200
Fax: (609) 346-8299
http://www.amwater.com
General counsel: W. Timothy Pohl
Approx. size: 10-15

**Ameritas Life Insurance Corp.**
5900 "O" Street
Post Office Box 81889
Lincoln, Nebraska 68501
Telephone: (402) 467-1122
http://www.ameritas.com
Executive Vice President, Legal and Governmental Affairs – Norman Kivosha
Approx. size: 5-10

**Ameritech Corporation**
30 South Wacker Drive
39th Floor
Chicago, Illinois 60606
Telephone: (800) 257-0902
http://www.ameritech.com
General counsel: Kelly R. Welsh
Approx. size: 5-10

**Amgen, Inc.**
One Amgen Center Drive
Thousand Oaks, California 91320-1789
Telephone: (805) 447-1000
Fax: (805) 480-9941
http://www.amgen.com
General Counsel: George A. Vandeman
Approx. size: 30-35

**AMR Corporation**
Dallas/Fort Worth Airport
Post Office Box 619616
Dallas, Texas 75261-9616
Telephone: (817) 931-1234
Fax: (817) 967-2937
http://www.amrcorp.com
General counsel: Anne H. McNamara
Approx. size: 40-45

**AmSouth Bank**
1901 6th Avenue North
Suite 920
Birmingham, Alabama 35203
Telephone: (205) 326-5319
Fax: (205) 583-4497
http://www.amsouth.com
General counsel: Stephen A. Yoder
Approx. size: 5-10

**Amsted Industries**
205 North Michigan Avenue
Boulevard Tower South – 44th Floor
Chicago, Illinois 60601
Telephone: (312) 645-1700
Fax: (312) 819-8484
http://www.amsted.com
General counsel: Thomas C. Berg
Approx. size: 5-10

**Amway Corporation**
7575 East Fulton Road
Ada, Michigan 49355
Telephone: (616) 787-6000
Fax: (616) 787-6709
http://www.amway.com
General Counsel: Craig N. Meurlin
Approx. size: 35-40

**Amwest Insurance Group**
5230 Las Virgenes Road
Post Office Box 4500
Calabasas, California 91302
Telephone: (818) 871-2000
Fax: (818) 871-2032
http://www.amwest.com
Approx. size: 10-14

**Anadarko Petroleum Corporation**
17001 Northchase Drive
Post Office Box 1330
Houston, Texas 77251-1330
Telephone: (281) 875-1101
http://www.anadarko.com
General counsel: J. Stephen Martin
Approx. size: 10-15

**Andersen Worldwide**
15th Floor
225 North Michigan Avenue
Chicago, Illinois 60601
Telephone: (312) 782-0225
http://www.arthurandersen.com
General Counsel: Jon N. Ekdahl
Approx. size: 45-50

**Anthem Blue Cross and Blue Shield of Connecticut**
370 Bassett Road
North Haven, Connecticut 06473-4201
Telephone: (203) 239-8526
http://www.anthembcbsct.com
Vice President/Law – Peter Thorkelson
Approx. size: 5-10

**Aon Corporation**
123 North Wacker Drive
Chicago, Illinois 60606
Telephone: (312) 701-3000
Fax: (312) 701-3888
http://www.aon.com
Approx. size: 35-40

**Apache Corporation**
2000 Post Oak Boulevard
Suite 100
Houston, Texas 77056-4400
Telephone: (713) 296-6000
http://www.apachecorp.com
General counsel: Zurab S. Kobiashvili
Approx. size: 5-10

**Applebee's International, Inc.**
4551 West 107th Street
Suite 100
Overland Park, Kansas 66207
Telephone: (913) 967-4000
Fax: (913) 341-1696
http://www.applebees.com
General counsel: Robert T. Steinkamp
Approx. size: < 5

**Applied Industrial Technologies**
One Applied Plaza
Post Office Box 6925
Cleveland, Ohio 44115-5056
Telephone: (216) 426-4000
Fax: (216) 426-4899
http://www.appliedindustrial.com
Approx. size: < 5

**Aramco Services Company**
9009 West Loop South
Post Office Box 4535
Houston, Texas 77210-4535
Telephone: (713) 432-5910
Fax: (713) 432-5913
http://www.aramcoservices.com
General counsel: S. E. McGinley
Approx. size: 5-10

**Arch Coal, Inc.**
Cityplace One
Suite 300
St. Louis, Missouri 63141
Telephone: (314) 994-2700
Fax: (314) 994-2734
http://www.archcoal.com
Approx. size: < 5

**Aristar, Inc.**
8900 Grand Oak Circle
Hidden River Corporate Park
Tampa, Florida 33637-1050
Telephone: (813) 632-4500
Fax: (813) 632-4599
http://www.aristar.com
General counsel: James R. Garner
Approx. size: 5-10

**Arm Financial Group, Inc.**
515 West Market Street
Louisville, Kentucky 40202
Telephone: (502) 582-7900
Fax: (502) 582-7995
http://www.armfinancial.com
General counsel: None designated
Approx. size: 5-10

**Armstrong World Industries, Inc.**
2500 Columbia Avenue
Post Office Box 3001
Lancaster, Pennsylvania 17604
Telephone: (717) 397-0611
Fax: (717) 396-6121
http://www.armstrong.com
General counsel: Deborah K. Owen
Approx. size: 10-15

**Arrow Electronics, Inc.**
25 Hub Drive
Melville, New York 11747
Telephone: (516) 391-1300
Fax: (516) 391-1230
http://www.arrow.com
General counsel: Robert E. Klatell
Approx. size: 5-10

**Arthur J. Gallagher & Co.**
Two Pierce Place
Itasca, Illinois 60143
Telephone: (630) 773-3800
http://www.ajg.com
General counsel: John C. Rosengren
Approx. size: < 5

**Asarco Incorporated**
180 Maiden Lane
25th Floor
New York, New York 10038
Telephone: (212) 510-2000
http://www.asarco.com
General counsel: Augustus B.
   Kinsolving
Approx. size: 10-15

**Asea Brown Boveri Inc.**
501 Merritt 7
Norwalk, Connecticut 06856
Telephone: (203) 750-2200
http://www.abb.com
General counsel: Richard M. Burt
Approx. size: 25-30

**Ashland Inc.**
50 East RiverCenter Boulevard
Covington, Kentucky 41012
Telephone: (606) 815-3333
http://www.ashland.com
General Counsel: David L. Hausrath
Approx. size: 40-45

**Association of International**
   **Automobile Manufacturers, Inc.**
1001 19th Street North
Suite 1200
Arlington, Virginia 22209
Telephone: (703) 525-7788
http://www.aiam.org
General counsel: Charles H. Lockwood, II
Approx. size: <5

**AT&T Wireless Services, Inc.**
7277 164th Avenue, N. E.
Redmond, Washington 90852
Telephone: (425) 580-6000
http://www.att.com
General counsel: Gregory P. Landis
Approx. size: 30-35

**Attorneys' Liability Assurance Society, Inc.**
311 South Wacker Drive
Suite 5700
Chicago, Illinois 60606-6622
Telephone: (312) 697-6900
Fax: (312) 697-6901
http://www.ababnet.org/legalservices/
   pl/alas.html
General counsel: Donald S. Breakstone
Approx. size: 10-15

**Attorneys' Title Insurance Fund, Inc.**
6545 Corporate Center Boulevard
Orlando, Florida 32822
Telephone: (407) 240-3863
http://www.thefund.com
General counsel: R. Norwood Gay, III
Approx. size: 5-10

**Automatic Data Processing, Inc.**
One ADP Boulevard
Roseland, New Jersey 07068
Telephone: (201) 994-5000
http://www.adp.com
General counsel: James B. Benson
Approx. size: 30-35

**AutoNation, Inc.**
110 Southeast 6th Street
20th Floor
Fort Lauderdale, Florida 33301
Telephone: (954) 769-7200
Fax: (954) 769-6328
http://www.autonation.com
General Counsel: James O. Cole
Approx. size: 15-20

**Autozone, Inc.**
123 South Front Street
Memphis, Tennessee 38103
Telephone: (901) 495-6500
http://www.autozone.com
General Counsel: Harry L. Goldsmith
Approx. size: 15-20

**Avery Dennison Corporation**
150 North Orange Grove Boulevard
Pasadena, California 91103
Telephone: (616) 304-2000
Fax: (616) 304-2251
http://www.averydennison.com
General counsel: Robert G. van
  Schooneberg
Approx. size: 5-10

**Avis Rent A Car, Inc.**
900 Old Country Road
Garden City, New York 11530-2128
Telephone: (516) 222-3000
Fax: (516) 222-4101
http://www.avis.com
General counsel: Karen C. Sclafani
Approx. size: 10-15

**Avnet, Inc.**
2211 South 47th Street
Phoenix, Arizona 85034
Telephone: (602) 643-2000
Fax: (602) 643-8848
http://www.avnet.com
General counsel: David R. Birk
Approx. size: 5-10

**Avon Products, Inc.**
1345 Avenue of the Americas
New York, New York 10105
Telephone: (212) 282-5000
http://www.avon.com
General counsel: Ward M. Miller, Jr.
Approx. size: 10-15

**Baker Hughes Incorporated**
3900 Essex Lane
Suite 1200
Houston, Texas 77027-5177
Telephone: (713) 439-8600
Fax: (713) 439-8472
http://www.bakerhughes.com
General counsel: Lawrence O'Donnell, III
Approx. size: 20-25

**Ball Corporation**
10 Longs Peak Drive
Broomfield, Colorado 80021-2510
Telephone: (303) 460-2586
Fax: (303) 460-2691
http://www.ball.com
General Counsel: Donald C. Lewis
Approx. size: 5-10

**Bank of America**
Bank of America Corporate Center
100 North Tryon Street NCI-007-20-01
Charlotte, North Carolina 28255
Telephone: (704) 386-7484
http://www.BankAmerica.com
General Counsel: Paul J. Polking
Approx. size: 200+

**The Bank of New York**
1 Wall Street
15th Floor
New York, New York 10286
Telephone: (212) 495-1784
http://www.bankofny.com
General counsel: not designated
Approx. size: 40-45

**The Bank of Tokyo-Mitsubishi, Ltd.**
1251 Avenue of the Americas
New York, New York 10020-1104
Telephone: (212) 782-4620
Fax: (212) 782-6420
http://www.btm.co.jp/index_e.htm
General counsel: Robert E. Hand
Approx. size: 5-10

**Bank United**
3200 Southwest Freeway
Suite 2600
Houston, Texas 77027
Telephone: (713) 543-6958
Fax: (713) 543-6469
http://www.bankunited.com
General counsel: Jonathon K. Heffron
Approx. size: 5-10

**Barclays Bank P.L.C.**
222 Broadway
10th Floor
New York, New York 10038
Telephone: (212) 412-3544
Fax: (212) 412-7519
http://www.barclays.com
General counsel: Guy C. Dempsey, Jr.
Approx. size: 5-10

**BASF Corporation**
3000 Continental Drive North
Mount Olive, New Jersey 07828-1234
Telephone: (201) 426-2600
http://www.basf.com
General Counsel: Thomas Y. Allman
Approx. size: 45-50

**Bass Hotels & Resorts, Inc.**
Three Ravinia Drive
Suite 2900
Atlanta, Georgia 30346
Telephone: (770) 604-2000
http://www.meetings.basshotels.com
General counsel: Robert D. Hill
Approx. size: 15-20

**Bausch & Lomb Incorporated**
One Bausch & Lomb Place
Rochester, New York 14604-2701
Telephone: (716) 338-6000
Fax: (716) 338-6007
http://www.bauschandlomb.com
General Counsel: Robert B. Stiles
Approx. size: 15-20

**Bayer Corporation**
100 Bayer Road
Pittsburgh, Pennsylvania 15205-9741
Telephone: (412) 777-2000
Fax: (412) 777-3802
http://www.bayer.com
General Counsel: Leslie F. Nute
Approx. size: 50-55

**Baxter International Incorporated**
One Baxter Parkway
Deerfield, Illinois 60015-4625
Telephone: (847) 948-2000
Fax: (847) 948-3948
http://www.baxter.com
General counsel: Thomas J. Sabatino, Jr.
Approx. size: 70-80

**Belk Stores Services, Inc.**
2801 West Tyvola Road
Charlotte, North Carolina 28217-4500
Telephone: (704) 357-1000
http://www.belk.com
General counsel: Ralph A. Pitts
Approx. size: <5

**Bell Atlantic**
1095 Avenue of the Americas
38th Floor
New York, New York 10036
Telephone: (212) 395-2121
http://www.bell-atl.com
General counsel: James R. Young
Approx. size: 120-130

**Bell Atlantic Mobile Systems, Inc.**
180 Washington Valley Road
Bedminster, New Jersey 07921-2120
Telephone: (908) 306-7000
Fax: (908) 306-6876
http://www.verizonwireless.com
General counsel: none designated
Approx. size: <5

**BellSouth Corporation**
1155 Peachtree Street, N. E.
Atlanta, Georgia 30309-3610
Telephone: (404) 249-2600
http://www.bellsouth.com
General Counsel: Charles R. Morgan
Approx. size: 180-190

**Bethlehem Steel Corporation**
1170 Eighth Avenue
Room 2018
Bethlehem, Pennsylvania 18016-7699
Telephone: (610) 694-2424
Fax: (610) 694-1753
http://www.bsco.com
General Counsel: William H. Graham
Approx. size: 15-20

**Berkshire Hathaway Group**
3024 Harney Street
Omaha, Nebraska 68131-3580
Telephone: (402) 536-3000
Fax: (402) 536-3031
http://www.berkshirehathaway.com
General counsel: Forrest N. Krutter
Approx. size: 5-10

**Berwind Group**
1500 Market Street
3000 Center Square West
Philadelphia, Pennsylvania 19102
Telephone: (215) 563-2800
http://www.berwindfinancial.com
General counsel: Pamela I. Lehrer
Approx. size: 5-10

**Bestfoods**
700 Sylvan Avenue
International Plaza
Englewood Cliffs, New Jersey 07632-9976
Telephone: (201) 894-4000
Fax: (201) 894-2193
http://www.bestfoods.com
General counsel: Hanes A. Heller
Approx. size: 15-20

**Beverly Enterprises**
5111 Rogers Avenue
Suite 40-A
Fort Smith, Arkansas 72919-0155
Telephone: (501) 484-8750
Fax: (501) 452-3760
http://www.beverlynet.com
General counsel: Robert W. Pommerville
Approx. size: 5-10

**BIC Corporation**
500 BIC Drive
Milford, Connecticut 06460
Telephone: (203) 783-2000
Fax: (203) 783-2108
http://www.bicworld.com
General counsel: Thomas M. Kelleher
Approx. size: <5

**Biomet, Inc.**
Airport Industrial Park
P.O. Box 587
Warsaw, Indiana 46581-0587
Telephone: (219) 267-6639
Fax: (219) 267-8137
http://www.biomet.com
General Counsel: Daniel P. Hann
Approx. size: 5-10

**Bituminous Casualty Company**
320 18th Street
Rock Island, Illinois 61201
Telephone: (309) 786-5401
Fax: (309) 786-7073
http://www.bituminousinsurance.com
Approx. size: <5

**The Black & Decker Corporation**
701 East Joppa Road
Towson, Maryland 21286
Telephone: (410) 716-3900
Fax: (410) 716-2660
http://www.blackanddecker.com
General counsel: Charles E. Fenton
Approx. size: 5-10

**Black Entertainment Television, Inc.**
1900 "W" Place, N. E.
One BET Plaza
Washington, D.C. 20018-1211
Telephone: (202) 608-2000
Fax: (202) 608-2515
http://www.bet.com
Approx. size: 5-10

**Block Drug Company, Inc.**
257 Cornelison Avenue
Jersey City, New Jersey 07302
Telephone: (201) 434-3000
http://www.blockdrug.com
General counsel: John E. Peters
Approx. size: 5-10

**Blue Cross & Blue Shield of Maryland, Inc.**
10455 Mill Run Circle
5th Floor
Owings Mills, Maryland 21117
Telephone: (410) 998-5960
Fax: (410) 998-5133
http://www.bcbmd.com
General counsel: John A. Picciotto
Approx. size: 10-15

**BlueCross BlueShield Association**
225 N. Michigan Avenue
Chicago, Illinois 60601
Telephone: (312) 297-6000
Fax: (312) 297-5867
http://www.bluecares.com
General counsel: Roger G. Wilson
Approx. size: 10-15

**The BOC Group, Inc.**
575 Mountain Avenue
Murray Hill, New Jersey 07974-2082
Telephone: (908) 464-8100
Fax: (908) 771-4775
http://www.boc.com
General counsel: James P. Blake
Approx. size: 15-20

**BOC Process Systems**
575 Mountain Avenue
Murray Hill, New Jersey 07974-2082
Telephone: (908) 665-2400
Fax: (908) 508-2735
http://www.boc.com
General counsel: Ferdinand Alvaro, Jr.
Approx. size: 5-10

**The Boeing Company**
7755 East Marginal Way South
Seattle, Washington 98108
Telephone: (206) 655-6000
Fax: (206) 544-2020
http://www.boeing.com
General counsel: Theodore J. Collins
Approx. size: 90-100

**Boise Cascade Corporation**
1111 West Jefferson Street
Boise, Idaho 83728-0001
Telephone: (208) 384-7460
Fax: (208) 384-4961
http://www.bc.com
General Counsel: John W. Holleran
Approx. size: 15-20

**Bombardier Capital Holdings Inc.**
12735 Gran Bay Parkway West
Suite 1000
Jacksonville, Florida 32258
Telephone: (888) 421-7758
Fax: (904) 288-1255
http://www.bombardier.com
General counsel: R. William Crowe
Approx. size: 10-15

**Booz, Allen & Hamilton, Inc.**
101 Park Avenue
New York, New York 10178
Telephone: (212) 697-1900
Fax: (212) 551-6562
http://www.bah.com
General counsel: Cornwell G. Appleby
Approx. size: 5-10

**Borders Group**
100 Phoenix Drive
Ann Arbor, Michigan 48108
Telephone: (734) 477-1100
Fax: (734) 477-1370
http://www.bordersgroupinc.com
General Counsel: Thomas D. Carney
Approx. size: 5-10

**Bovis, Inc.**
200 Park Avenue
New York, New York 10166
Telephone: (212) 592-6700
Fax: (212) 592-6988
http://www.bovis.com
General counsel: Mark D. Melson
Approx. size: 5-10

**Bowater Incorporated**
55 East Camperdown Way
P.O. Box 1028
Greenville, South Carolina 29602-1028
Telephone: (864) 271-7733
Fax: (864) 282-9468
http://www.bowater.com
General Counsel: Anthony H. Barash
Approx. size: 5-10

**Boyd Gaming Corporation**
2950 South Industrial Road
Las Vegas, Nevada 89109
Telephone: (702) 792-7200
http://www.boydgaming.com
General counsel: Brian A. Larson
Approx. size: 5-10

**BP Amoco Corporation**
200 East Randolph Drive
Chicago, Illinois 60601-7125
Telephone: (32) 856-6111
http://www.bp.com
General counsel: none designated
Approx. size: 100-110

**Branch Banking and Trust Company**
200 West Second Street
3rd Floor
Winston-Salem, North Carolina 27102
Telephone: (910) 773-2180
Fax: (910) 733-2189
http://www.bbandt.com
General counsel: Jerone C. Herring
Approx. size: 5-10

**Bridgestone/Firestone, Inc.**
50 Century Boulevard
Nashville, Tennessee 37214-3609
Telephone: (615) 872-5000
http://www.bridgestone-firestone.com
General Counsel: Gary A. Garfield
Approx. size: 20-25

**Brinker International, Inc.**
6820 LBJ Freeway
Dallas, Texas 75240
Telephone: (972) 980-9917
Fax: (972) 770-9456
http://www.brinker.com
General counsel: Roger F. Thomson
Approx. size: 5-10

**Bristol-Myers Squibb Company**
345 Park Avenue
New York, New York 10154-0037
Telephone: (212) 546-4000
http://www.bristolmeyers.com
General Counsel: John L. McGoldrick
Approx. size: 100+

**British Aerospace North America, Inc.**
15000 Conference Center Drive
Suite 200
Chantilly, Virginia 20151
Telephone: (703) 802-0080
Fax: (703) 227-1766
http://www.baesystems.com
General counsel: Charles E. Gaba
Approx. size: 5-10

**Brown-Forman Corporation**
850 Dixie Highway
P.O. Box 1080
Louisville, Kentucky 40201-1080
Telephone: (502) 585-1100
http://www.brown-forman.com
General Counsel: Michael B. Crutcher
Approx. size: 5-10

**Bull HN Information Systems Inc.**
300 Concord-530
Billerica, Massachusetts 01821-4186
Telephone: (978) 294-6000
Fax: (978) 294-4645
http://www.bull.com
General counsel: John P. Paone, Jr.
Approx. size: 5-10

**Burger King Corporation**
17777 Old Cutler Road
Miami, Florida 33157
Telephone: (305) 378-7095
Fax: (305) 378-7230
http://www.burgerking.com
General Counsel: W. Barry Blum
Approx. size: 10-15

**Buck Consultants, Inc.**
One Pennsylvania Plaza
New York, New York 10119-4798
Telephone: (212) 330-1000
Fax: (212) 695-4184
http://www.buckconsultants.com
General counsel: none designated
Approx. size: 20-25

**Budget Rent A Car Corporation**
4225 Napervile Road
Lisle, Illinois 60532
Telephone: (630) 955-1900
Fax: (630) 955-7810
http://www.drivebudget.com
General counsel: Robert L. Aprati
Approx. size: 5-10

**Brown Group, Inc.**
8300 Maryland Avenue
Post Office Box 29
St. Louis, Missouri 63166-0029
Telephone: (314) 854-4000
http://www.thebrowngroup.com
General counsel: Robert Douglas Pickle
Approx. size: <5

**Brunswick Corporation**
1 North Field Court
Lake Forest, Illinois 60045-4811
Telephone: (847) 735-4306
Fax: (847) 735-4050
http://www.brunswickcorp.com
General Counsel: Dustan E. McCoy
Approx. size: 10-15

**Burlington Resources Oil & Gas Company**
5051 Westheimer
Suite 1400
Houston, Texas 77056
Telephone: (713) 624-9000
Fax: (713) 624-9624
http://www.br-inc.com
General counsel: Frederick J. Plaeger, II
Approx. size: 10-15

**Burns International Security Services Corporation**
Two Campus Drive
Parsippany, New Jersey 07054
Telephone: (973) 267-5300
Fax: (973) 397-2021
http://www.burnsinternational.com
Approx. size: 5-10

**Business Laws, Inc.**
11630 Chillicothe Road
Chesterland, Ohio 44026
Telephone: (440) 729-7996
Fax: (440) 729-8190
http://www.businesslaws.com
General counsel: none designated
Approx. size: 5-10

**C. R. Bard, Inc.**
730 Central Avenue
Murray Hill, New Jersey 07974
Telephone: (908) 277-8267
Fax: (908) 277-8025
http://www.crbard.com
General counsel: Nadia C. Adler
Approx. size: 5-10

**Cablevision Systems Corporation**
1111 Stewart Avenue
Bethpage, New York 11714
Telephone: (516) 803-2000
Fax: (516) 803-1190
http://www.cablevision.com
General counsel: Robert S. Lemle
Approx. size: 5-10

**Caesars Palace**
3570 Las Vegas Boulevard South
Las Vegas, Nevada 89109
Telephone: (702) 731-7311
Fax: (702) 731-7869
http://www.caesars.com
General counsel: Marc H. Rubenstein
Approx. size: <5

**Carolina Power & Light Company**
411 Fayetteville Street Mall
Raleigh, North Carolina 27602
Telephone: (919) 546-6463
http://www.cplc.com
General Counsel: Robert B. McGehee
Approx. size: 10-15

**Carpenter Technology Corporation**
1047 North Park Road
Wyomissing, Pennsylvania 19610
Telephone: (610) 208-2000
http://www.cartech.com
General counsel: John R. Welty
Approx. size: 5-10

**Cantor Fitzgerald, L.P.**
One World Trade Center
New York, New York 10048
Telephone: (212) 938-5000
http://www.cantor.com
General counsel: Stephen M. Merkel
Approx. size: <5

**Capital Group Companies, Inc.**
333 South Hope Street
55th Floor
Los Angeles, California 90071
Telephone: (213) 486-9200
http://www.capgroup.com
General counsel: Solomon M. Kamm
Approx. size: 10-15

**California Federal Bank, a Federal**
**Savings Bank**
135 Main Street
20th Floor
San Francisco, California 94105
Telephone: (415) 904-4615
http://www.calfed.com
General counsel: Christie S. Flanagan
Approx. size: 20-25

**Campbell Soup Company**
Camden Place
Post Office Box 43
Camden, New Jersey 08103-1799
Telephone: (609) 342-4946
Fax: (609) 342-5216
http://www.campbellsoup.com
General counsel: none designated
Approx. size: 10-15

**Carrier Corporation**
One Carrier Place
Post Office Box 4015
Farmington, Connecticut 06034-4015
Telephone: (860) 674-3000
Fax: (860) 674-3265
http://www.carrier.com
General counsel: Robert E. Galli
Approx. size: 20-25

**Case Corporation**
700 State Street
Racine, Wisconsin 53404
Telephone: (414) 636-6011
http://www.casecorp.com
General counsel: Richard S. Brennan
Approx. size: 15-20

**Caterpillar Inc.**
100 N. E. Adams Street
Peoria, Illinois 61629-7310
Telephone: (309) 675-1000
http://www.cat.com
General Counsel: R. Rennie
Atterbury, III
Approx. size: 45-50

**Catholic Healthcare West**
1700 Montgomery Street
Suite 300
San Francisco, California 94111-1024
Telephone: (415) 438-5500
Fax: (415) 438-5726
http://www.chw.edu
General counsel: Robert L. Johnson
Approx. size: 15-20

**CB Richard Ellis, Inc.**
333 South Beaudry Avenue
Ninth Floor
Los Angeles, California 90017-5139
Telephone: (213) 613-3342
http://www.cbrichardellis.com
General counsel: Walter V. Stafford
Approx. size: 10-15

**CBS Corp.**
51 West 52nd Street
New York, New York 10019
Telephone: (212) 975-5123
http://www.cbs.com
General Counsel: Louis J. Briskman
Approx. size: 45-50

**Cendant Corporation**
6 Sylvan Way
Parsippany, New Jersey 07054
Telephone: (973) 428-9700
Fax: (973) 496-5331
http://www.cendant.com
General Counsel: James E. Buckman
Approx. size: 40-45

**Cenex Harvest States Cooperatives**
5500 Cenex Drive
Inver Grove Heights, Minnesota 55077
Telephone: (651) 306-3710
Fax: (651) 451-4554
http://www.cenexharveststates.com
General counsel: Debra A. Thornton
Approx. size: 5-10

**Centex Corporation**
2728 North Harwood
Dallas, Texas 75201-1516
Telephone: (214) 981-5000
Fax: (214) 981-6855
http://www.centex.com
Chief legal officer: Raymond G. Smerge
Approx. size: 15-20

**Central & South West Corporation**
1616 Woodall Rodgers Freeway
P.O. Box 660164
Dallas, Texas 75266-0164
Telephone: (214) 777-1000
http://www.csw.com
General counsel: Ferd. C. Meyer, Jr.
Approx. size: 5-10

**CH2M Hill**
6060 South Willow Drive
Englewood, Colorado 80222
Telephone: (303) 771-0900
http://www.ch2m.com
General Counsel: S. Wyatt McCallie
Approx. size: 5-10

**Charter Communications, Inc.**
12444 Powerscourt
Suite 100
St. Louis, Missouri 63131
Telephone: (314) 543-2400
Fax: (314) 965-6640
http://www.chartercom.com
General counsel: Curtis S. Shaw
Approx. size: 5-10

**Chicago Stock Exchange, Incorporated**
One Financial Place
440 South LaSalle Street
Chicago, Illinois 60605-1070
Telephone: (312) 663-2222
Fax: (312) 663-2231
http://www.chicagostockex.com
General counsel: Ellen J. Neely
Approx. size: 5-10

**Chicago Title Insurance Company**
245 South Los Robles Avenue
Suite 105
Pasadena, California 91101
Telephone: (626) 432-7600
http://www.ctic.com
General counsel: none designated
Approx. size: 5-10

**Chevron Corporation**
575 Market Street
P.O. Box 7643
San Francisco, California 94105
Telephone: (415) 894-7700
Fax: (415) 894-2248
http://www.chevron.com
General counsel: Harvey D. Hinman
Approx. size: 140-150

**Chicago Bridge & Iron Company N.V.**
1501 North Division Street
Plainfield, Illinois 60544-8984
Telephone: (815) 439-4475
Fax: (815) 439-6600
http://www.chicago-bridge.com
General counsel: Robert H. Wolfe
Approx. size: 5-10

**Chase Bank of Texas, National
   Association**
712 Main
26th Floor
Houston, Texas 77252-8045
Telephone: (713) 216-5887
Fax: (713) 216-7970
General counsel: Jeffrey B. Reitman
Approx. size: 15-20

**The Chase Manhattan Bank**
270 Park Avenue
New York, New York 10017
Telephone: (212) 552-0933
http://www.chase.com
General counsel: William H. McDavid
Approx. size: 150-160

**Chrysler Financial Company L.L.C.**
27777 Franklin Road
Southfield, Michigan 48034
Telephone: (248) 948-3062
Fax: (248) 948-3138
http://www.chryslerfinancial.com
General counsel: Christopher A. Taravella
Approx. size: 5-10

**Church Mutual Insurance Company**
3000 Schuster Lane
Merrill, Wisconsin 54452
Telephone: (715) 536-5577
http://www.churchmutual.com
General counsel: John F. Cleary
Approx. size: 5-10

**Chiron Corporation**
4560 Horton Street
Emeryville, California 94608-2916
Telephone: (510) 923-3274
Fax: (510) 654-5360
http://www.chiron.com
General counsel: William G. Green
Approx. size: 10-15

**Choice Hotels International, Inc.**
10750 Columbia Pike
Silver Spring, Maryland 20901
Telephone: (301) 979-5000
http://www.hotelchoice.com
General counsel: Michael J. DeSantis
Approx. size: 5-10

**Chick-Fil-A, Inc.**
5200 Buffington Road
Atlanta, Georgia 30349
Telephone: (404) 765-8000
Fax: (404) 765-8941
http://www.chick-fil-a.com
General counsel: Bureon E. Ledbetter, Jr.
Approx. size: 5-10

**Chiquita Brands International, Inc.**
Chiquita Center
250 East Fifth Street
Cincinnati, Ohio 45202
Telephone: (513) 784-8000
Fax: (513) 784-6691
http://www.chiquita.com
General counsel: Robert W. Olson
Approx. size: 10-15

**Cincinnati Insurance Company**
6200 South Gilmore Road
Fairfield, Ohio 45014
Telephone: (513) 870-2000
http://www.cinfin.com
General counsel: none designated
Approx. size: 10-15

**Circuit City Stores, Inc.**
9950 Mayland Drive
DRI 5
Richmond, Virginia 23233-1464
Telephone: (804) 527-4000
Fax: (804) 418-8248
http://www.circuitcity.com
General Counsel: W. Stephen Cannon
Approx. size: 10-15

**Circus Circus Enterprises, Inc.**
3950 Las Vegas Boulevard South
Las Vegas, Nevada 89119
Telephone: (702) 632-6720
http://www.circuscircus.com
General counsel: Yvette E. Landau
Approx. size: <5

**The CIT Group, Inc.**
650 CIT Drive
Livingston, New Jersey 07039-5795
Telephone: (973) 740-5234
Fax: (973) 740-5087
http://www.citgroup.com
General counsel: Ernest D. Stein
Approx. size: 60-70

**Citizens Communications**
3 High Ridge Park
Stamford, Connecticut 06905
Telephone: (203) 614-6500
Fax: (203) 614-4651
http://www.czn.com
General counsel: L. Russell Mitten
Approx. size: 10-15

**Claims Resolution Management
   Corporation**
8260 Willow Oaks Corporate Drive
Fairfax, Virginia 22031
Telephone: (703) 204-9300
Fax: (703) 205-6249
http://www.mantrust.org
General counsel: David T. Austern
Approx. size: 5-10

**CMS Energy Corporation**
330 Town Center Drive
Fairlane Plaza South – Suite 1100
Dearborn, Michigan 48126
Telephone: (313) 436-9200
Fax: (313) 436-9225
http://www.cmsenergy.com
General counsel: Rodger A. Kershner
Approx. size: 60-70

**CNA Insurance Companies**
Law Department 43S
CNA Plaza
Chicago, Illinois 60685
Telephone: (312) 822-2000
Fax: (312) 822-1186
http://www.cna.com
General Counsel: Jonathan D. Kantor
Approx. size: 25-30

**CNF Transportation Inc.**
3240 Hillview Avenue
Palo Alto, California 94304
Telephone: (650) 494-2900
Fax: (650) 494-8372
http://www.cnf.com
General counsel: Eberhard G. H. Schmoller
Approx. size: 10-15

**The Coastal Corporation**
9 Greenway Plaza
Houston, Texas 77046-0995
Telephone: (713) 877-1400
http://www.coastalcorp.com
General Counsel: Carl A. Corrallo
Approx. size: 75-85

**The Coca-Cola Company**
One Coca-Cola Plaza
Post Office Drawer 1734
Atlanta, Georgia 30301
Telephone: (404) 676-2121
http://www.coke.com
General Counsel: Joseph R. Gladden, Jr.
Approx. size: 160-170

**Coca-Cola Enterprises Inc.**
2500 Windy Ridge Parkway
Atlanta, Georgia 30339
Telephone: (770) 989-3000
http://www.coke.com
General counsel: John R. Parker, Jr.
Approx. size: 10-15

**Coldwell Banker/NRT Incorporated**
27271 Las Ramblas
Mission Viejo, California  92691
Telephone:  (714) 367-2060
Fax:  (714) 367-2080
http://www.coldwellbanker.com
http://www.nrtinc.com
General counsel:  Gregory V. Blackburn
Approx. size:  5-10

**Cole National Corporation**
5915 Landerbrook Drive
Suite 300
Cleveland, Ohio  44124
Telephone:  (440) 449-4100
http://www.colenational.com
General counsel:  Leslie D. Dunn
Approx. size:  5-10

**Colonial Pipeline Company**
945 East Paces Ferry Road
Atlanta, Georgia  30326
Telephone:  (404) 261-1470
http://www.colonialpipeline.com
General counsel:  Kalin Jones
Approx. size:  5-10

**Coltec Industries Inc.**
2550 West Tyvola Road
3 Coliseum Centre
Charlotte, North Carolina  28217
Telephone:  (704) 423-7000
General counsel:  Robert James Tubbs
Approx. size:  5-10

**Comdisco, Inc.**
6111 North River Road
Rosemont, Illinois  60018
Telephone:  (847) 698-3000
http://www.comdisco.com
General counsel:  Jeremiah M. Fitzgerald
Approx. size:  15-20

**Comerica Incorporated**
500 Woodward Avenue
33rd Floor
Post Office Box  MC 3391
Detroit, Michigan  48226
Telephone:  (313) 222-6115
http://www.comerica.com
General counsel:  George W. Madison
Approx. size:  25-30

**Compaq Computer Corporation**
20555 State Highway 249
Houston, Texas 77070-2698
Telephone: (281) 370-0670
Fax: (281) 514-6355
http://www.compaq.com
General Counsel: Thomas C. Siekman
Approx. size: 60-70

**Computer Associates International, Inc.**
One Computer Associates Plaza
Islandia, New York 11788-7000
Telephone: (516) 342-5224
Fax: (516) 342-4866
http://www.computerassociates.com
General counsel: Steven M. Woghin
Approx. size: 10-15

**Conectiv**
800 King Street
Post Office Box 231
Wilmington, Delaware 19899
Telephone: (302) 429-3758
Fax: (302) 429-3801
http://www.conectiv.com
General counsel: Peter F. Clark
Approx. size: 5-10

**Consolidated Edison Company of New York, Inc.**
4 Irving Place
Room 1810-S
New York, New York 10003
Telephone: (212) 460-4600
Fax: (212) 260-8627
http://www.coned.com
General Counsel: Richard A. Babinecz
Approx. size: 70-80

**Continental Airlines, Inc.**
Post Office Box 4607
Houston, Texas 77210-4607
Telephone: (713) 324-5131
Fax: (713) 324-5161
http://www.continental.com
General Counsel: Jeffery A. Smisek
Approx. size: 5-10

**Cooper Industries, Inc.**
600 Travis Street
Post Office Box 4446
Houston, Texas 77210
Telephone: (713) 209-8457
Fax: (713) 209-8991
http://www.cooperindustries.com
General counsel: Diane Kosmach Schumacher
Approx. size:10-15

**Coral Energy, LLC**
1301 McKinney Street
Suite 700
Houston, Texas 77010
Telephone: (713) 230-3000
Fax: (713) 230-2900
http://www.coralenergy.com
General counsel: Paul W. Chung
Approx. size: 10-15

**Cordant Technologies, Inc.**
15 West South Temple
Suite 1600
Salt Lake City, Utah 84101
Telephone: (801) 933-4200
Fax: (801) 933-4203
http://www.cordanttech.com
General counsel: Daniel S. Hapke, Jr.
Approx. size: 5-10

**Corning Incorporated**
One Riverfront Plaza
Corning, New York 14831
Telephone: (607) 974-8247
http://www.corning.com
General counsel: William D. Eggers
Approx. size: 10-15

**Covance Inc.**
210 Carnegie Center
Princeton, New Jersey 08540-6233
Telephone: (609) 452-4430
Fax: (609) 452-9865
http://www.covance.com
General counsel: Jeffrey S. Hurwitz
Approx. size: 5-10

**Cox Communications, Inc.**
1400 Lake Hearn Drive
Atlanta, Georgia 30319
Telephone: (404) 843-5000
http://www.cox.com
Senior Vice President, Legal and
Regulatory Affairs: James A. Hatcher
Approx. size: 10-15

**CSX Corporation**
901 East Cary Street
One James Center
Post Office Box 85629
Richmond, Virginia 23285
Telephone: (804) 782-1400
Fax: (804) 783-1355
http://www.csx.com
General counsel: Peter J. Shudtz
Approx. size: 10-15

**Cummins Engine Company, Inc.**
500 Jackson Street
Columbus, Indiana 47201
Telephone: (812) 377-5083
Fax: (812) 377-9713
http://www.cummins.com
General counsel: Pamela S. Carter
Approx. size: 5-10

**Cushman & Wakefield, Inc.**
The CBS Building
51 West 52nd Street
11th Floor
New York, New York 10019
Telephone: (212) 841-7500
http://www.cushmanandwakefield.com
General counsel: Kenneth P. Singleton
Approx. size: 10-15

**CVS Corporation**
One CVS Drive
Woonsocket, Rhode Island 02895
Telephone: (401) 765-1500
Fax: (401) 765-7887
http://www.cvs.com
General Counsel: Zenon Paul
Lankowsky
Approx. size: 10-15

**Dana Corporation**
4500 Dorr Street
P.O. Box 1000
Toldeo, Ohio 43615
Telephone: (419) 535-4500
http://www.dana.com
General Counsel: Martin J. Strobel
Approx. size: 15-20

**Dean Foods Company**
3600 North River Road
Franklin Park, Illinois 60131-2185
Telephone: (847) 678-1680
Fax: (847) 233-5501
http://www.deanfoods.com
General counsel: Dale Elliott Kleber
Approx. size: 5-10

**Deere & Company**
One John Deere Place
Moline, Illinois 61265-8098
Telephone: (309) 765-8000
Fax: (309) 765-5892
http://www.deere.com
General counsel: Frank S. Cottrell
Approx. size: 25-30

**Defense Research Institute**
150 North Michigan Avenue
Suite 300
Chicago, Illinois 60601
Telephone: (312) 795-1101
Fax: (312) 795-0747
http://www.dri.org
General counsel: none designated
Approx. size: 5-10

**Delaware North Companies,
Incorporated**
One Delaware North Place
438 Main Street
Buffalo, New York 14202
Telephone: (716) 858-5000
Fax: (716) 858-5056
http://www.delawarenorth.com
General Counsel: Bryan J. Keller
Approx. size: 5-10

**Dell Computer Corporation**
One Dell Way
Round Rock, Texas 78682-2244
Telephone: (512) 728-3504
Fax: (512) 728-8935
http://www.dell.com
General Counsel: William R. Sawyers
Approx. size: 35-40

**Deloitte & Touche LLP**
1633 Broadway
New York, New York 10019-6754
Telephone: (212) 489-1600
Fax: (212) 492-4201
http://www.dttus.com
General counsel: Philip R. Rotner
Approx. size: 25-30

**Delphi Automotive Systems**
5725 Delphi Drive
Troy, Michigan 48098-2815
Telephone: (248) 816-3409
Fax: (248) 649-9569
http://www.delphiauto.com
General Counsel: Not specified
Approx. size: 10-15

**Delta Air Lines, Inc.**
Hartsfield Atlanta International Airport
Atlanta, Georgia 30320
Telephone: (404) 715-2191
Fax: (404) 715-2233
http://www.delta.com
General Counsel: Robert S. Harkey
Approx. size: 35-40

**Deutsche Bank North America**
31 West 52nd Street
New York, New York 10019-6160
Telephone: (212) 469-8000
Fax: (212) 469-8173
http://public.deutsche-bank.de/global
General counsel: Troland S. Link
Approx. size: 25-30

**The Dial Corporation**
15501 North Dial Boulevard
Scottsdale, Arizona 85260-1619
Telephone: (602) 754-3425
Fax: (602) 754-1098
http://www.dialcorp.com
General counsel: Jane E. Owens
Approx. size: 5-10

**Discovision Associates**
2355 Main Street
Suite 200
Irvine, California 92614
Telephone: (949) 660-5000
Fax: (949) 660-1801
http://www.discovision.com
General Counsel: Not specified
Approx. size: 10-15

**Dole Food Company, Inc.**
31365 Oak Crest Drive
Westlake Village, California 91361
Telephone: (818) 879-6600
http://www.dole.com
General counsel: J. Brett Tibbitts
Approx. size: 5-10

**The Dow Chemical Company**
2030 Dow Center
Midland, Michigan 48674
Telephone: (517) 636-1000
http://www.dow.com
General Counsel: John G. Scriven
Approx. size: 10-15

**Dow Corning Corporation**
2200 West Salzburg Road
Midland, Michigan 48686-0994
Telephone: (517) 496-4000
Fax: (517) 496-8307
http://www.dowcorning.com
General counsel: James R. Jenkins
Approx. size: 30-35

**Duke Energy Corporation**
422 South Church Street
P.O. Box 1224
Charlotte, North Carolina 28201-1244
Telephone: (704) 382-8136
Fax: (704) 382-8137
http://www.dukeenergy.com
General Counsel: Richard W. Blackburn
Approx. size: 45-50

**The Dun & Bradstreet Corporation**
One Diamond Hill Road
Murray Hill, New Jersey 07974-1200
Telephone: (908) 665-5000
Fax: (908) 665-1409
http://www.dnb.com
Chief legal counsel: Nancy L. Henry
Approx. size: 60-70

**Dunkin' Donuts Incorporated**
14 Pacella Park Drive
P.O. Box 317
Randolph, Massachusetts 02368-2368
Telephone: (781) 961-4000
http://www.dunkindonuts.com
General Counsel: Lawrence W.
  Hantman
Approx. size: 5-10

**Dynegy Inc.**
1000 Louisiana
Suite 5800
Houston, Texas 77002
Telephone: (713) 507-6400
Fax: (713) 507-6808
http://www.dynegy.com
General Counsel: Kenneth E. Randolph
Approx. size: 25-30

**Eagle-Picher Industries, Inc.**
250 East Fifth Street
Suite 500
Post Office Box 779
Cincinnati, Ohio 45201
Telephone: (513) 721-7010
Fax: (513) 629-2572
http://www.epcorp.com
General counsel: David G. Krall
Approx. size: 5-10

**Eastman Chemical Company**
Post Office Box 511
Kingsport, Tennessee 37662-5075
Telephone: (423) 229-2000
Fax: (423) 229-4137
http://www.eastman.com
General counsel: Harold L. Henderson
Approx. size: 20-25

**ECS Claims Administrators, Inc.**
600 Eagleview Boulevard
Post Office Box 688
Exton, Pennsylvania 19341-0688
Telephone: (610) 458-7445
Fax: (610) 458-7448
http://www.ecsclaims.com
Approx. size: 15-20

**Edison Electric Institute**
701 Pennsylvania Avenue, N. W.
Washington, D.C. 20004-2696
Telephone: (202) 508-5000
Fax: (202) 508-5673
http://www.eei.org
General counsel: Edward H. Comer
Approx. size: 5-10

**EcoLab Inc.**
370 North Wabasha
St. Paul, Minnesota 55102
Telephone: (612) 293-2836
Fax: (612) 293-2573
http://www.ecolab.com
General counsel: Lawrence T. Bell
Approx. size: 5-10

**Ecology & Environment, Inc.**
369 Pleasant View Drive
Buffalo Corporate Center
Lancaster, New York 14086
Telephone: (716) 684-8060
Fax: (716) 684-0844
http://www.ecolen.com
Approx. size: <5

**EBAY Inc.**
2125 Hamilton Avenue
San Jose, California 95125
Telephone: (408) 558-7400
Fax: (408) 558-7514
http://www.ebay.com
General counsel: Michael R. Jacobson
Approx. size: 5-10

**EchoStar Communications Corporation**
5701 South Santa Fe Drive
Littleton, Colorado 80120
Telephone: (303) 723-1000
Fax: (303) 723-1699
http://www.echostar.com
General counsel: David K. Moskowitz
Approx. size: 5-10

**Edison Mission Energy**
18101 Von Karman Avenue
Suite 1700
Irvine, California 92612-1046
Telephone: (949) 752-5588
Fax: (949) 752-5624
http://www.edison.com/profileexa/
    eme/index.htm
General counsel: Raymond W. Vickers
Approx. size: 5-10

**E. I. du Pont de Nemours and Company**
Dupont Building
1007 Market Street
Wilmington, Delaware 19898
Telephone: (302) 774-1000
http://www.dupont.com
General Counsel: Stacey J. Mobley
Approx. size: 100+

**E. & J. Gallo Winery**
600 Yosemite Boulevard
P.O. Box 1130
Modesto, California 95353
Telephone: (209) 341-3111
http://www.gallo.com
General Counsel: Jack B. Owens
Approx. size: 8-10

**Electric Insurance Company**
152 Conant Street
Beverly, Massachusetts 01915
Telephone: (978) 921-0660
Fax: (978) 524-5218
http://www.electricinsurance.com
General Counsel: Elizabeth M
    Thompson
Approx. size: 10-15

**Electronic Data Systems Corporation**
5400 Legacy Drive
H3-3A-05
Plano, Texas 75024
Telephone: (214) 605-5500
Fax: (214) 605-5452
http://www.eds.com
General Counsel: D. Gilbert Friedlander
Approx. size: 100+

**Elf Atochem North America, Inc.**
2000 Market Street
Philadelphia, Pennsylvania 19103
Telephone: (215) 419-7000
http://www.elf-atochem.com
General counsel: Andrea E. Utecht
Approx. size: 15-20

**Eli Lilly and Company**
Lilly Corporate Center
Indianapolis, Indiana 46285
Telephone: (317) 276-2000
http://www.lilly.com
General Counsel: Rebecca O. Goss
Approx. size: 80-90

**El Paso Energy Corporation**
1001 Louisiana Street
Houston, Texas 77002
Telephone: (713) 420-3357
Fax: (713) 420-4099
http://www.epenergy.com
General Counsel: Britton White, Jr.
Approx. size: 40-45

**EMC Corporation**
P.O. Box 368
171 South Street
Hopkinton, Massachusetts 01748
Telephone: (508) 435-1000
http://www.emc.com
General Counsel: Paul T. Dacier
Approx. size: 10-15

**EMC Insurance Companies**
717 Mulberry Street
Post Office Box 712
Des Moines, Iowa 50303-0712
Telephone: (515) 280-2511
Fax: (515) 280-2895
http://www.emcins.com
General counsel: Richard W. Hoffmann
Approx. size: 5-10

**Emerson Electric Co.**
8000 West Florissant Avenue
P.O. Box 4100
St. Louis, Missouri 63136
Telephone: (314) 553-2000
http://www.emersonelectric.com
General Counsel: W. Wayne Withers
Approx. size: 25-30

**Engelhard Corporation**
101 Wood Avenue
Post Office Box 770
Iselin, New Jersey 08830-0770
Telephone: (732) 205-5527
Fax: (732) 548-7835
http://www.engelhard.com
General counsel: Arthur A. Dornbusch, II
Approx. size: 5-10

**Enron Corp.**
1400 Smith Street
Houston, Texas 77002
Telephone: (713) 853-6161
http://www.enron.com
General Counsel: James V. Derrick, Jr.
Approx. size: 150+

**Entergy Corporation**
639 Loyola Avenue
Post Office Box 61000
New Orleans, Louisiana 70161
Telephone: (504) 576-4214
Fax: (504) 576-4150
http://www.entergy.com
General counsel: Michael G. Thompson
Approx. size: 35-40

**Environmental Law Institute**
1616 P Street, N. W.
Washington, D.C. 20036
Telephone: (202) 939-3800
Fax: (202) 939-3868
http://www.eli.org
General counsel: none designated
Approx. size: 15-20

**Equifax Inc.**
1600 Peachtree Street, N. W.
Atlanta, Georgia 30309
Telephone: (404) 885-8000
Fax: (404) 885-8800
http://www.equifax.com
General counsel: Bruce S. Richards
Approx. size: 5-10

**Ernst & Young LLP**
787 Seventh Avenue
New York, New York 10019
Telephone: (212) 773-3800
Fax: (212) 773-3896
http://www.ey.com
General Counsel: Kathryn A. Oberly
Approx. size: 25-30

**The Estee Lauder Companies Inc.**
767 Fifth Avenue
New York, New York 10153
Telephone: (212) 572-3980
http://www.esteelauder.com
General counsel: Saul H. Magram
Approx. size: 10-15

**Ethyl Corporation**
330 South Fourth Street
Richmond, Virginia 23219
Telephone: (804) 788-5485
Fax: (804) 788-5519
http://www.ethyl.com
General counsel: Steven M. Mayer
Approx. size: 5-10

**Exxon Corporation**
5959 Las Colinas Boulevard
Irving, Texas 75039
Telephone: (214) 444-1000
http://www.exxon.com
General Counsel: Charles W. Matthews, Jr.
Approx. size: 250+

**Fair, Isaac and Company, Inc.**
120 North Redwood Drive
San Rafael, California 94903
Telephone: (415) 472-2211
Fax: (415) 492-9381
http://www.fairisaac.com
General counsel: Peter L. McCorkell
Approx. size: 5-10

**The Fairchild Corporation**
Washington Dulles International Airport
45025 Aviation Drive
Suite 400
Dulles, Virginia 20166-7516
Telephone: (703) 478-5800
Fax: (703) 478-5920
http://www.fairchildcorp.com
General counsel: Donald E. Miller
Approx. size: 5-10

**Fannie Mae**
3900 Wisconsin Avenue, N. W.
Washington, D.C. 20016
Telephone: (202) 752-7000
Fax: (202) 752-5023
http://www.fanniemae.com
General counsel: Thomas E. Donilon
Approx. size: 70-80

**Farmers Group, Inc.**
4680 Wilshire Boulevard
2nd Floor
Los Angeles, California 90010
Telephone: (323) 932-3200
Fax: (323) 964-8093
http://www.farmersinsurance.com
General Counsel: Jason L. Katz
Approx. size: 15-20

**Farmland Industries, Inc.**
3315 North Oak Trafficway
Post Office Box 7305, Dept. 62
Kansas City, Missouri 64116
Telephone: (816) 459-6000
http://www.farmland.com
General counsel: Robert B. Terry
Approx. size: 5-10

**Federal Home Loan Mortgage Corporation**
8200 Jones Branch Drive
McLean, Virginia 22102
Telephone: (703) 903-2600
http://www.freddiemac.com
General counsel: Maud Mater
Approx. size: 80-90

**FedEx Corporation**
942 South Shady Grove Road
Memphis, Tennessee 38120
Telephone: (901) 395-3382
http://www.fedex.com
Executive Vice President, Legal
    Department: Steven H. Taylor
Approx. size: 60

**Federated Department Stores, Inc.**
7 West Seventh Street
Cincinnati, Ohio 45202
Telephone: (513) 579-7000
http://www.federated-fds.com
General Counsel: Dennis J. Broderick
Approx. size: 25-30

**Fiduciary Trust Company International**
Two World Trade Center
94th Floor
New York, New York 10048
Telephone: (212) 466-4100
Fax: (212) 524-5029
http://www.fiduciarytrust.com
Chief corporate counsel: Carol K. Demitz
Approx. size: 5-10

**FINA, Inc.**
6000 Legacy Drive
Plano, Texas 75024
Telephone: (972) 801-2997
Fax: (972) 801-2570
http://www.totalfina.com/us/html/
    index.htm
General counsel: Cullen M. Godfrey
Approx. size: 15-20

**Fingerhut Companies, Inc.**
4400 Baker Road
Minnetonka, Minnesota 55343
Telephone: (612) 932-3220
Fax: (612) 932-3181
http://www.fingerhut.com
General Counsel: Michael P. Sherman
Approx. size: 5-10

**First Union Corporation**
301 South College Street
One First Union Center
Charlotte, North Carolina 28288-0630
Telephone: (704) 374-6611
Fax: (704) 374-3105
http://www.firstunion.com
General counsel: Mark C. Treanor
Approx. size: 5-10

**Fiserv, Inc.**
255 Fiserv Drive
Post Office Box 979
Brookfield, Wisconsin 53045
Telephone: (414) 879-5000
Fax: (414) 879-5532
http://www.fiserv.com
General counsel: Charles W. Sprague
Approx. size: 5-10

**Fisher Scientific International Inc.**
One Liberty Lane
Hampton, New Hampshire 03842
Telephone: (603) 926-5911
http://www.fisherscientific.com
General counsel: Todd M. DuChene
Approx. size: 5-10

**Fleming Companies, Inc.**
6301 Waterford Boulevard
Post Office Box 26647
Oklahoma City, Oklahoma 73126-0647
Telephone: (405) 840-7290
http://www.fleming.com
General counsel: David R. Almond
Approx. size: 5-10

**Florida Power Corporation**
3201 34th Street South
Post Office Box 14042
St. Petersburg, Florida 33733
Telephone: (813) 866-5785
Fax: (813) 866-4931
http://www.fpc.com/flpower
General counsel: Kenneth E. Armstrong
Approx. size: 5-10

**Fort James Corporation**
1650 Lake Cook Road
Post Office Box 89
Deerfield, Illinois 60015
Telephone: (847) 317-5000
Fax: (847) 236-3755
http://www.fortjames.com
General counsel: Clifford A. Cutchins, IV
Approx. size: 15-20

**Foster Wheeler Corporation**
Perryville Corporate Park
Clinton, New Jersey 08809-4000
Telephone: (908) 730-4000
Fax: (908) 730-5300
http://www.fwc.com
General Counsel: Thomas R. O'Brien
Approx. size: 20-25

**Ford Motor Company**
The American Road
Dearborn, Michigan 48121-1899
Telephone: (313) 322-3000
http://www.ford.com
General Counsel: John M. Rintamaki
Approx. size: 80-90

**Fortis Health Care & Time Insurance Company**
P.O. Box 3050
501 West Michigan Avenue
Milwaukee, Wisconsin 53201-3050
Telephone: (414) 271-3011
Fax: (414) 299-8438
http://www.health.us.fortis.com
General Counsel: Ann G. Mayberry-French

Approx. size: 10-15

**Fluor Corporation**
One Enterprise Drive
Aliso Viejo, California 92656-2606
Telephone: (949) 349-2000
Fax: (949) 349-4517
http://www.fluor.com
Managing general counsel: Robert R.
   Dryden
Approx. size: 25-30

**FMC Corporation**
200 East Randolph Drive
Chicago, Illinois 60601
Telephone: (312) 861-6000
http://www.fmc.com
General counsel: J. Paul McGrath
Approx. size: 5-10

**The Fremont Group**
50 Fremont Street
San Francisco, California 94105
Telephone: (415) 284-8700
Fax: (415) 512-7121
http://www.freemontgroup.com
General counsel: Richard S. Kopf
Approx. size: 5-10

**Fresenius Medical Care N.A.**
Two Ledgemont Center
95 Hayden Avenue
Lexington, Massachusetts 02420-9192
Telephone: (781) 402-9000
Fax: (781) 402-9171
http://www.fmcna.com
General counsel: Ronald J. Kuerbitz
Approx. size: 15-20

**Fox Group**
10201 West Pico Boulevard
Post Office Box 900
Beverly Hills, California 90213
Telephone: (310) 369-1234
Fax: (310) 369-7860
Deputy general counsel: Mary Anne
   Harrison
Approx. size: 10-15

**Freightliner LLC**
4747 North Channel Avenue
Portland, Oregon 97217-7613
Telephone: (503) 735-8000
Fax: (503) 735-5999
http://www.freightliner.com
General Counsel: James T. Hubler
Approx. size: 5-10

**Foundation Health Systems, Inc.**
21650 Oxnard Street
Woodland Hills, California 91367
Telephone: (818) 676-8989
Fax: (818) 676-8981
http://www.fhs.com
General counsel: none designated
Approx. size: 20-25

**Fox Channels Group**
1440 South Sepulveda Boulevard
Los Angeles, California 90025
Telephone: (310) 444-8123
Fax: (310) 914-8784
http://www.foxchannels.com
General Counsel: Daniel M. Fawcett
Approx. size: 5-10

**Frito-Lay, Inc.**
7701 Legacy Drive
Plano, Texas 75024
Telephone: (972) 334-7000
http://www.fritolay.com
General Counsel: Arthur F. Starrs, Jr.
Approx. size: 5-10

**Fruit of the Loom, Ltd.**
5000 Sears Tower
233 South Wacker Drive
Chicago, Illinois 60606
Telephone: (312) 876-1724
http://www.fruit.com
General Counsel: John J. Ray, III
Approx. size: 5-10

**Gannett Co., Inc.**
1100 Wilson Boulevard
Arlington, Virginia 22234
Telephone: (703) 284-6000
Fax: (703) 558-3897
http://www.gannett.com
General Counsel: Thomas L. Chapple
Approx. size: 10-15

**The Gates Rubber Company**
900 South Broadway
Denver, Colorado 80217
Telephone: (303) 744-1911
http://www.gates.com
General Counsel: James E. Nelson
Approx. size: 5-10

**Gateway 2000, Inc.**
4545 Towne Center Court
San Diego, California 92121
Telephone: (800) 846-2000
Fax: (619) 799-3413
http://www.gateway.com
General Counsel: Not designated
Approx. size: 15-20

**GenCorp Inc.**
175 Ghent Road
Fairlawn, Ohio 44333-3300
Telephone: (330) 869-4200
http://www.gencorp.com
General counsel: William R. Phillips
Approx. size: 5-10

**Genetech, Inc.**
1 DNA Way
South San Francisco, California 94080-
4990
Telephone: (650) 225-1719
Fax: (650) 952-9881
http://www.gene.com
General Counsel: Stephen G. Juelsgaard
Approx. size: 20-25

**General Dynamics Corporation**
3190 Fairview Park Drive
Falls Church, Virginia 22042-4523
Telephone: (703) 876-3000
Fax: (703) 876-3554
http://www.generaldynamics.com
General Counsel: David A. Savner
Approx. size: 30-35

**General Electric Company**
3135 Easton Turnpike
Fairfield, Connecticut 06431
Telephone: (203) 373-2211
Fax: (203) 373-3131
http://www.ge.com
General Counsel: Benjamin W.
  Heineman, Jr.
Approx. size: 500+

**General Mills, Inc.**
Number One General Mills Boulevard
Minneapolis, Minnesota 55426
Telephone: (612) 540-2311
http://www.generalmills.com
General Counsel: Siri S. Marshall
Approx. size: 10-15

**General Motors Corporation**
3031 West Grand Boulevard
Detroit, Michigan 48202
Telephone: (313) 974-1264
http://www.gm.com
General Counsel: Thomas A. Gottschalk
Approx. size: 100+

**Georgia-Pacific Corporation**
133 Peachtree Street, N. E.
Atlanta, Georgia 30303
Telephone: (404) 652-4893
Fax: (404) 584-1461
http://www.gapac.com
General Counsel: James F. Kelley
Approx. size: 35-40

**The Gillette Company**
Prudential Tower Building
39th Floor
Boston, Massachusetts 02199
Telephone: (617) 421-7863
Fax: (617) 421-8373
http://www.gillette.com
General Counsel: Richard K. Willard
Approx. size: 20-25

**Glaxo Wellcome, Inc.**
Post Office Box 13398
Research Triangle Park, North Carolina
27709
Telephone: (919) 483-2100
Fax: (919) 483-2871
http://www.glaxowellcome.com
General Counsel: Paul A. Holcombe, Jr.
Approx. size: 45-50

**Great Lakes Chemical Corporation**
One Great Lakes Boulevard
West Lafayette, Indiana 47906-5894
Telephone: (765) 497-6100
Fax: (765) 497-6660
http://www.greatlakeschem.com
General Counsel: John V. Lacci
Approx. size: 5-10

**GTE Service Corporation**
1255 Corporate Drive
Irving, Texas 75038-2518
Telephone: (972) 507-5338
http://www.gte.com
General Counsel: Ira H. Parker
Approx. size: 80-90

**GTECH Corporation**
55 Technology Way
West Greenwich, Rhode Island 02917-
1711
Telephone: (401) 392-1000
Fax: (401) 392-0391
http://www.gtech.com
General Counsel: Cynthia Anne
Nebergall
Approx. size: 5-10

**H. J. Heinz Company**
600 Grant Street
P.O. Box 57
Pittsburgh, Pennsylvania 15219
Telephone: (412) 456-5700
http://www.heinz.com
General Counsel: Lawrence J. McCabe
Approx. size: 15-20

**Hallmark Cards, Incorporated**
2501 McGee Trafficway
Legal Division #339
P.O. Box 419126
Kansas City, Missouri 64108
Telephone: (816) 274-5583
Fax: (816) 274-7171
http://www.hallamrk.com
General Counsel: Judith Whitaker
Approx. size: 10-15

**Hannaford Bros. Co.**
145 Pleasant Hill Road
Scarborough, Maine 04074
Telephone: (207) 883-2911
http://www.hannaford.com
General Counsel: Andrew P. Geoghegan
Approx. size: < 5

**Harley-Davidson Motor Company**
3700 West Juneau Avenue
Milwaukee, Wisconsin 53208
Telephone: (414) 342-4680
Fax: (414) 343-4089
http://www.harley-davidson.com
General Counsel: Gail A. Lione
Approx. size: 5-10

**Harrah's Entertainment, Inc.**
5100 West Sahara Boulevard
Suite 200
Las Vegas, Nevada 89146
Telephone: (702) 579-2300
Fax: (702) 579-2338
http://www.harrahs.com
General Counsel: Stephen H. Brammell
Approx. size: 15-20

**Hasbro, Inc.**
1027 Newport Avenue
Pawtucket, Rhode Island 02862-1059
Telephone: (401) 727-5757
Fax: (401) 727-5089
http://www.hasbro.com
General Counsel: Cynthia S. Reed
Approx. size: 15-20

**The Hearst Corporation**
959 Eighth Avenue
New York, New York 10019
Telephone: (212) 649-2011
http://www.hearst.com
General Counsel: Jonathan E. Thackeray
Approx. size: 15-20

**Hercules Incorporated**
Hercules Plaza
Wilmington, Delaware 19894
Telephone: (302) 594-5000
Fax: (302) 594-7252
http://www.herc.com
General Counsel: Richard G. Dahlen
Approx. size: 20-25

**The Hertz Corporation**
225 Brae Boulevard
Park Ridge, New Jersey 07656
Telephone: (201) 307-2000
Fax: (201) 307-2876
http://www.hertz.com
General Counsel: Harold E. Rolfe
Approx. size: 15-20

**Hewlett-Packard Company**
3000 Hanover Street
Mail Stop 20BQ
Palo Alto, California 94304
Telephone: (650) 813-3332
http://www.hp.com
General Counsel: Ann O. Baskins
Approx. size: 90-100

**Hoechst Marion Roussel, Inc.**
10236 Marion Park Drive
P.O. Box 9627
Kansas City, Missouri 64134-0627
Telephone: (816) 966-4000
http://www.hmri.com
General Counsel: Edward H.
    Stratemeier
Approx. size: 25-30

**Home Shopping Network, Inc.**
1 HSN Drive
St. Petersburg, Florida 33729
Telephone: (813) 572-8585
http://www.internet.net
General Counsel: James G. Gallagher
Approx. size: 5-10

**Honda North America, Inc.**
700 Van Ness Avenue
Torrance, California 90501
Telephone: (310) 781-4961
http://www.honda.com
General Counsel: Mark A. Brooks
Approx. size: 10-15

**Host Marriott Services Corporation**
6600 Rockledge Drive
Bethesda, Maryland 20817
Telephone: (301) 380-7000
Fax: (301) 380-7020
http://www.hmscorp.com
General Counsel: Joe P. Martin
Approx. size: 5-10

**Hughes Electronics**
200 North Sepulveda Boulevard
Mail Stop A110
El Segundo, California 90245-0956
Telephone: (310) 662-9940
http://www.hughes.com
General Counsel: Marcy J. K. Tiffany
Approx. size: 30-35

**Huntsman Corporation**
500 Huntsman Way
Salt Lake City, Utah 84108
Telephone: (801) 584-5700
Fax: (801) 584-5782
http://www.huntsman.com
General Counsel: Robert B. Lence
Approx. size: 5-10

**ING Insurance Operations – Atlanta**
5780 Powers Ferry Road
P.O. Box 105006
Atlanta, Georgia 30348-5006
Telephone: (770) 850-7780
Fax: (770) 541-3270
http://www.inggroup.com
General Counsel: B. Scott Burton
Approx. size: 5-10

**Ingersoll-Rand Company**
200 Chestnut Ridge Road
Woodcliff Lake, New Jersey 07675
Telephone: (201) 573-0123
http://www.ingersoll-rand.com
General Counsel: Patricia Nachtigal
Approx. size: 20-25

**Intel Corporation**
2200 Mission College Boulevard
Santa Clara, California 95052
Telephone: (408) 987-8080
http://www.intel.com
General Counsel: Tom Dunlap
Approx. size: 45-50

**Interdigital Communications
Corporation**
781 Third Avenue
King of Prussia, Pennsylvania 19406
Telephone: (610) 878-7800
Fax: (610) 878-7844
http://www.interdigital.com
General Counsel: William J. Merritt
Approx. size: 5-10

**International Paper Company**
Two Manhattanville Road
Purchase, New York 10577
Telephone: (914) 397-1500
Fax: (914) 397-1596
http://www.internationalpaper.com
General Counsel: William B. Lytton
Approx. size: 45-50

**Invensys**
4701 West Greenfield Avenue
Milwaukee, Wisconsin 53214
Telephone: (414) 643-3000
Fax: (414) 643-2311
http://www.apv.invensys.com
Division General Counsel: Irwin M.
  Shur
Approx. size: < 5

**The IT Group**
2790 Mosside Boulevard
Monroeville, Pennsylvania 15146-2792
Telephone: (412) 858-3906
Fax: (412) 858-3997
http://www.itcorporation.com
General Counsel: James G. Kirk
Approx. size: 5-10

**J. C. Penney Company, Inc.**
6501 Legacy Drive
Plano, Texas 75024-1117
Telephone: (972) 431-1201
Fax: (972) 431-1133; 1134
http://www.jcpenney.com
General Counsel: Charles R. Lotter
Approx. size: 30-35

**J. R. Simplot Company**
999 Main Street
Suite 1300
P.O. Box 27
Boise, Idaho 83707
Telephone: (208) 336-2110
Fax: (208) 389-7464
http://www.simplot.com
General Counsel: Ronald N. Graves
Approx. size: 10-15

**Kerr-McGee Corporation**
Kerr-McGee Center
Post Office Box 25861
Oklahoma City, Oklahoma 73125
Telephone: (405) 270-1313
Fax: (405) 270-2863
http://www.kerr-mcgee.com
General Counsel: Gregory F. Pilcher
Approx. size: 15-20

**King World Products. Inc.**
1700 Broadway
New York, New York 10019
Telephone: (212) 315-4000
Fax: (212) 974-0310
http://www.kingworld.com
General Counsel: Jonathan Birkhahn
Approx. size: 5-10

**Kinkos Inc.**
255 West Stanley Avenue
Ventura, California 93002-8000
Telephone: (805) 652-3187
Fax: (805) 641-4926
http://www.kinkos.com
General Counsel: Not designated
Approx. size: 5-10

**Koch Industries, Inc.**
4111 East 37th Street North
P.O. Box 2256
Wichita, Kansas 67201
Telephone: (316) 828-5500
Fax: (316) 828-5803
http://www.kochind.com
Associate General Counsel: Thomas J.
  Meek
Approx. size: 50-55

**Kohler Company**
444 Highland Drive
Kohler, Wisconsin 53044-1515
Telephone: (920) 457-4441
Fax: (920) 459-1583
http://www.kohlerco.com
General Counsel: Natalie A. Black
Approx. size: 5-10

**The Kroger Co.**
1014 Vine Street
Cincinnati, Ohio 45202
Telephone: (513) 762-4421
Fax: (513) 762-4935
http://www.kroger.com
General Counsel: Paul W. Heldman
Approx. size: 15-20

**Louisiana-Pacific Corporation**
111 S. W. Fifth Avenue
Suite 4200
Portland, Oregon 97204
Telephone: (503) 221-0800
Fax: (503) 796-0105
http://www.lpcorp.com
General Counsel: Gary C. Wilkerson
Approx. size: 10-15

**Loyola University of Chicago**
820 N. Michigan Avenue
Chicago, Illinois 60611
Telephone: (312) 915-6200
http://www.luc.edu
General Counsel: Ellen Kane Munro
Approx. size: 5-10

**Lexis-Nexis Group**
9443 Springboro Pike
P.O. Box 933
Dayton, Ohio 45401
Telephone: (937) 865-7068
Fax: (937) 865-1211
http://www.lexisnexis.com
General Counsel: Michael A. Jacobs
Approx. size: 5-10

**Lincoln National Corporation**
1300 South Clinton St.
P.O. Box 1110
Fort Wayne, Indiana 46801
Telephone: (219) 455-2000
http://www.lfg.com
General Counsel: Jack D. Hunter
Approx. size: 45-50

**Leggett & Platt, Incorporated**
#1 Leggett Road
Carthage, Missouri 64836
Telephone: (417) 358-8131
Fax: (417) 358-8449
http://www.leggett.com
General Counsel: Ernest C. Jett, Jr.
Approx. size: 10-15

**Levi Strauss & Company**
1155 Battery Street
San Francisco, California 94111-1230
Telephone: (415) 501-7064
Fax: (415) 501-7650
http://www.levistrauss.com
General Counsel: Albert F. Moreno
Approx. size: 5-10

**Lucent Technologies**
600-700 Mountain Avenue
Murray Hill, New Jersey 07974
Telephone: (908) 582-8504
Fax: (908) 582-6130
http://www.lucent.com
General Counsel: Richard J. Rawson
Approx. size: 5-10

**Marriott International, Inc.**
Marriott Drive
Washington, D.C. 20058
Telephone: (301) 380-9555
Fax: (301) 380-6727
http://www.marriott.com
General Counsel: Joseph Ryan
Approx. size: 75-80

**Mary Kay Inc.**
16251 Dallas Parkway
P.O. Box 799045
Dallas, Texas 75379-9045
Telephone: (972) 687-6300
http://www.marykay.com
General Counsel: R. Bradley Glendening
Approx. size: 5-10

**Mattell, Inc.**
333 Continental Boulevard
El Segundo, California 90245-5032
Telephone: (310) 252-3639
Fax: (310) 252-3861
http://www.mattel.com
General Counsel: Robert J. Normile
Approx. size: 5-10

**Maxxam Inc.**
5847 San Felipe
Suite 2600
Houston, Texas 77057
Telephone: (713) 975-7600
Managing Counsel: Erik A. Eriksson, Jr.
Approx. size: 5-10

**Mayo Foundation**
200 First Street, S. W.
Rochester, Minnesota 55905
Telephone: (507) 284-2650
http://www.may.edu
General Counsel: Jill Smith Beed
Approx. size: 15-20

**McDonald's Corporation**
One McDonald's Plaza
Oak Brook, Illinois 60523-1900
Telephone: (630) 623-3000
Fax: (630) 623-5865
http://www.mcdonalds.com
General Counsel: Jeffery B Kindler
Approx. size: 80-90

**The McGraw-Hill Companies, Inc.**
1221 Avenue of the Americas
New York, New York 10020
Telephone: (212) 512-2564
Fax: (212) 512-4827
http://www.mcgraw-hill.com
General Counsel: Kenneth M. Vittor
Approx. size: 25-30

**MediaOne Group**
188 Inverness Drive West
Suite 600
Englewood, Colorado 80112
Telephone: (303) 858-3588
Fax: (303) 858-3487
http://www.broadband.att.com
General Counsel: Frank M. Eichler
Approx. size: 20-25

**Medtronic, Inc.**
7000 Central Avenue, N. E.
Minneapolis, Minnesota 55432-3576
Telephone: (612) 514-4000
Fax: (612) 514-3074
http://www.medtronic.com
General Counsel: Ronald E. Lund
Approx. size: 5-10

**Mellon Bank Corporation**
One Mellon Bank Center
Room 1915
Fifth and Grant Street
Pittsburgh, Pennsylvania 15258
Telephone: (412) 234-5000
http://www.mellon.com
General Counsel: Robert J. Ratner
Approx. size: 75-80

**Merck & Co., Inc.**
One Merck Drive
P.O. Box 100
Whitehouse Station, New Jersey 08889
Telephone: (908) 423-1000
http://www.merck.com
General Counsel: Mary M. McDonald
Approx. size: 80-90

**Monsanto Company**
800 North Lindbergh Boulevard
St. Louis, Missouri 63167-7843
Telephone: (314) 694-1000
http://www.monsanto.com
General Counsel: R. William Ide
Approx. size: 75-80

**Morgan Stanley Dean Witter**
1585 Broadway
38th Floor
New York, New York 10036
Telephone: (212) 761-4000
Fax: (212) 761-8815
http://www.msdw.com
General Counsel: Donald G. Kempf, Jr.
Approx. size: 180+

**Microsoft Corporation**
One Microsoft Way
Redmond, Washington 98052-6399
Telephone: (425) 882-8080
Fax: (425) 936-7329
http://www.microsoft.com
General Counsel: Robert A Eshelman
Approx. size: 90-100

**Mobil Oil Company**
3225 Gallows Road
Fairfax, Virginia 22037
Telephone: (703) 846-3000
http://www.mobil.com
General Counsel: Samuel H.
  Gillespie, III
Approx. size: 140-150

**Metromedia Company**
Metropolitan Executive Towers
One Meadowlands Plaza – 6th Floor
East Rutherford, New Jersey 07073-2137
Telephone: (201) 531-8050
Fax: (201) 531-2803
http://www.metromedia.com
General Counsel: Arnold L. Wadler
Approx. size: 15-20

**Metropolitan Life Insurance Company**
One Madison Avenue
New York, New York 10010
Telephone: (212) 578-3111
Fax: (212) 578-3916
http://www.metlife.com
General Counsel: Gary A. Beller
Approx. size: 150+

**Morrison Knudsen Corporation**
[Washington Group International]
720 Park Boulevard
P.O. Box 73
Boise, Idaho 83712
Telephone: (208) 386-5000
Fax: (208) 386-5298
http://www.wgint.com
General Counsel: Richard D. Parry
Approx. size: 30-35

**Motient Corporation**
10802 Parkridge Boulevard
Reston, Virginia 20191-5416
Telephone: (703) 758-6000
Fax: (703) 758-6134
http://www.ammobile.com
General counsel: Randy S. Segal
Approx. size: < 5

**NAACP Legal Defense & Education**
**Fund, Inc.**
99 Hudson Street
Suite 1600
New York, New York 10013-2897
Telephone: (212) 965-2262
Fax: (212) 219-1594
http://www.naacp.org
President and Director: Elaine R. Jones
Approx. size: 5-10

**National Association of Broadcasters**
1771 N. Street, N. W.
Washington, D.C. 20036
Telephone: (202) 429-5430
Fax: (202) 775-3526
http://www.nab.org
General Counsel: Jack N. Goodman
Approx. size: 5-10

**National Geographic Society**
1145 17th Street, N. W.
Washington, D.C. 20036
Telephone: (202) 857-7449
Fax: (202) 429-5744
http://www.nationalgeographic.com
Senior Vice President: Terrence B.
Adamson
Approx. size: 5-10

**NCR Corporation**
101 West Schantz Avenue
Dayton, Ohio 45479
Telephone: (937) 445-2773
Fax: (937) 445-6227
http://www.ncr.com
General Counsel: Jonathan S. Hoak
Approx. size: 25-30

**Parker-Hannifin Corporation**
6035 Parkland Boulevard
Cleveland, Ohio 44124
Telephone: (216) 896-3000
Fax: (216) 896-4027
http://www.parker.com
General Counsel: Thomas A. Piraino, Jr.
Approx. size: 10-15

**Payless ShoeSource, Inc.**
3231 S.E. Sixth Street
P.O. Box 1189
Topeka, Kansas 66601
Telephone: (785) 233-5171
Fax: (785) 295-6084
http://www.paylessshoesource.com
General Counsel: William J. Rainey
Approx. size: 10-15

**Occidental Chemical Corporation**
Occidental Tower
5005 LBJ Freeway
P.O. Box 809050
Dallas, Texas 75380-9050
Telephone: (972) 404-3800
Fax: (972) 404-3957
http://www.oxy.com
General Counsel: Keith C. McDole
Approx. size: 15-20

**Oracle Corporation**
500 Oracle Parkway (Redwood Shores)
Redwood City, California 94065
Telephone: (415) 506-7000
Fax: (415) 506-7114
http://www.oracle.com
General Counsel: Daniel Cooperman
Approx. size: 45-50

**Nike, Inc.**
One Bowerman Dr.
Beaverton, Oregon 97005-6453
Telephone: (505) 671-6453
Fax: (503) 646 6926
http://www.nike.com
General Counsel: James C. Carter
Approx. Size 15-20

**Novartis Pharmaceuticals Corporation**
59 Route 10
East Hanover, New Jersey 07936
Telephone: (973) 781-8300
Fax: (973) 781-6477
http://www.pharma.novartis.com
General Counsel: Dorothy P. Watson
Approx. size: 10-15

**Pizza Hut, Inc.**
14841 Dallas Parkway
Dallas, Texas 75240
Telephone: (972) 338-7700
Fax: (972) 338-6803
http://www.pizzahut.com
General Counsel: Robert W. Millen
Approx. size: 5-10

**Polaroid Corporation**
784 Memorial Drive
Cambridge, Massachusetts 02139
Telephone: (781) 386-2000
http://www.polaroid.com
General Counsel: Thomas M. Lemberg
Approx. size: 15-20

**Philips Electronics North America
  Corporation**
1251 Avenue of the Americas, 20th Floor
New York, New York 10020-1104
Telephone: (212) 536-0620
Fax: (212) 536-0629
http://www.philips.usa.com
General Counsel: Belinda W. Chew
Approx. size: 40-45

**Pitney Bowes Inc.**
World Headquarters
1 Elmcroft Road
Stamford, Connecticut 06926-0700
Telephone: (203) 351-6480
http://www.pb.com
General Counsel: Sara E. Moss
Approx. size: 10-15

**Pechiney Plastic Packaging, Inc.**
8770 West Bryn Mawr Avenue
Chicago, Illinois 60631
Telephone: (312) 399-3000
http://www.pechiney.com
General Counsel: Mike J. Hoover
Approx. size: 5-10

**PeopleSoft, Inc.**
4460 Hacienda Drive
Pleasanton, California 94588
Telephone: (925) 225-3000
Fax: (925) 694-8427
http://www.peoplesoft.com
General Counsel: Anne S. Jordan
Approx. size: 15-20

**PricewaterhouseCoopers LLP**
1301 Avenue of the Americas
New York, New York 10019-6013
Telephone: (212) 707-6700
Fax: (212) 707-6717
http://www.pricewaterhousecoopers.com
General Counsel: Lawrence W. Keeshan
Approx. size: 40-45

**The Procter & Gamble Co.**
One Procter & Gamble Plaza
Cincinnati, Ohio 45202
Telephone: (513) 983-5940
Fax: (513) 983-4274
http://www.pg.com
General Counsel: Gary Hagopian
Approx. size: 30-35

**Provident Companies, Inc.**
1 Fountain Square
Chattanooga, Tennessee 37402
Telephone: (423) 755-1011
http://www.unum.com
General Counsel: F. Dean Copeland
Approx. size: 35-40

**Prudential Securities Inc**
One Seaport Plaza
31st Floor
New York, New York 10292
Telephone: (212) 214-1000
Fax: (212) 214-6517
http://www.prudentialsecurities.com
General Counsel: Kenneth W. Gerver
Approx. size: 5-10

**Ralston Purina Company**
Checkerboard Square
St. Louis, Missouri 63164
Telephone: (314) 982-1266
Fax: (314) 982-1288
http://www.ralston.com
General Counsel: James M. Neville
Approx. size: 15-20

**Recording Industry Association of America, Inc.**
1330 Connecticut Avenue, N. W.
Suite 300
Washington, D.C. 20036
Telephone: (202) 775-0101
Fax: (202) 775-7253
http://www.riaa.com
General Counsel: Cary Howard Sherman
Approx. size: 10-15

**Revlon Consumer Products Corp.**
625 Madison Avenue
16th Floor
New York, New York 10022
Telephone: (212) 527-5620
http://www.revlon.com
General Counsel: Robert K. Kretzman
Approx. size: 10-15

**The Rouse Company**
The Rouse Company Building
10275 Little Patuxent Parkway
Columbia, Maryland 21044
Telephone: (410) 992-6400
http://www.therousecompany.com
General Counsel: Gordon H. Glenn
Approx. size: 15-20

**Royal & SunAlliance**
9300 Arrowpoint Boulevard
Charlotte, North Carolina 28201
Telephone: (704) 522-2000
Fax: (704) 522-3200
http://www.royal-and-sunalliance.com
General Counsel: Joyce W. Wheeler
Approx. size: 5-10

**Ryder System, Inc.**
3600 Northwest 82nd Avenue
Miami, Florida 33166
Telephone: (305) 500-4591
Fax: (305) 500-3198
http://www.ryder.com
General Counsel: Vicki A. O'Meara
Approx. size: 10-15

**The St. Paul Companies, Inc.**
385 Washington Street
St. Paul, Minnesota 55102
Telephone: (651) 310-7911
Fax: (651) 310-8294
www3.StPaul.com
General Counsel: John A. MacColl
Approx. size: 75-80

**Sallie Mae, Inc.**
11600 Sallie Mae Drive
Reston, Virginia 20193-4798
Telephone: (703) 810-3000
Fax: (703) 810-7586
http://www.salliemae.com
General Counsel: Marianne M. Keler
Approx. size: 10-15

**Sears, Roebuck and Co.**
3333 Beverly Road
Hoffman Estates, Illinois 60179
Telephone: (847) 286-2500
Fax: (847) 286-4511
http://www.sears.com
General Counsel: Anastasia D. Kelly
Approx. size: 60-65

**Sempra Energy**
101 Ash Street
Suite 1200
San Diego, California 92101-3017
Telephone: (619) 696-4366
http://www.sempra.com
General Counsel: John R. Light
Approx. size: 35-40

**Schering-Plough Corporation**
One Giralda Farms
Madison, New Jersey 07940-1000
Telephone: (973) 822-7000
Fax: (973) 822-7048
http://www.schering-plough.com
General Counsel: Joseph C. Connors
Approx. size: 55-60

**Scientific-Atlanta, Inc.**
One Technology Parkway South
Norcross, Georgia 30092
Telephone: (770) 903-5000
http://www.sciatl.com
General Counsel: William E. Eason, Jr.
Approx. size: 5-10

**Salomon Smith Barney**
388 Greenwich Street
New York, New York 10013
Telephone: (212) 816-6000
http://www.smithbarney.com
General Counsel: Dov S. Schechter
Approx. size: 100-110

**SCANA Corporation**
1426 Main Street
Columbia, South Carolina 29201-2834
Telephone: (803) 748-3000
Fax: (803) 217-7931
http://www.scana.com
General Counsel: H. Thomas Arthur
Approx. size: 5-10

**Solutia Inc.**
575 Maryville Centre Drive
P.O. Box 66760
St. Louis, Missouri 63166-6760
Telephone: (314) 674-1000
Fax: (314) 674-2721
http://www.solutia.com
General Counsel: Karl R. Barnickol
Approx. size: 15-20

**Southern Company**
270 Peachtree Street, N. W.
Suite 1400
Atlanta, Georgia 30303
Telephone: (404) 506-5000
Fax: (404) 506-0629
http://www.southernco.com
General Counsel: Stephen A. Wakefield
Approx. size: 25-30

**Siemens Corporation**
153 East 53rd Street
56th Floor
New York, New York 10022
Telephone: (212) 258-4000
http://www.siemens.com
General Counsel: E. Robert Lupone
Approx. size: 70-75

**SmithKLINE Beecham Corporation**
One Franklin Plaza
Philadelphia, Pennsylvania 19101
Telephone: (215) 751-4000
Fax: (215) 751-5132
http://www.sb.com
General Counsel U. S.: Edward T. Lentz
Approx. size: 30-35

**Shaklee Corporation**
4747 Willow Road
Pleasanton, California 94588-2740
Telephone: (415) 954-3000
Fax: (415) 954-2702
http://www.shaklee.com
General Counsel: Edward W. Beck
Approx. size: < 5

**The Sherwin-Williams Company**
101 Prospect Avenue, N. W.
Cleveland, Ohio 44115
Telephone: (216) 566-2000
Fax: (216) 566-1708
http://www.sherwinwilliams.com
General Counsel: Louis E. Stellato
Approx. size: 15-20

Starwood Hotels & Resorts Worldwide, Inc.
777 Westchester Avenue
White Plains, New York 10604
Telephone: (914) 640-8100
Fax: (914) 640-8310
http://www.starwood.com
General Counsel: Thomas C. Janson, Jr.
Approx. size: 10-15

State Street Corporation
225 Franklin Street
Boston, Massachusetts 02110
Telephone: (617) 786-3000
Fax: (617) 664-4006
http://www.statestreet.com
Chief Counsel: Mitchell H. Shames
Approx. size: 25-30

Sprint Corporation
8140 Ward Parkway
Kansas City, Missouri 64114
Telephone: (913) 624-6556
http://www.sprint.com
General Counsel: Not designated
Approx. size: 110-120

SPX Corporation
700 Terrace Point Drive
Muskegon, Michigan 49440
Telephone: (616) 724-5000
Fax: (616) 724-5720
http://www.spx.com
General Counsel: Christopher J. Kearney, III
Approx. size: 5-10

Southern Farm Bureau Life Insurance Company
1401 Livingston Lane
P.O. Box 78
Jackson, Mississippi 39205-0078
Telephone: (601) 981-7422
Fax: (601) 982-9569
http://www.sfbli.com
General Counsel: Joseph A. Purvis
Approx. size: 5-10

The Southland Corporation
2711 North Haskell Avenue
P.O. Box 711
Dallas, Texas 75204
Telephone: (214) 828-7011
http://www.7-eleven.com
General Counsel: Bryan F. (Buck) Smith, Jr.
Approx. size: 10-15

**Steelcase Inc.**
901 44th Street, S. E.
Grand Rapids, Michigan 49508
Telephone: (616) 247-3385
Fax: (616) 248-7010
http://www.steelcase.com
General Counsel: Jon D. Botsford
Approx. size: 10-15

**Stone & Webster, Incorporated**
245 Summer Street
8th Floor
Boston, Massachusetts 02210
Telephone: (617) 589-5111
http://www.stoneweb.com
General Counsel: James P. Jones
Approx. size: 15-20

**The Stop & Shop Companies, Inc.**
1385 Hancock Street
Quincy, Massachusetts 02169
Mailing Address:
P.O. Box 369
Boston, Massachusetts 02101
Telephone: (617) 770-6001
Fax: (617) 770-6416
http://www.stopandshop.com
General Counsel: Peter M. Phillipes
Approx. size: 5-10

**Sunbeam Corporation**
2381 Executive Center Drive
Boca Raton, Florida 33431
Telephone: (561) 912-4100
Fax: (561) 912-4465
http://www.sunbeam.com
General Counsel: Steven R. Isko
Approx. size: 10-15

**Sunoco, Inc.**
1801 Market Street
10 Penn Center
Philadelphia, Pennsylvania
Telephone: (215) 977-3782
http://www.sunoco.com
General Counsel: Jack L. Foltz
Approx. size: 25-30

**Supervalu Inc.**
11840 Valley View Road
Eden Prairie, Minnesota 55344
Telephone: (612) 828-4000
Fax: (612) 828-4403
http://www.supervalu.com
General Counsel: Not designated
Approx. size: 5-10

**Sysco Corporation**
1390 Enclave Parkway
Houston, Texas 77077-2099
Telephone: (281) 584-1390
Fax: (281) 584-2510
http://www.sysco.com
General Counsel: Michael C. Nichols
Approx. size: 5-10

**T. Rowe Price Associates, Inc.**
100 East Pratt Street
Baltimore, Maryland 21202-1009
Telephone: (410) 345-6640
http://www.Troweprice.com
Chief Legal Counsel: Henry H. Hopkins
Approx. size: 10-15

**Teachers Insurance & Annuity Association**
730 Third Avenue
New York, New York 10017
Telephone: (212) 490-9000
http://www.tiaa-cref.org
General Counsel: Charles H. Stamm, III
Approx. size: 70-75

**Teco Energy, Inc.**
702 North Franklin Street
P.O. Box 111
Tampa, Florida 33602
Telephone: (813) 228-4111
http://www.tecoenergy.com
General Counsel: Sheila M. McDevitt
Approx. size: 5-10

**Tektronix, Inc.**
Law Department, 63-Law
26600 S. W. Parkway
P.O. Box 1000
Wilsonville, Oregon 97070-1000
Telephone: (503) 627-7111
Fax: (503) 685-4223
http://www.tek.com
General Counsel: James F. Dalton
Approx. size: 5-10

**Telcordia Technologies, Inc.**
445 South Street
Morristown, New Jersey 07960-6438
Telephone: (973) 829-2000
http://www.telcordia.com
General Counsel: Grant L. Clark
Approx. size: 10-15

**Tele-Communications, Inc.**
9197 S. Peoria Street
Englewood, Colorado 80112
Telephone: (720) 875-5500
http://www.broadband.att.com
Chief Counsel: Terrel E. Davis
Approx. size: 10-15

**Temple-Inland Inc.**
Post Office Drawer N
Diboll, Texas 75941
Telephone: (409) 829-2211
http://www.templeinland.com
General Counsel: M. Richard Warner
Approx. size: 10-15

**Tenet Healthcare Corporation**
3820 State Street
P.O. Box 31907
Santa Barbara, California 93130
Telephone: (805) 563-7000
Fax: (805) 563-7085
http://www.tenethealth.com
General Counsel: Christi Rocovich
Sulzbach
Approx. size: 25-30

**Texas Instruments, Incorporated**
13500 North Central Expressway
P.O. Box MS 241
Dallas, Texas 75243
Telephone: (214) 995-4855
http://www.ti.com
General Counsel: Richard J. Agnich
Approx. size: 5-10

**Textron Inc.**
40 Westminster Street
15th Floor
Providence, Rhode Island 02903
Telephone: (401) 421-2800
http://www.textron.com
General Counsel: Wayne W. Juchatz
Approx. size: 50-55

**Thermo Electron Corporation**
81 Wyman Street
P.O. Box 9046
Waltham, Massachusetts 02454-9046
Telephone: (781) 622-1000
Fax: (781) 622-1207
http://www.thermo.com
General Counsel: Seth H. Hoogasian
Approx. size: 10-15

**The Thomson Corporation**
One Station Place
Stamford, Connecticut 06902-6800
Telephone: (203) 969-8700
Fax: (203) 348-5718
http://www.thomson.com
General Counsel: Michael S. Harris
Approx. size: 10-15

**Time Warner Inc.**
75 Rockefeller Plaza
New York, New York 10019
Telephone: (212) 484-8000
http://www.timewarner.com
General Counsel: Christopher P. Bogart
Approx. size: 250+

**Tishman Speyer Properties**
520 Madison Avenue
6th Floor
New York, New York 10022
Telephone: (212) 715-0300
Fax: (212) 935-8239
http://www.tishmanspeyer.com
General Counsel: Bruce D. Saber
Approx. size: 5-10

**The TJX Companies, Inc.**
770 Cochituate Road
Framingham, Massachusetts 01701
Telephone: (508) 390-1000
Fax: (508) 390-2457
http://www.tjx.com
General Counsel: Jay H. Meltzer
Approx. size: 5-10

**Torchmark Corporation**
2001 Third Avenue South
Birmingham, Alabama 35233
Telephone: (205) 325-4200
http://www.torchmarkcorp.com
General Counsel: Not designated
Approx. size: 5-10

**Towers Perrin Forster & Crosby Inc.**
1500 Markeet Street
Center Square East
Philadelphia, Pennsylvania 19102-4790
Telephone: (215) 246-6120
Fax: (215) 246-4463
http://www.towers.com
General Counsel: Kevin C. Young
Approx. size: 5-10

**Toyota Motor Sales, U.S.A., Inc.**
19001 Southwestern Avenue
Suite A107
Torrance, California 90509
Telephone: (310) 468-4000
Fax: (310) 468-7808
http://www.toyota.com
General Counsel: Dian D. Ogilvie
Approx. size: 20-25

**Toys "R" Us, Inc.**
461 From Road
5th Floor
Paramus, New Jersey 07652-3524
Telephone: (201) 599-7880
http://www.toysrus.com
Vice President- Counsel: Michael L.
    Tumolo
Approx. size: 5-10

**Trans World Airlines, Inc.**
One City Centre
515 North 6th Street
St. Louis, Missouri 63101
Telephone: (314) 589-3227
http://www.twa.com
General Counsel: Kathleen A. Soled
Approx. size: 10-15

**Tribune Company**
435 North Michigan Avenue
Suite 600
Chicago, Illinois 60611-4001
Telephone: (312) 222-2491
Fax: (312) 222-4206
http://www.tribune.com
General Counsel: Crane H. Kenney
Approx. size: 5-10

**Tricon Restaurants International**
14841 North Dallas Parkway
Dallas, Texas 75240-2100
Telephone: (972) 338-8100
Fax: (972) 338-8104
http://www.triconglobal.com
General Counsel: Duncan H. Makeig
Approx. size: 5-10

**TrizecHahn Corporation**
BCE Place
181 Bay Street
Suite 3900
Toronto, Ontario M5J 2T3 Canada
Telephone: (416) 361-7200
Fax: (416) 361-7205
http://www.trizechahn.com
General Counsel: Robin A. Campbell
Approx. size: 15-20

**TRW Inc.**
1900 Richmond Road
Cleveland, Ohio 44124
Telephone: (216) 291-7000
Fax: (216) 291-7070
http://www.trus.com
General Counsel: William B. Lawrence
Approx. size: 40-45

**Tupperware Corporation**
14901 South Orange Blossom Trail
Orlando, Florida 32837
Telephone: (407) 826-5050
http://www.tupperware.com
General Counsel: Thomas M. Roehlk
Approx. size: 5-10

**Tyco International Ltd.**
The Gibbons Building
10 Queen Street
Suite 301
Hamilton HM 11, Bermuda
Telephone: (441) 292-8674
http://www.tycoint.com
General Counsel: Bernard J. Doherty
Approx. size: 45-50

**U. S. Office Products Company**
1025 Thomas Jefferson Street, N. W.
Suite 600E
Washington, DC 20007
Telephone: (202) 339-6700
Fax: (202) 339-6733
http://www.usop.com
General Counsel: Mark D. Director
Approx. size: < 5

**UGI Corporation**
460 North Gulph Road
King of Prussia, Pennsylvania 19406
Telephone: (610) 337-1000
Fax: (610) 992-3258
http://www.ugi.com
General Counsel: Brendan P. Bovaird
Approx. size: 10-15

**Unisys Corporation**
Township Line 2 Union Meeting Roads
Post Office Box 500
Blue Bell, Pennsylvania 19424-0001
Telephone: (215) 986-4011
http://www.
General Counsel: Harold S. Barron
Approx. size: 70-75

**United Airlines**
1200 East Algonquin Road
Elk Grove Village, Illinois 60007
Telephone: (847) 700-6250
Fax: (847) 700-4683
http://www.ual.com
General Counsel: Francesca Marciniak
    Maher
Approx. size: 15-20

**United Parcel Service**
55 Glenlake Parkway, N. E.
Atlanta, Georgia 30328
Telephone: (404) 828-6000
http://www.ups.com
General Counsel: Joseph R. Moderow
Approx. size: 25-30

**United Services Automobile**
    **Association (USAA)**
9800 Fredericksberg Road
Building C-3-W
San Antonio, Texas 78288-3056
Telephone: (210) 498-1888
Fax: (210) 498-0608
http://www.usaa.com
General Counsel: Bradford W. Rich
Approx. size: 30-35

**United States Filter Corporation**
40-004 Cook Street
Palm Desert, California 92211
Telephone: (760) 340-0098
Fax: (760) 346-4024
http://www.usfilter.com
General Counsel: Stephen P. Stanczak
Approx. size: 15-20

**United Steel Workers of America**
Five Gateway Center
Pittsburgh, Pennsylvania 15222
Telephone: (412) 562-2541
Fax: (412) 562-2574
http://www.uswa.org
General Counsel: Carl B. Frankel
Approx. size: 5-10

**United Technologies Corporation**
Post Office Box 109600
West Palm Beach, Florida 33410-9600
Telephone: (561) 796-2000
http://www.utc.com
Deputy General Counsel: David K. Ware
Approx. size: 5-10

**University of Alabama System**
1818 University Boulevard
Tuscaloosa, Alabama 35401-1518
Telephone: (205) 348-8345
Fax: (205) 348-0413
General Counsel: C. Glenn Powell
Approx. size: 15-20

**Univision Communication Inc.**
6701 Center Drive West
16th Floor
Los Angeles, California 90045
Telephone: (310) 348-3673
Fax: (310) 348-3679
http://www.univision.net
General Counsel: Sylvia R. Esquivel
Approx. size: 5-10

**USA Group**
30 South Meridian Street
Indianapolis, Indiana 46204-3503
Telephone: (317) 849-6510
Fax: (317) 951-5532
http://www.usagroup.com
Mailing address:
P.O. Box 7039
Indianapolis, Indiana 46207-7039
General Counsel: Edward R. Schmidt
Approx. size: 5-10

**Venator Group, Inc.**
233 Broadway
New York, New York 10279
Telephone: (212) 553-2000
http://www.venatorgroup.com
General Counsel: Gary M. Bahler
Approx. size: 10-15

**Viacom Inc.**
1515 Broadway
New York, New York 10036-5794
Telephone: (212) 258-6000
http://www.viacom.com
General Counsel: Deborah Chapin
Approx. size: 20-25

**VISA International**
Post Office Box 8999
San Francisco, California 94128-8999
Telephone: (650) 432-3200
http://www.visa.com
General Counsel: Bennett R. Katz
Approx. size: 15-20

**Volvo Group North America, Inc.**
570 Lexington Avenue
20th Floor
New York, New York 10022
Telephone: (212) 754-3300
http://www.volvo.com
General Counsel: Robert B. Mercer
Approx. size: 5-10

**Vulcan Materials Company**
1200 Urban Center Drive
P.O. Box 38504
Birmingham, Alabama 35238-5014
Telephone: (205) 298-3000
http://www.vulcanmat.com
Vice President, Law: William F. Denson, III
Approx. size: 5-10

**W. R. Grace & Co.**
7500 Grace Drive
Columbia, Maryland 21044
Telephone: (410) 531-4000
Fax: (410) 531-4367
http://www.grace.com
General Counsel: David B. Siegel
Approx. size: 25-30

**W. W. Grainger, Inc.**
100 Grainger Parkway
Lake Forest, Illinois 60045-5201
Telephone: (847) 535-1000
Fax: (847) 535-9243
http://www.grainger.com
General Counsel: James B. Baisley
Approx. size: 15-20

**Wachovia Corporation**
100 North Main Street
P.O. Box 3099
Winston-Salem, North Carolina 27150
Telephone: (336) 732-5782
http://www.wachovia.com
General Counsel: Kenneth W. McAllister
Approx. size: 25-30

**The Walt Disney Company**
500 South Buena Vista Street
Burbank, California 91521
Telephone: (818) 560-1000
Fax: (818) 560-1930
http://www.disney.com
General Counsel: Louis M. Meisinger
Approx. size: 150+

**Walter Industries, Inc.**
1500 North Dale Mabry Highway
Tampa, Florida 33607
Telephone: (813) 871-4851
Fax: (813) 871-4491
http://www.walterind.com
General Counsel: Edward A. Porter
Approx. size: 10-15

**Washington Gas Light Company**
1100 H Street, N. W.
Washington, DC 20080
Telephone: (202) 624-6544
Fax: (202) 624-6789
http://www.washingtongas.com
General Counsel: John K. Keane, Jr.
Approx. size: 15-20

**Washington Metropolitan Area Transit Authority**
600 Fifth Street, N. W.
Washington, DC 20001
Telephone: (202) 962-1234
Fax: (202) 962-2550
http://www.wmata.com
General Counsel: Not designated
Approx. size: 10-15

**Watson Wyatt Worldwide**
6707 Democracy Boulevard
Suite 800
Bethesda, Maryland 20812-1129
Telephone: (301) 581-4600
Fax: (301) 581-4935
http://www.watsonwyatt.com
General Counsel: Walter W. Bardenwerper
Approx. size: 5-10

**Wegmans Food Markets, Inc.**
1500 Brooks Avenue
P.O. Box 844
Rochester, New York 14603-0844
Telephone: (716) 328-2550
Fax: (716) 464-4636
http://www.wegmans.com
General Counsel: Paul S. Speranza, Jr.
Approx. size: < 5

**WellPoint Health Networks Inc.**
1 Wellpoint Way
Thousand Oaks, California 91362
Telephone: (805) 557-6110
Fax: (805) 557-6820
http://www.wellpoint.com
General Counsel: Thomas C. Geiser
Approx. size: 15-20

**Wendy's International, Inc.**
4288 West Dublin-Granville Road
P.O. Box 256
Dublin, Ohio 43017
Telephone: (614) 764-3100
http://www.wendys.com
General Counsel: Leon M. McCorkle, Jr.
Approx. size: 15-20

**Westfield Companies**
One Park Circle
Westfield Center, Ohio 44251-5001
Telephone: (330) 887-0980
Fax: (330) 887-0678
http://www.westfield-cos.com
General Counsel: Not designated
Approx. size: 5-10

**Westpoint Stevens Inc.**
507 West 10th Street
P.O. Box 71
West Point, Georgia 31833-1232
Telephone: (706) 645-4000
Fax: (706) 645-4396
http://www.westpointstevens.com
General Counsel: M. Clayton
    Humphries, Jr.
Approx. size: < 5

**Whirlpool Corporation**
2000 North M63
Benton Harbor, Michigan 49022-2692
Telephone: (616) 923-5000
Fax: (616) 923-3722
http://www.whirlpool.com
General Counsel: Daniel F. Hopp
Approx. size: 25-27

**Wilmington Trust Company**
Rodney Square North
Wilmington, Delaware 19890
Telephone: (302) 651-1000
Fax: (302) 651-8010
http://www.wilmingtontrust.com
General Counsel: Thomas P. Collins
Approx. size: 10-15

**Winn-Dixie Stores, Inc.**
5050 Edgewood Court
Jacksonville, Florida 32254
Telephone: (904) 783-5000
Fax: (904) 783-5138
http://www.winndixie.com
Mailing address:
P.O. Box B
Jacksonville, Florida 32203
General Counsel: E. Ellis Zahra, Jr.
Approx. size: 10-15

**Witco Corporation**
One American Lane
Greenwich, Connecticut 06831
Telephone: (203) 552-2820
Fax: (203) 552-2869
http://www.witco.com
General Counsel: Edgar J. Smith, Jr.
Approx. size: 10-15

**Wm. Wrigley Jr. Company**
410 North Michigan Avenue
Chicago, Illinois 60611
Telephone: (312) 644-2121
Fax: (312) 661-1267
http://www.wrigley.com
General Counsel: Howard Malovany
Approx. size: 5-10

**Xerox Corporation**
800 Long Ridge Road
P.O. Box 1600
Stamford, Connecticut 06904
Telephone: (203) 968-3000
http://www.xerox.com
General Counsel: Richard S. Paul
Approx. size: 20-25

**Zurich-American Insurance Group**
Zurich Towers
1400 American Lane
Schaumburg, Illinois 60196-1056
Telephone: (847) 605-6000
Fax: (847) 605-4356
http://www.zurichus.com
General Counsel: David Alan Bowers
Approx. size: 5-10

# GLOSSARY

## A Working Glossary of Legal Recruitment and Career Services Terms and Jargon

Reprinted with the permission of the National Association for Law Placement, Washington, D.C.
*www.nalp.org*

Professional jargon abounds in the field of legal recruitment and law school career services. To help those who are new to the plethora of acronyms and specialized terms, the 1995-96 NALP Publications Committee has developed the following glossary, based upon A Working Glossary of Various and Sundry Law Placement and Legal Recruitment Terms and Jargon, published by NALP, with revisions, since 1983.

Although somewhat inclusive, this brief glossary cannot feature every legal recruitment term or every law-related organization.

## A

**AALS:** Association of American Law Schools. An organization of law schools whose purpose is the improvement of the legal profession through legal education. This association serves as the law teachers' learned society and produces a monthly newsletter of teaching and administrative positions available at law schools nationwide.

**AALSA/APALSA:** Asian American Law Student Association/Asian Pacific American Law Student Association.

**ABA:** American Bar Association. Headquartered in Chicago, the ABA offers educational programs, publications, and services relating to all facets of the practice of law.

**ACCA:** American Corporate Counsel Association.

**ADA:** Americans with Disabilities Act.

**ADJUNCT PROFESSOR:** A part-time faculty member who is generally a practitioner.

**ADR:** Alternative Dispute Resolution. Methods other than going to court to solve problems among people, including counseling, mediation and arbitration.

**AILTO:** American Institute for Law Training within the Office.

**ALA:** Association of Legal Administrators.

**ALTERNATIVE CAREERS/LAW-RELATED CAREERS:** Law-related and/or non-legal career opportunities for J.D. graduates other than the practice of law.

**ANNUAL EDUCATION CONFERENCE NALP's:** annual conference, which offers a wide array of programming and includes the NALP annual business meeting.

**ASSOCIATE:** A lawyer who is an employee, as opposed to an owner, of a law firm. (See also Partner.)

**B**

**BAR EXAM:** The licensing examination required to become a member of the bar. While individuals may earn a J.D. degree, they may not practice law until they have passed a state's bar examination. Most states offer the bar exam twice a year, in February and July.

**BILLABLE HOURS:** The time lawyers work on a project for a client that can be charged to the client. Most employers require an established number of billable hours per lawyer (e.g., 35 billable hours a week). The number of billable hours required is a major area of concern and inquiry for both students and practicing lawyers.

**BLIND AD A:** job posting in which the employer is not named. Interested applicants forward resumes to post office boxes and are therefore unable to contact the employer directly.

**BLSA:** Black Law Students Association.

**BOOK AWARDS:** In some schools, when students earn the highest grade in a particular class it is said they booked the course. Often schools or outside organizations provide awards to students who earn this distinction e.g., the American Jurisprudence Award.

**BRANCH OFFICE:** An auxiliary office to a law firm's main office location.

**BUCKLEY AMENDMENT:** The Family Educational Rights and Privacy Act of 1974, which guarantees that students have the right of access to inspect and review any and all official records, files, documents, and other materials created during the period the individual was enrolled as a student at the institution. With limited exceptions, no personally identifiable information from the educational records of a student may be disclosed to any third party by an official or employee of the institution without the written consent of the student.

## C

**CALLBACK/FLYBACK:** The in-depth interview students have in an employer's office, generally after a preliminary screening interview with the employer.

**CAREER SERVICES DIRECTOR:** The professional responsible for the coordination of a school's career services program.

**CHAIRED FACULTY:** Faculty members whose salaries are supplemented by private endowments to the institution where they work. Individuals holding chaired positions are generally regarded as specialists in the areas in which they teach.

**CITY GROUP:** An association of local recruitment administrators (and sometimes career services personnel) in a particular city.

**CLASS RANK:** Class rank reflects an individual's academic performance as compared to his/her classmates. Some schools have chosen not to rank their students.

**CLE:** Continuing Legal Education. Additional education that lawyers take to stay abreast of current changes in the law. In some states, CLE courses are mandatory, especially if lawyers wish to designate themselves as specialists in particular areas of law.

**CLEO:** Council on Legal Education Opportunity. A program aimed at helping and encouraging economically and educationally disadvantaged students to enter law school and become members of the legal profession.

**CLINICAL EDUCATION:** Law school programs that provide students with practical and skills-oriented instruction. Under the supervision of a faculty member, students represent clients through specialized legal aid, prosecutorial, and defender clinics.

**CODE OF PROFESSIONAL RESPONSIBILITY:** The ethical guidelines for lawyers in conducting their professional activities. A Model Code sets forth basic standards, but guidelines are promulgated by each state and may vary from the Model Code.

**CONSORTIUM:** A consortium consists of several law schools (usually in one geographic region) that work cooperatively in such areas as cosponsorship of off-campus career fairs.

**CONTRACT ATTORNEY/TEMPORARY ATTORNEY:** Attorney hired for a specific project or for a finite period of time.

**COST SHARING:** In legal recruitment, the practice of employers sharing interview expenses for out-of-town interviewees.

## D

**DING LETTER/FLUSH LETTER:** Slang for an employment rejection letter.

**DIRECT CONTACT/RESUMES FORWARDED:** Two services most career services offices make available to employers. Direct Contact indicates that students must send their own letter to the employer in response to a posted position. Resumes Forwarded indicates that the career services office collects resumes from interested students for an available position and mails them collectively to an employer on a pre-determined date.

**DOG & PONY SHOW:** Slang for recruiting trips during which law school career planning personnel promote their institutions to employers or employers promote their organizations to law schools.

## E

**EEOC:** Equal Employment Opportunity Commission. The EEOC was established to work toward elimination of discrimination based on race, color, religion, sex, national origin, age, or disability status in hiring, promoting, firing, wages, testing, training, apprenticeship, and all other conditions of employment.

**ERSS:** The annual Employment Report and Salary Survey published by NALP, which consolidates data reported by law schools and provides aggregate information on salaries and types of employment obtained by graduates each year.

## F

**FEDERAL AGENCY HONOR PROGRAM:** A program sponsored by a federal agency e.g., Justice or Treasury Department for law students who meet specific academic standards or co-curricular activities. The Honor Program is often the only entry to the agency directly from law school.

**FEEDER SCHOOLS:** A term referring to schools at which a legal employer tends to recruit heavily and employ a large number of graduates. Also refers to undergraduate schools from which law schools enroll a large number of students.

**FELLOWSHIP:** A program that matches law graduates with public service organizations or with law school programs. Fellowships are variously funded and very competitive and are usually for a prescribed number of years following graduation.

**FIRM RESUME:** An informational brochure that employers provide to career services offices to acquaint law students with the employer's business, recruiting plans, summer clerk and associate programs, and so on.

## G

**GOING RATE:** The starting lawyer and summer clerk salary for any given city or market area.

## H

**HEADHUNTER/LEGAL SEARCH CONSULTANT:** An individual associated with a private placement agency, i.e., an individual who assists with the matching of a potential employee with an employer and who receives as a fee a percentage of the employee's starting salary.

**HIRING COMMITTEE:** A committee of lawyers that oversees the recruiting program and makes hiring decisions.

**HIRING ATTORNEY/HIRING PARTNER:** The attorney/partner who is chair of a legal employer's Hiring Committee.

**HISPANIC NATIONAL BAR ASSOCIATION:** A national association of Hispanic attorneys.

**HLSA:** Hispanic Law Students Association.

**HOLD LETTER:** Letter indicating to the student recipient that he/she is still under consideration for an offer.

## I

**IF YOU ARE IN TOWN . . . LETTER:** A fairly standard response to students who have written directly to out-of-town employers. The sense of the letter is that the firm is not willing to pay for the student's travel expenses but, if the student will be in town, the employer will grant an interview.

**IN-HOUSE COUNSEL:** This term refers to a lawyer who works for a business as the company lawyer. Generally, large corporations have sizeable legal departments and often will use outside counsel (e.g., law firms) for litigation or specialty work.

## J-K

**JAGC:** Judge Advocate General's Corps. The in-house counsel of the various armed forces.

**J.D./JURIS DOCTOR:** Degree awarded after three years of prescribed study in a law school.

**JOB FAIR/CAREER FAIR:** An off-campus interview program usually sponsored by several law schools to bring together students and employers in one centralized setting. Job fairs may appeal to employers and market students in specialty areas of practice e.g., intellectual property or may be designed to assist employers interested specifically in hiring minority students.

**JOINT DEGREE PROGRAMS:** A dual degree program leading to a J.D. degree in conjunction with another advanced degree e.g., M.B.A., Masters in Accounting., Ph.D., Masters in Public Health, etc.

**JUDICIAL CLERK:** A graduate who is employed by a judge to assist with research, writing, and review of opinions and orders, usually for a one- or two-year period. The level of prestige of the clerkship is often commensurate with the level of the court.

# L

**LL.B.:** Bachelor of Laws Degree. Equivalent to a J.D. degree, the LL.B. was the law degree conferred prior to establishment of the J.D.

**LL.M.:** Master of Laws Degree. An advanced degree beyond the J.D., often concentrated in a specialty area e.g., taxation, banking, etc.

**LALSA:** The Latin American Law Students Association.

**LATERAL HIRE:** An experienced lawyer who has been hired by a new employer, often at the same seniority level as in his/her prior position.

**LAW REVIEW/LAW JOURNAL:** A legal periodical published by law students presenting the results of research, analysis, and scholarly investigation of legal problems. Articles are written by law professors, practitioners, or established authorities from other fields, and notes and comments on recent judicial decisions are prepared by student members. Membership on some law reviews is limited to students who have demonstrated outstanding scholastic ability through grades or writing competitions; some journals are open to all interested students.

**LAW STUDENTS 3L, 4L:** These terms refer to first-year, second-year, third-year and fourth-year (part-time) law students, respectively.

**LAWYERING PROCESS:** A trend in law schools to provide students with instruction in better lawyering and alternative dispute resolution, e.g., interviewing, counseling, and negotiations.

**LEGAL MARKETING ASSOCIATION:** (formerly the National Law Firm Marketing Association).

**LEXIS-NEXIS:** Computer databases of cases, statutes, regulations, newspapers, journals, business magazines, and other materials used by lawyers in doing legal and non-legal research. NALP's National Directory of Legal Employers can be found on LEXIS, and users can link from this Directory to other LEXIS databases.

**L.L.P.:** Limited liability partnership. A legal organizational structure in which the liability of partners for the malpractice of another partner is limited.

**LOAN REPAYMENT ASSISTANCE PROGRAM/ LRAP:** Law school financial aid programs providing for the reduction or forgiveness of law school debts in return for work with public service organizations for a set period of time after graduation.

**LOTTERY:** Resume selection process whereby students are selected at random for interviews as an alternative to prescreening.

**LSAC/LSAS:** Law School Admission Council/Law School Admission Services. This organization is best known for its administration of the LSAT, but it also provides other resources for pre-law and law students and carries out research on topics such as law student debt loads.

**LSAT:** Law School Admission Test, a prerequisite for admission to most law schools.

# M

**MacCRATE REPORT:** A major study published in July 1992 by the ABA Task Force on Law Schools and the Profession: Narrowing the Gap (referred to as the MacCrate Report because the Task Force was chaired by Robert MacCrate). This report on the status of legal education focuses on the preparation of law students for the practice of law.

**MARTINDALE-HUBBELL:** A multi-volume directory (and database on-line on LEXIS ) of private law firms and in-house counsel for corporations that lists lawyers, biographical information, areas of practice, and representative clients.

**MASS MAILING:** A method of job hunting by which students send numerous employers the same letter. Some students are beginning to do mass mailings by e-mail, but, whether via conventional or electronic mail, mass mailings are generally not targeted carefully enough to achieve positive results.

**MENTOR:** A lawyer who assumes responsibility for teaching and guidance of a new lawyer or summer associate.

**MOOT COURT:** A co-curricular activity for students interested in the principles of written and oral advocacy. Students represent either the plaintiff or defendant in writing briefs and presenting oral arguments in a mock trial setting.

**MORAL FITNESS:** Prior to being permitted to sit for a state's bar exam, the state's Board of Bar Examiners attempts to ascertain the moral fitness of a bar candidate by doing extensive research into the individual's past.

**MPRE:** Multistate Professional Responsibility Exam, required in many states to practice law.

**MULTISTATE BAR EXAM:** An exam required by many states for admission to the bar that tests federal law as it applies to all states.

## N

**NACE:** National Association of Colleges and Employers (formerly the College Placement Council).

**NALP:** National Association for Law Placement. Founded in 1971, NALP is an organization of law schools and legal employers committed to the development and advancement of fair, effective, and efficient career services and recruitment practices. NALP works toward this goal by providing educational programs and materials to those involved in legal career services and recruitment and by establishing and maintaining standards.

**NALP BULLETIN:** A monthly newsletter from NALP providing informative articles, book reviews, and professional news.

**NALP TIMELINES:** Guidelines by which students should respond to offers of employment as prescribed in Part V of the NALP Principles and Standards.

**NALP FORM:** A questionnaire developed by NALP member organizations and used by career services directors to collect information about a legal employer's business and recruiting practices. The questionnaires are used by law schools to standardize the collection of employer information. Employers may also choose to have their NALP forms published in the annual Directory of Legal Employers (in print version and on CD-ROM) and in the on-line database available on LEXIS.

**NALPOfrs:** An acronym for the NALP Offer Reporting Service recruitment management software developed by NALP. Using NALPOfrs, employers can track the status of candidates and prepare useful management reports. Employers may also choose to participate in NALP's research on the legal employment market by reporting their recruiting activity confidentially to NALP.

**NALSA:** Native American Law Students Association.

**NALSC:** National Association of Legal Search Consultants.

**NAPIL:** National Association for Public Interest Law. An organization that works with student groups across the country to promote public service law through loan forgiveness programs, fellowships, educational programs, and an annual career fair.

**NATIONAL ASIAN PACIFIC AMERICAN BAR ASSOCIATION:** A national association for Asian/Pacific American attorneys.

**NATIONAL BAR ASSOCIATION:** A national association for African-American attorneys.

**NATIVE AMERICAN BAR ASSOCIATION:** A national association for Native American attorneys.

**NETWORKING:** The art of cultivating and developing contacts for the purpose of finding jobs.

**NLGLA:** National Lesbian and Gay Law Association.

## O

**OCI:** On-campus interviewing scheduled by an employer through the career services office at a school with students at the school. (See also On-Campus Interviews.)

**OF COUNSEL:** A lawyer who is not a partner of a firm but who has a formal relationship with the firm. For example, the term may be used for a senior partner of a law firm who has gone into semi-retirement or a lateral hire who may be in line for partnership after a prescribed amount of time with the firm. (See also Partner and Associate.)

**OFF-CAMPUS INTERVIEW PROGRAM:** A recruitment program in which students pay their own travel and lodging expenses to participate in employment interviews arranged in a different city by their career services office.

**ON-CAMPUS INTERVIEWS/OCI:** Typically, large law firms, corporations, and government agencies who recruit a year in advance for their hiring needs visit law school campuses during August through December to conduct employment interviews with law students for summer and full-time associate positions.

**ORDER OF THE COIF:** A national legal honor society, similar to Phi Beta Kappa for undergraduate institutions, in which membership is limited to the academic top 10% of each graduating class.

**OUTPLACEMENT:** Career and job search counseling provided to lawyers who are leaving a firm.

**OVERSUBSCRIPTION / OVERFLOW RESUMES:** Students who were unable to secure an on-campus or job fair interview with an employer and whose resumes are still provided to the employer on an overflow basis.

## P-Q

**PARALEGAL/LEGAL ASSISTANT:** An individual who has received either formal academic training or on-the-job training to assist lawyers with certain aspects of law practice. The responsibilities of paralegals vary from employer to employer.

**PART V:** The section of NALP's Principles and Standards that offers guidelines for the timing of offers and responses in law student recruitment.

**PARTNER:** A lawyer who has become an owner of the firm and is paid a percentage of the firm's profits that reflects the lawyer's contribution to the firm. Sometimes called a shareholder or equity member of the firm. (See also Associate and Permanent Associate.)

**P.C./P.A.:** Professional Corporation/Professional Association. A tax arrangement allowing partnerships to enjoy corporate benefits while retaining the other attributes of a partnership.

**PDC:** An acronym for the Professional Development Curriculum a curriculum of courses developed by the NALP Educational Programming Committee to provide foundational, intermediate, and advanced levels of training for legal recruitment, personnel, and career services professionals. Each Annual Education Conference offers a selection of PDC courses, as well as a wide range of additional seminars. Conference brochures provide information on the Professional Development Curriculum and identify PDC courses with a special symbol.

**PERMANENT ASSOCIATE/NON-EQUITY PARTNER:** A lawyer who is not considered on track for equity partnership but fulfills a specialty niche in the firm's practice.

**PIGGYBACKING:** Slang for a student building upon one out-of-town interview so that the trip results in several interviews for the student.

**PLACEMENT COMMITTEE:** A committee of faculty and students who serve as a resource pool for placement ideas and a sounding board for career services policy.

**POUNDING THE PAVEMENT/DOOR KNOCKING:** A job search method by which students call upon potential employers without previously arranging for an interview.

**PRESCREENING:** A procedure by which employers are permitted to review students' resumes prior to on-campus interviews and select the students they desire to interview.

**PRINCIPLES AND STANDARDS NALP's:** Ethical guidelines for career services directors, legal employers, and students regarding the law placement and recruiting process.

**PRO BONO/PRO PUBLICO PRACTICE:** Literally, for the public good, refers to time donated at no charge by lawyers in the community interest, including representation of the poor, charitable organizations, not-for-profit organizations, and other groups whose purposes are for the good of the general public.

**PROFIT CENTERS:** Refers to those departments in a law firm that tend to produce the most business and, thus, generate the most revenue for the firm.

### R

**RAINMAKER:** A lawyer who brings in a great deal of business for his/her firm.

**RECIPROCITY:** Agreements among law schools allowing students and/or graduates to use the career services offices at other schools. NALP periodically publishes a compilation of law school reciprocity policies.

**RECRUITMENT ADMINISTRATORS/ COORDI-NATORS:** A professional who is responsible for the coordination of an employer's legal recruiting program. This role may be assumed by a human resources or personnel administrator within a firm.

## S-T

**SPECTATOR ASSIGNMENTS:** Activities designed for summer law clerks that allow them to observe the firm's lawyers in action e.g., sitting in on a closing, observing a litigator in court, etc.

**SPLIT SUMMER:** A summer in which a law clerk works for more than one employer.

**STANDARD 213:** An accrediting standard of the ABA which states: The Law School should provide adequate staff, space, and resources, in view of the size and program of the school, to maintain an active placement service to assist its graduates to make sound career choices.

**STANDARD 215:** The ABA is in the process of refining accrediting Standard 215, which will serve as an ethical guideline for law school consumer information. NALP collaborated with the ABA Section on Legal Education to recommend standards for employment data furnished by law schools as consumer information.

**STUDENT BAR ASSOCIATION:** Student governing body of a law school.

**SUMMER ASSOCIATES/SUMMER CLERKS:** Law students employed as law clerks during the summer.

**SWEAT SHOP:** A law firm with the reputation for having its lawyers work long hours.

## U

**UP OR OUT POLICY:** Refers to a philosophy within many law firms whereby a lawyer either is made a partner after a stipulated associate period or leaves the firm.

## V

**VISITING PROFESSOR:** A faculty member who is on leave of absence from his/her institution so that he/she may teach at a different law school.

## W-X-Y-Z

**WESTLAW:** West Publishing Company's electronic databases of cases, statutes, regulations, newspapers, journals, business magazines and other materials used by lawyers in doing legal and non-legal research. WESTLAW includes the West Legal Directory (a database of attorneys throughout the country) and other databases which are useful to students in searching for possible employers and to career services and recruitment professionals.

**WRITE-IN APPLICATIONS:** Unsolicited letter and resume applications.

**WRITE-OFFS:** Billable client time that is subsequently not charged to a client.

**WRITING SAMPLE:** A piece of legal writing submitted to an employer by an applicant to demonstrate legal writing skills.

# INDEX